A special thanks to the
Drawing Near to God editing team.

"Drawing Near to God" Devotional 4th edition

ISBN-13: 978-0-9971243-3-0

Drawing Near to God
P.O. Box 1274
Mount Pleasant, SC 29465
(843) 284-4333
www.JoanneEllison.com

Draw near to God and He will draw near to you.

James 4:8

Joanne Ellison often refers to her ministry as a bridge that takes you from knowing about Jesus to having a personal relationship with Him.

Driven by a vision to motivate women to pursue a deeper relationship with God, Joanne founded Drawing Near to God Ministry in 2000 and has since reached tens of thousands of women through Christian radio and television, blogging, contributions to the Christian Broadcasting Network, social media, her weekly Bible teachings, livestreaming, speaking, books and other resources. She is the author of over 20 Bible study guides, the popular 365-day Bible devotional, *Drawing Near To God, Sitting at His Feet* devotional and *Tell Your Heart to Beat Again.*

She is a mother of three, grandmother of 11 and has been married for 45 years to Dr. Blount Ellison. Making her home in the Charleston area for most of her life, Joanne is a graduate of the College of Charleston and an active member of Saint Andrew's Church, Mount Pleasant, SC. In her free time, she enjoys spending time with her grandchildren and traveling with her husband.

Joanne is an engaging speaker, writer and Bible teacher. Her speaking style includes both vulnerability and humor and is rooted in her passion for the Bible. She often incorporates stories about her children, grandchildren and travels into her teachings - cycling through Portugal and Copenhagen as well as hiking mountains all over the States have provided many challenges and adventures! Joanne's teachings engage you from beginning to end, always including life application, so you can be both "hearers AND doers of the Word."

Joanne continues her love of learning by continuously studying the Scriptures, taking theology classes and spending precious quiet time with the Lord where great instruction and revelation come.

Joanne Ellison

DRAWING NEAR TO GOD

www.JoanneEllison.com

Drawing Near to God

To my family, without whose support and encouragement this book would not have been completed.

Missing the Mark

We all, like sheep, have gone astray, each of us has turned to his own way; and the Lord has laid on him the iniquity of us all.
Isaiah 53:6

The Greek word for sin is *hamartia,* which translates "missing the mark." When we sin, we miss the mark of obtaining God's best for our lives. My son loves to bow hunt for deer. In order to shoot the deer, he must first line up the animal in the "sight" of the bow or else he will miss the target. When we do not keep God "in sight," we fall prey to sin. We must align ourselves with God's Word in order to stay on target and hit the mark to assure that we are in God's will.

In what area of your life do you fall prey to "missing the mark"? Sometimes it is obvious to us where we are not in obedience to God's Word, and other times we must pray and ask the Holy Spirit to reveal any area where we fall short of God's will. I always find God to be faithful to show me when I ask and faithful to help me return to Him and get on track. Take a moment and ask the Lord to show you where you may have taken a wrong turn. He will be faithful to show you the way.

Trust in the Lord with all of your heart and lean not on your own understanding; in all your ways acknowledge Him and He will make your path straight. (Proverbs 3:2)

Heavenly Father,
I have sinned (fill in the blank) and have turned away from You. I long to follow Your will, and today I acknowledge that I have not trusted You in this area of my life. I bring You back in focus today acknowledging my weakness and turning to You for strength. I know that You alone are trustworthy to help me get back on track, and I rejoice in returning to You.
In Jesus' name, Amen

January 2

Removing the Grave Clothes

Jesus, once more deeply moved, came to the tomb. It was a cave with a stone laid across the entrance. "Take away the stone," he said. "But, Lord," said Martha, the sister of the dead man, "by this time there is a bad odor, for he has been there four days." Then Jesus said, "Did I not tell you that if you believed, you would see the glory of God?" So they took away the stone. Then Jesus looked up and said, "Father, I thank You that You have heard me. I knew that You always hear me, but I said this for the benefit of the people standing here, that they may believe that You sent me." When he had said this, Jesus called in a loud voice, "Lazarus, come out!" The dead man came out, his hands and feet wrapped with strips of linen, and a cloth around his face. Jesus said to them, "Take off the grave clothes and let him go."

John 11:38-44

The Lord of Life now comes to the tomb to confront his opponent, death, symbolized in the cave tomb before Him. When the stone is rolled back, Jesus prays and shows his personal intimacy with God the Father. He also demonstrates that his work is done in concert with God's will. Jesus cries out in a LOUD VOICE with authority. The Greek word is *kraugazo,* meaning "shout with authority." When Lazarus emerges from the tomb, he is bound in grave wrappings which were strips of fabric wound around his limbs and filled with burial spices. Jewish burials likewise tied the jaw closed and covered the face with a linen cloth. Can you imagine the scene? Mourners wailing, Jesus is angry, and Jesus shows His amazing authority and power over death by calling Lazarus out of the grave.

Jesus then tells the people to unbind Lazarus. Notice He tells others to unbind. Jesus tells us today although we cannot regenerate people, we can help free them from the wounds and destruction of the past. The strict ritual laws of purification would have caused the people to shrink back and not touch the unclean dead body. So it is for us. We find ourselves today in the same dilemma—are we willing to reach out to the unclean, the hurting, those who do not look like us or act like us? Are we willing to reach out and unwrap their grave clothes? The grave clothes are those things that represent death to our spiritual, physical, and emotional lives. In the most important sense, our grave clothes represent our unbelief or whatever holds us back from believing in Jesus and receiving salvation and eternal life.

Take a moment and ask your Father in heaven to begin the work of removing any area in your life that steals away the abundant life Christ has for you. Ask Him to send others to help you remove the grave cloths. Remember to give God the glory when He sets you free!

Heavenly Father,
You alone give life. You are the author of life and the One who sustains life by Your hand. I am struggling with a spirit of heaviness and sense that You are calling me to surrender my grave cloths. As You call me out from the grave of my circumstances, I rejoice that You will restore my life in great abundance.
In Jesus' name, Amen

January 3

Strangers in the World

Dear friends, I urge you, as aliens and strangers in the world, to abstain from sinful desires which war against your soul.
I Peter 2:11

Peter refers to Christians in the world as strangers whose citizenship is in heaven. Peter calls the readers to live as strangers in the world, abstaining from sin and glorifying God by good deeds. It is difficult to stand against the tide of society which opposes Christian values and rejects absolute Biblical truth.

Has the Lord asked you to do anything that seemed to alienate you from the things of the world? Peter tells us in *I Peter 2:6-8* that for those who believe, Jesus, the Cornerstone, is precious, but not so for those who are unbelievers. They reject Christ's message of salvation. Although believers are called to live as strangers in the world, in Christ we are to be "salt and light" as we stand firm and are prepared to give the reason for the hope that we have in Christ. *(I Peter 3:15)* The world has never needed Him more!

Heavenly Father,
Sometimes I feel like a fish out of water as I go through life. I know that You have called me to reflect Your values, Your ways, and Your love, but it is difficult. The world pulls me in another direction, and I feel alone sometimes trying to live a Christian life. Lord, give me the grace to follow You; give me the courage to stand for You; give me the love for all people and for Your world so that I will walk in humility and represent You well.
In Jesus' name, Amen

Joshua's Faithful Response

By faith Abraham, when called to go to a place he would later receive as his inheritance, obeyed and went, even though he did not know where he was going.
Hebrews 11:8

The Lord promised Joshua that He would be faithful to him just as He had been to Moses. But just as Moses had to be faithful to respond to God's call, so Joshua had to be obedient to follow the Lord's instructions. God told Joshua that He would give him every place where he set his foot. The Scriptures show us that God holds true to His promises. We often have a responsibility to respond in obedience in order for His promises to be fulfilled in us. The Lord promised the Israelites that if they obeyed His command *to love the Lord Your God, to walk in all His ways, and to hold fast to Him,* He would send rain on their land and cause them to prosper. (*Deuteronomy 11:22*) God continues to look for faithful men and women to whom He can entrust His promises.

Heavenly Father,
I pray that like Joshua I will be courageous to step out in faith wherever You send me knowing that You will be with me wherever I go. Thank You for going before me and for giving me every place I put my foot as I seek to spread the good news of Christ. Help me to obey Your Word and follow You in all of my ways. I claim Your promise that as I follow and obey You, You will send rain on my life to produce fruit for Your kingdom.
In Jesus' name, Amen

January 5

Seeking God

You will seek me and find me when you seek me with all your heart.
Jeremiah 29:13

Throughout the Scriptures, we learn that if we seek God, we will find Him; if we draw near to Him, He will draw near to us. *(Jeremiah 29:13, James 4:8)* For years I didn't understand the importance of seeking the Lord and intentionally drawing near to Him. I thought that it was God's job to move me closer to Him! As I study the Scriptures, I am now more aware that our relationship with God is similar to our relationships with friends. In order to grow closer to someone, we must spend time with him or her and communicate by both listening and sharing in order to learn more about each other. God created us to know Him intimately and to be His closest friend.

Do you know Him as your best friend, or are you just acquainted with Him? Choose today to make Him your best friend and draw near to Him—He is only a heartbeat away.

Heavenly Father,
You alone are the perfect friend. I have been disappointed by friends in the past and need a trustworthy friend. I choose today to seek You with all of my heart and to draw near to You in prayer and in meditating on Your Word. Help me to know the secrets of Your heart and remove the blocks that keep me from trusting You with my secrets.
In Jesus' name, Amen

A Gospel of Righteousness

What shall we conclude then? Are we any better? Not at all! We have already made the charge that Jews and Gentiles alike are all under sin. As it is written: "There is no one righteous, not even one; there is no one who understands, no one who seeks God. All have turned away, they have become worthless; there is no one who does good, not even one."
Romans 3:9-12

Righteousness is defined most clearly as "being in a right relationship with God." We are made right with God when we receive Jesus Christ as our Savior and the power of the gospel comes alive in our lives. The word "gospel" comes from the Old English meaning "good story" or "good news." The good news is that God provided salvation through the life, death, and resurrection of Jesus Christ. This gospel from God, according to Paul, reveals a righteousness that is by faith. (*Romans 1:17*) We live in a society today that encourages working hard in order to be successful. However, being "right" with God is dependent on our faith in Jesus Christ and not dependent on what we do. We must be willing both to believe in our hearts and confess with our mouths that God raised Jesus from the dead in order to be saved. *(Romans 10:9)* No amount of "doing" or "good works" can make us right with God.

Are you aware that no other religion claims we are saved on account of the work of *someone else*, that is the work of the cross through Jesus Christ? When I consider that God sent His only Son for each of us, I am humbled that He would lavish such an undeserving gift on humanity. How can we refuse His gift of righteousness imparted to us by faith?

Heavenly Father,
For years I have believed that I was in control of my life. I have tried to please You as I have tried to please others. I have believed a lie that it is in my "doing" that I am saved. As Your Word of truth breaks through into my life, help me to surrender my life to You and to believe the words of Christ: The work of God is this: to believe in the one He has sent. (John 6:29)
In Jesus' name, Amen

January 7

Salt and Light

. . .you are the salt of the earth. But if the salt loses its saltiness, how can it be made salty again? It is no longer good for anything, except to be thrown out and trampled by men. You are the light of the world. A city on a hill cannot be hidden. Neither do people light a lamp and put it under a bowl. Instead they put it on its stand, and it gives light to everyone in the house. In the same way, let your light shine before men, that they may see Your good deeds and praise Your Father in heaven.

Matthew 5:13-16

The Beatitudes describe the qualities of kingdom citizens. Jesus goes on to teach that His followers are to be "salt and light" to the world, penetrating society with the character of Christ. Salt is a preservative and a seasoning to flavor foods. Interestingly, most of the salt in Israel came from the Dead Sea and was full of impurities, causing it to lose some of its flavor. If we are to be "salt" to a needy world, we must ask the Lord to remove our impurities so that we don't lose our flavor or preserving properties. Also, we must continue to feed on His Word to become more like Him in order to be "salt and light" to the world around us. (*Romans 12:2*) Is the light of Christ shining out from you, or are you hiding the light of Christ within you?

Heavenly Father,
It is my desire to be a light to others around me. I desire to lead others to You, to help the hurting, the lonely, the sick and needy. As I step out in faith to be the hands and feet of Christ to those in need, cleanse my heart and my motives so that I can truly love them and be "salt and light" as You intended for me to be.
In Jesus' name,
Amen

Preparing for our Spiritual Journey

This is what the Lord says; "Stand at the crossroads and look; ask for the ancient paths, ask where the good way is, and walk in it, and you will find rest for your souls. But you said, 'We will not walk in it.'
Jeremiah 6:16

It is not uncommon for us to board a plane and take off on a trip with little consideration for what it takes for the plane to fly. On the wall of an air museum, it says that there are four elements of flight: gravity, lift, drag, and power. These same four elements affect us in our spiritual journey. If it were not for the force of gravity, we would never be able to complete our journey. God's Word provides the force of gravity for our lives in that it keeps us grounded. Lift is the element that enables the flight to take off. In our spiritual life, prayer provides our lift and the Holy Spirit provides our power. There is an element of drag in any flight caused by the size and shape of the plane, as well as the load. Many times in our lives, we have unnecessary baggage that can keep us from actually beginning our journey or hinder us as we move forward. Drag affects the ability for the other three elements to operate.

Often the baggage in our lives that creates drag is our determination to do things our way instead of waiting on God. Too often, we let the past haunt us and the future scare us as we prepare to move forward in our spiritual journey. As we prepare for our spiritual journey, we need to make sure that obstacles are removed that either stand in the way of our believing in Jesus as our Savior or in appropriating the promises of God to our lives.

Heavenly Father,
Thank you for Your Word that is my resource for living a godly life. Thank you for Your promise that You hear the prayers of the righteous. (Proverbs 15:29) Thank you that the Holy Spirit provides me with power for the journey of life. I pray that You will reveal and remove any unnecessary baggage that I carry around—any bitterness, unforgiveness, hard heartedness—so that I can fly in the promises of Your Word.
In Jesus' name, Amen

January 9

The Penitent Redeemed

...but I see another law at work in the members of my body, waging war against the law of my mind and making me a prisoner of the law of sin at work within my members. What a wretched man I am! Who will rescue me from this body of death?
Romans 7:23-24

Isaiah describes the condition of Israel as a nation filled with guilt. The human condition of our fallen nature perpetuates a cycle of sin where, like Paul, we do what we don't want to do. (*Romans 7:14-20*) The Israelites had forsaken the Lord, and their condition was seemingly hopeless. *Isaiah 1:27* gives us hope that the penitent will be redeemed. We sometimes feel hopeless and burdened with guilt, but Jesus Christ offers us a solution to our condition through His offer of forgiveness by His shed blood on the cross. *(Hebrews 9:22)*

Do you have the assurance that Christ has forgiven and redeemed your sins?

Heavenly Father,
Your Word says that ALL have sinned and fallen short of Your glory. (Romans 3:23) I recognize that I am part of the ALL who sins. Forgive me when I sin and forgive me when I fall short of turning back to You when I have fallen away. I accept You as my Savior and look forward to You as my Redeemer who brings me from the places of darkness into your glorious light. (I Peter 2:9)
In Jesus' name, Amen

January 10

People of Hope

But in your hearts set apart Christ as Lord. Always be prepared to give an answer to everyone who asks you to give the reason for the hope that you have. But do this with gentleness and respect.
I Peter 3:15

Peter encourages the persecuted scattered Christians to put their hope in Christ and to be prepared to express that hope to others. It is interesting to note that in the midst of persecution, the testimony of Christ spread like a wild fire. In the midst of the trials of life is often the time when our testimony of the faithfulness of Christ comes alive. People are best able to see the enduring life of Christ in us when we are suffering and yet still testifying of God's goodness.

Are you going through tough times right now? Use this opportunity to share the hope of Christ with others. Your testimony of standing with Christ through the trials will bear fruit that you may never see but will have lasting effect in the lives of others. When I am under persecution or suffering under a trial, I am tempted to have a "pity party" and then hope that someone will notice my suffering. When I take my eyes off self and place them on Jesus, remembering His trials, I am humbled and ready to testify of God's goodness. In no way does this minimize our sufferings, but it does give suffering a higher purpose and brings glory to God.

Heavenly Father,
Help me to keep my eyes on You during seasons of trials. Give me the courage to take my eyes off of self and look to You as my source of life and comfort. Give me opportunities to demonstrate your faithfulness to others.
In Jesus' name, Amen

January 11

Significance of Names

Lord, our Lord, how majestic is Your name in all the earth!
You have set Your glory above the heavens.
Psalm 8:1

In the beginning was the Word, and the Word was with God, and the Word was God. (John 1:1) Jesus was with the Father at the creation and was sent to earth to reconcile us to the Father. When Jesus came to earth, He revealed "in the flesh" the character of His Father. He demonstrated and proclaimed God's kingdom and gave us insight into the nature of God. At creation, God named Adam and Eve and then instructed Adam to name the animals. A name is an intimate thing and often identifies our relationship with individuals. For example, I have nicknames for each of my children because it identifies my unique and close relationship with each one. In the account in *Genesis 32,* Jacob wrestles with a man whom we identify as the pre-incarnate Christ. After Jacob wrestled with Him, the man changed Jacob's name to Israel, thus identifying him with the nation that God was establishing. The name Israel now defined who he was and what his purpose would be. God calls us by name. He asks us to call *Him* by name and to know His names that we might *know Him* better.

Heavenly Father,
Help me to believe Your Word that You have called me by name. (Isaiah 43:1) Help me to believe that my name is written on the palm of Your hand. (Isaiah 49:16) As I meditate on the truth of Your Word, enable me to live into Your Word by acknowledging the truth and breaking the lies I have believed. I am a child of the kingdom and You have called me by name into the purposes of God. And to that I say AMEN!
In Jesus' name, Amen

God Looks at the Heart

But now your kingdom will not endure; the Lord has sought out a man after his own heart and appointed him a leader of his people, because you have not kept the Lord's command.
I Samuel 13:14

The Lord looks down from heaven on the sons of men to see if there are any who understand, any who seek God. (Psalm 13:2) Seeking God is a fundamental heart requirement for a true spiritual leader. Saul became impatient when Samuel did not come when he told Saul he would come to Gilgal. So Saul decided not to wait any longer and made a burnt offering to the Lord. It seems like a harmless thing to do while he was waiting, doesn't it? In fact, it seems like a godly thing to offer a sacrifice to the Lord, seeking Him in the face of danger! Samuel told Saul that what he did was foolish and that he had disobeyed the Lord. Saul's kingdom would be taken away and given to a man *"after God's own heart."*

God wants us to surrender our hearts to Him and to His love. He tells us to seek Him with all of our hearts and to love and obey Him. Have you determined in your heart to do this? God looks at the heart when He calls leaders. As we examine the fruit of our lives and the words that come forth from our mouths, we are able to see what is stored in our hearts. It is always a good idea periodically to have a "heart" checkup to be sure that there are no "spiritually clogged arteries."

Heavenly Father,
I pray that You will give me a "heart" checkup. Like David I pray that You will examine my heart and see if there is anything offensive in me. (Psalm 139:23-24) Help me to not grow weary or impatient in doing the things You have called me to do and to willingly obey You. Though I often fall short of loving You with all of my heart, soul, and mind, I do seek to do so and to walk in Your ways.
In Jesus' name, Amen

January 13

God's Promises

Your promises have been thoroughly tested, and Your servant loves them.
Psalm 119:140

God promised Abram that his offspring would inherit the land. However, Abram had to obey by leaving his home, not knowing where he was going. God protected Abram's offspring, forming the nation of Israel and leading them throughout the centuries towards the fulfillment of His promise. If Abram had not forged ahead in spite of his fears, he never might have left Ur. From the moment he took his first step of faith, God reassured him and his descendants that He would be with them every step of the way as they sought to be obedient.

Abram's step of faith was the first step towards the fulfillment of God's promise to him. Later, God asked Abraham, God's new name for Abram, to demonstrate his faith by being willing to sacrifice his son, Isaac. Abraham knew that God had promised to form the nation of Israel from his seed, Isaac. But once again, God was looking for Abraham's obedience, faith, and trust. What holds you back from stepping out in faith and obeying something the Lord has asked you to do?

Heavenly Father,
I have heard You call my name; I have heard You call me into Your purposes, but I fear forging ahead. What holds me back? Why am I so distressed about following where You call? I feel inadequate and fear rejection by You and others. Why do You call me to do the impossible? Help me to believe Your truth in my heart that I can do all things through Christ who strengthens me. (Philippians 4:13)
In Jesus' name, Amen

A Gospel of Power

I am not ashamed of the gospel, because it is the power of God for the salvation of everyone who believes…
Romans 1:16

According to Webster's dictionary, the word "power" has the following synonyms: *authority, jurisdiction, control, command, dominion.* The gospel is the power of God for salvation and it has authority, jurisdiction, control, and dominion over our lives for salvation if we choose to believe. Salvation is defined as the saving of man from the power and effects of sin. Salvation is one of the main themes in the Scriptures. From God's perspective, salvation includes the total work of God in bringing people from condemnation to justification, from death to eternal life. From the human perspective, it incorporates all of the blessings that being in Christ brings both in this life and the life to come. In putting "power and salvation" together, we see that the gospel has the power, authority, jurisdiction, and dominion to save us from sin and death and to enable us to live a life of freedom in Christ. Paul writes that he is not ashamed of the gospel because it is powerful and effective for those who believe.

In today's world, people are seeking freedom from the chains of sin and weight of condemnation. Jesus offers just that. Paul was not ashamed to share the gospel because he knew firsthand as a persecutor of Christians how the Lord touched him and led him from a life of bondage to a life of freedom in Christ. Where do you need to see God's power at work in your life?

Heavenly Father,
I feel powerless to stand against the tide of life. I feel as though the tide is pulling me under, and I am overwhelmed with the things I have to do and the limited time to do them. I pray for Your power to accomplish those things that YOU have called me to do. Give me discernment to know what I need to let go of. Thank

you that in You is all power and dominion to lead the life that You have called me to live. Help me to throw off the guilt of trying to please everyone else and give me the grace to only desire to please You.
In Jesus' name, Amen

Rebellion and the Fall

And the LORD God said, "The man has now become like one of us, knowing good from evil. He must not be allowed to reach out his hand and take also from the tree of life and eat, and live forever." So the LORD God banished him from the Garden of Eden to work the ground from which he had been taken.

Genesis 3:22-23

Throughout the ages, mankind has rebelled against God, seeking to be equal to God. Although we are made in God's image, repeatedly we have sought to be above God, our Creator. Often it is subtle, but always it leads to our downfall because we were created by God to be under His care and authority. When we come out from under His authority by rebelling against Him, we suffer the consequences. Read the story of the fall of man in the garden in *Genesis 3* and the subsequent fall in *Genesis 11* at the Tower of Babel. How do you fall into the trap of seeking to be like God?

Heavenly Father,
Why is it that I like to be in control of my own life? In truth, some days I am pretty good at it but other days I feel as though I am out of control. Your Word teaches me to surrender to You, but it is so difficult to give up control. Forgive me for my stubbornness of heart and help me to know that letting go gives You opportunity to work in my life. Help me to begin each day by surrendering to You. After all, You are much better at taking care of me than I am.
In Jesus' name, Amen

January 16

Honoring His Name

Ascribe to the Lord the glory due his name; worship the Lord in the splendor of his holiness.
Psalm 29:2

The *Psalms* inspire us to praise and honor the name of the Lord. As we seek God, He will reveal His character to us through His names. Let us learn to honor Jehovah God, Adonai, El Shaddai, Jehovah Nissi, Jehovah Shalom, and His many other names. He is our Master, our Sufficiency, our Banner, our Peace. As His names are revealed to us, we cannot help but praise and honor Him for who He is to us. The psalmists were full of praise for His name. Jesus taught His disciples to pray by hallowing (honoring) the Lord.

We are called to honor His name, *the name that is above every name. (Philippians 2:9)* Take the time to look for the names of God in Scripture. Often when a person in Scripture encountered God, a characteristic of God was revealed to him. Take Abraham, for instance. God told him to sacrifice his only son, and in his obedience Abraham prepared to do so. But an angel of heaven appeared and released him from the sacrifice. God saw that Abraham was prepared to obey, even by giving up his only son. Abraham discovered that God was his provider as the lamb for the sacrifice appeared. That day Abraham came to know God as Jehovah Jirah, his provider.

What name of God do you need to know today? Draw near to Him and encounter His love and presence in the area of your need. He will surely reveal His name to you.

Heavenly Father,
Reveal Yourself to me, Lord as I relinquish control. Help me to know You in a deeper way today and to honor Your holy name.
In Jesus' name, Amen

January 17

A People of Grace

Concerning this salvation, the prophets, who spoke of the grace that was to come to you, searched intently and with the greatest care, trying to find out the time and circumstances to which the Spirit of Christ in them was pointing when he predicted the sufferings of Christ and the glories that would follow.
I Peter 1:10-11

The prophets spoke of a time of grace when the Messiah would come bringing salvation to the people. They predicted His sufferings and the glory that would follow. *(I Peter 1:10-11)* Grace has been defined as "unmerited favor"—God's favor that we do not deserve. It is only through belief in the death and resurrection of Jesus Christ and receiving Him into our lives through forgiveness of sin that we have salvation. The magnificent hymn, *Amazing Grace,* always brings me to tears as I reflect on how merciful the Lord has been to me.

Amazing Grace! How sweet the sound that saved a wretch
like me! I once was lost, but now am found;
Was blind, but now I see.

How have you experienced God's abundant provision of grace in your life? Grace transforms us. Grace humbles us. Grace empowers us.

Heavenly Father,
Forgive me where I have taken Your grace in vain. Forgive me where I have not recognized Your grace in my self-centered world. Help me to remember the high cost You paid for me to have forgiveness and grace extended to me and help me to be a person that extends love and grace to others in return.
In Jesus' name, Amen

January 18

Sincere Worship

...let us draw near to God with a sincere heart in full assurance of faith, having our hearts sprinkled to cleanse us from a guilty conscience and having our bodies washed with pure water.
Hebrews 10:22

Burnt offerings were offered every morning and every evening for all of Israel. *(Exodus 29:38-42)* The Hebrew name "minhah" for burnt offerings means "gift" or "sacrifice." The Israelites worshipped God through sacrificing animals. God speaks through Isaiah telling the Israelites that their burnt offerings are meaningless. *(Isaiah 1:11-13)* God looks at our hearts to see if our attitude of worship is sincere or if we are simply going through the motions. Jesus replaced the Old Testament sacrifices once and for all. *(Hebrews 10:10)*

How does knowing this encourage you to receive Jesus as the sacrifice for your sins and help you to worship God with a new heart? I pray that God will pierce our hearts and our worship will grow in sincerity and purity.

Heavenly Father,
Do I really know what worship means? When I read the Scriptures, am I worshipping You? When I pray, am I worshipping You? As I go through the routine of life, could that be worshipping You? Yes, I believe that in all things, in all circumstances, I am to live my life honoring, praising and worshipping You. To separate the life I lead from worshipping You would be impossible. I pray that I would grow in my desire to worship You with my whole life.
In Jesus' name, Amen

January 19

God Anoints His Leaders

So he sent and had him brought in. He was ruddy, with a fine appearance and handsome features. Then the Lord said, "Rise and anoint him; he is he one."
I Samuel 16:12

The word anoint comes from the Hebrew word *masah,* which means to "anoint, smear, consecrate." It occurs approximately 70 times in the Old Testament. It is used most frequently in the sense of a setting apart for an office or function. When Jesse's youngest son, David, came in from the fields, the Lord told Samuel to "rise and anoint him." So Samuel took the horn of oil and anointed David in the presence of his brothers. Then the Spirit of the Lord came upon David in power. Later, *Isaiah 61* describes the Spirit of the Lord coming to anoint one who would bring freedom to the captives. Jesus Christ tells the people in the synagogue that He is the fulfillment of that prophecy: *The Spirit of the Lord is on me because He has anointed me to preach good news to the poor. He has sent me to proclaim freedom for the prisoners. (Luke 4:18)* Then He sent the anointing of His Holy Spirit to be upon us as believers and to enable us to be courageous leaders. *(I John 2:20, Isaiah 61:1-2)* At Pentecost, the Holy Spirit came like "tongues of fire," resting on the believers. After Pentecost, we saw Peter, who had denied Christ out of fear three times, become one of the most courageous leaders for Christ that we have ever known. Anointed by the Holy Spirit, Peter was empowered to witness about the saving grace of Jesus Christ. He no longer cowered in fear for his life, but instead he became bold and was willing to give his all for Christ. Are you willing to do the same?

Heavenly Father,
Fill me with Your Holy Spirit that I might be like Peter and boldly tell others about You. Give me the heart of David that I might demonstrate Your power through my life. Help me to remember that apart from Your Holy Spirit I am powerless to live a godly life and continue to fill me daily with Your Holy Spirit.
In Jesus' name, Amen

January 20

Effective Gospel

Now you, if you call yourself a Jew; if you rely on the law and brag about your relationship to God; if you know his will and approve of what is superior because you are instructed by the law; if you are convinced that you are a guide for the blind, a light for those who are in the dark, an instructor of the foolish, a teacher of infants, because you have in the law the embodiment of knowledge and truth – you, then, who teach others, do you not teach yourself? You who preach against stealing, do you steal? You who say that people should not commit adultery, do you commit adultery? You who abhor idols, do you rob temples?
Romans 2:17-22

Paul experienced firsthand the effect of the gospel which was the "good news" of Jesus Christ. He described how he persecuted the church and how the grace of God snatched him from his former way of life. He began to proclaim the power of the gospel to save. Paul was a zealous preacher who knew that the gospel would provide a way to be made "right" with God and that it was powerful and effective to change lives. The world today needs the radical life changing effects of hearing and believing the gospel. Paul's first century world was in need of the gospel and he preached to both Gentiles and Jews. In *Romans 2:17,* Paul points out that the Jews were self-righteous, bragging on their reliance on the law. He understood this because he was once self-righteous relying on his heritage, his learning, and his position in society. Paul points out to his fellow Jews that though they had a physical circumcision as a sign of being a Jew, they needed a spiritual circumcision of the heart to indicate that they truly belonged to God. Paul teaches that both Jews and Gentiles are sinners *(Romans 3:9)* and that the gospel is effective only if they believe that Jesus Christ is the way to salvation and have a right relationship with God. The gospel is only effective if they believe and then obey.

What about you? Do you see the fruit of the gospel or "good news" of Jesus Christ in your life? Are you more patient and humble, seeking to serve others rather than being served? Ask the Lord to soften your heart to walk in the truth of His Word.

Heavenly Father,
Help me to not just be a "hearer" of the word but a "doer" (James 1:22). I pray that my life will reflect the "good news" of the gospel and that others will see Christ both in my words and in my actions.
In Jesus' name, Amen

January 21

Our Response to Others

My command is this: Love each other as I have loved you. Greater love has no one than this, that he lay down his life for his friends
John 15:12-13

The three tribes (the Reubenites, Gadites, and the half-tribe of Manasseh) had to leave their place of rest east of the Jordan, which had already been given to them, in order to go and help the other tribes fight the enemy: But to the Reubenites, the Gadites, and the half tribe of Manasseh, Joshua said, remember the command that Moses the servant of the Lord gave you. The Lord your God is giving you rest and has granted you this land. Your wives, your children, and your livestock may stay in the land that Moses gave you east of the Jordan, but all your fighting men, fully armed, must cross over ahead of your brothers. You are to help your brothers until the Lord gives them rest as he has done for you and until they too have taken possession of the land that the Lord your God is giving them. (Joshua 1:12-15) It would have been easy for these three tribes to stay in the land that God had given them and not fight to help their brothers attain the land ascribed to them by God. Each of us is on a journey to grow in our faith, and we need the body of Christ to help us grow in our faith. It is essential that we encourage one another in the faith and help one another to possess the land that the Lord is giving us.

What is the land that God is giving us? Spiritually speaking the Lord is calling us to grow into the *likeness* of Christ and walk in the fullness of our calling. We all need help along the way, and although it is easy to be concerned only with our own journey of faith, God is calling us to help our "brothers and sisters" in Christ to possess the land and to ultimately find rest in Christ. Jesus tells us today that we are to love one another and to lay our lives down for one another. One way we can do this is to help others be victorious in their Christian walk, just as the tribes of Israel helped each other. What are some ways you can encourage someone who is struggling in his/her walk with the Lord? Who do you need to encourage this week?

Heavenly Father,
Help me to remember that I am not alone in this journey of faith. Open my eyes and heart to help others by encouraging and fighting for them to walk in the promises o God's Word.
Help me to fight the "me first" world that I live in and to be willing to help others helping others to possess their "promised land."
In Jesus' name, Amen

January 22

Fighting the Opposition

Your servant has killed both the lion and the bear; this uncircumcised Philistine will be like one of them, because he has defied the armies of the living God.
I Samuel 17:36

As Christians, we are enlisted in God's army and we take our orders from our Commander-in-Chief. He has called us to "advance His kingdom" forcefully. (Matthew 11:12) Often we are so busy fighting our own battles that we miss the one that the Lord has called us to fight. Paul tells us that we "struggle not against flesh and blood but against rulers, against the authorities, against the powers of this dark world and against the spiritual forces of evil in the heavenly realms." (Ephesians 6:11) We are told to put on the full armor of God to stand against the schemes of the evil one. The good news is that the Lord equips us for battle with His Word, His truth, and His full armor. I have come to realize that I am most effective in serving the Lord when I am aware that the Lord is with me and the battle is His: This is what the Lord says to you: Do not be afraid or discouraged because of this vast army. For the battle is not yours but God's. (II Chronicles 20:15)

We must trust Him to defeat the giants in our life. What prevents you from having this same attitude of trust?

Heavenly Father,
I have enlisted in Your army as a believer in Jesus Christ. Sometimes life seems to be one battle after another, and I get weary and discouraged. Help me remember that You are always with me and that the battle belongs to You.
In Jesus' name, Amen

Salvation Through Faith

Praise be to the God and Father of our Lord Jesus Christ! In his great mercy he has given us new birth into a living hope through the resurrection of Jesus Christ from the dead, and into an inheritance that can never perish, spoil or fade – kept in heaven for you, who through faith are shielded by God's power until the coming of the salvation that is ready to be revealed in the last time.
I Peter 1:3-5

We have an inheritance of salvation that we receive through our faith in Jesus Christ. Salvation, according to Webster's dictionary, means "the saving of man from the power and effects of sin." Peter explains three dimensions of salvation which are: the new birth, the sanctifying work of the Holy Spirit, and our inheritance in heaven. *(I Peter 1:1-5)* Peter begins his first letter by giving the recipients of this letter an understanding that it is only through faith in Jesus Christ that they can receive salvation and live a life worthy of their calling. Also, it is the only way they could rejoice while enduring persecution and suffering. How true that is today as we seek to bring Christ into a world that often rejects the message of salvation. At the core of our lives lies faith, and *without faith it is impossible to please God.* (*Hebrews 11:6*)

Does your life reflect the three dimensions of salvation by new birth, transformation and hope for eternal life? Sometimes we are so busy living our lives that we forget the amazing inheritance we have in Christ that never spoils or fades. It is so easy to get caught up with the things of daily living, working for things that will not last. The one thing that lasts forever is our inheritance of salvation through faith. Seek today to bring others to this lasting inheritance.

Heavenly Father,
Sometimes I am so busy with life that I forget that You ARE life. Sometimes I forget that the most important relationship I have is with You and I work for things that are not lasting. Help me to remember that my lasting inheritance is in You and give me the opportunities to lead others to You.
In Jesus' name, Amen

January 24

The Majesty of God

Lord, our Lord, how majestic is Your name in all the earth!
You have set Your glory above the heavens.
Psalm 8:1

When the prophet Isaiah had a vision of God seated on His throne, he was undone. God's majesty and His holiness caused him to cry out, *Woe to me! I am ruined! For I am a man of unclean lips, and I live among a people of unclean lips, and my eyes have seen the King, the Lord Almighty. (Isaiah 6:1-5)* Isaiah recognized that he could not stand before the God of all Ages, before His majesty and holiness, and not have his sins exposed. As I read through this passage in *Isaiah,* I close my eyes and imagine the Lord, high and lifted up, and my standing before Him with my life exposed. I, too, cried out with Isaiah, "Woe to me! I am ruined!" Then I remember Immanuel, God with us, the One whom God sent to restore me and to enable me to be in His presence. With great relief and awe, I thank God for making a way for me to draw near to Him through His Son Jesus Christ. When we catch but a glimpse of God's glory, His holiness, and His majesty, we are forever changed. Thank God for His transforming Presence in our lives!!

Jesus has made a way for us to approach God's throne of grace boldly and with confidence. *(Hebrews 4:16)* Yet when we approach Him, though now accessible, we approach a holy God with reverent awe. His Presence is consuming; His Presence is transforming. Do you approach Him in reverence and fear? Yes, He is approachable through the work of the cross. But let us never forget His majesty and holiness.

Heavenly Father,
As I approach You in prayer, as I approach You in the Word, as I approach You in the circumstances of life, I pray that I never lose sight of Your majesty and awe. I pray for a reverential fear of the Lord to seek to honor You in my life. Lord, my Lord, how majestic is Your name in all the earth!

In Jesus' name, Amen

January 25

God's Workings Through Ordinary People

But the Lord said to Samuel, "Do not consider his appearance or his height, for I have rejected him. The Lord does not look at the things man looks at. Man looks at the outward appearance, but the Lord looks at the heart."
I Samuel 16:7

In *I Samuel 16:1-7*, we read that God looks at the heart, not the outward appearance. God is not a respecter of persons. David was the least likely of Jesse's sons to be selected to be king; however, God was looking at his heart and he was chosen to be king of all of Israel. Rahab was earnestly willing to help the Israelite spies because she recognized and acknowledged that their God was sovereign. *(Joshua 2:9-11)* God saw her heart and He worked through her to protect and save Israel's spies. Rahab remained faithful to God's instruction given to her by the Israelite spies. Through her faithfulness, she and those in her household were saved. The Lord continues to search for those who have faithful hearts and are willing to be open to knowing and following His ways. God works through ordinary people. He especially gives power and grace to those who are willing to acknowledge their sins and their weaknesses. In *II Corinthians 12:7-10*, Paul describes his weaknesses as a "thorn in his flesh," and yet God used Him mightily. God looks at the heart, and He pours out His grace on humble hearts.

As you examine your life, are you able to see your weaknesses as an opportunity for the Lord to use you? Do you seek to have a humble servant's heart in all that you do? God is looking for this type of person to use—ordinary people like you and me—but extraordinary in submission to God.

Heavenly Father,
I have looked at my life as ordinary and wondered if You could use me. I have seen my weaknesses as obstacles to serving You. I pray that You will give me a

humble heart to serve You daily as You see fit. I am Yours. My life belongs to You.

In Jesus' name, Amen

January 26

Restoration of God's Kingdom on Earth

For God so loved the world that he gave his one and only Son, that whoever believes in him shall not perish but have eternal life.
John 3:16

When Adam and Eve rebelled against God in the garden, the consequence was separation from God. They had enjoyed fellowship with God, but because of their sin, they were separated from Him. The love of God our Creator is the strongest force on earth, and it was that love that sent His Son Jesus to restore man's relationship to God. I marvel at the love of our Father, who sacrificed His Son Jesus to die for our sins and provided the way for us to come back into fellowship with Him! Jesus came and preached, *Repent, for the kingdom of Heaven is near (Matthew 4:17).* He called humanity to turn from their sins, to turn back to God, and to advance God's kingdom on earth. Did you know that God, the Creator of all things, loves us beyond any words that we can express? He longs for us to be in fellowship with Him, working together to bring His truth to the world. What a privilege it is to be in partnership with Him!

God is in the business of restoring us first in relationship to Him through His Son, and then in relationship with ourselves and others. Often it is through suffering that we draw near to God, and often it is through our relationships that we suffer. But God has promised that He will not only restore us, but also use our brokenness to bring restoration to others: *And the God of all grace, who called you to His eternal glory in Christ, after you have suffered a little while will Himself restore you and make you strong. (I Peter 5:10)*

It is the love of God, the strongest force on earth that does the restoring. Like a house in need of repair, we need repair from the damage done by the world, ourselves, and others. Are you willing to allow Him to do some renovation on your heart?

Heavenly Father,

Thank you for sending Your Son, Jesus Christ to restore Your kingdom on earth. Thank you that You love me enough not to allow me to perish but to have eternal life. I choose to surrender to the transforming work of renovation on my heart and my life.
In Jesus' name, Amen

January 27

His Powerful Word

For the word of God is living and active. Sharper than any double-edged sword, it penetrates even to dividing soul and spirit, joints and marrow; it judges the thoughts and attitudes of the heart.
Hebrews 4:12

In the beginning God created the heavens and the earth. (Genesis 1:1) The earth was formless, empty, and dark. *Elohim said, Let there be light, and there was light. (Genesis 1:3)* Each time He spoke forth His word, God was creating the heavens and the earth. His love was the force and power, the cause of all, and His word was the agent in achieving His purpose to create. He spoke all into being: the sky, the waters, vegetation, stars, sun, and moon. His powerful spoken word called forth sea creatures, living creatures, and most importantly man. God's word that goes forth from His mouth will not return empty, but will accomplish what God desires and achieve the purpose for which it was sent. *(Isaiah 55:11)* Are you aware that there is power in the words that we speak? Our words have the power to bring life or death. (*Proverbs 18:21*) In reflecting on this, I shudder to think of the power that my negative words have had on the lives of others! But I am also keenly aware that my positive encouraging words have the power to influence lives for good. When I see that my words are not encouraging and uplifting, it is time to have a "spiritual heart" examination. King David best describes the process: *Search me, O God, and know my heart; test me and know my anxious thoughts. See if there is any offensive way in me, and lead me in the way everlasting. (Psalm 139:23-24)*

Are you aware of the power of your words for destroying or for
building up? Ask the Lord to examine your heart when you find that your words are negative. The Lord God created the world with His words and they brought forth life. How amazing it is when our words bring forth life as well!

Heavenly Father,

I desire to speak words that are encouraging and uplifting to others. Often it is easier to speak kindly to those who are not closest to me. Help me to first edify You, Lord, with my words; then help me to uplift those who are closest to me. Examine my heart when I struggle with my tongue and lead me to repentance.
In Jesus' name, Amen

January 28

Guilty as Charged

This righteousness from God comes through faith in Jesus Christ to all who believe. There is no difference, for all have sinned and fall short of the glory of God… Romans 3:22-23

Paul addresses the deliberate nature of mankind in disobedience and rebellion against God. I often wonder how Paul would be received today. He would likely be shunned by the world of psychology, sociology, and maybe even theology. His premise that mankind is sinful, rebellious, and disobedient against God goes against the school of thought claiming our depraved condition is a result of environment, genetics, and social issues. Paul claims that God has revealed His presence to mankind in plain ways such as in nature. But man has turned away from Him, worshipping the creation rather than the Creator. As a result, man deliberately practices immorality and idolatry. It seems as though Paul speaks directly to our society today. His message is just as applicable today as it was to the 1st century church.

Where are you in rebellion or disobedience to God? Have you blamed it on your past circumstances, your family or friends? We are affected by our past, however the Lord desires for us to receive His healing and to step out in faith to do His will. Where have you been chained to the past or fearful of the future? Has this inhibited your obedience to God? Remember that the Lord will heal and deliver you, freeing you to serve Him in obedience. As we walk with Christ knowing we are "guilty as charged," let us never forget that He has paid the price for our freedom. That enables us to follow the Lord in obedience and find peace and rest in walking in obedience.

Heavenly Father,
Thank you for the price You paid for my sins. Thank you for the freedom through redemption that You give me to serve You in obedience. Help me not to look at the bondage of my sin, but to look to You for forgiveness.

In Jesus' name, Amen

January 29

Trusting God's Deliverance

"The Lord who delivered me from the paw of the lion and the paw of the bear will deliver me from the hand of this Philistine."
Saul said to David, "Go, and the Lord be with You." I Samuel 17:37

David had seen God come to his aid when he kept his father's sheep. When a lion or a bear came and carried off a sheep from the flock, David went after it, struck it, and rescued the sheep from its mouth. He had seen the Lord deliver the sheep from harm's way using him as the means of deliverance. He had confidence that if God could empower him with supernatural strength to deliver the sheep from a lion and a bear, He would certainly deliver him from the giant. What an attitude of trust! The truth is that as we grow in our understanding of God's character, we learn that God is for us: *"If God is for us, who can be against us?" (Romans 8:31)* David was confident that God was *for* him because even as a shepherd boy, he had sought the Lord. During the long days and nights in the fields, he had gazed at the stars and knew that Elohim God had created them. He had watched the sheep under his care and knew that he was under the care of His Great Shepherd. He had fought the lion and the bear because he knew that HIS Great Shepherd would fight the lions and bears in his life.

Do you trust the Lord to deliver you from the giants in your life—the fears, the anger, the insecurities that plague you? As you study the story of David and the giant, take time to give the Lord your "giants." He will destroy them with but a single stone because He is for you. You are *His beloved child!* Trusting the Lord is the key to being delivered from our enemies. Perhaps you are presently going through a difficult time in a relationship, or you are struggling with a sin, or your life seems beset with problems. Scripture gives you hope to *trust in the Lord with all your heart and lean not on your own understanding. In all your ways acknowledge Him, and He will make your paths straight. (Proverbs 3:5-6)*

Heavenly Father,
I am surrounded with the "lions and bears" of life. I am confused, angry, and fearful. Your Word promises me that You will deliver me from my enemies. I am counting on You. I have nowhere else to turn. -In Jesus' name, Amen

January 30

Faith Tested

In this you greatly rejoice, though now for a little while you may have had to suffer grief in all kinds of trials. These have come so that your faith – of greater worth than gold, which perishes even though refined by fire – may be proved genuine and may result in praise, glory and honor when Jesus Christ is revealed.
I Peter 1:6-7

You may wonder why a good God would allow His children to suffer. The Scriptures are full of stories of men and women who suffered for their faith. Jesus said, *Blessed are you when people insult you, persecute you, and falsely say all kinds of evil against you because of Me. Rejoice and be glad for great is your reward in heaven. (Matthew 5:11)* Peter was addressing the impact salvation had on one's life and how often it produced suffering and persecution. Clearly suffering will test our faith, but the Lord will use the suffering to produce character in us. *(James 1:2-40)* As children of God, He wants our suffering to produce a harvest of righteousness.

You may be thinking, "Is there an easier way?" In my life, it has been mostly through hard times that I have grown closer to the Lord. During these times, He has strengthened my faith and increased my ability to help others. In the western world, we do not see persecution for our faith as openly as Christians do in other countries. However, it is present, though more subtle, when we take a stand on issues that run counter to Biblical teachings. As the tide seems to be shifting against Christian views, we see the importance of gaining a Biblical perspective to stand against the tide. What is your greatest obstacle in sharing your faith?

Heavenly Father,
It is so hard to take a stand for You in this world. My faith is tested each day as I try to live a Christian life. Why is it so difficult? Am I fearful of being persecuted for my faith? Strengthen me in Your Word and give me the courage and perseverance to stand against the assaults on my faith.

In Jesus' name, Amen

January 31

Faith

If you do not stand firm in your faith, you will not stand at all.
Isaiah 7:9b

There are two kinds of faith: saving faith (believing in Jesus and receiving Him as Savior) and faith to participate with God in His activities on earth (being co-workers with God). When we accept Jesus Christ as our Lord and Savior, we must take a leap of faith believing that He is who He says He is, the Son of God, our Savior and Redeemer. Our faith from that point must continue to be exercised in order to participate with God's activities on earth. James 2 says that faith without action is dead faith, so we must exercise our faith to have genuine faith. I am a member of a gym and I try to go three times a week to lift weights. The more I lift, the easier it becomes and then I am able to increase the weights as I build up my strength. The same is true for our faith: the more we exercise our faith, the stronger it becomes and the more we will see evidence of God working in our midst. Sometimes God tests our faith. If we pass the test, our faith is strengthened. Abraham was tested by God to see if he would trust God and obey Him, even if it meant sacrificing his son. One day God called out to him and told him to sacrifice Isaac, the child of promise. He was the child of promise because it was through Isaac that the Lord was going to form the nation of Israel. Isaac and Abraham went to the mountain prepared to obey God, but God intervened and sent a ram from the thickets to be the sacrifice (*Genesis 22:1-18*). Abraham passed the test.

Has God been testing your faith? Has He asked you to sacrifice something that you consider sacred–off limits to God? Remember the words in Isaiah: *if you do not stand firm in your faith, you will not stand at all.* (Isaiah 7:9) Your faith will be tested, but God has allowed it so that your "faith muscles" will become stronger.

Heavenly Father,
I recall times when my faith was tested and I turned and ran the other way. I did not know the reward of allowing You to strengthen me through obedience. I recall

other times when my faith was tested and I stood my ground trusting that You would deliver and strengthen me. Help me, dear Lord, to persevere through my tests of faith, trusting You to make me stronger. - In Jesus' name, Amen

February 1

Purposeful Witnesses

And I will ask the Father, and he will give you another Counselor to be with you forever—the Spirit of truth. The world cannot accept him, because it neither sees him nor knows him. But you know him, for he lives with you and will be in you.
John 14:16-17

Webster's dictionary defines "purpose" as *intention* or *determination.* To be purposeful is to be intentional or deliberate in accomplishing a goal. Over the past few years, much has been written on being "purposeful" in living. Most of the writings have one thing in common: in order to accomplish something, you have to give it thought, set a goal, and then move forward with purpose to do it. It doesn't do any good to have a plan if you aren't intentional about carrying it out. So it is with being a witness for Christ. The Holy Spirit guides us in what to say, gives us insight on how to do it, and leads us to the person or persons who are ready for the Word. But God does not speak for us. We must take the initiative and be obedient.

Do you believe that the Holy Spirit lives in you? As a believer, He is resident within you seeking a surrendered life. He is your Counselor, the Spirit of truth, and will lead you and guide you in your pursuit of God. Have you surrendered to Him asking the Holy Spirit to be released in your life as the "light force," the transforming power of life within you? As you pray daily for the infilling of the Holy Spirit, the Lord will transform you, empower you, and guide you into truth. Jesus told the woman at the well: *If you knew the gift of God and who it is that asks you for a drink, you would have asked Him and He would have given you living water. (John 4:10)* Ask the Lord to give you this living water today…His Spirit to fill you and to release His gifts within you *…but whoever drinks the water I give him will never thirst. (v.14)*

Heavenly Father,

Fill me with Your Holy Spirit. Stir up the gifts of Your Spirit within me so that I might be a powerful witness to Your holy name. When the waters seem to subside within me, fill me afresh and anew so that I can walk in Your will and Your ways. Help me to draw near to You and to receive the water that You give so that I might never thirst again.
In Jesus' name, Amen

February 2

One Spirit

If you have any encouragement from being united with Christ, if any comfort from his love, if any fellowship with the Spirit, if any tenderness and compassion, then make my joy complete by being like-minded, having the same love, being one in spirit and purpose. Do nothing out of selfish ambition or vain conceit, but in humility consider others better than yourselves. Each of you should look not only to your own interests, but also to the interests of others.
Philippians 2:1-4

Unity with Christ is defined by humility. As believers, if we have been united with Christ, the fruit of this union will be evident in the way we are united with others, being one in spirit and purpose and humbly serving others. Throughout the Old Testament, God's law served to point out sin and keep the Israelites united in purpose serving God. After Jesus came and offered us salvation through the forgiveness of our sins, His Holy Spirit continued the work of uniting all believers as one with one purpose—to love the Lord and to love our neighbor as ourselves (the Great Commandment). As Ezra read the Word, the people were convicted of their sin and were transformed as they responded in obedience. As we apply the message of unity to our lives, let us keep in mind that Jesus Christ has brought us together to love, to serve, and to continue the work of advancing His kingdom.

With whom do you feel divided or conflicted? You may not agree on issues, or circumstances may be such that you cannot be in agreement, however the Lord calls us to humbly walk with others. To love, encourage, and serve others regardless of differences perceived or real. The law of love supersedes our "right to be right" or our desire to get even. The Word teaches us that love covers a multitude of sins. (I Peter 4:8) Love will bring unity and purpose to our lives; love will cover our sins and draw us together. It is the most powerful force on earth.

Heavenly Father,

Help me to be like-minded, having the same unity of love, being one in spirit and purpose with other believers. Help me to do nothing out of selfish ambition or conceit; to look to the interest of others and value their opinion. Help me remember that Christ lives in me for the purpose of being united to share the good news of Jesus Christ and break down the walls of disunity that cause His kingdom to be divided. - In Jesus' name, Amen

February 3

Christian Standard of Living

Now when He saw the crowds, He went up on a mountainside and sat down. His disciples came to him, and he began to teach them…
Matthew 5:1-2

The Sermon on the Mount is the first of five discourses in *Matthew.* It contains the Beatitudes, which describe a state of blessedness or well-being for those who share in the kingdom. *(Matthew 5:1-12)* The meaning of blessed is different from the word happy, which is derived from "hap," meaning by chance, a joy often dependent on outward circumstances. Blessedness, derived from the Greek word "makarios," refers to the distinctive, spiritual joy of those who share in the salvation of the kingdom of God. It is a direct result of living *for* God and working *with* Him to establish His kingdom on earth. The Beatitudes describe ethical standards by which we are to live.

There are a variety of views on whether or not this was an actual sermon that Jesus preached or a composite of all of His teachings. Regardless, a standard of Christian living is set forth that can only be fulfilled by the power of God and our dependency on Him. How gracious the Lord is to give us all that we need to live kingdom lives and to help us when we fall short of His standards! The Beatitudes set forth a standard of living that is impossible to live without the power of the Holy Spirit. Take a moment and ask the Lord each day to fill you with His Spirit to empower you to live this blessed kingdom life.

Heavenly Father,
Thank you for Your Word that teaches me that my happiness is not just "by chance" and that my joy is complete in You alone. I desire to live for You, Lord, and not for myself. My life is yours to use as You wish. Fill me with Your life giving Spirit that I might live for You alone knowing that true joy comes from You.
In Jesus' name, Amen

His Covenant Word

For the Lord your God is a merciful God; He will not abandon or destroy you or forget the covenant with your forefathers, which he confirmed to them by oath.
Deuteronomy 4:31

The name of God, Elohim, is formed from the Hebrew word "Alah" to "swear" and describes One who stands in a covenant relationship ratified by an oath. We see in this name the mystery of the covenant relationship of the Trinity, but we also see the covenant relationship God has with His people. We first see the covenant relationship between man and God in Genesis. God establishes a covenant with Noah; although evil mankind will perish in the flood, Noah's seed will live. (Genesis 6:17-18) We see the covenant relationship between God and Abram when God promised him an heir. This seemed humanly impossible because his wife Sarai was beyond childbearing years. However, Sarai had a son because God is always faithful to His covenant word. We continue to see His covenant at work in the lives of Isaac, Jacob, and Moses. These everlasting covenants with His people have been a source of strength throughout the ages. Although God's children are often rebellious and turn away from Him, Elohim, Creator God, never forsakes the covenant He established with them. We may suffer the consequences when we turn from God, but He will never forsake His covenant with us. When we serve Him wholeheartedly, turning back to Him when we fall away, He is always there to restore us. What hope does that give you that Elohim will be faithful to His covenant with you even if you are disobedient?

Heavenly Father,
You alone are faithful. You never break your Covenant of love with me. Forgive me Lord, when I break my Covenant with You in rebellion and sin. Thank you for undeserved grace, unmerited forgiveness, and Your unconditional love that is

unprecedented. I am so grateful that though I am undeserving, You never abandon me.
In Jesus' name, Amen

Spiral of Sin

For although they knew God, they neither glorified Him as God nor gave thanks to him, but their thinking became futile and their foolish hearts were darkened. Although they claimed to be wise, they became fools and exchanged the glory of the immortal God for images made to look like mortal man and birds and animals and reptiles.
Romans 1:21-23

Paul says that mankind is without excuse in knowing, acknowledging, and worshipping God because God has plainly made Himself known to them in creation. Their choice to exchange God's immortal glory for images made to look like mortal man, birds, and animals begins an inevitable process of spiritual decline and immorality. The spiral of sin begins when we turn our hearts from the Living God towards images created to our likeness. It is interesting to note that we become like the gods we choose to worship and serve. At this point, God gives us over to whatever we choose to worship. For example, if we worship money, we may be driven to give all our time, energy, and heart to make more money. Jesus addressed this in *Matthew 6:24*: *"No one can serve two masters. Either he will hate the one and love the other, or he will be devoted to the one and despise the other. You cannot serve both God and money."* In *Romans 1:21-32*, we can see the spiral of sin as the Gentiles were given over to the sinful desires of their hearts. Their actions resulted in sexual impurity, exchanging God's truth for a lie, and becoming filled with wickedness, envy, murder, strife and malice. We must always be certain that in every area of our lives we put the Lord first, worshipping and seeking Him alone, and not allow the things we worship other than God to become paramount.

Heavenly Father,
Forgive me for crafting my own "idols" of worship—money, success, power. Forgive me Lord, for anything or anyone that I put in the place of my

relationship with You. I find myself over and over turning to false idols—things that lure my heart away from You. Sometimes I even put relationship with others before You, or fear man rather than fear You. Help me to throw off everything that encumbers my relationship with You and lead me in your everlasting ways.
In Jesus' name, Amen

February 6

Faith Proved Genuine

Now faith is being sure of what we hope for and certain of what we do not see.
Hebrews 11:1

Hebrews 11, the great chapter of faith, describes the men and women of God who were commended for their faith in the "unseen." When we place our trust in God's promises, we are also rewarded. (v. 6) When my daughter went through her rebellious years, I remember clinging to God's promises that He would be with her, that He would strengthen her, and that one day, He would use her in a mighty way. He has been true to His promise! At the time, all I saw were the problems but God's promise grew in my heart; what was not a present reality became a reality in my heart. I urge you to cling to God's promises and let them be the benchmark of your life. Let Jesus Christ assure you that the certainty of His resurrection will grow in your heart, just as certainly as His promises will prevail!! *Though you have not seen Him, you love Him; and even though you do not see Him now, you believe in Him and are filled with an inexpressible and glorious joy, for you are receiving the goal of your faith, the salvation of your souls.(* I Peter 1:8-9)

Heavenly Father,
Thank you for the assurance of what I hope for through faith. Thank you, Lord, that You alone are faithful to fulfill Your promises and purposes. Help me to cling to You in the tough times and to hold to the promises of Your Word. Fill me with "inexpressible joy," knowing that in all things You prevail.
In Jesus' name, Amen

February 7

Mercy

Then Peter came to Jesus and asked, "Lord, how many times shall I forgive my brother when he sins against me? Up to seven times?" Jesus answered, "I tell you, not seven times, but seventy-seven times. Therefore, the kingdom of heaven is like a king who wanted to settle accounts with his servants. As he began the settlement, a man who owed him ten thousand talents was brought to him. Since he was not able to pay, the master ordered that he and his wife and his children and all that he had be sold to repay the debt. The servant fell on his knees before him. 'Be patient with me,' he begged, 'and I will pay back everything.' The servant's master took pity on him, canceled the debt and let him go. But when that servant went out, he found one of his fellow servants who owed him a hundred denarii. He grabbed him and began to choke him. 'Pay back what you owe me!' he demanded. His fellow servant fell to his knees and begged him, 'Be patient with me, and I will pay you back.' But he refused. Instead, he went off and had the man thrown into prison until he could pay the debt. When the other servants saw what had happened, they were greatly distressed and went and told their master everything that had happened. Then the master called the servant in. 'You wicked servant,' he said, 'I canceled all that debt of yours because you begged me to. Shouldn't you have had mercy on your fellow servant just as I had on you?'"
Matthew 18:21-33

Jesus said, *Blessed are the merciful, for they will be shown mercy. (Matthew 5:7)* Webster describes "mercy" as *kind, compassionate,* and *forgiving* treatment. Sometimes we need to extend mercy to others; often we need to extend mercy to ourselves. It is easy to forget that we live under the Covenant that grace bought for us by the blood Jesus shed on the cross. It is through this Covenant that we are able to *approach the throne of grace with confidence*, knowing that we will receive mercy and grace *(Hebrews 4:16)*

Is there someone to whom you need to extend grace and mercy today? Remember that the Lord extended His hands on the cross offering undeserved mercy. It is through His example and compassion that we are called to do the same with others.

Heavenly Father,
It is too difficult to be merciful to others who have stabbed me in the back, been dishonest, or caused me harm. It is not within me to extend mercy to those who have hurt me. But when I consider what You have done for me, how You willingly went to the cross to offer me forgiveness for my sins, how can I do anything less than offer mercy to others? Fill me with Your agape love, compassion and mercy today.
In Jesus' name,
Amen

February 8

God's Faithfulness to Cover Our Sins

But if we walk in the light, as He is in the light, we have fellowship with one another, and the blood of Jesus, His son, purifies us from all sin.
John 1:7

The early church fathers viewed the scarlet cord as a type (symbol) of Jesus' atonement (forgiveness for sins by the shed blood of Jesus Christ). Throughout the Scriptures, the importance of Jesus' atonement is presented in different ways. Jesus represents the Lamb of God in the story in Exodus where the blood of the lamb was put on the door posts to save the Israelites' firstborn sons from certain death. Jesus shed His blood so that we could also be saved from spiritual death by coming into a right relationship with His Father.

You do not have to hang a scarlet cord outside your door like Rahab did to demonstrate her faith. *(Joshua 2:21)* Yet, it is important for each of us to recognize the importance of our atonement through Jesus' shed blood for us. Remember that as God used Rahab, He can and will use you if you are willing. Determine to deal with anything that holds you back from having the faith that enables you to be used by God.

Heavenly Father,
Forgive me when I take your grace in vain. Today, I symbolically place a "scarlet cord" over my life indicating that I am Yours, covered in the blood of Jesus. Help me to remember that though it may seem risky to place my faith in You at times, You are worth it all.

In Jesus' name,
Amen

A Love for God's Word

Oh, how I love your law!
I meditate on it all day long.
Your commands make me wiser than my enemies,
for they are ever with me. I have more insight than all my teachers,
for I meditate on your statutes.
Psalm 119:97-99

Psalm 119 is a devotional on the Word of God. The author was devoted to God's Word. He hid the Word in his heart so that he would not sin. *(v.11)* He submitted his life to the correction of the Word. Throughout *I* and *II Samuel,* David *"inquired of the Lord."* He sought the Lord before battles and often went to the priests for counsel. Saul, on the other hand, sought counsel from the witch of Endor. When Saul inquired of the Lord, He did not answer him, perhaps because Saul had been disobedient to the instructions of the Lord. Therefore, Saul sought counsel from the witch of Endor to find out the outcome of the battle. *(I Samuel 28:7)*

Courageous leaders need to recognize that the answers to their problems are found in God and His Word. They need to turn to the Lord in prayer and to His Word for counsel. More and more people are searching for answers. They are turning to psychics, horoscopes, and crystal balls. As leaders, we have an awesome responsibility to encourage people in our sphere of influence to turn to God's Word for help.

Heavenly Father,
Sometimes I simply do not want to take the time to read Your Word. Sometimes I read Your Word and I walk away having heard it, yet not responding. I desire to meditate on Your Word and have Your Word transform my hard heart. As I meditate on Your Word, help me to respond in obedience.
In Jesus' name,
Amen

February 10

Acknowledging God's Greatness

Lord, let your ear be attentive to the prayer of this your servant and to the prayer of your servants who delight in revering your name. Give your servant success today by granting him this favor in the presence of this man.
Nehemiah 1:11

Nehemiah models prayer for us in a compelling way. His prayer contains four significant elements:

- Devotes days to fasting and prayer as he waits on the Lord to lead him
- Acknowledges that God is an awesome, covenant-keeping God
- Repents of his sins and the sins of the Israelites
- Reminds the Lord of His promises to the Israelites if they return to Him

After Nehemiah's commitment to pray and fast, the door opens for him to share with the King of Persia the predicament of the Jewish people. When we wait on the Lord with prayer and fasting, acknowledging His greatness and His promises to us, God opens doors that no man can open. Today during my prayer time I asked the Lord to open a door for me to have a conversation with one of my daughters. I knew that I had to wait on the timing of the Lord and the wisdom of the Lord. He opened the door later that day and I was aware of His goodness and faithfulness. When I try to resolve conflicts and to devise solutions for problems, I have forgotten to pray first. I was reminded today that the Lord longs for His children to allow Him to bring resolution to their conflicts and solutions to their problems. This week, take your problems to the Lord in prayer using Nehemiah's model, and trust in His faithfulness to be attentive to your prayer. (*Nehemiah 1:11*)

Heavenly Father,
I acknowledge today that You are an awesome, Covenant-keeping God. I repent for the times I have not trusted You or believed that You are the problem solver. I release to You today the concerns of my heart and wait on You for my deliverance.
In Jesus' name,
Amen

Powerful Witnesses

But you will receive power when the Holy Spirit comes on you; and you will be my witnesses in Jerusalem, and in all Judea and Samaria, and to the ends of the earth.
Acts 1:8

In the gospel of *John*, Jesus promises to send His Holy Spirit when He leaves earth to go back to His Father. He promises He will not leave them (or us) on earth as orphans without power and guidance to live the Christian life. As I grow older, I often think I ought to have enough experience to deal with most things, but this is not the case. It is true that the Lord gives us wisdom when we ask, but usually life continues to be so challenging. I have realized that I need to rely on the Holy Spirit to guide and help me throughout each day. I challenge you to join me in beginning each day with a simple prayer: "Lord, please fill me today with your Holy Spirit." All day long we need to ask the Lord to refill us because we "leak." It is the power of the Holy Spirit that enables us to live the Christian life and be effective witnesses for God.

Heavenly Father,
I want to be bold for You, but I shrink back in fear of being rejected. I pray to share my faith story in an unimposing and humble way. I fear that I will not say the right words, or that my actions will betray me as I share my testimony of faith. Fill me with Your Holy Spirit who empowers and strengthens me to do Your will.
In Jesus' name,
Amen

February 12

The Just Judge

God "will give to each person according to what he has done." To those who by persistence in doing good seek glory, honor and immortality, He will give eternal life. But for those who are self-seeking and who reject the truth and follow evil, there will be wrath and anger.
Romans 2:6-8

God's judgment of Jew and Gentile alike was based on whether or not God's will was being done. It was based on impartiality and truth. Possession of the law did not give the Jew an advantage over the Gentiles. According to Paul, God is an impartial judge who rewards each person according to his or her works. Jews who sin while possessing the law were judged by that standard. Gentiles not under the law were judged by their conscience.

We are not under the law, but under grace. On this side of the cross, the key to escaping judgment is a matter of the heart worked out by evidence of a new life. Does your heart defy you by your words? ...*For out of the overflow of the heart the mouth speaks. (Matthew 12:34)* Each day it is good to do a "heart check." I do this by reviewing my day and observing how I responded to daily stresses, to concerns of others, to my children, my friends. It is easy to see what is in my heart when I observe what I have said or how I have behaved. *Proverbs 4:23* warns us to guard our hearts: *Above all else, guard your heart, for it is a wellspring of life.* Are you willing to have the Lord examine your heart today and ask for His forgiveness for every careless word or action that denied His love to others? He is a just judge who will not condemn but forgive.

Heavenly Father,
Forgive me today where I have spoken harshly to others. My heart is transparent before You and You alone know how to perform spiritual heart surgery. Guard my heart, O Lord, and fill me with Your love for others. Thank You that You are a just judge, giving me mercy I do not deserve.
In Jesus' name,
Amen

The Grace of God

The Word became flesh and made his dwelling among us. We have seen his glory, the glory of the One and Only who came from the Father, full of grace and truth. John testifies concerning him. He cries out, saying, "This was he of whom I said, 'He who comes after me has surpassed me because he was before me.' From the fullness of his grace we have all received one blessing after another. For the law was given through Moses; grace and truth came through Jesus Christ.
John 1:14-17

God's grace, His unmerited favor, was poured out on us at the cross. He redeemed us with His precious blood. (*I Peter 1:19*) *I Peter 1:13* tells us to set our hope on God's grace and to be prepared for action. In the language of the first century, it meant to gather up your long flowing garments and be ready for physical action. We are called to action by setting our minds for action, by being self-controlled, and by setting our hope in God's grace. Peter is calling us to have active faith as we pursue holiness—by being obedient and by not conforming to the world. (v.14) God calls us to "be holy as He is holy," living in reverent fear of Him and in obedience to His Word.

What is the stumbling block that keeps you from accessing God's grace? Perhaps you are ashamed of a past sin, a present sin. Perhaps you believe that God's grace is for everyone else, but not for you. As Jesus walked to the cross, He thought of YOU; as He hung on the cross, He thought of YOU; as He rose from the grave, He thought of YOU. He only has eyes for you, His beloved child. God's ways are not our ways. We think He only has the capacity or time to love just a few people, or to extend grace to a chosen few. His love and acceptance are beyond our understanding. Though he hates sin, He loves us individually and never forsakes us. Turn to Him... no, run to Him; He is waiting to shower you with His grace.

Heavenly Father,
I am ashamed of the things that I have done, and the things that I have left undone. I do not deserve Your grace and do not feel Your love. Today I refuse to believe the lie that You do not have enough love to go around or that You have

favorites. You came to this earth filled with grace and truth, and I choose to believe that I am the one that You love forever and ever.
In Jesus' name,
Amen

February 14

The Creative Godhead

Then God said, "Let us make man in our image, in our likeness, and let them rule over the fish of the sea and the birds of the air, over the livestock, over all the earth, and over all the creatures that move along the ground.
Genesis 1:26

Elohim, Creator God, by His spoken word created the heavens and the earth. He created mankind and entered into a covenant relationship to which He has been faithful in spite of mankind's rebellion throughout the centuries. The Hebrew ending for Elohim is plural because it describes the Trinity: the Father, the Son, and the Holy Spirit. At the beginning of creation, God said, "*Let* **us** *make man in our image, after our own likeness". (*Genesis 1:26) We also see the work of the Holy Spirit: *The Spirit of God moved upon the face of the earth. (*Genesis 1:21) and the presence of Jesus: *For by Him all things were created.* (Colossians 1:16) God is the Architect, Jesus the Builder, and the Holy Spirit is the One who breathes the life of God into the structure. As Elohim, He is the Father, Son, and Holy Spirit, present at the creation, present now, and will be present forever!

Heavenly Father,
The understanding of the Trinity is complex to me. To know You as Father, Son and Holy Spirit is the desire of my heart. Father, I desire to know Your love; Son, I desire to know You as the branch connected to the vine; Holy Spirit, I desire to know You as the breath of life.
In Jesus' name,
Amen

February 15

The Head and the Tail

The Lord is angry with all nations; his wrath is upon all their armies. He will totally destroy them, he will give them over to slaughter.
Isaiah 34:2

Throughout the book of *Isaiah*, the prophet condemns the leadership of the people. In *Isaiah 10*, the lawmakers issued "oppressive decrees" and withheld justice. The elders of Israel (the head) and the prophets (the tail) were misguiding the people. *(Isaiah 9:15-16)*

Christian leaders are called to set an example for the ungodly. It is our responsibility to be leaders in our society today, exemplifying the character of Christ. As I write, an interesting image comes to mind. I think about traveling with young children. Before take-off, the pre-flight instructions include what to do if there is oxygen loss and how you are to assist children. First you secure the oxygen mask over your nose, and then you help your child put on his/her oxygen mask. As Christian leaders, we can only be effective in leading others by first insuring that we are "breathing in the Holy Spirit." *Isaiah 11* describes what the oxygen of the Holy Spirit is like: wisdom, understanding, counsel, power, and fear of the Lord. When we walk with a "full tank," we can help others draw from the springs of salvation and offer them the oxygen tank of life that we have stored up. Who are you leading, and what can you do to improve in your leadership skills?

Heavenly Father,
Fill me with Your Holy Spirit. I breathe in Your life as oxygen for my soul. And after I am filled with Your Spirit, pour out Your life through me. Help me to be a courageous leader exemplifying the character of Christ. Open doors today so that I may lead others to You.
In Jesus' name,
Amen

Fruit of Christian Living

But when he saw many of the Pharisees and Sadducees coming to where he was baptizing, he said to them: "You brood of vipers! Who warned you to flee from the coming wrath? Produce fruit in keeping with repentance. And do not think you can say to yourselves, 'We have Abraham as our father.' I tell you that out of these stones God can raise up children for Abraham. The ax is already at the root of the trees, and every tree that does not produce good fruit will be cut down and thrown into the fire.
Matthew 3:7-10

God called Israel to live distinct and holy from other nations, primarily in the external matters of the Law. However, Jesus calls His people to a holiness that proceeds from the heart. Holiness is the fruit of a personal relationship with God. Jesus came as the fulfillment of the Law; therefore, New Testament living is based on actions that proceed from a transformed heart through a relationship with Christ. *Matthew 7:18* describes our lives of obedience to Christ as trees bearing good fruit: *A good tree cannot bear bad fruit, and a bad tree cannot bear good fruit.* I have a vegetable garden that is beginning to show blossoms, the first sign of the fruit to come. As we spend time with the Lord in His Word and through prayer, we will begin to see the blossoming of our spiritual lives and ultimately the fruit will come. The soil of our hearts needs to be tilled up, and the seeds of the life of His Word need to be watered in us as we seek to be holy and fruitful in Christ. The Lord desires that we all bear fruit for His kingdom. We do that by living lives consistent with the standards that Jesus set forth in the Sermon on the Mount. The apostle Paul reminds us to put off our old self, corrupted by deceitful desires, and to be made new in the attitude of our minds by putting on the new self, created to be like God in true righteousness and holiness. *(Ephesians 4:22)*

How about you? Are you beginning to see the blossoms of Christ in your life? Are you beginning to see fruit? Ask the Lord to till up the soil of your heart and be faithful to meditate on His Word and obey. He will be faithful to produce a crop of new life in you. His life in you will draw others to Christ as well.

Heavenly Father,
I desire to bear fruit in Your name. Create in me a clean heart, Lord. Destroy those things in me that are not holy. Lead me to draw from the springs of water in Your Word and produce the fruit of love, goodness, compassion and holiness.
In Jesus' name,
Amen

Connection to Others

My command is this: Love each other as I have loved you. Greater love has no one than this, that he lay down his life for his friends.
John 15:12-13

We must be connected to Jesus, the Vine, if our lives are to be spiritually fruitful. He is our source of strength, sustenance, authority, and power. Paul exemplifies a man who drew from the Living Vine. He also exemplifies a man who was connected to others as an outflow of his relationship with Christ. In *Acts 22,* we read about the other believers who treasured His friendship and valued His life. In *Acts 22* and *23,* we see Paul attempt to connect with his fellow Jews as he calls them "brothers." He showed respect to the "rulers of the people" *(Acts 23:5)* and sought to bring unity to all people through the gift of God's love and salvation. Some chose to connect with him and others chose to defy him. So it is with us as we relate to people around us.

Who are the people that God has brought into your life—your spouse, children, friends, family members? Examine those relationships and take each one to prayer asking the Holy Spirit to guide and direct you. Seek first to be intimately connected to Jesus, and He will cause those relationships to thrive. I know when I have heeded God's Word to "remain in Him" because I see the fruit of my obedience in my relationships with others: *Remain in me, and I will remain in you. No branch can bear fruit by itself; it must remain in the vine. (John 15:4)*

As you go through your week, seek a connection with the Lord and with others. You will see the fruit of honesty, vulnerability, truthfulness and compassion in your relationships because this is the character of Christ in you, the connection seen between the vine and the branch.

Heavenly Father,
Your Word says to seek Your kingdom and righteousness first. (Matthew 6:33) It is the desire of my heart to seek You above all other relationships. As the vine is connected to the branches, help me to reflect this connection of my life in Christ

to others.
In Jesus' name, Amen

The Lord's Battle

Saul replied, "You are not able to go out against this Philistine and fight him; you are only a boy, and he has been a fighting man from his youth." But David said to Saul, "…The Lord who delivered me from the paw of the lion and the paw of the bear will deliver me from the hand of this Philistine."
I Samuel 17:33-37

I Corinthians 1:27 reveals the truth that the Lord uses our weaknesses to display His strength. I am certain that the people who watched David thought he was foolish to fight the Philistine giant. But God chose the foolish things of the world to shame the wise; God chose the weak things of the world to shame the strong. David may have appeared foolish, but he knew that the battle was the Lord's. It was the Lord who would defeat the giant. In *I Samuel 30*, David continued to demonstrate his reliance on the Lord when he reminded the men who battled the Amalekites that it was the Lord who had protected them, not their own ability or strength. When we believe that the battle is ours and fight in our own strength, we often feel defeated. Though we may seemingly win the battle, we become weary or burned out. When we allow the Lord to fight our battles, trusting in Him and stepping out in faith, He reveals to us that though we are weak, we are strong in Him. Paul came to this same conclusion when he battled an unknown thorn in the flesh. Three times he pleaded with the Lord to take it away, and the Lord responded: *My grace is sufficient for you, for My power is made perfect in weakness. (II Corinthians 12:9)* Take a moment and pray for the faith to believe that God's grace is sufficient for every battle you face.

Heavenly Father,
I have been in a battle facing my own "giants" of fear of insecurity, lost hope, and fear of failure. Help me to stand on the promise of Your Word that when I am weak, You are strong; when I feel inadequate to stand against the "giants," You will fight for me. Thank you that all of the battles I face are fought in Your strength.
In Jesus' name, Amen

February 19

Repentance

...let your ear be attentive and your eyes open to hear the prayer your servant is praying before you day and night for your servants, the people of Israel.
Nehemiah 1:6

A key component of Nehemiah's prayer was repentance. He identified with the sins of the people and repented, both for his own sins and for theirs, for their unfaithfulness towards God. Israel's history was replete with God's people turning from God to idolatry and pagan practices. Repeatedly the Lord reminded them that if they turned back to Him, He would redeem them. Time and time again we see this pattern repeated: unfaithfulness and disobedience, turning back to God, and God redeeming His people. Nehemiah confessed their sins of disobedience against God's commands that were given to Moses. *(v.7)* God has promised us as well that if we return to Him in repentance he will heal and deliver us: *...if my people who are called by my name will humble themselves and pray and seek my face I will hear from heaven and will forgive their sin and will heal their land. (II Chronicles 7:14)* Nehemiah repented and reminded God of His promise to gather His people back when they turned to Him in repentance.

Where do you need to turn back to God? Have you been so busy that you haven't sought Him in prayer? Have you sinned and refused to come back to Him thinking that you have strayed so far away that it is impossible for you to return? God's Word says that sin is not to be our master because we are not under the law, but under grace. *(Romans 6:14)* Where has sin had mastery over you? Turn back today and receive God's grace. The Lord is always waiting with open arms.

Heavenly Father,
I repent that I have strayed far from You. I have been disobedient to Your Word and have fallen away. Thank you for Your promise that if I humble myself and turn back to You, You will receive me with open arms.
In Jesus' name, Amen

Profession and Practice

Now if you call yourself a Jew; if you rely on the law and brag about your relationship to God; if you know his will and approve of what is superior because you are instructed by the law; if you are convinced that you are a guide for the blind, a light for those who are in the dark, an instructor of the foolish, a teacher of infants, because you have in the law the embodiment of knowledge and truth – you, then, who teach others, do you not teach yourself? You who preach against stealing, do you steal?
Romans 2:17-21

The Jews were governed by the Mosaic Law, and Paul argues in this passage that what the Jews considered to be assets (i.e. relying on the law and their status as God's chosen nation) became liabilities when there was no connection between profession and practice. The same principal that governed God's judgment in *Romans 2:1-16* applied to both the Gentiles and the Jews. Paul, once a self-righteous Jew, skillfully sets forth a series of questions addressing the issues of hypocrisy for the Jews who bragged about the law but dishonored God by breaking the law. *(v.23)* As I study this passage, I can think of so many ways I have dishonored the Lord by not obeying His Word. As you study this passage, consider ways that your profession of faith does not match the practice of your faith. Together, let us ask the Lord to soften our hearts so that what comes out of our mouths and how we live our daily lives will be in line with God's Word.

Heavenly Father,
I can see ways that what I profess I do not practice. Help me to line up Your Word with my life and give me a willing heart to follow You in both word and deed. Forgive my hypocrisy, and strengthen my resolve to be more like You.
In Jesus' name, Amen

February 21

Strategic Witnesses

"But you will receive power when the Holy Spirit comes on you; and you will be my witnesses in Jerusalem, and in all Judea and Samaria, and to the ends of the earth."
Acts 1:8

Jesus sent His Holy Spirit at Pentecost to empower believers to be witnesses for Christ. Today, we also have the Holy Spirit and access to His power as believers. When we want to accomplish something, we set goals for ourselves and outline strategies or ways that will enable us to accomplish our goals. The same is true with being a witness for Christ. Jesus tells the believers that they will be His witnesses in Jerusalem, Judea, Samaria, and to the ends of the earth. He starts with the city they are in and moves out to farther and farther places.

Applying this pattern of witnessing for Christ in your own lives, consider setting a goal to be a witness to those nearest you, such as family members and then beyond. Being a witness does not mean quoting Scripture—it means living the truth of the Scripture. Sometimes it is more difficult to express the love of Christ to family members than to outsiders, but just as the disciples were challenged to begin in Jerusalem, close to home, we must also begin with home. Jesus was laying a strategy before us—first Jerusalem, then Judea and Samaria. Are you willing to be a witness at home and serve family members first? Are you willing to go beyond the comfort of home and reach out to others? The Lord will lead you by His Holy Spirit and enable you to be His hands and feet on earth.

Heavenly Father,
Sometimes I am a better witness to those outside of my family than to my own family members. Give me patience with my family, seeking their interests above my own. And help me to reach out to others beyond my home to share the love of Christ.
In Jesus' name, Amen

Jehovah, The Righteous Judge

...let the LORD judge the peoples.
Judge me, O LORD,
according to my righteousness,
according to my integrity,
O Most High.
Psalm 7:8

The word Jehovah is formed from two tenses of the Hebrew verb "havah," *to be*, and meaning "One who is what He is," reflecting the words of God to Moses, I AM WHO I AM. *(Exodus 3:14)* Inherent in this name is His holiness and self-existence. Jehovah is the expression of God's being, and therefore we see Him as holy, just, and true. In *Genesis 2 and 3*, we begin to see God as Jehovah who commands Adam and Eve not to eat the fruit of the tree of the knowledge of good and evil. God is placing a requirement on Adam and Eve to be holy by being obedient to His commands. They failed the test, and we are introduced in God's Word to JEHOVAH God, the Judge, as He disciplines His people. Because He is holy, He requires that we be holy. (*Leviticus 20:24-25*)

Are you able to say as King David did: *judge me, O Lord, according to my righteousness?* Are you willing to stand before Jehovah, the Righteous Judge and, like David, say: *Search me, O God, and know my heart; test me and know my anxious thoughts. See if there is any offensive way in me, and lead me in the way everlasting.*

Heavenly Father,
Search my heart, O Lord, and examine my thoughts; test my ways, and see if there is any offensive way in me.
In Jesus' name, Amen

February 23

The Holiness of God

"Who among the gods is like you, O LORD? Who is like you – majestic in holiness, awesome in glory, working wonders?"
Exodus 15:11

Peter 1:15-16 challenges us to be holy as God is holy. The text continues by describing what it means to be holy and set apart: to live as strangers on earth in fear of the Lord. In *I Peter 1:1*, stranger is defined as "exile"—a person living temporarily on earth, but whose home is in heaven. I Peter 1:18 reminds readers that we are redeemed not with perishable things such as silver or gold, but with the precious blood of Christ. Consequently, we are not to take lightly the holiness of God, but to pursue holiness because God is holy. What an opportunity we have to bring God's light into a dark world by being a holy people who are set apart for God! The Word of God teaches us to fear the Lord; that the fear of the Lord is the beginning of wisdom. *(Proverbs 1:7)* Fear of the Lord implies our revering Him, honoring Him, and knowing Him as majestic and holy. Though we are called to intimacy with Christ, we must approach Him with reverence. Moses heard the voice of God in the burning bush and was told to remove his sandals. *(Exodus 3:5)* Perhaps his sandals represented the places Moses had been that were not holy—the places where he had been defiled. He removed his sandals to stand before a holy God.

What are your sandals that represent the things that defile a holy God—a sinful relationship, an unholy business partnership, a sin that you refuse to give over to God? The Lord is calling you as a child of God to remove your sandals and stand before Him, the majestic, awesome God.

Heavenly Father,
Thank you that through Christ I am able to approach Your throne of grace with confidence. (Hebrews 4:16) Help me to remember that as I approach You, I approach You as a holy, majestic God. Thank you that when I come to You

stained with sin, You receive me, wash me, and place on my feet sandals of holiness.
In Jesus' name, Amen

February 24

Healing the Sick

He sent forth his word and healed them; he rescued them from the grave.
Psalm 107:20

In *Matthew 8 and 9*, we read that Jesus healed a man with leprosy, cured a centurion's servant, healed Peter's mother-in-law, cast out demons, and healed a paralytic. As we read through these accounts, Jesus demonstrates and proclaims the kingdom of God. Today we still see evidence of the kingdom, yet we often discount the "miraculous" that happens around us. I have started praying daily that the Lord will open my spiritual eyes to see His kingdom power and enable me to demonstrate and proclaim His kingdom. *Jeremiah 17:5-14* tells us that we must have confidence in the Lord in order to be healed. Do you have blocks that hinder your spiritual or physical healing? What are they? Ask the Lord to remove obstacles that hinder your confidence in His healing power.

Heavenly Father,
I confess that when I pray "Your kingdom come, Your will be done," too often I do not believe Your kingdom will really break through. Increase my faith as I pray that Your kingdom comes to earth, knowing that Your awesome power is at work.
In Jesus' name, Amen

Moving Into the Promised Land

Yet he did not waver through unbelief regarding the promise of God, but was strengthened in his faith and gave glory to God…
Romans 4:20

God told Joshua to lead the Israelites across the Jordan River. *(Joshua 1)* They had to cross the Jordan in order to enter and live in the Promised Land. The Jordan River, for us, represents the obstacles we must cross to move into our Promised Land, our place of victory, peace, and rest in the Lord. I believe there is a twofold meaning of the Promised Land: as unbelievers, crossing into the Promised Land represents our acceptance of Christ as our Savior and receiving the gift of eternal life. As believers who have accepted Christ into our lives, crossing into the Promised Land is the process of appropriating the promises of God to our lives. Moses, Joshua's mentor and leader, had died. Joshua was now faced with leading the Israelites into the Promised Land. Had he wavered in unbelief, he might have turned back. God spoke to Joshua, reminding him that he would be with him wherever he went: *Be strong and courageous. Do not be terrified; do not be discouraged for the Lord your God will be with you wherever you go. (Joshua 1:9)* Joshua could have chosen to turn back in unbelief, but he chose to believe that God was with him and that he was called to lead God's people. We must also be strengthened in our faith by the Word of God. He calls us to step out in faith and believe His Word. What promises in His Word have you chosen not to believe? Are you discouraged or terrified about something? Where God calls you, He will not fail you. His promises are true today just as they were for Joshua, but you must choose to believe.

Heavenly Father,
The truth is that I am discouraged today. I have tried to put up a good front, but I am tired and beaten down. Help me not to waver in unbelief regarding Your promises. Give me strength and courage to step out in faith and believe that, like Joshua, You will be with me wherever I go.
In Jesus' name, Amen

February 26

A Faithful Remnant

Repent, then, and turn to God so that your sins may be wiped out, that times of refreshing may come from the Lord...
Acts 3:19

The son of King Ahaz was called Shear-jashub, which means "a remnant shall return." The House of David had to eat curds and honey, the food of poverty, because the invading Assyrian army decimated the countryside. They learned, however, through this difficult time to "refuse evil and choose good." Shear-jashub represents the return of the remnant back to the Lord and thus back to a time of prosperity. (*Isaiah 10*) The Lord has promised throughout the ages that if we turn from evil and seek to obey the Lord, He will bring us back from captivity. There has always been a faithful remnant who has continued to turn to the Lord. I pray that we will all be a part of the faithful! Jesus looked out over Jerusalem and said that He longed to gather the chicks like a mother hen. He longed to draw the Jews to Himself, the well of salvation, a place of security, peace, and deliverance. The people of Jerusalem rejected Jesus just as the people of Isaiah's time had rejected God.

Let us be a people who are willing to go forth with joy, drawing from the well of salvation as a part of the faithful remnant. (*Isaiah 12:3)* As we repent and daily turn to the Lord, He will refresh us. When I sin against the Lord and others and turn back to Him in prayer and repentance, I imagine a huge waterfall raining down on me washing and refreshing my weary soul. Do you need to stand under the waterfall of his grace?

Heavenly Father,
Thank you for the gift of repentance. Thank you that You will wash and cleanse me from my sins. Just as I bathe every day, help me to wash in Your cleansing Word. Jesus told His disciples that they were cleansed by His words: "you are already clean because of the Word I have spoken to you." (John 15:3) Cleanse me with Your Word and lead me to new life.
In Jesus' name, Amen

Willfulness or Willingness

If you fear the LORD and serve and obey him and do not rebel against his commands, and if both you and the king who reigns over you follow the LORD your God – good! But if you do not obey the LORD, and if you rebel against his commands, his hand will be against you, as it was against your fathers.
I Samuel 12:14-15

Willfulness leads to disobedience. Pride and self-centeredness cause us to do what we want rather than to follow what God wants us to do. Saul discovered this when he disobeyed the Lord twice. His disobedience cost him the kingdom. The first time he disobeyed by not waiting on the Lord. The second time, he rebelled by sparing King Agag and the best sheep and cattle, all of which God had instructed him to destroy. Saul was serving his own interests, and then he gave an excuse for what he did. *(I Samuel 15:22)* He even blamed his willfulness on others. How like Saul we are! The consequences for King Saul were great. Likewise, the times that I have disobeyed the Lord have caused me sorrow and pain. God knows what is best for us and knows that we are like "sheep that go astray." *(I Peter 2:25)* Our Good Shepherd, however, brings us back, cares for our wounds, and forgives our sins when we willingly turn to Him. We need to turn from willfulness to willingness to follow God who loves us so deeply.

What has the Lord told you to do that you have refused to do? Disobedience can cause our hearts to be hardened, and little by little the voice of the Shepherd grows faint. Our spiritual ears become dull and our spiritual eyes grow dim when we continue to defy the Lord.

Heavenly Father,
I determine today to do Your Will. Help me to turn my willfulness into willingness, and I ask Your blessing on my obedience.
In Jesus' name, Amen

February 28

Prayer of Faith

The LORD has heard my cry for mercy;
the LORD accepts my prayer.
Psalm 6:9

In the first chapter of *Nehemiah*, we see that faith was a key component of Nehemiah's prayer; he did not doubt that God would be faithful to His promises. Nehemiah knew of the unfaithfulness of the Israelites to God, but he also knew of God's faithfulness to them throughout the years. He reminds the Lord of His promise to return the exiles to Jerusalem so that He could have a dwelling place. Jesus commended people for their faith, indicating that their faith had been a catalyst for God's response. Nehemiah knew that God was consistent, faithful, and trustworthy, and so he placed his faith in God, not in the circumstances at hand. It is so easy for us to look at the circumstances that we are praying about instead of being like Nehemiah and looking to God and His faithfulness to hear and answer our prayer. Nehemiah looked to God for the solution to the problems in Jerusalem. He had compassion on the people in Jerusalem who were in trouble and disgrace, living in a city with broken-down walls. Yet rather than seeking his own solutions, he sought the Lord and was certain that God would provide them with a solution.

We, like the city of Jerusalem, have "broken-down" walls in our lives; broken relationships, financial stress, and an inability to receive God's love. It is tempting to try to find our own solutions. The Lord is looking to raise up a people who will turn to God in prayer and trust that God will be faithful to His promises.

Heavenly Father,
I release my broken-down places to You. I ask for Your wisdom and direction in the mending of broken walls. You alone are faithful and able to help me to find solutions to my struggles. Forgive me where I have tried to take care of things myself rather than turning to You.
In Jesus' name, Amen

God's Faithfulness to Israel

Have I not commanded you? Be strong and courageous. Do not be terrified; do not be discouraged, for the LORD your God will be with you wherever you go.
Joshua 1:9

God has demonstrated His faithfulness throughout the ages. He promised never to forsake His people. The Israelites, however, often forsook God. They worshipped graven images, made idols and hardened their hearts to God. The Lord continually reminded the Israelites to turn from their wicked ways and back to Him, but throughout their history they were rebellious time and time again.

How like the Israelites we are! We continue to worship Him with our lips but forsake His ways. We become self-absorbed, or the world absorbs our time and devotion. The Lord continually calls us back to Himself, reminding us that He will faithfully take us back. Think about your most faithful and trustworthy friend. Has he ever let you down? I have told my two sisters that even though my intentions are good, I will let them down from time to time. *Proverbs 18:24* says that there is a friend who sticks closer than a brother. Jesus Christ is that friend—the perfect friend. He is always there, always faithful and trustworthy. In today's passage, God told Joshua to be courageous because He would never leave him. Joshua was facing the challenge of his life, and God knew he needed a friend, someone who would help him face obstacles as he entered the Promised Land.

As you face a trial or obstacle, keep in mind that God is with you and will never let you down. Friends may break promises, but He is always true to His Word.

Heavenly Father,
I have been so disappointed in friends. I fear letting anyone get too close. You called Your disciples friends and You demonstrated friendship with the greatest sacrifice of all—Your life. Help me to know You as my friend, the faithful One, and to be open to friendships with others.
In Jesus' name, Amen

March 2

The Word of God

For you have been born again, not of perishable seed, but of imperishable, through the living and enduring word of God.
I Peter 1:23

The Word of God is living and enduring. I love the Word of God! As I read, meditate, and study God's Word, I am learning more about the love of Christ, His transforming power, and the Holy Spirit's conviction. I pray, "Lord, change me through Your Word. Bring correction, healing, and truth to my life." Peter describes our experience as *born again, not of perishable seed, but of imperishable, through the living and enduring Word of God. (I Peter 1:23)* Did you know that the Word of God goes out and never returns empty? When God's Word is spoken, read and received, it will always accomplish a purpose in your life: *…so is my word that goes out from my mouth; it will not return to me empty, but will accomplish what I desire and achieve the purpose for which I sent it. (Isaiah 55:11)* We are often careless with our words—perhaps offering to call or pray for someone but not following through. Our words may not always find fulfillment of purpose, but God's Word will always be fulfilled. Paul understood the significance of God's Word and admonished the early Christian believers to allow the Word of God to dwell richly within them. *(Colossians 3:16)* Try taking a scripture passage each day and meditate on it all day long. God's Word, when planted in the fertile soil of our hearts, will always bear fruit.

Heavenly Father,
Your Word is a lamp to my feet and a light to my path. (Psalm 119:105) Forgive me where I have been careless with my words, where I have spoken without thinking, or promised something and never followed through. Help me, Lord, to choose my words wisely and to follow through with what I say. I thank you that You always keep Your Word. Help me to do the same.
In Jesus' name, Amen

Bread of Life

I am the bread of life. He who comes to me will never go hungry, and he who believes in me will never be thirsty.
John 6:35

Jesus demonstrated that He was the Bread of Life by feeding five thousand people by multiplying five loaves of bread and two fish. He demonstrated that He was the Bread of Life that could feed their spiritual hunger. One day the disciples were crossing over the eastern shore of the Sea of Galilee. The disciples had forgotten to bring a loaf of bread along to eat, and Jesus heard them discussing this among themselves. The disciples had just witnessed a miracle when Jesus multiplied the fishes and loaves of bread, and yet they still did not understand that He WAS the Bread of Life—the One who could provide them with both physical and spiritual bread. Jesus said: *Why are you talking about having no bread? Do you still not see or understand? Are your hearts hardened? Do you have eyes but fail to see, and ears but fail to hear? When I broke the five loaves for the five thousand, how many basketfuls of pieces did you pick up? (Mark 8:17-19)*

In what way do you need to meet Jesus as the Bread of Life? Do you need provision financially, or do you have concerns for the future? Do you struggle knowing that He can multiply your resources and provide you with "bread"? Do you know Him as the Bread of Life who is able to quench your spiritual hunger? The disciples did not understand. They had just seen a miracle of multiplication and yet they still worried about their "lack." The Lord is calling you today to meet Him as the Bread of Life. Trust Him to fill where you have lack and to satisfy you where you are thirsty and hungry.

Heavenly Father,
Help me to know You as the Bread of Life. Forgive me where I have limited the possibilities with You. I release to You my concerns and fears and ask You to reveal Yourself to me today as the Bread of Life.
In Jesus' name, Amen

March 4

The Journey of Surrender

Then the Lord said, "Rise and anoint him; he is the one." So Samuel took the horn of oil and anointed him in the presence of his brothers, and from that day on, the Spirit of the LORD came upon David in power.
I Samuel 16:12-13

Paul warns us: *Be very careful, then, how you live. (Ephesians 5:15)* The Scripture teaches that surrendering to God is an ongoing journey; it is not a destination. When David was anointed by Samuel, it was just the beginning of his journey from tending sheep to leading a nation. David walked step by step in his journey of surrender, following the path to which God had called him. His spiritual journey was ignited by his relationship with God, and courage was an outgrowth of that relationship. *(I Samuel 17:48-49)* The fuel for the journey of surrender was provided by the ongoing guidance of the Holy Spirit. *(I Samuel 16:13)* Some of the experiences David had were easier than others. Yet David was described as having a *heart after the Lord's heart. (I Samuel 13:14)* The most difficult thing for me to do is to be patient and wait on the Lord once I sense that He is calling me to do something. Time and time again, the Lord reminds me that His timing is perfect and I must wait on Him to give me the "green light." The problem is I forget that I am on a journey with God, and I get impatient to arrive at my destination. David was anointed king, but he had to endure years of working for King Saul and years of torment at the hand of Saul before he became king.

Has the Lord anointed you to do something? Are you certain of His call, but every time you step out in faith, you fail or doors do not open? The Lord is more concerned with the journey than the destination. He may be growing trust and patience in you. He may be waiting for the perfect timing that will enable you to fulfill the call. Place your trust in Him and wait. He has a plan, a perfect plan.

Heavenly Father,
I am so impatient. I have waited for so long for You to move in my life. You placed a dream in my heart and it has yet to be fulfilled. I have tried to make it

happen to no avail. Have Your way in my life, Lord. I surrender to Your Will and Your perfect timing.
In Jesus' name, Amen

March 5

Presenting the Problem

The king said to me, "What is it you want?" Then I prayed to the God of heaven, and I answered the king, "If it pleases the king and if your servant has found favor in his sight, let him send me to the city in Judah where my fathers are buried so that I can rebuild it."
Nehemiah 2:4-5

Nehemiah approached the king with the fear of the Lord and with submission to the God-given authorities. He humbly asked the king for the resources he needed to complete his mission in Jerusalem. It is obvious that through his time of prayer and fasting, the Lord gave him a strategy to go forward in order to help restore Jerusalem's broken-down walls. We also have "broken-down" walls in our lives. The Lord longs to restore those broken-down places where the world and the evil one continually weaken our defenses and make us ashamed, angry, hurt, disappointed, fearful, or even hopeless. Nehemiah models for us how a Godly man approached the devastation in Jerusalem. His first step was to fast and pray. Then he waited for God to open the door of opportunity so he could begin the process of stepping out in faith and putting his God-given plan into action. As believers, we have the Holy Spirit to lead, guide and direct our paths. In the places of devastation in our lives—those broken-down places—the Lord will direct us through His Holy Spirit when we turn to Him in prayer. He will give us the mind of Christ to show us what to do and when to do it. Even more importantly, it is GOD who will provide the resources we need to restore our lives. The Lord is gracious and compassionate, and, like Nehemiah, we are able to say: *the gracious hand of my God was upon me and the king granted my requests. (Nehemiah 2:8b)*

Has the Lord laid something on your heart that needs to be done? Does it seem like an impossible task? Nehemiah was faced with rebuilding a city that had been burned down—a formidable task! He did not dwell on the negative possibilities but sought the Lord in prayer, and the God of the impossible told him what to do. If you are faced with a problem, seek the Lord. He will give you the wisdom you need.

Heavenly Father,
I am faced with an impossible task. I do not have the resources, the time, or the ability to accomplish it. I cry out to You for wisdom, strength, time and ability to accomplish what is before me.
In Jesus' name, Amen

March 6

God's Kindness Leads to Repentance

Or do you show contempt for the riches of his kindness, tolerance, and patience, not realizing that God's kindness leads you toward repentance?
Romans 2:4

It is God's kindness that leads us to repentance. He is patient, desiring that none should perish. As I meditate on this Scripture, I am reminded of how often I am miserable in my sin and how the Lord does not always offer me relief from my misery. He offers me, instead, the gift of forgiveness. He longs for to us to come back to Him in repentance and restoration of fellowship. Paul writes that an unrepentant heart stores up wrath for the day of God's judgment. Consider a loving parent who patiently leads a child towards repentance. When my children were young, I tried to give them every opportunity to tell me the truth when I knew they had disobeyed me. I often would tell them that the consequences would be far greater if they failed to be truthful. Our loving Father is infinitely more patient with us, desiring that we turn back to Him. Paul, a zealous Jew, understood the self-righteousness of the Jews. He knew of their temptation to judge the Gentiles and yet to not live up to the standard of God's Word themselves. Although the Gentiles did not live by the law, they were judged by God according to the light that had been revealed to them, the truth of God's Word, and their deeds. God, the impartial judge, waited for them to repent. He waits for us as well. His kindness leads us to repentance. How irresistible His love is!

Heavenly Father,
Thank you that it is Your kindness that leads to repentance. I am miserable in my sin, and I know that You have allowed me to feel this way so that I will turn back. Your love reaches down and lifts me up.
In Jesus' name, Amen

Jehovah, The Holy One

The Lord said to Moses, "Speak to the entire assembly of Israel and say to them: 'Be holy because I, the LORD your God, am holy."
Leviticus 19:1-2

Jehovah is a holy God, and He expects us to be a holy people. When Adam and Eve sinned and disobeyed God, the consequences of their sin caused mankind to be separated from God forever. Jesus Christ came as our holy sacrifice, making grace available to us, because we fall short of keeping the law and the requirements of holiness. Where sin abounds, grace abounds all the more, but that does not give us permission to live an unholy life. We are called to be holy as He is holy. When we fall short and turn back to the Lord, He forgives, cleanses, and restores us. Holiness is not something we achieve; holiness is something that we must yearn for. Only God is holy, but as His people, set apart, He calls us to strive for holiness.

How do we do this? It is not by our "works," not by our formulas for holiness (to fast and pray more often), but by our willingness to gaze at the beauty of our Lord. As we gaze at HIS holiness, we become aware of our sinfulness. Like Isaiah, we say: *Woe to me! I cried. I am ruined! For I am a man of unclean lips and I live among a people of unclean lips and my eyes have seen the King. (Isaiah 6:5)*

May the cry of your heart be like King David: *One thing I ask of the Lord, this is what I seek: that I may dwell in the house of the Lord all the days of my life, to gaze upon the beauty of the Lord and to seek Him in His temple. (Psalm 27:4)*

Heavenly Father,
You alone are holy. When I gaze at You in Your holiness, I see my need to be cleansed. I stand before You yearning for holiness. Forgive me, for I am a man of unclean lips. Restore me with the righteousness of Christ.
In Jesus' name, Amen

March 8

The Self-Sufficiency of Babylon

You have forgotten God your savior; you have not remembered the Rock, your fortress.
Isaiah 17:10

The nations in the time of Isaiah were filled with turmoil. The city of Babylon is seen throughout both the Old and New Testaments as a city plagued with pride and self-sufficiency. Babylon symbolizes the world powers arrayed against God's kingdom. Throughout the ages, we see other cities and nations plagued by self-sufficiency, finding no need for God. And as individuals, we also fall prey to self-sufficiency. We tend to forget God, our Savior; we forget our Rock, our Fortress. *(Isaiah 17:10)* Yet, when we catch but a glimpse of God's glory, His holiness, and His majesty, we are forever changed. Thank God for His transforming Presence in our lives! Pride is the besetting sin of humanity. Adam and Eve fell prey to pride when they ate of the tree of knowledge of good and evil. They wanted to know as much as God. The nations fell into confusion when their pride caused them to build the tower of Babel to be like God. Often I do a "pride" check. I forget that it is the Lord who calls me, the Lord who enables me to do His will. Like the Israelites, I forget to give God the glory for my accomplishments: *My people have committed two sins: They have forsaken me the spring of living water, and have dug their own cisterns, broken cisterns that cannot hold water. (Jeremiah 2:13)* God's people had forgotten Him and had become self-sufficient. They no longer asked where their God was who brought them out of Egypt, and they worshipped idols.

It is easy for us to forget it is the Lord who works in and through us—that we can do nothing apart from Him. *(John 15:5)* Always do a "pride" check when you are accomplishing great things. Remember that it is the Lord who causes all of us to prosper and who grants us success.

Heavenly Father,

You alone deserve all glory and honor. Forgive me, Lord, when I take the glory for what You have accomplished through me. I thank you for every gift and resource You have given me, and I offer them all back to You.
In Jesus' name, Amen

March 9

All Under the Power of Sin

What shall we conclude then? Are we any better? Not at all! We have already made the charge that Jews and Gentiles alike are all under sin.
Romans 3:9

Paul says that all people are under the power of sin. Speaking to the 1st Century church, he uses language that reflects the domination of the Jews by the ruling power, the Romans. Paul describes humanity as being *under* sin, as opposed to *committing* sin. This reflects his determination to show sin as bondage and enslavement. People are imprisoned under sin, unable to be set free by anything that they can do. Knowing this, God sent our Liberator, Jesus Christ, The One who has the power to free us from our sins. After defining the privileges of being a Jew, Paul concludes that in spite of these privileges, Gentiles and Jews alike are under sin: *There is no one righteous, not even one…* (v.10). He then describes, through a series of Old Testament quotations, what that looks like. (vv.10-18) Keep in mind that God is faithful, and although we fall into sin, His faithfulness continues to draw us back to Him.

Have you ever thought of sin as being "bondage"? The Israelites were slaves, in bondage in Egypt for 400 years. Moses led them out of Egypt. Their crossing the Red Sea to freedom is a picture of the freedom we have in Christ as believers. Imagine the scene: the horses and chariots of Egypt chasing the Israelites who were filled with confusion, fear, and perhaps even terror. It seemed a certainty that the Egyptians would catch up with them. Moses, God's leader, raises his staff and the waters part, enabling the Israelites to cross over on the dry seabed. Jesus raised His staff (the cross) and enabled us to cross over from the bondage of sin into the freedom of new life in Him. The terror of the enemy is drowned in the sea. What sin is chasing you today? Raise the cross of God's righteousness in your life and cross over into freedom.

Heavenly Father,
I am chased by enemies that torment me with lies. I struggle, thinking I will never be set free. As I look to Your cross, I see You carrying my burdens, my struggles

and my sin. Thank you for delivering me from my enemies. In Jesus' name, Amen

March 10

Christ, The Living Stone

...built on the foundation of the apostles and prophets, with Christ Jesus himself as the chief cornerstone. In Him the whole building is joined together and rises to become a holy temple in the Lord. And in Him you too are being built together to become a dwelling in which God lives by his Spirit.
Ephesians 2:20-22

Paul reminded the Ephesians that as Gentiles they were once separated from Christ, excluded from citizenship in Israel, foreigners to the covenants of the promise, and without hope. *(Ephesians 2:11-12)* Now they were brought into the promises of God through the blood of Jesus. As fellow citizens with God's people and members of God's household, their "spiritual houses" were built on the foundation of the apostles and prophets with Christ as the chief cornerstone. As believers, we have been joined together to become a holy temple for the Lord—a dwelling place for His Holy Spirit. The body of Christ is built on the cornerstone of Christ Jesus. As the Lord builds on His foundation, we are joined together as one building. Paul describes the building in another way as he describes the gifts of the Holy Spirit that each of us possesses: *Now the body is not made up of one part but of many. If the foot should say, because I am not a hand, I do not belong to the body. And if the ear should say because I am not an eye, I do not belong to the body; it would not for that reason cease to be a body. (I Corinthians 12:16)* Paul explained to the early church that God was building His temple, His body, each with a unique role to play and that they needed one another in order to have the body function properly. It is the same for us today. Christ is still building His body, the church, and we need one another to function as a whole.

Are you connected to the body of Christ, or have you isolated yourself from other believers? Together we encourage, build up, and exercise the unique gifts God has given us. Together we can make a difference in the world.

Heavenly Father,

Join me together with other members of the body of Christ. Help me, as a part of Your body, to build on Christ, the Cornerstone, and to become a place in which God dwells.
In Jesus' name, Amen

March 11

Obedience From The Heart

But Samuel replied: "Does the LORD delight in burnt offerings and sacrifices as much as in obeying the voice of the LORD? To obey is better than sacrifice, and to heed is better than the fat of rams."
I Samuel 15:22

The words of Christ to His Father *not as I will but as You will... (Matthew 26:39)* demonstrate that obedience was the spiritual attitude of Christ. True obedience begins in the interior life. Too often we are more concerned with the things we do rather than with the attitude of our heart. In the scripture above, Saul thought that because he had made a sacrifice to God, he was pleasing God. But his heart was not obedient, as pointed out by Samuel. David was described as a man after God's own heart. *(I Samuel 13:14)* In the *Psalms*, David said that he loved God's law. *(Psalm 119:97,127)* Being obedient to God requires a diligent search of the Scriptures so that we know what God commands. Then we need to incorporate the Word into our lives. *Micah 6:8* provides an accurate description of what obedience involves: *He has showed you, O man, what is good. And what does the Lord require of you? To act justly and to love mercy and to walk humbly with your God.* Allow the Holy Spirit to give you the strength and power to have an obedient heart.

Have you been sacrificing for God and calling it obedience? God tells us in His Word that God is looking for obedience, not sacrifice. Sometimes we work so hard for God and sacrifice so much that we forget He is looking for a humble heart willing to simply love and follow Him.

Heavenly Father,
I have been trying to work for You, thinking that what You have required of me is sacrifice. But all You require is a humble heart of love that seeks to know You and to love You through obedience. Help me show my love for You through obedience.
In Jesus' name, Amen

Power From the Spirit

They saw what seemed to be tongues of fire that separated and came to rest on each of them. All of them were filled with the Holy Spirit and began to speak in other tongues as the Spirit enabled them.
Acts 2:4

Pentecost was the 50th day after the Sabbath of Passover Week. It was also called the Feast of Weeks, the Feast of Harvest, and the Day of First Fruits. The Israelites were instructed by God to celebrate the Feast of Harvest by giving to God the first fruit of the crops they had harvested. Jesus Christ, raised from the dead, is the "first-fruits"—the one who is the way for us to have eternal life and the guarantee of our resurrection. (I Corinthians 15:23) On Pentecost, the Holy Spirit that was promised by Jesus descended on those gathered. It is not surprising that He sent His Holy Spirit at Pentecost because it symbolizes the celebration we have in Christ, the first-fruits. Growing in our relationship with Christ is dependent on our continual willingness to yield to and be dependent upon the Holy Spirit. The Holy Spirit is the One who leads us into the truth of God's Word, who guides us in our daily lives, and who empowers us to live the Christian life as effective witnesses for Christ.

Have you allowed the Holy Spirit to have His way in your life? Pray for your personal "Pentecost" daily so that the Lord can live His life through you.

Heavenly Father,
I yield to Your Holy Spirit. Empower me to be a witness for Christ in my home, at work, and in my relationships. Fill me with Your life-giving Spirit so that I can be a light to those You have called me to.
In Jesus' name, Amen

March 13

Gathering Resources

And my God will meet all your needs according to his glorious riches in Christ Jesus.
Philippians 4:19

Paul writes in his letter to the Philippians that God will supply all their needs according to His glorious riches in Christ Jesus. It is critical to understand that the Lord supplies *all* our needs. I would tell my younger children that I would supply their needs—food, clothing, shelter—but if they wanted to buy "things," they would need to work to buy them. Often I would pay for half of their "wants," but they knew that I would always supply all of their needs to the best of my ability. Our Lord has promised, through His Son Jesus Christ, to supply all of our needs. Jesus puts it this way in *Matthew 6:26*: *Therefore I tell you do not worry about your life, what you will eat or drink; or about your body, what you will wear. Is not life more important than food, and the body more important than clothes? Look at the birds of the air; they do not sow or reap or store away in barns, and yet your heavenly Father feeds them. Are you not much more valuable than they?*

When rebuilding Jerusalem, Nehemiah knew that God would supply all of the resources he needed to complete his God-given assignment. He knew that wherever God called him, He would provide what was needed to accomplish the task. The Lord has called us to live sacrificial lives for God and for others. We are only able to do this when we love the Lord God with all of our hearts, souls, minds, and strength. Jesus tells us in His Word that when we seek Him and His righteousness first, all other things will be added. Nehemiah sought God first, and he was able to approach a pagan king to obtain the supplies that he needed.

What is it that you need today? Ask the Lord to supply your needs and to help you to recognize His provision. Seek wisdom in areas where you seem to be lacking—finances, relationships, work. He promises that He will meet every need according to His glorious riches in Christ Jesus.

Heavenly Father,
I am struggling with anxiety and worry concerning a need that I have (fill in the blank).
I have sought my own solutions to meet that need. Today I come to You in faith and ask You to give me wisdom concerning my lack, and I will trust You to provide what I need.
In Jesus' name, Amen

March 14

Readying Our Feet With the Word of God

. . .and with your feet fitted with the readiness that comes from the gospel of peace.
Ephesians 6:15

We must be alert, ready, and watchful at all times to fight the schemes of the enemy. Peter tells us that *the devil prowls around like a roaring lion looking for someone to devour. (I Peter 5:8)* The Roman soldier of that time wore protection, even on his feet. If his feet were disabled, it would be difficult, if not impossible, to fight in battle. Just like the soldiers, we must wear "spiritual armor" on our feet. *Ephesians 6:15* says we are to have our *feet fitted with the readiness that comes from the gospel of peace.* The Word of God is the means of "readying" our feet for action. Jesus used the Word of God to fight the enemy when He was in the wilderness. When the devil challenged Him to turn the stones into bread after a prolonged period of fasting, Jesus used Scripture as His weapon against him. *(Matthew 4:4)*

We must read the Word, study the Word, meditate on the Word, and know the Word so that we will be armed and ready for any battle with the enemy. When many of the disciples deserted Jesus, He asked the twelve disciples if they too wished to leave Him. Peter answered: *Lord, to whom shall we go? You have the words of eternal life. (John 6:68)*

Jesus' words bring us life. Where do you need to be revived? As you read His Word today, ask the Holy Spirit to bring life into any area that seems lifeless.

Heavenly Father,
Like Peter, I believe that there is nowhere else to go for the words of eternal life except to You. I pray that You will "ready" my feet with Your Word, protect me against the lies of the enemy, and prepare me to stand in the hope that Your Word brings. -In Jesus' name, Amen

March 15

Jehovah, The Promise Keeper

The LORD is faithful to all his promises and loving toward all he has made.
Psalm 145:13b

Moses was full of excuses when the Lord asked him to deliver His people out of Egypt. God began to reveal himself as Jehovah when Moses began to question Him. Moses had no understanding of the Lord as Jehovah, the Promise Keeper. When Moses was on the mountain receiving the Ten Commandments from the Lord, the people began to worship other gods. Jehovah saw their idolatry, and, as the Righteous Judge, was prepared to destroy them. Moses reminded God of His promise to make the Jewish people into a nation, and the Lord relented and did not destroy the people. *(Exodus 32:11-13)* Jehovah remembered and kept His word to preserve His people. Moses returned from the mountain and gave the people an opportunity to repent. Those who did not were killed. In *Exodus 33*, we see Jehovah, the Promise Keeper, once again keeping His promise to go with Moses to lead the people out, even though He had said He would not go with those "stiff-necked people." The intimacy that Moses found with Jehovah is seen as the Lord answers his request.

Do you know Jehovah God as the "promise keeper"? Is there a promise in His Word that you continue to cling to, wondering if it will ever be fulfilled in your life? A precious friend of mine told me that God may not answer your prayer when you want Him to, but He will always answer on His time. Our time frame is not always the same as God's. Give Him your disappointments and impatience, and choose to trust Him as the Promise Keeper.

Heavenly Father,
You have planted a dream in my heart. Every day I pray, waiting for the fulfillment of that dream. I have grown impatient and have been disappointed. Forgive me, Lord, for not trusting You as the Promise Keeper. I choose to wait on Your perfect timing for the fulfillment of my dream.
In Jesus' name, Amen

The Materialism Of Tyre

On the great waters came the grain of the Shihor; the harvest of the Nile was the revenue of Tyre, and she became the marketplace of the nations.
Isaiah 23:3

Tyre was the main seaport along the Phoenician coast. Part of the city was built on two rocky islands one-half mile from shore. The ships of Tarshish were laden with goods and the wealth of the nations. Nebuchadnezzar captured the mainland city (572 BC), but the island was not taken until Alexander the Great destroyed it in 332 BC. The city of Tyre represents a nation that was full of pride in its wealth. She had become the marketplace for the nations. The Lord brought Tyre low and humbled "the pride of her glory." Today, we see the pride and wealth in many nations, particularly in the United States. As individuals, we can easily be caught up in the "tyranny of Tyre." God judges materialism in nations and in our personal lives. The Lord's unfailing love, however, draws us to repentance when we see the tyranny of materialism. There is no silver, gold, or diamond that is more precious than the Lord.

What is your most valued possession? Whatever comes to mind first may be the thing that the Lord wants you to lay on the altar. He is a jealous God and has told us in His Word not to worship anything else above Him: *You shall have no other gods before me. You shall not make for yourself an idol in the form of anything in heaven or on the earth beneath, or in the waters below. You shall not bow down to them or worship them; for I the Lord your God am a jealous God…. (Deuteronomy 5:7-9)* Jesus knew that our possessions could be like "gods" that occupy our time and our hearts. He told the rich young ruler that if he wanted to inherit the kingdom, he needed to sell all of his possessions. The young man walked away.

What possession do you value above God? One easy test to see if you value something more than God is to look at where you spend your time, your treasure, and your talent. God is a jealous God, desiring that you have no other "gods" above Him. Consider today anything you have put before Him.

Heavenly Father,
I recognize that my heart has been held captive by other things. I have found comfort in food, money and possessions. Forgive me where I have been consumed by other things, and help me instead to be consumed with You.
In Jesus' name, Amen

Humility Exhibited

Do nothing out of selfish ambition or vain conceit, but in humility consider others better than yourselves.
Philippians 2:3

After David was anointed to be king, he enrolled in the school of "hard knocks," otherwise known as the school of humility. He learned to be subservient to his master, the king. King Saul became jealous of David: *When the men were returning home after David had killed the Philistines, the women came out from all of the towns of Israel to meet King Saul with singing and dancing with joyful songs and with tambourines and lutes. As they danced they sang:; Saul has slain his thousands and David his tens of thousands (I Samuel 18:6-7).* King Saul's jealousy of David's military success turned into an obsession and he tried to kill David. David was pursued by Saul and had to hide from him, but the Lord used this to grow humility in David. David had opportunities to kill Saul, but in obedience and humility, he would not touch God's anointed. Persecution, even the jealousy of others, though painful, can be a perfecting tool in God's hands. David found success wherever he went. He was successful in defeating the enemies of Israel, yet he never tried to elevate himself in the eyes of the people. We can learn so much from reading the *Psalms.* Many were written by David as he faced difficulties. God used the difficult times to help David develop humility.

As we read through the *Psalms,* we enter into the agony David felt as Saul relentlessly pursued him to take his life. Spend time this week meditating on the *Psalms,* apply them to your life, and recognize the truth in God's Word: *God opposes the proud, but gives grace to the humble. (James 4:6)* How we need His grace to help us develop the humility we need to be courageous leaders!

Heavenly Father,
Your Word tells me that You oppose the proud but give grace to the humble. I pray that I will not resist those things in my life that humble me and cause me to surrender completely to You.
In Jesus' name, Amen

March 18

God's Gracious Hand

Remember the instruction you gave your servant Moses, saying, 'If you are unfaithful, I will scatter you among the nations…
Nehemiah 1:8

In the first chapter of *Nehemiah,* we see Nehemiah's complete dependence on the Lord. He turned to God in his distress over the state of affairs in Jerusalem. He reminded the Lord of His promises to meet the needs of His people who return to Him in repentance. Nehemiah humbly repented on behalf of himself and the people of Jerusalem who had turned from God. He sought the Lord through prayer and fasting. He knew that the Lord was trustworthy to supply the needs in just the right time for him to accomplish the task. Doors flew open when Nehemiah's prayers filled the heavens and poured over King Artaxerxes, who became God's instrument of supply. Nehemiah waited on God's timing. When he received the resources he needed, he quickly proclaimed that it was only by God's gracious hand that he had received the resources.

The Lord longs to be gracious to us as we turn to Him. He has an infinite supply of resources, and when we cry out to Him, He supplies what we need. Are you feeling empty, lonely or afraid? Jesus Christ is the answer to all of your needs. He stands at the door, knocking to come in and supply you with a banquet to satisfy your thirst and hunger. Are you willing to open the door and let Him in?

Heavenly Father,
I pray for Your gracious hand to be upon me. As I struggle with my fears and insecurities, I ask You to open doors and supply my needs. You alone are able to meet those needs within me.
In Jesus' name, Amen

Witnesses In Word and Actions

After he was raised from the dead, his disciples recalled what he had said. Then they believed the Scripture and the words that Jesus had spoken.
John 2:22

According to Webster's dictionary, to "proclaim" means "to declare publicly through speech or in writing." Peter and John healed a crippled man outside the temple and the people were astonished and amazed. Peter's response to the onlookers was: *Why do you stare at us as if by our own power or godliness we made this man walk?* (*Acts 3*) Peter boldly proclaimed that it was Jesus who healed the man. Many of us have witnessed the Lord heal people both physically and spiritually but have hesitated to share it with others for fear that they wouldn't believe or understand. Recently, I had several people pray for my foot that had not healed completely after a severe injury. Although the accident happened many months ago, I was still experiencing pain. After they prayed, my foot was significantly better and has continued to progress. Immediately, I shared this with people who I knew were believers, but I hesitated to share it with those who perhaps wouldn't believe me. After my friends prayed with me, the Lord overcame my hesitation. He gave me a boldness to tell people I didn't even know and proclaim Him as the rightful Healer.

Are you afraid to tell others what God has done in your life? Why is it so easy to fear what people think of us? Fear keeps us from sharing our "God" stories—sharing those things that the Lord has done in our lives. Years ago, I saw a friend from childhood who told me that she heard I had become "religious." I tried to act as unspiritual as I could so that she would think differently of me. I did not like her label. It didn't take long for the Lord to convict me, and I realized I simply need to be an *authentic* Christian. I have become a better witness for Christ as I have sought to be myself—throwing off all labels and simply living my life for Him. It is freeing to know that I don't have to convince anyone that Jesus is my Lord; they will *see* He is my Lord. Actions speak far more than words.

Are you willing to let your life be an open book for others, sharing the good news with your actions, only using words when necessary?

Heavenly Father,
Help me to be a witness for You in thought and deed. Let my words reflect my heart, and may my heart be filled with love for You and for others.
In Jesus' name, Amen

Believers as Living Stones

Don't you know that you yourselves are God's temple and that God's Spirit lives in you?
1 Corinthians 3:16

The Holy Spirit builds believers into "spiritual houses." We are changed from "glory to glory," becoming more like Christ as we yield to the building process. When our house was being built for my family, I watched as the foundation was laid. The workmen took special care as they lay the first cement blocks. After the foundation was in place, the rest of the house went up rather quickly. We need to follow the example of the workmen and take special care to lay the proper foundation for our "spiritual houses," beginning with Jesus Christ as the Cornerstone. I heard about a company that specializes in rebuilding foundations by first locating the problem and then fixing it. I began to think about what it would take to rebuild the foundation of my present home. It would be an enormous task in both cost and time. But the Lord waits patiently to repair the cracks in the foundation of our spiritual lives as we yield to Him as the master builder. It can be an enormous costly and timely job, but Jesus has paid the price and given up His very life so that He can become our spiritual foundation. Paul writes to the church in Corinth describing the building process: *For no one can lay any foundation other than the one already laid, which is Jesus Christ. If any man builds on this foundation using gold, silver, costly stones, wood or straw or hay, his work will be shown for what it is. (I Corinthian 3:11-13)*

On what are you building your spiritual foundation? There will come a day when your foundation will be tested. Until that day, allow the Lord to do the building and repair where there is damage in your spiritual life. The Lord is the master builder and He is building a place where He can dwell within you. Do you have a godly foundation? If so, allow the Lord to continue building the house. If your foundation is faulty, ask Him today to tear it down and build up His foundation in you so that your "spiritual house" will be able to withstand any storm.

Heavenly Father,
I offer You my life, to build a place in which You can dwell. I know I have crowded You out of my life in many ways, but now I want You to have first place in my life. Destroy those things in my life that have caused me to build on a foundation other than You. Take Your rightful place on the throne of my life as the Cornerstone.
In Jesus' name, Amen

March 21

Spurring One Another On

And let us consider how we may spur one another on toward love and good deeds. Let us not give up meeting together as some are in the habit of doing, but let us encourage one another and all the more as we see the day approaching.
Hebrews 10:24-25

As you study God's Word from the book of *Hebrews,* discover the value of being involved in a Christian community. The writer of Hebrews tells us to consider how we may spur one another on living a fruitful Christian life. A significant part of that is meeting together, both in our times of celebration on Sundays as well as other times of sharing life together. Consider asking the Lord for a Christian friend or friends whom you can trust as prayer partners. Prayer partners give us the support, caring, and love of other believers. Let your prayer partners encourage you, pray with you, and keep you accountable as you strive to discover and obey God's will for you. As you recognize God's instructions for you from spending time in His Word, share your joys, concerns, and challenges with your prayer partners. Pray for each other daily. Study God's Word together and learn how it applies to your lives. This kind of interaction is a vital part of our journey with the Holy Spirit. Having accountability partners who are willing to invest in your life will help you to discern God's will. Christian friends spur you on when you are faced with life's challenges and pick you up when you are discouraged: *Two are better than one, because they have a good return for their work: If one falls down, his friend can help pick him up! But pity the man who falls and has no one to help him up! (Ecclesiastes 4:9)*

Are you willing to be vulnerable and become involved with a Christian community? Are you willing to submit your life to trusted friends and allow them to speak into your life? For some people, it will not be difficult to do that; for others, it will be a challenge. Our society today encourages independence, and we are becoming more and more isolated from one another. The Word teaches us to be in community, helping, encouraging, and discerning together the will of God.

Heavenly Father,
I have isolated myself from other believers and recognize my need to be in Christian fellowship. Lead me, Lord, to the place of community to which You are calling me. Help me to find Christian friends to support me in my Christian life. Enable me to be a support to others as well in their journey of faith.
In Jesus' name, Amen

Remain in My Love

When they had finished eating, Jesus said to Simon Peter, "Simon son of John, do you truly love me more than these?" "Yes, Lord," he said, "you know that I love you." Jesus said, "Feed my lambs." Again Jesus said, "Simon son of John, do you truly love me?" He answered, "Yes, Lord, you know that I love you." Jesus said, "Take care of my sheep." The third time he said to him, "Simon son of John, do you love me?" Peter was hurt because Jesus asked him the third time, "Do you love me?" He said, "Lord, you know all things; you know that I love you."
John 21:15-17

Jesus asks Peter if he loves (agape) Him. Peter answers of course he loves (filios—brotherly love) Him. Jesus asks him again, and again Peter answers the same way. Then a third time Jesus asks Peter if he loves (agape) Him. Jesus recognizes that Peter does not yet understand, or have as part of his experience, the agape love of the Father. At this point in his relationship with Jesus, he was only able to love Him with brotherly love, much like he would a friend. It wasn't until Pentecost that Peter could know and receive Christ's love through the empowering and enabling of the Holy Spirit. Jesus met Peter where he was. Jesus meets us where we are and then works toward our knowing and receiving this kind of love. Obedience and love go hand in hand. As we remain in God's love, obedience is the fruit. We *want* to obey. Jesus uses Himself as the example of being obedient to His Father. It was love for us and obedience to the Father that held Him to the cross. The cycle goes like this: God loves the Son; the Son loves us; the Son obeys the Father; we obey the Son. As a result, our joy is made complete: *As the Father has loved me, so have I loved you. Now remain in my love. (John 15:9)*

Jesus desires that you receive His agape love today: intimate love, the same as He has with His Father. He longs for us to love Him with more than brotherly love, with agape love. He describes this relationship in John: *Remain in me and I will remain in you. No branch can bear fruit by itself; it must remain in the vine. (John 15:4)* As believers, we are the branches connected to the vine. The branches cannot live apart from the vine. As you receive God's love, you, the branch, will bear much fruit.

Heavenly Father,
Help me to receive Your love and respond by loving You and having an intimate relationship with You. I have held back my heart in response to Your love, and I ask You to break down the walls that keep me from both receiving and responding to Your love.
In Jesus' name, Amen

Obeying God's Word

On the second day of the month, the heads of all the families, along with the priests and the Levites, gathered around Ezra the scribe to give attention to the words of the Law. They found written in the Law, which the LORD had commanded through Moses, that the Israelites were to live in booths during the feast of the seventh month and that they should proclaim this word and spread it throughout their towns and in Jerusalem: "Go out into the hill country and bring back branches from olive and wild olive trees, and from myrtles, palms and shade trees, to make booths"-as it is written. So the people went out and brought back branches and built themselves booths on their own roofs, in their courtyards, in the courts of the house of God and in the square by the Water Gate and the one by the Gate of Ephraim. The whole company that had returned from exile built booths and lived in them. From the days of Joshua son of Nun until that day, the Israelites had not celebrated it like this. And their joy was very great. Day after day, from the first day to the last, Ezra read from the Book of the Law of God. They celebrated the feast for seven days, and on the eighth day, in accordance with the regulation, there was an assembly.
Nehemiah 8:13-18

In obedience to God's Word, the people celebrated the Day of Atonement, always celebrated on the tenth day of the month, and the Feast of Tabernacles from the fifteenth to the twenty-first. The people celebrated with great joy: *The whole company that had returned from exile built booths and lived in them. From the days of Joshua son of Nun until that day, the Israelites had not celebrated it like this. And their joy was very great. (v.17)* During the seven days of the feast, the Jews lived in booths made of branches. It was a time of remembering the wandering in the wilderness, the goodness of the Lord, and His promised future kingdom. The people rejoiced in God's Word, and there was a new willingness to obey His Word. At the Water Gate, revival had begun and the people enjoyed fellowship, feasting, and hearing the Word of God. True revival begins when God's Word is proclaimed and His people respond. During the course of the history of the church, there have been spiritual revivals. People turn back to God, acknowledge Him as Lord, and are revived by His Holy Spirit: *If anyone is thirsty, let him come to me and drink. Whoever believes in me, as the*

Scripture has said, streams of living water will flow from within him. (John 7:37) It was at another Feast of Tabernacles that Jesus said those words, centuries after Ezra had read God's Word, and the people responded. Jesus Christ *is* the Water Gate for all who choose to believe in Him today.

Where have you been disobedient to God's Word? Do you sense that the Lord is asking you to forgive someone and you have stubbornly been refusing? Is He asking you to trust Him in an area of your life? Like the Israelites, when you obey, you will be filled with joy and celebration.

Heavenly Father,
Forgive me where I have disobeyed Your Word. I am committed to following through with Your instructions today. Fill me with Your joy as I seek to do Your will.
In Jesus' name, Amen

El Shaddai, Our Fruitfulness

"But blessed is the man who trusts in the LORD, whose confidence is in him. He will be like a tree planted by the water that sends out its roots by the stream. It does not fear when heat comes; its leaves are always green. It has no worries in a year of drought and never fails to bear fruit.
Jeremiah 17:7-8

God told Abram that he would make him into a great nation, that he would be the father of many nations, and that his descendants would be as numerous as the stars in the sky. (*Genesis 12:2 and 22:17)* His wife Sarai became restless waiting on the promise of God and decided to ensure that God's Word would be fulfilled as promised. She told Hagar, her servant, to sleep with Abram, and she conceived, bearing a son named Ishmael. Abram and Sarai did not know God as El Shaddai, the One who would make them fruitful, so they produced a son "of the flesh." God's promise to Abram still remained the same, that Sarai would have a son in her old age. He promised a son of the "spirit," and Sarai bore a son named Isaac from whom the nation of Israel came forth.

Why do we fall into the trap of taking things into our own hands? I think it is because we do not have a full revelation of El Shaddai, our fruitfulness. We must guard against the temptation to try to fulfill God's Word to us by ourselves. We might end up with Ishmael, a child of the "flesh."

Have you tried to make something happen that the Lord promised would happen? As you wait on the Lord to fulfill His promises, there may be things that He asks you to do, but remember to always rely on the Holy Spirit to lead the way. So often I am tempted to make things happen that I believe the Lord has promised. Waiting on the Lord and His timing always births an "Isaac." Doing things my way leads to an "Ishmael," and Ishmael was sent out to the desert. If you find yourself in the desert, ask the Lord if you have not believed His word to fulfill His promise. Choose today to trust Him.

Heavenly Father,

I find myself eager to make things happen that I believe are Your will. Help me to pray more earnestly, to wait patiently, and to trust that You will lead the way. In Jesus' name, Amen

Sent Out By God

He called His twelve disciples to him and gave them authority to drive out evil spirits and to heal every disease and sickness.
Matthew 10:1

Jesus sent out the twelve disciples and gave them the authority to *drive out evil spirits and to heal every disease and sickness. (Matthew 10:1)* He told them to go to the Jews first, preaching that the kingdom of heaven is near. The evidence of the kingdom would be seen as the disciples proclaimed and demonstrated the kingdom. Before ascending into heaven, Jesus instructed the apostles about the kingdom and told them to wait for the gift of the Holy Spirit to empower them to carry out His work. (*Acts 1*) On the day of Pentecost, 120 believers were filled with the Holy Spirit. Today, God continues to fill and send out believers to demonstrate that indeed the *kingdom of God is near. (Matthew 4:17)* The kingdom of God is the rule and reign of God on earth. As the gospel is preached, the kingdom of God draws near. Jesus declared that the kingdom was near when He came to earth; He demonstrated the kingdom and He commissioned believers to advance His kingdom on earth: *From the days of John the Baptist until now, the kingdom of heaven has been forcefully advancing and forceful men lay hold of it. (Matthew 11:12)* The kingdom was, the kingdom is, and the kingdom will be when Jesus Christ returns. As believers, we participate in the advancement of His kingdom as we spread the "good news" of Jesus Christ and demonstrate His goodness through prayer and faith.

Have you been simply waiting until Jesus returns for His kingdom to arrive? Perhaps you are content knowing you have received Jesus as your Lord and Savior but are unsure if you wish to participate in His activities on earth. The fullness of His Holy Spirit is here, guiding you and empowering you to actively participate with what He is doing as the world prepares for Him to return. Are you willing to pray for the sick or to reach out to the lost? He has prepared you to step out in faith and advance His kingdom. He is still working on earth and the harvest is plentiful: *Then He said to His disciples, "The harvest is plentiful but the workers are few. Ask the Lord of the harvest, therefore to send out workers into His harvest field." (Matthew 9:35-38)*

Heavenly Father,
Forgive me for being complacent about the advancement of Your kingdom. I desire to be Your hands and feet on earth, preparing for Your return. Increase my faith to spread Your word, lay hands on the sick and believe that Your kingdom is not just for the future, but Your kingdom is here now.
In Jesus' name, Amen

Response to Assault

But an evil spirit from the LORD came upon Saul as he was sitting in his house with his spear in his hand. While David was playing the harp, Saul tried to pin him to the wall with his spear, but David eluded him as Saul drove the spear into the wall.
I Samuel 19:9-10

As Saul sought to take David's life, David asked Jonathan, Saul's son, what he had done to cause Saul to be so angry that he would want to kill him. David knew that he was innocent of wrongdoing, yet he knew that Saul was the king and therefore he would not touch God's anointed. *(I Samuel 24:10)* After being anointed by Samuel to be king, David spent his early years running and hiding from Saul. The passage in *I Samuel 19* describes an evil spirit that came upon Saul as he was sitting with the spear in his hand. David eluded him as he had many times before. David was wronged. He had done nothing to deserve this kind of treatment from Saul, yet he was not going to retaliate.

In my own life, I have experienced times when I have felt the pain of spears and have wanted to get even. We must see things, however, from the perspective of heaven and replace our retaliation spears with the mantle of love. Courageous leaders know that to be like Jesus, they must abandon selfish ambition and vain conceit. It is by God's supernatural grace that we are able to retreat and not seek revenge. If we want to lead others, we must love courageously and depend on God to protect and deliver us.

Has someone wronged you? Perhaps someone has said things about you that were not true and damaged your reputation. The Lord may call you to bring the truth into the light and confront the person. He may ask you to do nothing. Regardless, we are called to be like Christ in our attitudes: *Blessed are you when people insult you, persecute you and falsely say all kind of evil against you because of me. (Matthew 5:11)* James tells us that we should consider our trials as joy because the Lord will use them to develop our character in Christ: *Consider it pure joy, my brothers, whenever you face trials of many kinds, because you know that the testing of your faith develops perseverance. Perseverance must finish its work so that you may be mature and complete, lacking in nothing. (James 1:2-4)* The Lord may be calling you to pray for the person who has insulted or wronged you. He may be asking you to lovingly confront the offense. But regardless of His ultimate plan, He uses our willingness to not retaliate to grow Christlike character in us. Although constraining ourselves from retaliation goes against our human nature, God will see us through.

Heavenly Father,
I want to justify my actions and retaliate against those who wrong me. Release me from my anger and lead me in prayer.
In Jesus' name, Amen

Destroying the Works of the Devil

He who does what is sinful is of the devil, because the devil has been sinning from the beginning. The reason the Son of God appeared was to destroy the devil's work.
I John 3:8

Scripture tells us that Jesus came to destroy the works of the devil. *(I John 3:8)* In *Matthew 12*, the Pharisees, the religious leaders of the day, accused Jesus of healing a demon-possessed man by power given to him by Beelzebub, prince of demons. Jesus explained to them that their logic was distorted. He came to drive out demons, so why would He be in partnership with the prince of demons? He told them, *If Satan drives out Satan, he is divided against himself. How can his kingdom stand? (Matthew 12:26)* He continued to explain to them that He drove out demons by the Spirit of God, demonstrating to them that the kingdom of God was at work. As believers, we are co-workers with the Holy Spirit in destroying the works of the devil. We are in partnership with God and work together to bring His kingdom power to earth. When I realize that I am to be united with God against the enemy, it motivates me to allow the Holy Spirit to drive out those things in my life that are not pleasing to God. By doing this, I can be more effective in my partnership with God. Jesus made it very clear to His disciples, and likewise to future believers, that the enemy is always prowling around seeking to destroy believers. *(I Peter 5:8)* One way he is successful in doing that is to have us live with a *mixture* of God's ways and his ways. Jesus commands us to *live as children of light* and to *have nothing to do with the fruitless deeds of darkness.* (*Ephesians 5:8-11*) In this way, we can be part of the kingdom of God, working together with Christ to destroy the works of the devil.

Where are you in conflict with God's ways and the ways of man and the world? Are you willing to partner with God in destroying anything in your life that is a mixture of God's ways and the world's ways?

Heavenly Father,

Forgive me where there is a mixture of Your ways and the ways of the world in my life. I surrender to Your work in me, driving out those things in my life that are not pleasing to You. My desire is to partnership with You and bring Your kingdom power to earth.
In Jesus' name, Amen

The Righteousness of God

But now a righteousness from God, apart from law, has been made known, to which the Law and the Prophets testify. This righteousness from God comes through faith in Jesus Christ to all who believe.
Romans 3:21-22

The 1st century Jews understood the righteousness of God as being inherently tied to God's faithfulness to His covenant people, the Jews. The Jews thought that their righteousness was linked to the fact that they were God's covenant people. However, the law was only meant to be a tool that pointed them to God. The Jewish people thought that their possession of the law was enough to make them righteous, and yet Jesus told his disciples that their righteousness must surpass the righteousness of the Pharisees in order to enter the kingdom of God: *For I tell you that unless your righteousness surpasses that of the Pharisees and the teachers of the law, you will certainly not enter the kingdom of heaven. (Matthew 5:20)* In essence, Jesus recognized the Pharisees as those who were so caught up in the law and their own righteousness that they missed seeing Him as the fulfillment of the law. Paul clarifies to the Jews that *now* (note the word *now*) righteousness apart from law has been made known, and this righteousness comes from faith in Jesus Christ. (*v.21*) Even today it is easy for us to think that we must earn our way into a right relationship with God. We learn this at an early age when we receive credit for the good things we do. But there is nothing we can *do* to earn salvation other than believe in the One who can save.

Heavenly Father,
I surrender my life to You. I know that my righteousness is like a filthy rag. I thank you that I am righteous through Your Son, Jesus Christ. Forgive me where I have strived to "get it right" or to be in good standing with You apart from Christ.
In Jesus' name, Amen

March 29

A People in Transition

When you see the ark of the covenant of the LORD your God, and the priests, who are Levites, carrying it, you are to move out from your positions and follow it. Then you will know which way to go, since you have never been this way before.
Joshua 3:3-4

When the Israelites crossed the Red Sea under the leadership of Moses, the Hebrew word "*nasa,*" which means to "*enter*" or "*walk,*" was used to signify the crossing of the Red Sea. When the Israelites crossed the Jordan River, however, the Hebrew word "*abar,*" meaning "*to cross*" or "*to pass,*" was used.

In our personal lives, we enter or walk into different seasons of our lives. This is not necessarily brought on by an abrupt change, crisis, or a significant event. Sometimes, we simply take the next step and the transition is smooth. There are times, however, when the transition is not smooth. The Israelites were in transition, crossing over into the Promised Land. This would be a totally new experience for them, unlike anything they had done before and unlike anywhere they had lived before. There are times when we, like the Israelites, have to transition into unfamiliar territory. We become "abar" people, claiming new territory and inheriting promises brought on by radical change. Although change can be jolting and unexpected, God is with us as we follow Him.

As Christians, we continue to face crossover experiences, journeying into places we have never been before. The Lord uses these times to stretch us and to change our character to be more like His. Are you in a time of transition? Trust the Lord to go before you as He did the Israelites. Be encouraged when God takes you to the other side. There will be a fruitful land waiting for you.

Heavenly Father,
I do not like change. I observe friends who embrace change with joy, and others who experience change gracefully. I do not do either. Help me to trust You in this time of transition in my life. Give me hope and encouragement that You are with me as I go.
In Jesus' name, Amen

March 30

Going Down to Egypt

Trust in the Lord with all your heart and lean not on your own understanding.
Proverbs 3:5

Woe to those who go down to Egypt for help, who rely on horses, who trust in the multitude of their chariots and in the great strength of their horseman, but do not look to the Holy One of Israel, or seek help from the Lord. (Isaiah 31:1) These are words penned by the prophet Isaiah describing Israel's reliance on Egypt, which represented wealth, false security, prosperity, and human wisdom. It is interesting to me that in former years, the Israelites had served as slaves to the Egyptians who were hard taskmasters. Yet they quickly wanted to go back to Egypt when the going got rough: *But the people were thirsty for water there, and they grumbled against Moses. They said, "Why did you bring us out of Egypt to make us and our children die of thirst? (Exodus 17:3)* How quickly the Israelites forgot their life of slavery as they remembered the "benefits" of Egypt.

We can easily become enslaved by forgetting the Lord and relying on "things" or "human wisdom" to bring us peace and understanding. Our only true peace comes through trusting in the Lord. God, in His infinite mercy and love, sent us Jesus Christ to be *a precious Cornerstone for a sure foundation. (Isaiah 28:16)* We are promised that when we put our trust in Him, Egypt cannot have a hold on us.

What have you put your trust in? What things represent the "chariots and horses" of Egypt? Egypt's wealth lured the people into thinking that freedom comes from wealth, when in fact they were enslaved in the midst of an affluent society. Their security was in the things that Egypt represented, but they had forgotten their God. The Lord is calling you to trust in Him alone; only in Him is there true freedom.

Heavenly Father,
I have trusted in the things of this world to give me peace and security. The more I have, the less I look to You as my source of peace and freedom. Help me to keep my eyes on You and not be lured into false security by the things of this world.
In Jesus' name, Amen

March 31

Stumbling In The Dark

A stone that causes men to stumble and a rock that makes them fall.
1 Peter 2:8

To those who respond in faith, the Stone is "precious," just as it is precious to God. But to those who reject Jesus Christ as the Messiah, He becomes a stumbling block. Peter compares the response of unbelievers to Christ with the disobedience of the people of Israel and Judah. God became their source of judgment rather than their salvation. Peter, writing to God's elect, admonishes them to be rid of all deceit and hypocrisy, envy and slander. He reminds them that they are being built into a "spiritual house" that will be evidenced by offering spiritual sacrifices.

Does your life reflect your belief that Jesus Christ is a precious treasure? What spiritual sacrifices have you been offering Him? Peter identifies spiritual sacrifices as a declaration of praises to God for bringing us out of darkness and into His light. Recently, a beautiful young woman gave birth to a baby boy. He is struggling with an illness, fighting for his little life. Jesus is precious to her and she clings to Him as she continues to praise and worship her Lord. For those who do not know Christ, it is difficult to understand her faith. Jesus is a stumbling block to them, and yet so very precious to her!

What causes you to stumble in your spiritual life? Are you able to declare praises to God even when things are difficult in your life? The Lord becomes precious to us as we learn to trust Him in *all* circumstances. What do you need to praise Him for today?

Heavenly Father,
I have been self-centered, allowing circumstances to cloud my desire to praise You. Build my spiritual house into a house of praise and thanksgiving, removing the stumbling blocks that cause me to fall. Help me to be a pure vessel, rid of all deceit, hypocrisy, envy, and slander so that others may see in me the treasure of God.
In Jesus' name, Amen

The Message of Repentance and Salvation

This is what the Sovereign LORD, the Holy One of Israel, says: "In repentance and rest is your salvation, in quietness and trust is your strength, but you would have none of it."
Isaiah 30:15

In the Scripture reading today, Isaiah describes repentance and rest as the fruit of our salvation and quietness and trust as our strength. The Israelites did not repent, and their lives reflected the loss of peace and rest. They continued to disobey God and ultimately ended up in captivity where they lost their confidence and peace and were weakened in spirit. Salvation, meaning "wholeness," is available to us through Jesus Christ. When we turn to Him in faith, He not only offers us eternal life, but He also offers freedom from the bondage of our sins which brings us peace and quiets our soul.

After Peter healed the beggar, he spoke boldly about Christ whom they, the Jews, had killed. He called on them to repent so that their sins could be forgiven. I don't know about you, but if I had been standing there, I would have been spellbound until he came to the part about my killing the Son of God! It took supernatural courage for Peter to speak so boldly. Are we willing to love people enough to tell them the good news that Jesus died for their sins and offers them forgiveness? It doesn't matter what we have done; there is nothing so terrible that He will not forgive if we repent from our sins and turn to Him.

Have you lost your peace or your confidence? Ask the Lord to show you if there is an area in your life where you are in disobedience and repent (turn back to God). You will find that in repentance and rest is your salvation, and in quietness and trust you will find your strength.

Heavenly Father,

I confess that I have disobeyed You (fill in the blank). I turn back to You and ask You to restore my strength and quiet my soul. Forgive me, Lord, for my willfulness and bring me out of captivity and into Your loving arms.
In Jesus' name, Amen

Work of the Holy Spirit

All this I have spoken while still with you. But the Counselor, the Holy Spirit, whom the Father will send in my name, will teach you all things and will remind you of everything I have said to you.
John 14:25-26

Before Jesus left this earth, He told his disciples that He would send His Holy Spirit to instruct them and to remind them of all that He had taught them. He told them that they would be at peace knowing the Holy Spirit would be their constant companion and guide into truth. The Holy Spirit also searches our hearts to see if there is any damage that is hindering our spiritual growth. Nehemiah, like the Holy Spirit, searched out the damaged walls in Jerusalem in order to repair them. Repairing the walls would protect the city from their enemies. The walls had been nearly destroyed by the conquering Babylonians, and now his task was to assess the damage and plan a strategy to rebuild. As he set out at night to view the damage, he went through the Valley Gate. Likewise, the Holy Spirit "inspects" our walls. The Lord says that our walls are ever before Him: *See, I have engraved you on the palms of my hands; your walls are ever before me. (Isaiah 49:16)* The Holy Spirit often works in the times that we are in the "valley," those times of despair, frustration, and hopelessness. He examines the dark places, assessing the damage, and sets out to repair and restore the broken-down places. Paul understood that the difficult times are opportunities for the Lord to work "good" in us, growing in us the character of Christ. *(Romans 5:1-5)* Nehemiah understood that when examining the damage to the walls, it was necessary to first examine the gates. The gates are the entry points for the enemy. If the gates are broken down, the enemy has access to the city. If our gates are broken, the enemy has access to our thought life, and this will be reflected in our actions. Nehemiah represents the Holy Spirit, systematically seeking to build and repair any place where the enemy could potentially enter our lives.

Ask the Holy Spirit to inspect your heart and identify areas that may be broken—in need of forgiveness or in need of giving forgiveness—any area where you harbor bitterness, anger, lack of self-control, or hurt. Invite Him into those areas to repair the brokenness, and He will deliver you out of the hands of the enemy and into the loving arms of God.

Heavenly Father,
Repair the broken down gates of my life where the enemy has had access. Where I lack love for others, forgive me; where I am bitter, forgive me; where I seek revenge, forgive me. I invite You into any area of my life to repair the brokenness so that I can be free to love You and others.
In Jesus' name, Amen

Willingness to Assume Responsibility

As for you, show kindness to your servant, for you have brought him into a covenant with you before the LORD. If I am guilty, then kill me yourself! Why hand me over to your father?
I Samuel 20:8

David questioned Saul's son, Jonathan, regarding the wrongs he committed against his father. He knew that he was innocent but was willing to ask the hard questions. Courageous leaders ask the hard questions. They are willing to right a wrong and to assume responsibility for their actions. In other words, a leader must realize that the buck stops with him or her. In *Courageous Leadership*, Bill Hybels explains that one of the principles of becoming an effective leader is self-leadership. He describes how leaders must have "checks and balances" in their development by asking, "Am I developing my gifts?" "Is my character submitted to Christ?" "Is my vision clear?" The one question that stood out to me as I read the list was, "Is my pride subdued?" David's questions to Jonathan reflected an attitude of humility and self-examination. Courageous leaders must be willing to continually ask themselves and others under their leadership if they are on course, then assume the responsibility to adjust when they have veered.

Are you guilty of doing something that would not be pleasing to the Lord? Be willing to have Him examine your heart like David: *Search me, O God, and know my heart; test me and see if there is any offensive way in me, and lead me in the way everlasting. (Psalm 139:23-24)*

Heavenly Father,
Sometimes I am afraid to ask You to search my heart. I fear what You will find. Help me to surrender to Your loving search, knowing that You will lead me in the way everlasting.
In Jesus' name, Amen

April 4

Ordinary Men With Extraordinary Power

When they saw the courage of Peter and John and realized that they were unschooled, ordinary men, they were astonished and they took note that these men had been with Jesus.
Acts 4:13

Acts 4:13 describes the reaction of the people when they realized that Peter and John were unschooled, ordinary men. They were astonished that these ordinary men had been with Jesus. This passage gives both hope and courage to live boldly and to follow Christ where He leads. When I spend time with the Lord, I gain confidence and feel as though I could climb Mount Everest. That may be a bit of an exaggeration; however, when I cling to the Lord, spending time in His Word and talking with Him in prayer, my perspective changes from saying "I can't do it," to *I can do all things through God who strengthens me.* (*Philippians 4:13*)

When I sensed the Lord calling me to teach His Word, I felt so inadequate. I was like the disciples in many ways—unschooled (had not been to seminary) and very ordinary! I have been so dependent on the Lord to teach me His Word and to give me the ability to teach others. The more I depend on Him, the more He shows up! My hope is that people will be astonished at how the Lord can use an ordinary, untrained woman to teach His Word! I also hope that others will know that I have been with Jesus. What hope we have in knowing that the Lord uses ordinary men and women to accomplish His purposes on earth!

What about you? Do you sense that the Lord is calling you to do something but you feel inadequate? Hang out with Jesus and He will equip you and anoint you to do whatever He calls you to do. People will be astonished at how He uses ordinary people like you and me.

Heavenly Father,
I have been afraid to step out in faith and do what I sensed You were calling me to do. I feel inadequate and I fear failure. But today I place all of my inadequacies in Your hands and choose to spend time with You. I acknowledge that it is from

my time with You that I will be transformed into an extraordinary person who can accomplish anything with Your strength!
In Jesus' name, Amen

April 5

Places of Vulnerability

The thief comes only to steal and kill and destroy; I have come that they may have life, and have it to the full.
John 10:10

Jesus said that He came to give us abundant life. When we live our lives in brokenness, we are only able to live partially. Jesus came to set us free from the power of sin and death and to destroy the works of the devil. He set us free through His shed blood on the cross and has called us to live in that freedom. Our hurts and our brokenness keep us in bondage and prevent us from living the abundant life. We have areas of vulnerability in our lives. It is the desire of Christ to set us free and to close the door where the enemy has access. One particular area of vulnerability is our thought life. The battle begins there because it is often the most vulnerable part of our being. If the enemy can get us to agree with him, and not with the Word of God, then he brings us death. If we agree with God's Word, then the Lord imparts life to us. That is why it is so important for us to study and meditate on God's Word, so that when our thought life tries to deceive us, we can stand firm on God's truth. We must keep in mind that Jesus Christ paid a high price to bring us freedom: *Now the Lord is Spirit, and where the Spirit of the Lord is there is freedom. (II Corinthians 3:17)*

Ask the Lord to heal areas of vulnerability in your life. Often that must begin with forgiveness. We are most vulnerable in areas where we need to forgive. Examine your thought life to see if your thinking is being influenced by unforgiveness. The Holy Spirit longs to direct your thoughts, and where He is, there is complete freedom!

Heavenly Father,
Expose those vulnerable areas in my life where the enemy has access. I thank You for the abundant life that You have promised me and for the freedom You bring.
In Jesus' name, Amen

April 6

Abstaining From Sin

Dear friends, I urge you, as aliens and strangers in the world, to abstain from sinful desires, which war against your soul.
I Peter 2:11

The passage in *I Peter 2:11* urges readers to live *as aliens and strangers in the world, to abstain from sinful desires, which war against your soul.* We also must live in submission to the Holy Spirit, seeking to live in such a way that those who do not believe in Christ will see our good deeds and glorify God. *(v.12)* In order to live as strangers in the world, we must be familiar with God's ways, and our standard must be God's Word. Last summer I kayaked in a river off the ocean. When I got to a certain place in the river, the tide of the ocean began to pull me and I had to use all of my strength to steer the kayak back into calm waters. Eventually, I pulled over to the shore because I was too tired to fight it any longer. The tide pulling me to danger is like the world trying to lure us into being disobedient to God's Word. God's Word is like the river, gently leading us, teaching us God's ways and keeping us out of harm's way. We may fight the tide, but sometimes the tide pulls at us so hard we are forced to go to shore and leave the peace of the river. Jesus told the woman at the well that He was living water. He is still living water today that gives us peace in the tides of the world in which we live.

Do you have a sin that is pulling you further and further away from the security of God's loving river? *I Peter 2* challenges us to live as strangers in this world, conforming to God's ways and His will. It is not always easy to go against the tide, but the benefits far outweigh the struggle.

Heavenly Father,
Your ways are not the ways of the world. I find myself tempted to sin, and I have become dull to Your Word. Help me to establish my life on the standard of Your Word and keep me protected in Your living water.
In Jesus' name, Amen

April 7

Grace and Truth

The fear of the Lord is the beginning of wisdom. For the law was given through Moses; grace and truth came through Jesus Christ
John 1:17

The Pharisees (the keepers of the law) were trying to trap Jesus to see if He would obey the law and agree to the stoning of the woman caught in adultery: *If any one of you is without sin, let him be the first to throw a stone at her. (John 8:7)* Jesus demonstrated a higher law of grace by pointing out that we are all sinners in need of a Savior. Grace is receiving what we don't deserve. It is easy to see how the Pharisees were so caught up with the law that they did not apply grace, but as Christians, we also fall into the trap of being self-righteous and legalistic. Why is it so easy to point a finger at others while refusing to see our own wrongdoings? Jesus condemned the hypocrisy of this: *Why do you look at the speck of sawdust in your brother's eye and pay no attention to the plank in your own eye? (Matthew 7:3)* The Pharisees were accusing the adulterous woman of her sin, but they refused to look at their own sin. Jesus exhibited grace, undeserved by the prostitute, and He spoke truth to the Pharisees. They must have been cut to the quick when He showed them their guilty sinful hearts.

What about you? Do you quickly judge others of their sin and disregard the sin in your own life? Have you judged someone harshly, attempting to remove the "sawdust" out of their eye when a plank remains in your own eye? The Lord is full of grace and truth, and as we seek to be more like Him, we will relate to others through the lens of grace.

Heavenly Father,
I have judged (fill in the blank) harshly. I have condemned this person and have refused to look at my own heart. Help me to walk in grace and truth, to speak the truth in love, and to walk in the power of Your mercy and grace.
In Jesus' name, Amen

God's Leading

See, the ark of the covenant of the Lord of all the earth will go into the Jordan ahead of you.
Joshua 3:11

The Israelites had to cross over the Jordan at flood tide. The river was swollen by the spring rains and melting snow from the Lebanon Mountains. During most of the year, the Jordan River was about 100 feet wide. However, during the spring flood season, the usually narrow river overflowed its banks and swelled to be a mile wide. The Israelites had no physical way to cross the Jordan. They needed the power of God to do what they were helpless to do. In the same way, God works in our lives today. God promises to go before us in times of transition, preparing the way for us and remaining with us each step of the way. I imagine that the Israelites looked at the swollen Jordan River and back at the shore again and were afraid. The Promised Land was just ahead on the other side of the Jordan, but was it worth the risk? God promised them that if they would trust Him, He would send His Presence (represented by the ark) ahead of them. His Presence would part the river and lead the way.

It is often when things seem impossible, when the rivers of life are at a breaking point, that fear immobilizes us. Consider those things that seem impossible to you today. Perhaps your child is rebelling or your marriage is failing. Look up and see the ark of God's Presence beckoning you to follow. He will lead the way and part the turbulent waters. Your part is to step out in faith; His part is to carry you across.

Heavenly Father,
I am afraid of the swollen river of my circumstance. Why must I cross over when it seems so impossible? It would be so much easier to wait until the waters subside to deal with things. I realize that it requires more faith for me to trust You when things seem impossible. Increase my faith to trust You and to follow Your lead.
In Jesus' name, Amen

April 9

Promises Received By Faith

Then they asked him, "What must we do to do the works God requires?"
John 6:28

God's promises are true and He is the Promise Keeper. *Hebrews 10* tells us that *He who promised is faithful.* We sometimes use human standards to consider what faithfulness means. In today's society, we see marriages that have failed due to unfaithfulness, friendships that have been lost because of broken promises, and businesses that have failed because they have been proven untrustworthy. Paul writes to the Jews and Gentiles using Abraham as an example of a man who was considered righteous because he believed God and his promises. When the crowd asked Jesus what they must *do* to be right with God, He responded that they must believe in Him. The first promise we have from God is that all the promises are ours if we simply believe. Seem too easy? In today's world of "doing" and "performance," it does seem too easy to simply believe and receive God's promises by faith. Paul explains in the fourth chapter of *Romans* that before Abraham underwent circumcision, he believed. Circumcision did not make him "right" with God. Abraham's faith alone justified him, and in turn he was the beneficiary of God's promises. Our unwavering faith in Jesus Christ puts into our "accounts" the promises of God in His Word. What promises are you waiting for because you have failed to believe?

Heavenly Father,
You alone are faithful to Your Word. Forgive me where I have not believed that the promises in Your Word are for me. Help me to believe like Abraham with unwavering faith.
In Jesus' name, Amen

April 10

Parable of the Sower

But the one who received the seed that fell on good soil is the man who hears the word and understands it. He produces a crop, yielding a hundred, sixty or thirty times what was sown.
Matthew 13:23

Jesus began to teach the disciples from a boat on the Sea of Galilee. This is sometimes known as His Sermon on the Sea. It is very likely that it was springtime when the Lord was telling this story, and probably those listening could see a sower on the hillside going forth to sow. Perhaps they could see where the seeds were being scattered: on a path, on rocky places, among thorns and thistles, and on good soil. Jesus explains the parable of the sower first by telling them that the seed represents the message of the kingdom, an invisible, spiritual, heavenly kingdom that goes beyond what we can comprehend with our five senses. The seed of the kingdom refers to God's promise of power and righteousness *for the salvation of everyone who believes. (Romans 1:16-17)* The key to the seed bearing fruit is the condition of the soil. Similarly, our hearts must be prepared if we are to receive the Word of God. Jesus explains the parable: *When anyone hears the message of the kingdom and does not understand it, the evil one comes and snatches away what was sown in his heart. (Matthew 13:19)* The seed that falls on rocky places is the man who hears the Word and receives it with joy, but because he has no root, he quickly falls away when trouble comes. The seed that falls among thorns is the man who hears the Word, but the worries of this life choke it out. But the seed that falls on good soil is the man who hears the Word and understands it. The Word bears fruit in his life yielding thirty, sixty or one hundred times what was sown.

Has the Word of God born fruit in your life? Is the soil or the condition of your heart tilled and ready to receive God's Word? Or is your heart hardened so that the seed is choked out by the cares of the world? If you are willing to allow the Lord to prepare your heart, you will find that His Word will transform your life, and you will know the joy that His Word brings.

Heavenly Father,
You know the condition of my heart. I surrender my heart to you, to till and prepare it to receive Your Word. Where my heart is hard, soften it so that the seed of Your Word will find a place prepared to yield a harvest of righteousness.
In Jesus' name, Amen

El Shaddai, Our Protector

If you make the Most High your dwelling – even the LORD, who is my refuge – then no harm will befall you, no disaster will come near your tent.
Psalm 91:9-10

Psalm 91 describes El Shaddai, God Almighty, as our place of protection, our refuge, and our fortress. El Shaddai means "many breasted one," and inherent in the meaning is a mother who nourishes her child. El Shaddai is the One who will cause the godly not to fear and provide a safe haven for those who trust Him. The men and women of faith came to know God as El Shaddai when they were faced with trials and tribulations. Think about Joseph, thrown into a pit by his brothers, sold into slavery, thrown into prison, yet was always hidden under the shadow of the Almighty. What about King David who was ruthlessly pursued by his enemies, and yet God protected and hid him? Today, I read an e-mail from an amazing woman of God who shared her story of knowing God as El Shaddai. She has been like Job, afflicted with physical suffering and yet is always looking to her God as her security, her safe haven. She writes that in every trial, Her God is with her, sustaining her and keeping her under the shadow of His Presence.

What about you? Have you allowed the Lord Almighty to reveal Himself to you as your Protector? Do you fear that you are all alone, left vulnerable to circumstances or people beyond your control? Look to El Shaddai and know that He will care for you as a mother cares for her child: *But Zion said, "The Lord has forsaken me, the Lord has forgotten me. Can a mother forget the baby at her breast and have no compassion on the child she has borne? Though she may forget, I will never forget you. See I have engraved you on the palms of my hands. (Isaiah 49:15-16)* God is with you; God is your shelter and the One who nourishes you. His name is El Shaddai.

Heavenly Father,

I have felt forsaken, alone, rejected and afraid. I want to know You as El Shaddai. I run to the safety of Your arms and trust that, when everyone else forsakes me, You will still be there.
In Jesus' name, Amen

Taking Hold of God's Kingdom

From the days of John the Baptist until now, the kingdom of heaven has been forcefully advancing and forceful men lay hold of it.
Matthew 11:12

Jesus told the followers of John the Baptist, *From the days of John the Baptist until now, the kingdom of heaven has been forcefully advancing and forceful men lay hold of it.* In Greek, "forcefully advancing" can be taken as active or passive. In the passive sense, it refers to "suffering violent attacks." This means that violent people were attacking the kingdom. This is certainly true. However, in the active sense, it would mean that people were actively advancing the kingdom of God. The idea here is that the Church has been in a war throughout the centuries. Opposing forces have sought to destroy the Church, or at least to limit the advancement of the message of the gospel. Today, some people point to the seemingly intolerant stance that Christians have taken, that of believing that the only way to enter God's kingdom is by believing in Jesus Christ and receiving Him into your life. Increasingly, there is a greater emphasis on and acceptance of other religions. Jesus tells us, "*I am the way and the truth and the life. No one comes to the Father except through Me." (John 14:6)* As a body of believers, we have the advantage of living on this side of the cross, knowing that Jesus Christ, the Son of David, came to bring salvation. The church must stand firm in this truth and continue to advance the kingdom of God forcefully.

Have you found yourself in situations with people who find Christians intolerant? Do you find yourself defensive of your faith rather than being on the offense? As you live your life for Jesus, there will always be people who do not wish to believe that Jesus Christ is the only way to the Father; however, He clearly said: *I am the way and the truth and the life. No one comes to the Father except through me. (John 14:6)* Opposing forces have tried to limit and even extinguish the message of the kingdom, but the message and the Church have prevailed. The King of the kingdom will return some day, and His question will be: *...when the Son of Man comes, will He find faith on the earth? (Luke 18:8)* As we advance the good news of Jesus Christ and His kingdom, we exhibit genuine faith that will stand the test of time.

Heavenly Father,
I have been frustrated and discouraged at times as I attempt to share my faith. It is so difficult to be rejected because of my faith. Give me courage to stand up for what I know is true in Your Word, coupled with conviction to stay the course. When You return, I truly want You to see in me the genuine faith that You deserve.
In Jesus' name, Amen

Gates at Entry Points

By night, I went out through the Valley Gate toward the Jackal Well and the Dung Gate, examining the walls of Jerusalem, which had been broken down and its gates, which had been destroyed by fire.
Nehemiah 2:13

Nehemiah inspected the walls and discovered that the gates had been burned down (*2:17*). He encouraged the Jews to rebuild the walls so that they would no longer be in disgrace and reminded the people that the gracious hand of the Lord was on them to help them accomplish the task. Grace is a state of unmerited favor, and *dis*grace is loss of grace. Nehemiah said that the burned down gates caused disgrace, and it was the grace of God that enabled them to rebuild the gates. The Lord offers us grace as He builds back the broken-down gates of our lives. Gates represent an opening, a place of entry in our spiritual lives, where the enemy seeks to come into our lives to wreak havoc or destruction. He goes after the vulnerable places—places of hurt, disappointment, bitterness, and discouragement. The easiest entry point or gateway is through our thought life. If the enemy can enter our thought life, he then has access to our lives. Agreement with God's Word rebuilds the gate and closes it to the harmful effects of the world, the flesh and the devil. Jesus refers to Himself as the gate. *(John 10:7)* He is the gate through which we enter as believers, and His Word guards the gates of our lives.

Are there broken-down gates in your life? Does the enemy have access to any part of your life? Claim the promises of God, and He will rebuild every broken-down gate of your life.

Heavenly Father,
I am aware of the broken-down gates of my life. Where anger and hurt reside, the enemy has had access to my life. Heal my hurt, rebuild the broken-down places, and enable me to live into the promises of Your Word.
In Jesus' name, Amen

April 14

The Kingdom Proclaimed

Day after day, in the temple courts and from house to house, they never stopped teaching and proclaiming the good news that Jesus is the Christ.
Acts 5:42

In the early church, the Apostles devoted themselves to prayer, teaching, fellowship, and the "breaking of bread." The results of their lives together celebrating the Kingdom of God turned the world upside down. Their lives were radically devoted to Jesus and to each other, and the church grew rapidly. Miraculous signs and wonders were commonplace, and most importantly, *The Lord added to their number daily those who were being saved. (Acts 2:42)* If we are willing to experience our faith together, modeling the early church and proclaiming the Kingdom, I am convinced we will see the radical power of God at work and people giving their lives to Christ in ways we have not seen before. The key elements that were catalysts for growth were: devotion to the teachings of Christ, fellowship, sharing bread, and prayer. This describes groups of people who were willing to "do life together." They were a community that shared the gospel, had meals together, and were dedicated to prayer. Christian community is essential to the development and nurturing of our faith. We need the body of Christ to help us grow through studying the Word, prayer, and fellowship. Are you a part of a body of believers that offers you this kind of community? Attending church is essential to our spiritual growth, but the real work is done in community and fellowship within a small group of devoted followers of Jesus Christ where you have accountability in the working out of your faith.

Heavenly Father,
Thank you for the model of the early church—a body of believers who were devoted to You and to one another. Help me to find a small group of believers to encourage my spiritual growth and enable me to see the demonstration of Your kingdom on earth today.
In Jesus' name, Amen

Remembering the Past

So Joshua called together the twelve men he had appointed from the Israelites, one from each tribe, and said to them, "Go over before the ark of the LORD your God into the middle of the Jordan. Each of you is to take up a stone on his shoulder, according to the number of the tribes of the Israelites, to serve as a sign among you. In the future, when your children ask you, 'What do these stones mean?' tell them that the flow of the Jordan was cut off before the ark of the covenant of the LORD. When it crossed the Jordan, the waters of the Jordan were cut off. These stones are to be a memorial to the people of Israel forever.
Joshua 4:4-7

Setting up memorial stones was a common Old Testament practice. Many times when a significant event occurred in the life of the people of Israel, they would use stones to mark the place where an event occurred. The Israelites had left Egypt, wandered for 40 years, and now were at the dawn of a new day as they entered the Promised Land. The Lord wanted them to remember that God had been with them from their departure from Egypt to the parting of the Red Sea; from their wanderings in the desert to the edge of the Jordan River. He had supplied them with food and with shoes that never wore out. Although the Israelites grumbled and complained, He never forsook them. Their idolatry denied one generation of Israelites entrance into the Promised Land, but their descendants crossed over. Joshua had seen how quickly the Israelites forgot their God both in good times and in difficult times. Joshua wanted them to remember what God had done. He wanted their children to know what the stones signified. Today, we use memory markers such as pictures, souvenirs, or gifts to remind us of special events that are especially meaningful. I often write down in my journal answered prayers so that I can remember the faithfulness of God. Memorials help us to remember God's blessings and encourage us to go forward in our journey of faith.

Can you recall a time when the Lord opened up a river of blessings for you? After the Jordan River parted and the Israelites crossed over, the memorial stones were a reminder that God had delivered them from the bondage of Egypt into the Promised Land.

God's promises in His Word are true for us today. He parts the rivers in our lives and asks us to enter into His promises. In order to grow in our faith, we must trust God to part the sea and remember to thank the Lord for what He has done.

Heavenly Father,
I quickly forget Your faithfulness after You have answered my prayers until the next time when I again cry out to You in prayer. Forgive me for my ungratefulness. Carve a memorial stone of remembrance on my heart so that I will always remember Your faithfulness to me.
In Jesus' name, Amen

Unwavering Faith

Against all hope, Abraham in hope believed and so became the father of many nations, just as it had been said to him, "So shall your offspring be." Without weakening in his faith, he faced the fact that his body was about a hundred years old – and that Sarah's womb was also dead. Yet he did not waver through unbelief regarding the promise of God, but was strengthened in his faith and gave glory to God, being fully persuaded that God had the power to do what he had promised. This is why "it was credited to him as righteousness."
Romans 4:18-22

What causes your faith to waver? What circumstances are beyond your control? Do you have disappointments in life or health or financial issues that seem insurmountable? God told Abraham that he would be the father of many nations, yet he and his wife were childless and Sarai was beyond the child-bearing years. Paul writes that Abraham did not waver in his belief regarding the promise of God and that he was fully persuaded that God would fulfill His promise. His faith credited him with righteousness. If God told me at hundred years old that I was going to have a child, I think I would fail the test of unwavering faith! I would think that perhaps He was talking about adoption, or I would be like Sarai and laugh. One thing is for certain, I would not give my handmaiden to my husband in order to have a child!! And besides, the last time I looked, I didn't have any handmaidens. Although those things sound preposterous to me, there are other ways that I have disregarded God's promises or tried to take things into my own hands to make them happen. Take, for example, my desire for my son to marry a godly woman. The Lord has made it clear in His Word that He will protect and watch out for my children, but that has not stopped me from trying to pick out his wife! Paul, by using Abraham's faith as an example to us, shows us that God will credit us with righteousness when we believe in Jesus Christ, and He will fulfill His promises to us when we have the faith to believe.

What promises do you doubt that the Lord will fulfill? Are you willing to believe and put your hope in His fulfillment of them?

Heavenly Father,

Your Word is filled with promises. You have promised to never forsake me and to fulfill all of Your promises. Why do I try so hard to make things happen? Why do I feel as though You are not going to answer my prayers? Help me to be like Abraham, who believed You when You said that You would make him the father of many nations. It seemed like an impossible promise, but You are the God of the impossible!
In Jesus' name, Amen

April 17

Aligning with God

...He restores my soul. He guides me in paths of righteousness for His name's sake.
Psalm 23:3

Once the Lord shows us that we are on the wrong path, it is essential that we agree with His plan, change our course, and follow His way. Isaiah warned the people that they were obstinate because they carried out their own plans rather than the plans of the Lord, forming an alliance not by His Spirit. *(Isaiah 30:1)* They consulted with the Pharaoh of Egypt, aligning themselves with ungodly advice (human wisdom and reasoning) and sought the protection of the Pharaoh. Their sin, according to Isaiah, was like a *high wall, cracked and bulging, collapsing suddenly. (Isaiah 30:13)* We, too, have our "high walls" built on human reasoning and unholy alliances. The Lord is calling us to depend on Him, to trust Him, and to come into agreement with His Word laid forth in the Scriptures. The rebellious people in Isaiah's day told the prophets to tell them only pleasant things and to stop confronting them with the Holy One of Israel *(Isaiah 30:10)*.

In our nation today and in our personal lives, we can hear the cry of many saying, "Don't tell me any more bad news about God's judgment; don't confront me with the truth of Scripture." I pray that the Lord will help us to be willing to align ourselves with His truth. May we also be willing to confront the places of complacency in our own spiritual lives and be willing to agree with His purposes and plans.

Heavenly Father,
Lead me and guide me today. If I am going in the wrong direction, opposed to Your plan and Your will, help me to change my course and follow You. I am often just like the Israelites—obstinate and unwilling to follow Your way. Help me to depend on Your Holy Spirit to guide me and keep me from rebellion.
In Jesus' name, Amen

April 18

Submitting to Authority

Submit yourselves for the Lord's sake to every authority instituted among men…
1Peter 2:13

The word "submit" comes from the Greek word *hupeiko,* meaning "to yield." The culture in which we live suggests to us that we must be in control of our own destiny. Leading submitted, humble lives seems to be synonymous with being weak in character. However, yielding to the Lord and to those in authority actually strengthens us to live successful lives. When we yield ourselves completely to Christ, we love others and have their best interest at heart. We become people who are God-centered and not self-centered. Yielding to the authority of God allows us to live in peaceful surrender to a loving God who knows what is best for us and for others. The verses in this section of *I Peter* challenge us as we seek to understand the meaning of submission in our lives.

Where are you struggling with submission to authority? I remember teaching one of my children to yield at an intersection when she was learning to drive. My child, who always tested me, would come to yield at a stop sign or intersection and always inch her way out without first coming to a stop and looking both ways. Yielding requires us to slow down or perhaps stop and allow others to go ahead of us. The Lord has given us people in authority such as parents, government officials and our bosses, to whom we must be willing to submit. God is our ultimate authority, and as we learn to yield and surrender ourselves to Him, we will likewise learn to submit to others. We are actually strengthened as we learn to humbly do so.

Heavenly Father,
It seems safer to be in control of my own life. I struggle with surrendering to You and I realize that the root of my fear is lack of trust. Forgive me, Lord. Today I surrender to You. Give me the grace to surrender to those who are in authority over me and help me to extend grace to those over whom I have authority.
In Jesus' name, Amen

Parable of the Weeds

But while everyone was sleeping, his enemy came and sowed weeds among the wheat, and went away.
Matthew 13:25

In the first parable about sowing, the Word of God was sown and fell on four different conditions of soil. The parable of the weeds, however, is not about sowing the Word of God; it is about Jesus sowing the good seed, "the sons of the kingdom," into the world. The "sons of the kingdom" are scattered to preach the gospel to every creature. (*Mark 16:15*) In this parable, the field represents the world. Into this field of good seed (the wheat), the evil one planted his seed (the weeds), the "sons of the evil one." Thus, the people of the kingdom live side by side with the people of the evil one until the end of the age when Jesus separates them out and the weeds, the "sons of the evil one," are burned.

Are you a "son of the kingdom," influencing your world with the truth of Christ? Jesus teaches us in this parable that "the righteous will shine like the sun in the kingdom of their Father." (v.42) As sons of the kingdom, we grow up next to the weeds of the world, but we are called to shine with Christ's light in the harvest fields.

Where is your harvest field? We are called to bloom where we are planted—in our workplace, in our homes, and in our relationships. This week, consider where God has planted you and remember that as a "son of the kingdom" you are bringing Christ's Presence everywhere you go.

Heavenly Father,
You have called me to "bloom" where I am planted. As a son of the kingdom, help me to shine in a world filled with "weeds." Give me favor and influence (fill in the blank with your harvest field) and give me the courage to boldly proclaim Your Name.
In Jesus' name, Amen

April 20

El Shaddai, Our Place Of Surrender

Therefore, I urge you, brothers, in view of God's mercy, to offer your bodies as living sacrifices, holy and pleasing to God – this is your spiritual act of worship.
Romans 12:1

Abram met El Shaddai face to face when he was 99 years old. The Lord appeared to him and said, "I am God Almighty; walk before Me and be blameless." *(Genesis 17:1)* What hope that gives us as we seek to know this divine side of God as our El Shaddai. The Lord never stops revealing Himself to us no matter how old we are! God told Abram that after that day his name would be changed to Abraham. The Hebrew letter "h" was added to his name—the chief letter of His own name, Jehovah, the letter that when pronounced sounds like a breath of air. We, too, must receive God's breath of life, His Holy Spirit, in order to know El Shaddai. The Lord may reveal Himself to us as El Shaddai, our Protector and our Fruitfulness, but only when we are willing to surrender ourselves completely to His breath of life (Holy Spirit) will we know the fullness of El Shaddai. El Shaddai means "many breasted one," like a woman who offers breast milk to her baby. All of the nutrients the child needs are available in the mother's milk. El Shaddai is our place of nourishment, the place where we hide, the place where we are secure. As we offer ourselves to the Lord as living sacrifices, let us be ever mindful that El Shaddai will carry and sustain us. *(Romans 12:1)*

Are you burned out with work, with your family, maybe even with your spiritual walk with Christ? We all go through the valleys of life where we need to regroup, be refreshed and hide in the arms of our El Shaddai. Like a mother nourishes her child, so the Lord will nourish you. If you are in a valley today, seek the Lord and run into His loving arms.

Heavenly Father,
I am tired; I am struggling just to keep my head above water. I know that what I need is You. You are the only source of life and refreshment, and I come running back to You. Like a baby in Your arms, I surrender to You, El Shaddai.
In Jesus' name, Amen

Fighting God's Battles

And he became more and more powerful, because the LORD God Almighty was with him.
2 Samuel 5:10

David became more powerful *because* the Lord was with Him. *Matthew 6:33* reminds us to *seek first His Kingdom and His righteousness, and all these things will be given to you as well.* David's vision and the purpose of his life was to seek the Lord: *One thing I ask of the Lord, this is what I seek; that I may dwell in the house of the Lord all the days of my life, to gaze upon the beauty of the Lord and to seek Him in His temple. (Psalm 27:4)* As courageous leaders, our one goal and our whole purpose should be to seek the Lord, to love Him more each day, and to serve Him with our whole heart. We are warriors for God when we pursue Him and actively follow His commands. The wars in which David participated as he led God's people give us a picture of the spiritual war that we fight as we allow the Lord to grow His kingdom in us. Jesus made it clear that we would need His Holy Spirit when He left the earth. His Spirit would lead us into truth, convict us of error, and give us the power we need to struggle against the opposition. *(John 16)* Praise God that we are able to be courageous warriors for Christ as His Holy Spirit enables us to fight the good fight! *(I Timothy 6:12)*

The Lord is always with you fighting your battles. What battle do you face today that you need to remind yourself that it is His to fight? Our greatest weapon of warfare is staying close to Christ, seeking Him daily. As our life's purpose becomes intimacy with Christ, we will find ourselves immune to the battles of life. Yes, the struggles of life will still come, but we will see that our God goes before us and fights for our lives.

Heavenly Father,
Help me to be like King David who sought You with all of his heart. David faced many battles, but he always kept You in his line of vision. Thank you for Your promise that the battle belongs to You and help me to remember that my armor is secure when I stay close to You.
In Jesus' name, Amen

April 22

Repairing Our House

Come let us rebuild the wall of Jerusalem, and we will no longer be in disgrace.
Nehemiah 2:17b

Nehemiah inspected the walls of Jerusalem and discerned what needed to be done. He gathered the people and prepared a plan of action to accomplish the work. Godly leaders not only delegate the work to be done, but also are involved in the work themselves: *Come let US rebuild the wall of Jerusalem and we will no longer be in disgrace. (Nehemiah 2:17b)* Nehemiah simply told the people there was work to be done and together they could do it. Some of the people began directly in front of their houses. *Above the Horse Gate, the priests made repairs, each in front of their own house. (v.28)*

Sometimes the walls of our house are in disrepair and the enemy has come in to wreak havoc. The Lord has given us His Holy Spirit to bring healing and repair to the damaged places of our lives so that we can more effectively have the freedom to serve the Lord. The people of Jerusalem repaired the walls in front of their own houses, implying that we must not neglect our own household and repair the broken-down places in order to more effectively serve others. At the end of the day, I am so tired and sometimes it is easy to neglect my husband. I know that he will understand, so I make him my last priority. If I allow this attitude to continue, I begin to see walls break down, that is, relationship walls. God is forever reminding me that I must rebuild the walls of our relationship by investing the time.

Take an inventory of your life. Are there any areas of your life in need of repair? Don't wait until the wall is completely broken down. Broken down walls allow the enemy to easily come in. In Nehemiah's time, there were watchmen on the walls who looked to see if the enemy was approaching. The Holy Spirit is your watchman. Allow Him to show you any places of vulnerability that need repair.

Heavenly Father,

I have neglected (fill in the blank). I recognize the need for repair in this area of my life. Please forgive me for not turning to You sooner. Help me to yield to the work that You need to do in my life to bring restoration.
In Jesus' name, Amen

April 23

Disobedience to God

If you obey my commands, you will remain in my love, just as I have obeyed my Father's commands and remain in his love.
John 15:10

Ananias and Sapphira were disciples of Christ who sold their land to help fulfill the mission of the early church: *None claimed that any of his possessions was his own, but they shared everything they had* (*Acts 4:32*). Ananias and Sapphira kept part of the money for themselves and lied about it, claiming to have given it all. Peter rebuked them saying, *You have not lied to men, but to God.* Over the past few weeks, I have been more aware of how easy it is to stretch the truth to make a point or to avoid the truth so that I do not have to deal with something. As Christians, we need to be committed to being 100% truthful all of the time! When we are not, we are lying to God, not just to men.

Obedience to God's commands, according to *John 15:10*, has the benefit of causing us to remain in God's love. God never stops loving us, but when we are disobedient, we draw away from His love. We may be ashamed or our hearts may be hardened, but whatever the reason for our disobedience, it causes us to be apart from His love.

What has God asked you to do that you are unwilling to do? Have you disobeyed God and find yourself struggling to know His love? He is waiting for you to return to Him in obedience. He longs for you to know the extent of His love. Paul puts it this way: *For I am convinced that neither death, nor life, neither angels nor demons, nor any powers, neither height nor depth, nor anything else in all creation, will be able to separate us from the love of God that is in Christ Jesus our Lord. (Romans 8:37-39)* If God's love is ever present and you are not experiencing that love, ask Him to show you if you are being disobedient to his commands. If so, return to Him in repentance and obedience, and you will remain in His love.

Heavenly Father,
I find myself in a place of emptiness, wondering if You care or even love me at all. Yet Your Word is clear that nothing separates me from Your love. So, I am asking You to show me any area of my life where I am in disobedience to Your Word. Forgive me, Lord, and lead me to obedience so that I can remain in Your love.
In Jesus' name, Amen

April 24

Fading Memories

Only be careful, and watch yourselves closely so that you do not forget the things your eyes have seen or let them slip from your heart as long as you live. Teach them to your children and to their children after them.
Deuteronomy 4:9

We read in *Judges 2:8-15* that it only took one generation after the Israelites crossed the Jordan River for the people to forget what the Lord had done for them. It is no wonder that the Israelites had to be reminded over and over again of God's laws and His faithfulness. The ease with which the Israelites forgot God's faithfulness emphasizes to us the importance of remembering God's faithfulness. One way to remember what God has done is to continue to thank and praise Him. Tell your children what He has done. A grateful heart is a sure remedy for remembering what God has done and for building up our faith. We must face the fact that it is also easy for us to move away from God's precepts and from recognizing and remembering His faithfulness. We are like sheep, prone to wander away from our Shepherd, and we must be diligent to remember the things that our eyes have seen (v.9).

Keep a daily journal of the ways that God has answered your prayers. When you are prone to wander, read through your entries. The Israelites witnessed an awesome miracle when the Jordan River was parted at flood tide, enabling them to pass through into the Promised Land. It is hard to believe that it only took one generation for them to forget what He had done.

Today begin your journal of "remembrance." Teach your children to remember what God does daily, and thank the Lord for all He has done.

Heavenly Father,
I am prone to wander, and like the Israelites I am prone to complain and forget all that You have done for me. Help me to have a grateful heart—a heart that worships and praises You daily—for You are an awesome and faithful God.
In Jesus' name, Amen

First Assault: Weak Resources

The Lord turned to him and said, "Go in the strength you have and save Israel out of Midian's hand. Am I not sending you?
Judges 6:14

The first assault that King Sennacherib of Assyria used against the people of God began with the question, "On what are you basing this confidence of yours?" *(Isaiah 36:4)* This is the same question posed to us today as believers, and it would be wise for us to evaluate exactly in what or in whom we place our confidence. The field commander serving as spokesperson for King Sennacherib pointed out that the people of Jerusalem were depending on Egypt, a splintered reed. *(Isaiah 36:6)* Egypt was known for her resources, particularly her massive army and chariots of horses. If the people of Jerusalem had put their confidence in Egypt, they would have failed. But through the strong godly leadership of their king, Hezekiah, they chose to believe that God would deliver them. It is an easy trap for us to fall into when we look at our meager or seemingly weak resources to defend ourselves against the assaults of the enemy. But we must remember, like Hezekiah, that He will surely come and save us!

The question still remains today: "on what are you basing this confidence of yours?" If we are fearful, tired, stressed or frustrated, it is easy to see that we have placed our confidence in ourselves. Whatever you are facing today, place your confidence in the Lord and remember *to go in the strength you have.* Where God sends you, *HE* gives you the resources you need to complete the job. If you are finding yourself in a losing battle, take a moment to evaluate in what or in whom you have placed your confidence. If it is in God, and He has sent you to battle, He will never fail you.

Heavenly Father,
I repent of my self-confidence. I have trusted in my own abilities and resources and forgotten that all of these things are gifts from You. I surrender my situation to You and I surrender my life, gifts, and talents on the altar of God. You alone are my source of strength.
In Jesus' name, Amen

April 26

Credited with Righteousness

Then the word of the LORD came to him: "This man will not be your heir, but a son coming from your own body, will be your heir. He took him outside and said, "Look up at the heavens and count the stars – if indeed you can count them." Then he said to him, "So shall your offspring be." Abram believed the Lord and he credited it to him as righteousness.
Genesis 15:4-6

Paul writes that if justification by faith proved true for Abraham, it was also true for the Jews and the Gentiles and for us today. When we put our hope and faith in Jesus Christ, when we choose to believe that He was delivered over to death for our sins and was raised from the dead *(Romans 4:24)*, we are given a credit statement that says "paid in full." I am always elated when my credit card statement has a zero balance. By believing in Jesus Christ, God writes across the statement of our lives "debt canceled!" We are credited with righteousness and justified before God. God's grace and His unmerited favor are imputed to us, and we can only offer ourselves back to Him in gratitude. Undeserving as we are, we can offer ourselves to the Lord as "living sacrifices" *(Romans 12:1)* and freely surrender to the God of grace.

Each time I read *Genesis 15: 4-6*, I am reminded that Abraham not only believed *in* God, He *believed* God. You see, we can believe that God exists, that He is the Creator of the universe. We can believe in His Son, sent to die for our sins, but we must go one step further and believe God—that is, believe in His promises and believe that His Word is true. Abraham was an old man and his wife Sarai was beyond child bearing years, but Abraham, knowing and believing in God, also believed God's Word, and he was credited with righteousness.

Do you believe God? Do you believe that what He has told you He will fulfill? What promise are you waiting for God to fulfill? Today chose to trust and believe God.

Heavenly Father,
I have been waiting on a promise for a long time. Today I choose to trust You to fulfill Your promise. Like Abraham, I believe Your Word because You are a trustworthy God.
In Jesus' name, Amen

April 27

Living in Harmony

Finally, all of you, live in harmony with one another; be sympathetic, love as brothers, be compassionate and humble.
1 Peter 3:8

I Peter 3:8 describes the way we are to live in fellowship with all people. We are to live in harmony with sympathy, compassion and humility. Scripture encourages us to *do good to all people, especially to those who belong to the family of believers. (Galatians 6:10)* Earlier, Peter told the readers to live their lives before men abstaining from sin, and becoming an example to the unbeliever. Christ becomes a person with human hands and a human heart when we show His love by reaching out to others. What a privilege it is to share Christ with others and to love people where they are. This does not mean that as Christians we are to compromise our beliefs in any way. *I Peter* continues by exhorting us not to repay evil for evil or insult for insult. This is difficult to do, but that does not excuse us from being obedient to God's Word.

Who today needs your sympathy, your compassion, your love? God's Word is clear that you must reach out to those in need, especially to the family of believers. Ask the Lord to show you who needs you to come alongside them and be willing to go the extra mile to show them Christ's love.

Heavenly Father,
I know that You are asking me today to reach out to (fill in the blank). I have been unwilling to do this up until now, but I realize that You are calling me to obedience. Help me to live in harmony with others, showing sympathy, compassion and humility. Help me to be more like You.
In Jesus' name, Amen

Parable of the Mustard Seed

He told them another parable: "The kingdom of heaven is like a mustard seed, which a man took and planted in his field. Though it is the smallest of all your seeds, yet when it grows, it is the largest of garden plants and becomes a tree, so that the birds of the air come and perch in its branches.
Matthew 13:31-32

The mustard seed that is planted in this parable has two inherent qualities. First, it is the smallest seed used by the Israelites, yet it could grow into a plant as large as a tree. Second, the seed has pungent, biting, burning properties. Both of these traits have significance as Jesus compared a mustard seed to His kingdom. The mustard seed's unusual growth is unnatural, and so it is with believers as we grow in Christ. It is a supernatural growth, both in individual believers and in the Church worldwide—the Church that provides shelter and a haven for a lost world. Also, just as the pungent, biting, and burning trait of the mustard seed is used in seasoning, so the message of God's kingdom is used in transforming society.

When I think of the smallness of the mustard seed, I think of humility. God's Word teaches us that He *gives grace to the humble (James 4:6)* and produces growth and power beyond human reasoning so that we can have an impact on the world in which we are sown. When I look at my mustard seed of faith I am reminded of God's Word: *If you have the faith as small as a mustard seed you can say to this mulberry tree be uprooted and planted in the sea, and it will obey you. (Luke 17:6)* Jesus told this to his disciples after they asked him to increase their faith. I can identify with mustard seed faith because at times my faith seems so small. It is harder, however, for me to identify with my mustard seed of faith as being able to move a tree! Yet this is what Jesus says. Our faith may be as small as a mustard seed, but like that little seed, it can grow supernaturally into a huge tree by the power of the Holy Spirit.

Perhaps you have looked at your faith as being so small you might as well bury it and not bother to water it. Pray for God to increase your faith, water it with prayer and the reading of God's Word, and like the mustard seed in the parable, it will grow.

Remember that it only takes the faith of a mustard seed to move mountains: *I tell you the truth, if you have faith as small as a mustard seed you can say to this mountain, move from here to there and it will move. Nothing will be impossible for you. (Matthew 17:20)*

Heavenly Father,
I pray that You would increase my faith. I offer to You my "mustard seed" faith for increase and growth. Help me to remember that what I see as a small seed can move mountains in my life and in the lives of others.
In Jesus' name, Amen

Our Provision and Example

But Abram said, "O Sovereign LORD, what can you give me since I remain childless and the one who will inherit my estate is Eliezer of Damascus?"
Genesis 15:2

The first time we see the name Adonai used is in *Genesis 15:2* where Abram calls on Adonai Jehovah to give him the assurance that God's promise to bless him would be fulfilled. He cries out to Adonai and says, "What can you give me since I remain childless?" Adonai begins to reveal that He is Abram's Provision as He promises to give him a son and offspring as numerous as the stars. As we grow in our understanding of Adonai as our Provision, we learn to trust Him. We become confident that He has the resources and ability to provide for our needs, and we learn that we can call on Him when we are in need. In many ways, the parent/child relationship is similar to our relationship with Adonai. I remember a time when one of my children asked me to do something that was out of the range of possibility for me. When I hesitated, she said, "But Mom, you can do *anything*!" She had complete confidence that I could, would, and had the resources to do it! The Old Testament Hebrew Adonai is the counterpart for the Greek New Testament "Kurios" (Lord). Jesus Christ is the Christian's Lord and Master. *"Ye call me Master and Lord: and ye say well; for so I am" (John 13:13 KJV).*

Do you know Jesus as your Lord and Master? You may know Him as Savior and as Redeemer, but do you know Him as Adonai? Today, He is calling you into a deeper relationship with Him as Lord. Are you willing to surrender?

Heavenly Father,
I know You as Savior, I have seen You at work as my Redeemer, redeeming the things that I have lost or reclaiming the things that were hopeless. Today I desire to know You as my Master. I realize that this requires me to surrender in ways that I have not been willing to do. Help me to know You as Adonai.
In Jesus' name, Amen

April 30

Front Line Leadership

In the past, while Saul was king over us, you were the one who led Israel on their military campaigns. And the Lord said to you, 'You will shepherd my people Israel, and you will become their ruler.'
II Samuel 5:2

David led the people in battle while Saul was king over Israel. The Lord told David that he would shepherd the people of Israel and become their king. David continued to fight with his army as their leader when he became king. *II Samuel 5* describes how David and his men captured the "fortress of Zion," the city of David, known as Jerusalem. Courageous leaders are willing to fight alongside their soldiers. They are willing to be on the front line of battle while fighting for their beliefs. When David chose not to go with his army to war, he got into trouble. His leadership suffered as he sought to cover up his affair with Bathsheba and made plans to have her husband killed. Leaders who are unwilling to be part of the battle to which they are called can find themselves in compromising positions. Temptation overtook David when he left his place of obedience. As leaders, we must be willing to fight on the front lines until the battle is won!

Where has God called you to be a leader? Have you been willing to lead others as a fellow worker, or have you been unwilling to get in the middle of the work and the battles? As a leader, we must never set ourselves above others. We are called to work humbly with others, setting an example of servant leadership. David fought alongside those he led because he did not consider himself more highly than others. Jesus is our prime example of servant leadership: *Who being in the nature of God did not consider equality with God something to be grasped, but made Himself nothing, taking the very nature of a servant… (Philippians 2:6-7)*

Who are you leading? Are you willing to take front line leadership and humbly serve others?

Heavenly Father,
Your Son Jesus Christ humbled Himself and became obedient to death. He laid down His life for others in a way that is unimaginable for me. Help me to be a leader willing to serve others and not be self-serving. Help me to be like Jesus.
In Jesus' name, Amen

May 1

Using God-Given Gifts

We have different gifts, according to the grace given us. If a man's gift is prophesying, let him use it in proportion to his faith.
Romans 12:6

No one person could have accomplished the work of repairing the walls and gates of Jerusalem. Nehemiah's effective leadership helped him survey the damage, prepare a plan, and seek the cooperation of the people to carry it out. He formulated a plan and then sought people for assignments according their gifts. He knew it would take craftsmen, priests, and a vast array of people to accomplish the task. As the leader, he had the awesome job to identify who was to do what job according to their skills and gifts. As the body of Christ, we must work together to do the work of the kingdom. We must identify our gifts and be willing to use them for the glory of God. Paul, in his letter to the Romans, describes the body of Christ and how it functions: *Just as each of us has one body with many members, and these members do not all have the same function, so in Christ we who are many form one body, and each member belongs to all the others. (Romans 12:4)*

Recently I attended a conference in St. Louis, Missouri. I am not a seasoned traveler, and my friend, a flight attendant for almost 30 years, accompanied me. Due to poor weather conditions, our plane was delayed, and suddenly there was pandemonium as thousands of people were going to miss their connections. My friend used both her professional experience and her communication gifts to negotiate alternative plans. Watching her during this real-life turmoil reminded me of the body of Christ and the value of working together. She used her travel experience to ensure our return home. It was a negotiation for which I had no experience, and had I been by myself, I would still be in St. Louis! Nehemiah joined the people in the work of rebuilding the walls, each using his or her gift to the glory of God. We are also called to work together as members of one body, each with different gifts to build God's kingdom.

Heavenly Father,

I am not certain of the gifts that You have given me to use for Your glory. I am anxious to serve You and to be a part of the body exercising my gifts. Lead, guide and direct me both in knowing where I am called and in knowing what gifts You have given me to use. Forgive me where I have not used the gifts You have given me in order to build Your kingdom.
In Jesus' name, Amen

May 2

Boldness For Christ

...but they could not stand up against his wisdom of the Spirit by whom he spoke.
Acts 6:10

Acts 6:10 tells us that opposition to the gospel *could not stand up against his (Stephen's) wisdom or the Spirit by which he spoke.* I remember a turning point in my walk with Christ when I was faced with standing up for what I believed God was telling me to do. For years I avoided conflict; I was a people-pleaser and would even get stomach aches if I had to take a stand. After I broke through my fear of man, my life in Christ changed significantly. The enemy tries to hold us back from boldness in Christ by reminding us that we may be rejected, not liked, or misunderstood. Breaking free of his tormenting thoughts was like being delivered by an angel similar to that in *Acts 5:19* when the prison doors were opened for the Apostles. When they got out of jail, they were free to preach the *full* message of life in Christ. *(Acts 5:20)*

Are you free enough to do this? *Proverbs 29:25* says that the fear of man will prove to be a snare. Are you ensnared by the fear of man? Ask the Lord to make you a God-pleaser and not a people-pleaser. God will deliver you from fear of man, and no opposition will be able to stand against the wisdom of God in you. You will be free to share the full message of life in Christ.

Heavenly Father,
I confess that I have sought to please friends, family members, co-workers. Forgive me that I have feared man and placed my fear of rejection above my love for You. It is so difficult to give up old patterns of behavior. Deliver me from my fear of rejection and help me to boldly live my life to please You alone.
In Jesus' name, Amen

Approaching the Throne of Grace

Let us then approach the throne of grace with confidence, so that we may receive mercy and find grace to help us in our time of need
Hebrews 4:16

The first two verses in *Romans 5* celebrate our access into the Presence of God: *Therefore, since we have been justified through faith, we have peace with God through our Lord Jesus Christ, through whom we have gained access by faith into this grace in which we now stand.* It is through our faith in Jesus Christ that we have the right to approach His throne of grace with confidence to receive mercy. (*Hebrews 4:16*) Having laid the foundation for justification by faith, Paul writes that we can access the grace of God and His powerful Presence where God's love, peace, and hope are poured out on us. The God of all creation desires to have a personal, intimate relationship with us and has provided a way for us to enter in through His Son. I am utterly amazed at the love of God the Father who seeks to lavish His children with the promise of peace, joy, goodness, and love! How great is such a love!

As a child when I had been disobedient, my mother told me that she would tell my father what I had done when he got home. Although I feared that he would be angry with me, I always knew that whether I had been good or bad, I could always approach him and find a place of mercy. Although there would be consequences to my behavior, I could approach him with confidence knowing he would still love me. Our Father in heaven has given us access to His throne of grace. Do you have the confidence to approach him knowing you will receive His grace and mercy?

Heavenly Father,
Thank you that I have direct access to Your throne room. I long to approach Your throne with confidence, but sometimes I am fearful of Your anger or disapproval. Help me believe Your Word that when I approach You, You will always receive me with undeserved mercy.
In Jesus' name, Amen

May 4

Christ Revealed

But what about you?" He asked. "Who do you say I am?" Simon Peter answered, "You are the Christ, the Son of the living God.
Matthew 16:15-16

Jesus asked His disciples: *Who do people say the Son of Man is?(Matthew 16:13)* They replied: *Some say John the Baptist; others say Elijah; and still others, Jeremiah or one of the prophets.* Jesus asked the question a second time, directing it this time to the disciples, and Peter responded: *You are the Christ, the Son of the Living God.* Jesus replied that God the Father revealed this profound truth to Peter. We also know Christ as He is revealed to us through the Holy Spirit. He opens our eyes to know Christ is the Son of God. After Peter revealed that he knew Jesus was the Son of God, Jesus gave him the keys to the kingdom. As Jesus is revealed to us, the keys to the kingdom are given to us. *(Matthew 16:19)*

Today I noticed that one of my keys had fallen on the floor. I sensed the Lord saying, "Joanne, remember you have the keys to my kingdom." One of the keys that unlocks the doors of His kingdom rule on earth is faith. Peter exercised his faith when he believed that Jesus was the Son of God, and in turn Jesus entrusted him with the keys of the kingdom.

What are some of the other keys besides faith? Prayer is a key to kingdom rule. When we pray to ask God to bring heaven to earth—*Your kingdom come, your will be done, on earth as it is in heaven (Matthew 6:10)*—we pray to invite God's perfect will and His kingdom rule into the situation that is our point of prayer.

What about you? Who do you say that Jesus is? Is He just a teacher, a prophet, a miracle worker, or is He the Son of Man? Like Peter, when we believe that Jesus is the Son of God, we are given the keys to the kingdom.

Heavenly Father,

I place my trust in You as the Son of God. I ask You to increase my faith and enable me to use the keys to the kingdom to unlock Your truth through Your Word and through prayer.
In Jesus' name, Amen

May 5

Remembering Our Spiritual Milestones

Remember the wonders he has done, his miracles, and the judgments he pronounced
I Chronicles 16:12

Whether you have just embarked on your spiritual journey or have been journeying for many years, I hope that you have recognized the importance of remembering spiritual milestones. It is important not only to remember these milestones, but also to share them with others. In the book of *Joshua*, we learn about God's protection, His promises, and His principles that assist us in our spiritual journey as they did the Israelites. We have seen God's hand at work in memorable ways as He guided the Israelites from slavery in Egypt to claiming their inheritance of the Promised Land. Throughout their journey, they established different memorials that they continued to share with each other and with their children. They set the example for us the importance of sharing with others what wonderful works God has accomplished in our lives.

Take the time to begin a journal for remembering spiritual milestones. For example, recently my sister got married. For years I had prayed that the Lord would send her someone who would love her as Christ loves the church. After several months of dating, she told me that her husband-to-be told her that his wish was to love her in that way. The Lord not only answered our prayers, He answered them in a specific way! For both my sister and me, this was a spiritual milestone. God increased our faith in prayer, and His faithfulness will be forever ingrained on my heart.

As you journey with the Lord, write down your spiritual "markers"—those things that have helped you grow in your faith—so that when you think you are not growing in your faith, you can look back and see that the Lord has always been at work.

Heavenly Father,

Some days I wonder if I am just treading water in my faith journey. I want to grow spiritually and will begin today to journal all of the ways You answer my prayers. Open up the "eyes of my heart" to see the many ways You are at work in my life.
In Jesus' name, Amen

May 6

Taking a Risk

For whoever wants to save his life will lose it, but whoever loses his life for me will save it.
Luke 9:24

The Israelites had to take a risk when they stepped into the swollen waters of the Jordan River. Such a risk involves trusting God to go before us even when we do not see Him. Wandering in the wilderness brought about the death of an entire generation of people. They were unwilling to surrender and trust God to take them into the Promised Land, which was to be a place of freedom. It was the next generation who chose to believe God's promise and obey. They were the ones who entered into the freedom and new life that God had promised them.

In the same way, before we actually risk taking the first step in obeying what God wants us to do, we must be willing to trust God that He will be faithful to buoy us as we carry out the decision to be obedient. Just as God went with the Israelites, He will go with us. It is risky to step out in faith, believing with our "spiritual eyes" and not seeing with our physical eyes. We have been taught to see and then believe, but faith means that I believe, *then* I see. The Word teaches us that if I want to save my life, I must lose it. This is another "kingdom principle" that defines our spiritual life. The world teaches us to preserve our lives; the Lord teaches us to be willing to lay our lives down. Again, risky business!

As the Israelites crossed the Jordan River and went into the Promised Land, they did it together. Today, we need Christian companions on our journey of faith to help encourage us along the way. As you cross the swollen rivers of your circumstances, take a friend along in prayer to assist you as you lay down your life and cross over. Jesus Christ has promised that He will lead the way.

Heavenly Father,
Why is it so difficult to take a risk? I edge out to the bank of obedience and then fear pushes me back to shore. Help me to step out in faith and trust You with my life. I surrender all my fears and unbelief.
In Jesus' name, Amen

May 7

Our Source of Power

You may say to yourself, "My power and the strength of my hands have produced this wealth for me." But remember the LORD your God, for it is he who gives you the ability to produce wealth, and so confirms his covenant, which he swore to your forefathers, as it is today.
Deuteronomy 8:17-18

There are two stories in the Old Testament that demonstrate Adonai as the One who gives us power to accomplish the things He calls us to do. Joshua, after experiencing a great victory at Jericho, anticipated a victory at Ai, but God's people were defeated due to sin in the camp. Joshua called out to his Master, Adonai, reminding Him that he needed His power to conquer the Promised Land. *(Joshua 7:1-8)* His prayer is based on his servant relationship with God. Another man named Gideon was fearful of the Midianites who were oppressing his people. When the angel of the Lord came to Gideon, he said, *if the LORD is with us, why has all this happened to us? (Judges 6:13)* Gideon recognized that his Master could give him guidance and power. The angel of the Lord promised Gideon God's help and gave him the directions to be victorious. The Lord Adonai, our Master, wants to give us His power that is available through our relationship with Him.

Joshua and Gideon knew that only with God's power could they defeat their enemies. What enemy do you face that requires the power of God? Remember that it is God who defeats our enemies and gives us the power to face all opposition.

Heavenly Father,
Forgive me where I have said that it is my power that has protected me from my enemies. You alone are my source of life and power. I call on You, Adonai, to help me live a victorious life. Thank you, Lord, for You alone produced power and strength for my hands.
In Jesus' name, Amen

Determination and Hard Work

It was he who gave some to be apostles, some to be prophets, some to be evangelists, and some to be pastors and teacher to prepare God's people for works of service, so that the body of Christ may be built up until we all reach unity in the faith and in the knowledge of the Son of God and become mature, attaining to the whole measure of the fullness of Christ. Then we will no longer be infants, tossed back and forth by the waves, and blown here and there by every wind of teaching and by the cunning and craftiness of men in their deceitful scheming. Instead, speaking the truth in love, we will in all things grow up into him who is the Head, that is, Christ. From him the whole body, joined and held together by every supporting ligament, grows and builds itself up in love, as each part does its work.

Ephesians 4:11-16

Paul, discussing unity and maturity as goals of the church, describes Jesus Christ as the Head who holds the body (joined by supporting ligaments) together. The body of Christ must grow, building one another up as they work together. The body of Christ must be determined to work together to accomplish the common goal of building God's kingdom. As Nehemiah gathered the people together, he knew that although he was the leader, he was dependent on God to give him direction. As he motivated the people of Jerusalem to action, he reminded them that the "gracious hand of God" was upon him. *(Neh 2:18)* He trusted God to lead them, but he knew that it would take the faith of the people, plus determination and hard work, to rebuild the wall. James describes faith in action: *In the same way, faith by itself, if it is not accompanied by action, is dead. (James 3:17)* As the body of Christ, we must be determined to work hard demonstrating our faith in God and be determined to follow the call of God. The people of Jerusalem knew that the Lord had sent Nehemiah and the supplies they needed to build the wall. Now it was time to put their faith to action.

Are you connected to a body of believers? God ordained believers to work together, encouraging one another to use our gifts for His glory. For years I did not realize the value of being joined with the body and the support that is offered through this connection to other believers. I remember praying as a team for someone when I came to understand the importance of the "supporting ligaments." My team partner could minister to this individual from her own experiences, and I marveled at how the Lord worked through her. I was able to fill in the gaps with the gifts that the Lord had given me. I knew that day that God had a purpose in sending out the disciples "two by two." Determination and hard work are needed to fulfill our calling, but without working with others as part of the body of Christ, it is easy to burn out. All of us are called to prepare God's people for "works of service," and in so doing, we will all reach the whole measure of the fullness of Christ.

Heavenly Father,
Help me to know my place in the body of Christ and to use my gifts for Your glory. Thank you that You never intended for me to work alone. Help me to be a supporting "ligament" to build up the body of Christ.
In Jesus' name, Amen

Love Covers Sin

Above all, love each other deeply, because love covers over a multitude of sins.
I Peter 4:8

In this passage from *I Peter,* Peter exhorts the believers to love each other deeply because love covers a multitude of sins. Eugene Patterson's *The Message* puts it this way: *Most of all, love each other as if your life depended on it. Love makes up for practically anything.* It goes on to say, *Be quick to give a meal to the hungry, a bed to the homeless—cheerfully. Be generous with the different things God gave you, passing them around so all get in on it; if words, let it be God's words; if help, let it be God's hearty help. That way, God's presence will be evident in everything through Jesus, and He'll get all the credit as the One mighty in everything—encores to the end of time. (I Peter 4: 7-11)* What an incredible description of love in action! Amidst the suffering of the persecuted Church, Peter is challenging them to love and reach out with God's grace to all! This passage of Scripture has challenged me over the years because when I am suffering, it is difficult for me not to be self-centered! Yet our God, in the person of Jesus Christ, loved us so much as He walked to the cross; He loved us so much as He suffered on the cross; He loved us so much as He forgave us on the cross. What a love divine! As His disciples, we are called to love by forgiving and by serving. In so doing, God will be glorified.

Meditate on these words: *Most of all, love each other as if your life depended on it.* Do you love as if your life depended on it? Are you aware that your love covers a multitude of sins? As we love God and He loves through us, we are actually covering our sins and the sins of others. God's "agape" unconditional love won for us on the cross pours over our mistakes, our sins, our wounds, our resentments. Only His love is powerful enough to break through our lives and offer us true forgiveness. How amazing is His love! How awesome is His faithfulness!

Heavenly Father,
While I was yet a sinner, You died for me. It was love that held You to the cross; it was love that was powerful enough to raise You from the dead; it was love that will bring You back again. Help me to receive Your love.
In Jesus' name, Amen

May 10

Demonstration of Miracles

His intent was that now, through the church, the manifold wisdom of God should be made known to the rulers and authorities in the heavenly realms.
Ephesians 3:10

Matthew 14 and *15* recount the miracles of Jesus feeding the five thousand and the four thousand who had come to hear Him teach. We also read in these chapters the accounts of Jesus walking on water and stilling the storm. The response of the disciples was to worship Him and to proclaim, *Truly You are the Son of God! (Matthew 14:33)* Paul describes the insight he has into the mystery of Christ made known to Him by the Spirit of God in *Ephesians 3:3*: *Surely you have heard about the administration of God's grace that was given to me for you, that is the mystery made known to be by revelation.* He preaches *not with words of human wisdom, lest the cross of Christ be emptied of its power. (I Corinthians 1:17)* Paul knew that God's grace was at work through the cross. Understanding the power of Christ demonstrated through the cross and the resurrection enables us to grab hold of the power demonstrated in the kingdom of God. Throughout the gospels we read about the miracles Jesus performed. Jesus told His disciples that when He came to earth God's kingdom had arrived. Evidence of that kingdom was seen in signs, wonders, and miracles.

As believers, the kingdom is within us; therefore, the power of the kingdom is the power of Christ within us. As we read the stories of the miracles written so long ago, let us keep in mind that the same power that was demonstrated then is available to us now if we open our "kingdom eyes" to see and believe.

Heavenly Father,
Paul understood that it was not his persuasive words that had power, but it was the power of the Spirit. (I Corinthians 2:4) Help me to grab hold of this truth, that You are just as powerful today as You were when You walked this earth. I release to You all unbelief that keeps me from seeing a demonstration of Your signs and wonders today.
In Jesus' name, Amen

May 11

God's Prevailing Power

Do your best to present yourself to God as one approved, a workman who does not need to be ashamed and who correctly handles the word of truth.
II Timothy 2:15

Often we are confused about whether or not something is from God. We long to know God's will, and we long to discern if something is of God. A Pharisee named Gamaliel figured out this dilemma. The Sadducees made the Apostles appear before the Sanhedrin, the supreme Jewish court, to be questioned by the high priest concerning their bold preaching of the gospel. The priests had given the Apostles strict orders not to teach about Jesus, but the Apostles disregarded their orders. God told them to "Go, tell the people the full message of this new life," and the Apostles obeyed. The Sadducees were furious with them, but Gamaliel simply said, "If it is from God, you will not be able to stop them." This is a great guideline or test for us when we are uncertain if something is of God. We simply need to remember that if the activity is of human origin, it will fail. If it is of God, it will prevail.

Are you faced with a decision to make? Have you prayed and sought the will of God and still are unsure? There are some practical ways to line up with the will of God. Using the analogy of navigation lights, you must line up the range markers in order to stay in the channel. To stay in the channel of God's will, there are several markers that are helpful:

a. It will line up with Scripture.
b. Circumstances will line up.
c. The peace of the Lord will be your plumb line.

There are other ways to line up with the will of God, but these three are significant as you seek to know God's will. Sometimes you are still unsure if it is God's will, but there are no apparent roadblocks. At times like that, I often choose to step out in faith, trusting that the Lord will turn me back if I am on the wrong path: *Trust in the Lord with all of your heart; lean not on your own understanding; in all your ways acknowledge Him and He will make your path straight. (Proverbs 3:5)* At other times I wait on the Lord until I have more direction: *The Lord is faithful; if you seek Him you will find Him. (Jeremiah 29:13)*

Heavenly Father,
I am struggling with a difficult decision. I keep praying and still have no direction. Help me to trust You in this and not depend on my own wisdom. Help me to seek Your wisdom and direction, believing that You will answer.
In Jesus' name, Amen

May 12

Confession of Sin

Those of Israelite descent had separated themselves from all foreigners. They stood in their places and confessed their sins and the wickedness of their fathers. They stood where they were and read from the Book of the Law of the LORD their God for a quarter of the day, and spent another quarter in confession and in worshiping the LORD their God.
Nehemiah 9:2-3

The Israelites were convicted of their sin and rebellion against God as they heard the Word of God read. They spent the next quarter of the day in worship and confession of their sins! The formation of a new man began to take place as the people worshipped in one accord and confessed their sins. Collaborative worship and confession draws God's people together and bridges the gap between a holy God and sinful man. It is interesting to note that just as Nehemiah had modeled repentance to them by confessing his own sins and the sins of his forefathers (*Nehemiah 1:6),* the people now confessed their sins and the sins of their forefathers. As God's people, we are called to identify not only with the sins of our forefathers, but our sins as well, and seek God's forgiveness. During their time of confession, the Israelites remembered that the Lord had been gracious and forgiving to them throughout the centuries: *But in your great mercy you did not put an end to them or abandon them, for you are a gracious and merciful God. (9:31)*

When we acknowledge and turn away from our sins in repentance, we begin to see clearly the goodness of the Lord and His mercy toward us. He never forsakes us even though we forsake and turn away from Him. I am reminded daily of how easily I turn from the Lord and how gracious and merciful He is to take me back when I return. We are like sheep that easily go astray, but we have a Great Shepherd who leads us back to safety. (*Isaiah 53:6*)

Heavenly Father,
Sometimes it is so difficult to repent. Pride keeps me from turning away from my sin and back to You. Forgive me, Lord, for my stubbornness and pride. I ask You to give me a teachable heart, willing to surrender daily to Your care.
In Jesus' name, Amen

Fighting the Good Fight

Timothy, my son, I give you this instruction in keeping with the prophecies once made about you, so that by following them you may fight the good fight.
I Timothy 1:18

Paul writes in his letter to Timothy to *fight the good fight.* He tells him to do this by loving from a pure heart, a good conscience, and a sincere faith. (*I Timothy 1:5*) Love is one of the keys to fighting the good fight. It is a powerful weapon against all evil. Brennan Manning says, "In every encounter we either give life (love) or we drain it. There is no neutral exchange." Love is a way to fight the good fight. It helps us to resist the evil one who plants seeds of destruction. Another way to be strong in power and resist the "devil's schemes" is to put on the full armor of God daily. *(Ephesians 6:10-18)* The disciples of Christ had to fight hard to hold on to their faith amidst the persecution and trials of being a Christian. Paul, however, describes the fight as a "good fight"—one worth fighting for, one worth giving your life for.

Are you tired of the "good fight"? Have you sought to live a godly life but feel like a failure? Remember that Jesus never came to make us perfect. He came as the perfect sacrifice to draw us to Himself and make us holy. Swimming against the tide of society in a post-Christian world can be tiring, but the fight is worthwhile and the rewards are great. Jesus puts it this way: *In this world you will have trouble. But take heart! I have overcome the world. (John 16:33)*

Heavenly Father,
I am tired of fighting the good fight. Sometimes it doesn't even feel like a "good" fight. It is difficult to live my life for You. Some of my friends do not understand my desire to live for You. In the workplace and at home, I feel alone as I try to live as Christ did. I pray for Christian friends to encourage me in this journey so that I will be strengthened as I seek to live for You.
In Jesus' name, Amen

May 14

Wilderness Christians

I will give you a new heart and put a new spirit in you; I will remove from you your heart of stone and give you a heart of flesh.
Ezekiel 36:26

When the Israelites left Egypt, the Egyptians saw God's power displayed as He brought about their release. For forty years, however, the Israelites lived in the desert lacking faith and power, complaining, and longing to return to Egypt. When the Israelites finally crossed the Jordan River, God once more displayed His power. When the Amorite and Canaanite kings along the coast heard how the Lord had dried up the Jordan enabling the Israelites to cross over, their *hearts melted and they no longer had the courage to face the Israelites. (Joshua 5:1)* Joshua then reinstated two Covenantal ceremonies: circumcision and the Passover. All of the sons of the Israelites were circumcised as a mark of the Covenant with God. When this was done, the reproach (shame, disgrace) of their time in slavery in Egypt was removed as they finally left the desert and moved into the Promised Land.

Wilderness Christians are like the Israelites—unable to display God's power because of their self-reliance. Wilderness Christians end up going around the same mountain again and again because they do not trust God.

Are you a wilderness Christian? Do you find yourself waking up in the morning thanking God for the day or complaining? I fell under conviction recently as I awoke each morning complaining about something that was on my mind. I sensed the Lord saying to me, "Joanne, as long as you start your days complaining, you will stay in the wilderness; the wilderness is a place of defeat, not victory." Since that day, I now begin each day with a word of thanksgiving to God. Start your days with a prayer of thanksgiving and see how quickly you will leave the wilderness and enter into the Promised Land.

Heavenly Father,
I have been stuck in the wilderness. I desire to enter into Your promises and trust You to take me there on the road of thankfulness. I do not wish to be like the

Israelites who quickly forgot all that You did for them. Help me to recall Your goodness and give me a grateful heart.
In Jesus' name, Amen

May 15

Our Helper

So we say with confidence, "The Lord is my helper; I will not be afraid. What can man do to me?"
Hebrews 13:6

Moses had a servant/master relationship with God. When he was commissioned by God to go to Pharaoh and demand the release of God's people, he lamented, *O my Lord, I have never been eloquent. (Exodus 4:10)* When God was commissioning Jeremiah to be a prophet to the nations, Jeremiah lamented, *Ah, Sovereign LORD (Adonai), I do not know how to speak; I am only a child. (Jeremiah 1:6)* Often when God calls us to do something, we are afraid of failure and we are disobedient to the very thing that God asks us to do. Fear is a strong tool that the enemy uses to keep us from obeying God. As we grow on our journey with Christ, the Lord desires to rid us of all fear of failure. His goal is for us to say with confidence, *The Lord is my helper; I will not be afraid. What can man do to me? (Hebrews 13:6)* Fear of man is the other stumbling block in our willingness to obey God. *Proverbs 29:25* says that the fear of man is a snare and when we fear man we are trapped into disobedience.

What is the Lord calling you to do today that requires obedience? Do you know the Lord as your Helper? Ask the Holy Spirit to examine your heart and see what keeps you from obedience. Repent, and quickly step out in faith. When you do, you will find the Lord as your Helper ready to lead you into success.

Heavenly Father,
Forgive me for fearing man and for my fear of failure. Help me to know You as my Helper and lead me into obedience.
In Jesus' name, Amen

Ridicule

When Sanballat heard that we were rebuilding the wall, he became angry and was greatly incensed. He ridiculed the Jews, and in the presence of his associates and the army of Samaria, he said, "What are those feeble Jews doing? Will they restore their wall? Will they offer sacrifices? Will they finish in a day? Can they bring the stones back to life from those heaps of rubble—burned as they are?"
Nehemiah 4:1-2

The first time that Nehemiah is ridiculed by his enemies, he responds by telling them that the God of heaven will give his people success. (*2:20*) In chapter 4, when Sanballat ridiculed the Jews, Nehemiah prayed. When Sanballat, Tobiah, the Arabs, and the Ammonites plotted to fight against Jerusalem, Nehemiah prayed and posted guards around the work. Prayer and watchfulness emphasize that faith and action go hand in hand to combat the enemy's ridicule and plans of destruction. In *I Samuel 17,* the story of David and Goliath demonstrates another godly man's response to ridicule. The giant hurled insults at David, and David sought and trusted his God with the response. Jesus Christ was insulted, mocked, and ridiculed by those who sought to kill Him, and yet He did not try to defend Himself. He prayed to His Father in heaven and kept His eyes on the task that was given Him.

So often we get caught up in an emotional response when we are insulted, and yet in God's Word, there are countless examples of responding by first turning to God. The next time you are insulted or ridiculed, look to the Lord for counsel and pray for wisdom before you respond. Consider this Scripture the next time you find yourself in this position: *If your enemy is hungry, give him food to eat; if he is thirsty, give him water to drink. In doing this, you will heap burning coals on his head, and the Lord will reward you. (Proverbs 25:21-22)*

Heavenly Father,
Sometimes when I seek to do Your will, I get trapped by ridicule and unbelief. At times I have found myself being my harshest critic. Help me to stand firm in Your Word and trust You to deliver me from ridicule. Fill me with grace to respond to insults by turning to You.
In Jesus' name, Amen

May 17

Offering a Sacrifice of Praise and Thanksgiving

Through Jesus, therefore, let us continually offer to God a sacrifice of praise—the fruit of lips that confess his name. And do not forget to do good and to share with others, for with such sacrifices God is pleased.
Hebrews 13:15-16

The Amplified Bible describes a sacrifice of praise: *Through Him, therefore, let us constantly and at all times offer up to God a sacrifice of praise, which is the fruit of lips that thankfully acknowledge and confess and glorify His name. Do not forget or neglect to do kindness and good. (Hebrews 13:15-16)* Praise and thanksgiving as a form of worship begin with our knowing the love of God. David knew the Good Shepherd from the time he was a shepherd in the fields. As King of Israel, he continued to praise and thank God for His hand upon his life and the people of Israel. After the Lord had delivered David from the hand of his enemies and from Saul, he praised God in song: *I call to the Lord, who is worthy of praise, and I am saved from my enemies. (II Samuel 22:4)* God is indeed worthy of our praise and thanksgiving! Many of the psalms reflect the theme of praise. They reflect Israel's awareness that praise must follow deliverance when God is to be honored. Praise sprang up from David's heart of thankfulness to the Lord for his deliverance.

Over the years I have learned that praising and thanking God takes the focus off of me and turns it to God. In the "me first" world, I easily am caught up with thinking that the world revolves around me. When I had my first child, I had my first lesson in self-sacrifice. My child was totally dependent on me and I came to know the rewards of living my life for someone else. Jesus Christ laid down His life for us—the ultimate act of sacrifice—and He thereby set an example for us of sacrifice. We now must offer our lives back to Him in praise and thanksgiving. Yes, this is a sacrifice when going through difficult times, but the reward is great. As we praise, honor and thank Him, our circumstances may not change, but the peace of the Lord will fill our hearts.

Heavenly Father,
Help me to remember to praise You in all circumstances. My heart's desire is to focus on You and not be self-centered. I willingly offer You my life as a sacrifice of praise and thanksgiving.
In Jesus' name, Amen

May 18

Sharing the Good News

But in your hearts set apart Christ as Lord. Always be prepared to give an answer to everyone who asks you to give the reason for the hope that you have. But do this with gentleness and respect, keeping a clear conscience, so that those who speak maliciously against your good behavior in Christ may be ashamed of their slander.
I Peter 3:15-16

We are called to share our faith at all times. *(II Timothy 4:2)* It is our responsibility, and indeed should be our delight, to share the hope that God gives us. Peter exhorts the persecuted body of Christ to set their heart apart for Christ and always be prepared to give an answer for why we have such hope. He also tells them they should share the gospel with gentleness and respect. To me, this is one of the key signs of a mature Christian—one who faithfully and joyfully shares his life in Christ with others in a gentle and respectful way. Often that is done with few words and with much love in action. You may have heard what Francis of Assisi said, "Preach the gospel always; when necessary, use words."

Today's Scripture tells us to always be prepared to answer anyone who asks you to give the reason for the hope of Christ that lives within you. What must you do to be prepared to share your faith story? Read God's Word to prepare your mind and heart to share your faith. Take time to journal your story; the story of how you came to faith may also be helpful. Just as we collect all the ingredients we need to cook a meal, so we must prepare in advance the tools that we need to share the good news. People tell me all the time that they are afraid of sharing their faith. If you take the time of preparation to tell the greatest story on earth, the Lord will fill you with His Holy Spirit and speak through you.

Heavenly Father,
I pray that You will give me opportunities to share my faith with others. Help me to prepare to share my faith in a gentle, respectful way that reflects the love of Christ.
In Jesus' name, Amen

Demonstration of Healing

Remember your leaders, who spoke the word of God to you. Consider the outcome of their way of life and imitate their faith. Jesus Christ is the same yesterday and today and forever.
Hebrews 13:7-8

In *Matthew 15,* we read about the Canaanite woman who cried out to Jesus to heal her daughter possessed by a demon. At first Jesus did not answer her, but her insistent cries caused the disciples to implore Jesus to send her away. Jesus explained to her that He was sent *only to the lost sheep of Israel.* However, because of the woman's great faith, Jesus healed her daughter. I am always awed by the faith of this woman, someone who was not Jewish but had faith to believe that Jesus could heal! She is such a great example of the key component to receiving the healing power of Christ: she believed. Throughout the generations since Jesus' resurrection, tradition, human reasoning, and confusion have caused God's people to settle for less than believing, proclaiming, and demonstrating the kingdom of God. Scriptures teach us that *Jesus Christ is the same yesterday, today, and forever. (Hebrews 13:8)* Why, then, would we not expect to see the demonstration of His kingdom today?

When Jesus healed the woman's daughter, he demonstrated that "the kingdom was near." As we pray, believe, and expect to see God's kingdom today, our eyes open to see the works of God. Do you cry out to God for healing and expect Him to heal? Do you cry out to God for deliverance and expect Him to deliver you? Jesus is the same today as He was yesterday, and He responds to the prayers of the faithful.

Heavenly Father,
I have been discouraged by unanswered prayer, and over time I have believed that You would not heal me. Forgive me for my unbelief and for turning away from faith in You. I turn back to You and cry out for healing, and like the woman of faith I receive Your healing power.
In Jesus' name, Amen

May 20

The Church Scattered

But you will receive power when the Holy Spirit comes on you; and you will be my witnesses in Jerusalem, and in all Judea and Samaria, and to the ends of the earth.
Acts 1:8

I am utterly amazed at how God carries out His plans! The first part of the eighth chapter of *Acts* tells us that after the stoning of Stephen, the church, all except for the Apostles, scattered throughout Judea and Samaria. Remember what Jesus' last words were before He was taken up into heaven: *When the Holy Spirit comes on you, you will be my witnesses in Jerusalem, and in all Judea and Samaria, and to the ends of the earth. (Acts 1:8)* It seemed as though the church was on the run, yet the Lord had planned for the church to spread. The persecution, which could have brought defeat or squelch the Christian movement, actually enabled the church to grow. God always has a plan even when things look hopeless. He can even use the difficult things in our lives *to work together for good. (Romans 8:28)*

What are the things in your life that seem to be hopeless? Is your marriage failing? Are your finances at risk? Are you suffering from depression or a feeling of hopelessness? The Lord majors in the impossible. He is an expert in taking the negative things of our lives and turning them around for good. He offers us hope when things seem hopeless. He waits for you to turn over those things that seem impossible and look to Him as the source of life.

This week I was overwhelmed with my responsibilities. It seemed as a line of endless tasks demanded my attention and time. As I sought the Lord, He reminded me of His Word in *John 16:33: In this world you will have trouble. But take heart! I have overcome the world.* Beloved children of God, Jesus Christ overcame every trial we could ever face. Turn to Him as your source of hope and He will not fail to lift you up.

Heavenly Father,
My life seems to be like the early church—scattered and defeated. What appeared like disaster turned the early church into the most formidable institution ever

known to man: the church, the body of Christ. Help me to fix my eyes on You and not on my out-of-control life. Help me to remember that what seems to be impossible is not impossible for You.
In Jesus' name, Amen

May 21

Developing Character through Suffering

Not only so, but we also rejoice in our sufferings, because we know that suffering produces perseverance; perseverance, character; and character, hope. And hope does not disappoint us, because God has poured out his love into our hearts by the Holy Spirit, whom he has given us.
Romans 5:3-5

True peace, joy, and hope come from being reconciled to God the Father through Jesus Christ. We gain access by faith into this grace in which we now stand. (*v.2*) Paul concludes that the grace of God poured over us enables us to stand against the storms of life and rejoice in the hope of the glory of God. He continues to underscore that suffering will produce Christ-like character in us and calls us to persevere and to grab hold of the hope that God pours into our lives. Paul helps us understand how we are able to celebrate in the midst of suffering. He shows us the steady progression of the Christian life: patience to character and from character to hope.
As I meditate on these verses, I am reminded of how the Lord gave me hope and assurance in the midst of storms in my life. No matter what circumstances have placed you in turbulent waters, the Lord will set your course to provide you a way to safety in His arms. All the while He is growing in you a hope in Him, and He will see you back safely to the shore.

What circumstances seem beyond your control at the moment? Cry out to God and He will pour His love into your heart, giving you a hope that will never disappoint. (*v.5*)

Heavenly Father,I am pressed in on all sides, stressed with daily life and circumstances that I face. I pray that during this season of trial I will develop perseverance, character, and hope. Your hope never disappoints—Your love never fails to free my soul.
In Jesus' name, Amen

Life through Christ

But the gift is not like the trespass. For if the many died by the trespass of the one man, how much more did God's grace and the gift that came by the grace of the one man, Jesus Christ, overflow to the many!
Romans 5:15

Judgment and condemnation entered through the sin of the one man, Adam, and with it were the effects of death and separation from God. Likewise, the gift of God through Jesus Christ brought justification and grace to many. Paul explains that the gift of righteousness is Christ's gift to humanity through His death and resurrection. Sin reigned in death and now grace reigns through righteousness to bring eternal life through Jesus Christ. (*v.21*) Imagine the scene when Jesus died on the cross. At that moment the veil, the shroud of death over humanity, was lifted, and we now have access through our faith in Jesus into a "right" relationship with God.

I often speak with people who have broken relationships with family members or friends. Though we are not always able to restore our broken relationships, we are called to forgive. Jesus Christ offered us the ultimate gift of grace, offering us forgiveness for our sins and reconciliation with the Father. As we live our lives free of the shroud of death in our sins and broken relationships, let us always remember that our Lord stands at the door knocking; He has provided us access to restoration in our daily lives. He offers us a new life of freedom in Him. In *The Message*, Peterson puts it this way: *Just as one person did it wrong and got us in trouble with sin and death, another person did it right and got us out of it. But more than just getting us out of trouble, He got us into life! (Romans 5:15)*

Heavenly Father,
Thank you for sending Your Son Jesus Christ who offers me the gift of freedom from my sin, healing of relationships, and forgiveness that I do not deserve. Help me remember to turn to You knowing that You paid the ultimate price of laying Your life down so I could walk in freedom.
In Jesus' name, Amen

May 23

Open Our Spiritual Eyes and Ears

As he went along, he saw a man blind from birth. His disciples asked him, "Rabbi, who sinned, this man or his parents, that he was born blind?" "Neither this man nor his parents sinned," said Jesus, "but this happened so that the works of God might be displayed in him. As long as it is day, we must do the works of him who sent me. Night is coming, when no one can work. While I am in the world, I am the light of the world." Having said this, he spit on the ground, made some mud with the saliva, and put it on the man's eyes. "Go," he told him, "wash in the Pool of Siloam" (this word means "Sent"). So the man went and washed, and came home seeing.
John 9:1-7

Jesus healed the blind man by putting mud on his eyes. The Pharisees accused Jesus of being a sinner and not being from God because He healed the blind man on the Sabbath. They questioned the blind man, looking for any hole in the man's story. They were insulted when the blind man told them: *Whether he is a sinner or not, I don't know. One thing I do know. I was blind and now I see. (John 9:25)* The Pharisees stubbornly refused to believe that Jesus was from God, and the blind man was certain of only one thing: this man Jesus had healed him. Jesus then asked the blind man if he believed in the Son of Man, the name Jesus most commonly titled Himself. The man answered that he did not know Him but would like to believe. At that point, Jesus revealed to the blind man that He was the Son of God who had performed this miracle and that He had come so that the blind could see. Having just healed a physically blind person, Jesus reveals that He had come to open the eyes of the spiritually blind. He inferred that the Pharisees were spiritually blind, claiming to see but walking in spiritual darkness.

The Lord calls out to you today to open your spiritual eyes and ears. Just as he healed the blind man, he longs to open your eyes to know Him. Paul prayed: *I pray that the eyes of your heart may be enlightened. (Ephesians 1:18)* Pray that the eyes of your heart will be open to know Christ and that your ears would be attentive to His Word.

Heavenly Father,

Open the eyes of my heart for understanding. Remove any places of "spiritual blindness" and allow me to hear and obey You.
In Jesus' name, Amen

May 24

The Self-Sufficiency of Babylon

You have forgotten God your Savior; you have not remembered the Rock, your fortress. Isaiah 17:10

The nations that raged in the time of Isaiah were filled with turmoil. The city of Babylon is seen throughout both the Old and New Testaments as a city plagued with pride and self-sufficiency. Babylon symbolizes the world powers arrayed against God's kingdom. Throughout the ages, we see other cities and nations plagued by self-sufficiency, finding no need for God. Individually, we fall prey to being self-sufficient and tend to forget God, our Savior, forgetting our Rock, our Fortress. *(Isaiah 17:10)* I can so easily be trusting in the Lord, praying for Him to guide and direct me and suddenly find myself on the road to self-trust. I may start out praying and seeking His guidance, but when the road splits, I choose on my own which road to take. The Lord requires us to seek Him every step of the way. Self-sufficiency is valued in our society today, but God wants us to be God-reliant. The Israelites repeatedly turned to idolatry, forgetting God, their fortress and Rock. They ended up in Babylon at one point in history because they turned away from Jehovah God. But each time God restored His people when they turned back to Him.

Are you presently in a place of being self-sufficient? Have you determined that you can do all things for yourself, or are you depending on God to strengthen you and give you wisdom and direction? Turn back to Him and He will show you where you got off *His* path and lead you as you depend on Him.

Heavenly Father,
I have been self-sufficient and full of pride. I acknowledge that I need You to lead me and to guide me in daily life. Forgive me for forgetting that You are my Rock and fortress; forgive me for taking charge of my life and not allowing You to direct my path.
In Jesus' name, Amen

Removing the Reproach of Egypt

Then the LORD said to Joshua, "Today I have rolled away the reproach of Egypt from you." So the place has been called Gilgal to this day.
Joshua 5:9

Wilderness Christians are often unable to display God's power because they are self-reliant and not God-reliant. When the Israelites left Egypt, the Egyptians saw God's power displayed as He brought about their release. For forty years, however, the Israelites lived in the desert, lacking faith and power, complaining, and longing to return to Egypt. When the Israelites finally crossed the Jordan River, God once more displayed His power. The Amorite and Canaanite kings along the coast, who had been skeptical of the power of God, now saw God's power displayed as the Israelites crossed the Jordan River. The reproach (disgrace, discredit) was removed as the Israelites finally left the desert and moved into the Promised Land.

There have been times when I wandered in the wilderness because of my disobedience to the Lord. I had a sense that the Lord was calling me to a place of obedience, and it either wasn't convenient or I did not bother to obey. At these times, I find myself wandering in a dry place, feeling separated from God but unwilling to seek Him. Those are the times where I find myself complaining and grumbling, wondering why God has abandoned me. The truth was that I had abandoned Him! God's Word says that He never forsakes us.

Are you in a "wilderness place"? Have you seen God intervene in your life like the Israelites, and yet you are wandering in a dry place having forgotten His display of power in your life? The Lord seeks to remove the disgrace that has kept you in that place and move in powerful ways in your life. Be willing to step out in faith and cross your personal "Jordan." He will part the sea of your circumstances and take you into the place of His promise.

Heavenly Father,

I am tired of feeling defeated. I have seen You work in my life in the past but do not see evidence of You at work now. I am in a wilderness full of self-pity and complaining. Forgive me, Lord, and lead me over the Jordan into agreement with Your promises for my life. -In Jesus' name, Amen

May 26

Confidence in God to Fulfill His Promise

Yet he did not waver through unbelief regarding the promise of God, but was strengthened in his faith and gave glory to God, being fully persuaded that God had power to do what he had promised.
Romans 4:20-21

God promised Abraham that his descendants would be as numerous as the stars. We see Abraham's complete confidence in God to fulfill His promise when he said to his servants, *Stay with the donkey while I and the boy go over there. We will worship and then we will come back to you. (Genesis 22:5)* How confident Abraham was! Although God had called him to sacrifice his son on the mountain, he had confidence they would BOTH return! Abraham knew God as the Promise Keeper, the Great Jehovah, who always kept His word. When we grow in our knowledge of the character of God to keep His promises, our life of faith radically turns to a life of peace, trust, and security. We have all experienced disappointment when friends have let us down. They have broken a promise to us and we have lost trust in them. God, unlike people, never breaks His promises. He told Abraham that He would have descendants as numerous as the stars, and Abraham not only believed Him, but did not waver in unbelief!

Have you been hurt by broken promises—a broken marriage, broken relationship, broken trust at work? The Lord wants you to have confidence in Him to fulfill all of the promises in His Word. He alone is faithful and true to His Word.

Heavenly Father,
I have been struggling with disappointments based on broken promises (fill in the blank). I want to be free of my hurt, so I choose to forgive these individuals (fill in the blank) who have broken trust with me. I turn to You, the great Promise Keeper, knowing that in You alone will I find peace.
In Jesus' name, Amen

Fatigue and Discouragement

After I looked things over, I stood up and said to the nobles, the officials and the rest of the people, "Don't be afraid of them. Remember the Lord, who is great and awesome, and fight for your brothers, your sons and your daughters, your wives and your homes."
Nehemiah 4:14

There were four causes for Nehemiah's potential discouragement: loss of strength, loss of vision, loss of confidence, and loss of security. We can see the loss of strength in the following passage: *Meanwhile, the people in Judah said, "The strength of the laborers is giving out and there is so much rubble that we cannot rebuild the wall." (Neh 4:10)* We become discouraged when the work is half done and it appears there is another mountain of work to do. The enemy tried to discourage them by making them feel overwhelmed with the task ahead. Another form of discouragement, loss of vision, is seen when the people look around and only see rubbish. They suddenly lose the vision of the completed wall. Vision is often lost when the task seems overwhelming. Loss of confidence is seen when their motivation is lost: *...we ourselves cannot build the wall. (v.10)*

Have you ever begun a task that you thought the Lord was calling you to and after getting it halfway done, you begin to doubt and lose confidence that you ever heard Him call you to do it? Many God-given visions are lost when God's people stop short due to loss of confidence. Lastly, discouragement found a place in the Jews who were rebuilding the wall when they lost their sense of security: *Also our enemies said, before they know it or see us, we will be right there among them and will kill them and put an end to their work.* (*Nehemiah 4:11*)

As Christians, we must be aware of the tactics of the enemy to discourage and fatigue us so that we will discontinue God's work. Just remember Nehemiah's words of encouragement as you go through those difficult times: *Don't be afraid of them. Remember the Lord who is great and awesome, and fight. (v.14)*

Heavenly Father,

I am discouraged and overwhelmed with life right now. I look at the work that I have to do and have lost vision and enthusiasm to complete it. Help me to trust You to give me the strength to complete the tasks before me.
In Jesus' name, Amen

Suffering for the Gospel

Dear friends, do not be surprised at the painful trial you are suffering, as though something strange were happening to you. But rejoice that you participate in the sufferings of Christ, so that you may be overjoyed when his glory is revealed.
I Peter 4:12-13

Peter writes to his dear friends, fellow believers who are scattered and persecuted because of their belief in Jesus Christ. *I Peter* is thought to have been written during the reign of Emperor Nero, no later than 67 or 68 A.D. Emperor Nero was an egocentric emperor who sought to make a name for himself. Most historians agree that he was responsible for the fire in July of 64 A.D. that destroyed most of the city of Rome. It is thought that he destroyed the buildings in order to make room to build monuments and palaces to establish his name in history. When the populace discovered this, they were incensed and ready to revolt. As a result, Nero blamed the Christians for burning the city, which began the persecutions. It was during that time that the Christians were dipped in tar and burned as torches to light the gardens of Nero. They also were thrown to lions and were tied up in leather bags and thrown into water so that when the bags shrank, they were squeezed to death. It seems unbelievable that these things could have happened to the people of God. In the world today, that type of persecution seems foreign to us. However, we must not be blind to the fact that in many countries, Christians are still being martyred for their belief in Jesus Christ.

You may not be experiencing the severe persecution for your faith that others around the world are experiencing. You may, however, be suffering for the gospel in other ways. *I Peter* is a reminder that no matter what trial you are going through, whether it has been caused by your faith or whether there is another source for your suffering, it is a time to rejoice. In rejoicing, the glory of God will be revealed.

Heavenly Father,
The trial that I am going through seems more than I can bear. Give me the strength to rejoice that I am participating in Your sufferings. Though it is

unnatural to give praise in the midst of suffering, it is my desire to bring You glory.
In Jesus' name, Amen

Demonstration of the Kingdom Within

Once, having been asked by the Pharisees when the kingdom of God would come, Jesus replied, "The kingdom of God does not come with your careful observation, nor will people say, 'Here it is,' or 'There it is,' because the kingdom of God is within you.
Luke 17:20-21

The Pharisees questioned Jesus; they wanted to know when the kingdom of God would come. Jesus replied that *the kingdom of God does not come with careful observation, but that the kingdom of God is within you. (Luke 17:20-21)* Can you imagine the Pharisees as they considered what Jesus had said? They were the religious leaders of the day, the ones who had all of the answers concerning spiritual issues, and yet they were being confronted with an answer that ran contrary to the very core of their religious conduct. Up until that point, they had been espousing God's law and seeing to it that the Jewish people did not disregard the law. Jesus, observing their behavior, recognized that they were more concerned with the law, the external religious rules, than the internal issues of the heart. (*Matthew 23:25*) In *Matthew 15*, Jesus confronts the Pharisees and teachers of the law with their traditions and rules. He explains that they should be more concerned about breaking the higher commands of God than in trying to keep their traditions.

This is an indictment on us today as well as we divide ourselves on issues of tradition and disregard the spiritual issues that are going on in us internally, like evil thoughts, slander, and sexual immorality. *(Matthew 15:19)* It is tempting to focus on the external, but Jesus challenges us today to examine our hearts to insure that we are clean before God.

Heavenly Father,
Help me to be more concerned with internal issues of my heart than with external religious rules. Transform my life so that I can be more like You and help me to have a pure heart.
In Jesus' name, Amen

May 30

The Holy Spirit's Guidance

But when he, the Spirit of truth, comes, he will guide you into all truth. But he will not speak on his own; he will speak only what he hears, and he will tell you what is yet to come.
John 16:13

Think back on *Acts 3:8* when Peter, "*filled with the Holy Spirit,*" spoke boldly proclaiming the kingdom of God and faith in Jesus Christ. The Holy Spirt empowered him to speak and empowered the Apostles to carry on the work of spreading the gospel. Many years ago, I prayed for the Lord to fill me with His Spirit because I felt that I needed help to grow in my faith. I acknowledged Jesus as my Lord and Savior, but I felt a lack of power to live the Christian life. The Lord showed me that I had not made room in my life for the Holy Spirit to lead the way in every area of my life. I acknowledged that the Holy Spirit resided in me and allowed His life-changing power to work in me. Now every day I ask the Lord to fill me with His Spirit, and I like to say, "Move over self and make room for the King of Kings!" The Holy Spirit led the people of the first century church, and He will still lead us today if we yield to Him daily or any time we take back control of our lives.

Are you seeking guidance? The Holy Spirit will lead you and guide you into truth. (*John 16:13*) Ask the Lord to fill you with His life giving Spirit and he will reveal to you what is to come.

Heavenly Father,
Fill me daily with Your Holy Spirit. Empower me like the apostles to boldly proclaim the kingdom of God. Lead and guide me into truth as I seek to do Your will.
In Jesus' name, Amen

Joshua's Faithful Response

...the Lord said to Joshua, "Moses my servant is dead. Now then, you and all these people, get ready to cross the Jordan River into the Land I am about to give to them...As I was with Moses so I will be with you; I will never leave you nor forsake you."
Joshua 1:1-5

The Lord promised Joshua that He would be faithful to him just as He had been to Moses. But just as Moses had to be faithful to respond to God's call, so Joshua had to be obedient to follow the Lord's instructions. God told Joshua that He would give him every place where he set his foot. The Scriptures show that God holds true to His promises to be fulfilled in us. The Lord promised that the Israelites that if they obeyed His command *to love the Lord your God, to walk in all His ways, and to hold fast to Him*, He would send rain on their land and cause them to prosper. (*Deuteronomy 11:22*) God continues to look for faithful men and women to whom He can entrust His promises.

God has promised to never leave you or forsake you. Has he asked you to step out in faith and serve Him in some way? Is He leading you in a direction that you have never been? The Lord always makes good on His promises but He waits for you to step out in faith. Trust Him and He will see you through.

Heavenly Father,
I am fearful of stepping out in faith in (you fill in the blank(s). Give me the courage to trust You and the willingness to obey.
In Jesus' name, Amen

June 1

Misunderstanding Grace

What shall we say, then? Shall we go on sinning so that grace may increase? By no means! We died to sin; how can we live in it any longer?
Romans 6:1-2

We have been justified through faith in Jesus Christ and now stand under the shadow of His grace. We are able to rejoice in our circumstances because we know that grace enables and empowers us to live a victorious life. Paul clarifies that grace must not be misunderstood or misused. I have often heard it said that it is easier to ask for grace than permission. In other words, do what you want to do, and then seek forgiveness and grace. Paul is concerned that people might take liberties and misuse the gift of grace. He reminds the early Christians that they have been baptized into Christ Jesus' death and resurrection, and as a result they were empowered to live a new life, a life free of the bondage to sin. Paul points out in *Romans 3:20* that the law made them conscious of sin. The law raised God's standard of righteous living, but the people were unable to follow the law. Jesus proclaims in *Matthew 5:17* that He has come not to abolish the law but to fulfill it. When we identify with Jesus' death and resurrection, we have the power through grace to live in obedience to God's will. We are no longer under law, but under grace. Paul writes that we are united with Jesus in His resurrection, enabling us to not be slaves to sin but to count ourselves dead to sin and alive in Christ. I, for one, want to shout out this good news to a world that seems to be heading for self-destruction, with people offering their lives to sin rather than to righteousness. We have been given freedom from the bondage of sin, and Paul points out the way for us to live our lives in the power of grace.

What about you? Have you recognized and received the gift of God's grace—undeserved yet freely given? Today, acknowledge and receive the gift. Whenever you fail or fall into sin, quickly turn back and stand under the shadow of His grace.

Heavenly Father,

Help me to recognize the precious gift of grace, allowing this undeserved gift to shape my life of obedience in You.
In Jesus' name, Amen

June 2

Doing God's Will

Peter and the other apostles replied: We must obey God rather than men!
Acts 5:29

The apostles were brought before the Sanhedrin, the supreme Jewish court consisting of 70 to 100 men. Imagine the scene: the members of the Sanhedrin sitting in a semicircle, backed by three rows of disciples of the "learned men," with the clerks of the court standing in front. How intimidating this must have been for the apostles! The apostles were brought before the Sanhedrin to be questioned by the high priest. They reminded the apostles that they had been told not to teach in the name of Jesus, yet the apostles had continued to do so: "*You have filled Jerusalem with your teaching and are determined to make us guilty of this man's blood." (Acts 5:28)* The members of the Sanhedrin were concerned that they would be blamed for the death of Jesus. Peter and the other apostles replied that they must obey God and not man. When the Sanhedrin heard this, they were furious and wanted to put them to death. Obedience to God's will always costs us something: our reputations, our position of influence, rejection, maybe even our very life. The apostles knew that those things waned in comparison with obedience to God. Obedience meant that they would stay close to their Savior, and their lives were consumed with knowing Him and making Him known to the world.

Are you willing to count the cost of obedience to Christ? It may cost you your job, relationships that are contrary to God's best will for you, or other sacrifices that are hard to make. The apostles were beaten for disobeying their orders to stop talking about Jesus, but they left rejoicing because they had shared in the sufferings of Christ. (*v.41*) What would you have done if you were in their places?

Heavenly Father,
I am willing to count the cost of obeying You. I want to be like he apostles who never stopped teaching and preaching the good news of Jesus Christ. (v.42) I no longer wish to live protecting my own self interests. I want to live totally surrendered to You.
In Jesus' name, Amen

Signs of the End of the Age

'Now learn this lesson from the fig tree: As soon as its twigs get tender and its leaves
come out, you know that summer is near.
Matthew 24:32

Jesus warned the disciples to beware of people who claim to be the "Christ." He also told them to watch for signs that point to His second coming: wars, famines, earthquakes, false prophets, and the increase of wickedness. Some of these events listed in *Matthew 24* were fulfilled in Jesus' time, some later, and some are to be fulfilled in the future. The Lord holds all things in His hand and promises to one day establish His kingdom on earth forever; but in the meantime, we see evidence of the "twigs getting tender." Jesus uses this analogy of the fig tree to demonstrate to his disciples that when these things happen (wars, famines, earthquakes, etc), they are signs of the end of the age. He then reminds them, and subsequently present-day disciples of Christ as well, that His words will never pass away: *Heaven and earth will pass away, but my words will never pass away. (v.35)*

As followers of Christ, we must pay attention to the signs of the end of the age. It is apparent that we have seen many of the "birth pangs" already: *Nation will rise up against nation, and kingdom against kingdom. There will be famines and earthquakes. (v.7)* It is comforting to know that Jesus Christ, the King of God's kingdom, has warned us of what is to come, and at the end of the age, He will return. We need not fear as we see some of the signs of His return. No, indeed! We should pray for God's kingdom to come and for His will to be done.

Heavenly Father,
I am afraid when I read the words in Matthew 24 describing the end of the age. I fear that I have become so accustomed to this world that I am not ready for the consummation of Your kingdom to come. Prepare my heart to be caught up with You and not with the things of this world, knowing that one day when You return, I will finally feel right at home.
In Jesus' name, Amen

June 4

Rejoicing in God's Word

Then Nehemiah the governor, Ezra the priest and scribe, and the Levites who were instructing the people said to them all, "This day is sacred to the LORD your God. Do not mourn or weep." For all the people had been weeping as they listened to the words of the Law. Nehemiah said, "Go and enjoy choice food and sweet drinks, and send some to those who have nothing prepared. This day is sacred to our Lord. Do not grieve, for the joy of the LORD is your strength." The Levites calmed all the people, saying, "Be still, for this is a sacred day. Do not grieve." Then all the people went away to eat and drink, to send portions of food and to celebrate with great joy, because they now understood the words that had been made known to them.
Nehemiah 8:9-12

As the Word of God was read, the people's initial response was conviction and sorrow. They mourned over their sins. Nehemiah told the people to stop mourning and rejoice in the freedom that God's Word brings. God's Word always brings conviction, but as we respond in faith and obedience, we are free to rejoice. Ezra read the Word and the people responded by lifting their hands in worship and bowing to the ground: *Ezra praised the Lord, the great God; and all the people lifted their hands and responded, "Amen! Amen!..." (v.6)* When the people began to understand the Word, they responded by mourning because they realized the goodness of the Lord and recognized how they had rebelled against him.

When was the last time you wept as you read God's Word? It is more powerful than a two edged sword and divides the truth from lies for us. (*Hebrews 4:12*) Before I read God's Word, I ask the Holy Spirit to convict me of truth, to search my heart, and to show me where I have sinned against Him. I am always convicted by His Word, and repentance draws me back to Him again in rejoicing. What an awesome God we serve! He sent His Son Jesus Christ to die for our sins, offering us forgiveness through repentance and freedom from the bondage of sin! Nehemiah knew that God's people needed a fresh start, and the only place to start anew was to be washed clean with God's Word. After the people wept, Ezra told them to rejoice because the joy of the Lord was to be their strength. (*v. 10*) We, too, are strengthened through the joy of obeying God's Word.

Heavenly Father,
Forgive me for reading Your word as if it was just another book. I pray that the motive of my heart for reading and meditating on Your Word is to know You more and to be changed and transformed in the reading. Pierce my heart with Your Word.
In Jesus' name, Amen

June 5

Revelation of the Cross

From that time on Jesus began to explain to his disciples that he must go to Jerusalem and suffer many things at the hands of the elders, chief priests and teachers of the law, and that he must be killed and on the third day be raised to life. Peter took him aside and began to rebuke him. "Never, Lord!" He said. "This shall never happen to you!" Jesus turned and said to Peter, "Get behind me, Satan! You are a stumbling block to me; you do not have in mind the things of God, but the things of men." Then Jesus said to his disciples, "If anyone would come after me, he must deny himself and take up his cross and follow me. For whoever wants to save his life] will lose it, but whoever loses his life for me will find it. What good will it be for a man if he gains the whole world, yet forfeits his soul? Or what can a man give in exchange for his soul?
Matthew 16:21-26

Jesus began to explain to His disciples that He must go to Jerusalem and suffer many things. *(Matthew 16:21)* He was beginning to prepare them for His ultimate death on the cross. He knew His assignment on earth was to set the captives free and that His death and resurrection would complete this assignment. He explained to His disciples that they must follow Him by taking up His cross and surrendering their lives to Him. Peter did not see God's highest plan—that Jesus' suffering on the cross would produce the fruit of life. He was responding to Christ through "the eyes of the flesh" rather than the "eyes of the spirit." Jesus rebuked Peter, knowing that this kind of thinking was a stumbling block to His mission. He told His disciples that as they took up the cross themselves, they would find life. How strange it must have seemed to the disciples to hear that in their suffering like Christ, they would find life!

The kingdom of God is revealed to us as we surrender our lives to Christ, take up His cross daily, and follow Him. Have you denied picking up the cross of Christ because you have reservations about surrendering your life? Remember that, like Peter, you must see things through "kingdom lenses," lenses that help you see that self-denial brings true life.

Heavenly Father,

Like Peter, I have not understood what it means to take up Your cross. I have taken the easy way out in my spiritual walk, doing those things that do not demand that I surrender everything. Today, I surrender my life to You and take up Your cross. I desire for the life of Christ to live in and through me.
In Jesus' name, Amen

June 6

The Promise of the Counselor

If you love me, you will obey what I command. I will ask the Father and he will give you another Counselor to be with you forever—the Spirit of truth.
John 14:15

Jesus tells his disciples that He will not leave them as orphans when He goes to the cross. He promises to send the Counselor to teach them and guide them. The promise is conditional, however; they have to love and obey Him. He says that loving Him will lead to obedience, which in turn leads to His promise of the Holy Spirit. He promises to never leave them as orphans, and He gives them assurance that one day they will be filled with His Spirit as He abides (makes His home) in them.

This is one of the most exciting and liberating passages in the Scripture for me, knowing that if I love and obey Jesus, He will send His Spirit to live in me! I need never feel alone, I need never worry about getting lost, because He is with me and He will guide me. I am one of those "directionally challenged" people in the world. My friends all know that I am clueless when it comes to directions. They are always willing to draw maps, lead me to places, or give me any assistance I need to ensure that I get to my destination. Though I am challenged in the natural with direction, I have confidence in my spiritual direction. The Holy Spirit guides me into truth, directs my path, and comes alongside my life to empower me.

How about you? Have you given your life over to Jesus Christ and allowed Him to fill you with His life-giving Spirit? Have you believed that He *is* guiding you throughout the day, and that He is your counselor? Take a moment to ask the Lord to fill you with His Spirit today.

Heavenly Father,
I have felt so alone, without direction and seeking truth. Fill me with Your Holy Spirit as I love and obey You and seek To follow Your direction.
In Jesus' name, Amen

Trust in God to Know What is Best

Trust in the LORD with all your heart and lean not on your own understanding.
Proverbs 3:5

Learning to trust that God knows what is best for me has been the turning point of my faith. Believing that Elohim, my Creator, knows exactly what I need and when I need it has been life-changing. Faith to trust in God begins with the knowledge that He is our Creator. Who could know better what is best for us than the One who not only created us, but also loves us with a perfect love? As we grasp that truth, the next step is to know Jehovah Jireh as our Provider. Abraham met Jehovah Jirah one day on Mount Moriah. God told him to saddle up his donkey, take His only son Isaac, and sacrifice him on the altar as a burnt offering. Abraham obeyed and started up the mountain. I cannot imagine what must have been going through his head: "…but Lord, this is the promised son—remember? This is the son you promised when you told me I would be the Father of many nations. Did you forget? Have you gone mad?" He may have been thinking those things but we do know for sure that he obeyed. He also demonstrated in his words that he trusted that the Lord would deliver his son: *He said to his servants, stay here with the donkey while I and the boy go over there. WE will come back to you. (Genesis 22:5)* He expected Isaac to return with him because he trusted His God! Perhaps he thought that God would provide another sacrifice (which he did), or perhaps he thought that he would raise his son from the dead. Regardless, we see that he trusted Jehovah to provide for him.

God will provide what we need, exactly when we need it. We have only to ask and allow Him! He may not make provision according to our timetable, but he answers according to His plan. Perhaps you remember the show "Father Knows Best." It was one of my favorite shows, and I looked forward to watching it every week. The father in the show was full of wisdom, and the children respected him. As we grow in our knowledge of Jehovah Jireh, we will learn to trust that He truly knows best!

In what circumstances do you need to meet Jehovah Jireh? God's Word says to trust the Lord with all of your heart and He will provide by making your path straight.

Heavenly Father,
I desire to trust You with (fill in the blank.) Every time I think I have let go, I realize that I haven't. My fear keeps getting in the way of trusting You. Just as Abraham was fully persuaded that You would keep Your promise, help me to trust Your Word as Jehovah Jirah, my Provider.
In Jesus' name, Amen

Courageous Living

Be on your guard; stand firm in the faith; be men of courage; be strong.
I Corinthians 16:13

Paul faced the possibility of losing his life when the storm took his ship off course. God sent an angel to assure Paul that he would make it to Rome in order to stand trial before Caesar. *(Acts 27:24)* The angel told him not to be afraid because God had a purpose for his life, and not even a storm could thwart His purposes. The ultimate purpose of the Lord was for Paul to get to Rome so that the gospel could be taken into that area.

We, too, sometimes feel as though we have been shipwrecked. The struggles of life throw us off course, and fear can easily set in. Remembering God's promises in His Word gives us courage and keeps us on course. Storms may try and take us off course, but God's purpose in the storm, once completed, will strengthen us. God does not desire for us to be shipwrecked, but He does allow the storms to cause us to turn to Him. He has a purpose for your life and you must not fear. As you turn to Him, He sets your course and your destiny to be fulfilled.

Paul tells the church in Corinth to be on guard and stand firm in the faith. (*I Corinthians 16:13*) He had experienced severe opposition as he, himself, had stood firm in his faith and convictions. He knew how difficult it could be when opposition threatened to defeat him. Yet he stood firm in his faith. God is calling you to do the same. When the storms of life come, call on the Lord to keep you from shipwreck and take courage, for you are not alone. He will never leave or forsake you. That is His promise!

Heavenly Father,
As I hold tightly to the boat of life, I am being tossed and turned and I live in fear of being thrown overboard or shipwrecked. Strengthen me in Your Word and give me the courage to see the storm through.
In Jesus' name, Amen

June 9

Wearing the Wedding Garments

Rather, clothe yourselves with the Lord Jesus Christ, and do not think about how to gratify the desires of the sinful nature.
Romans 13:14

Paul tells us in *Romans* to clothe ourselves with the Lord Jesus Christ. Jesus has prepared a banquet feast for us—a wedding celebration. He is the bridegroom, and when we accept Him as our Lord and Savior, we become His bride. As we live our lives as Christians, we are to clothe ourselves with the character of Christ as we await His coming again. He will return for His bride, and there will be quite a celebration...*for the wedding of the Lamb has come and His bride has made herself ready. (Revelation 19:7)*

Paul writes that we must prepare ourselves for the return of the Lord and the end of this age. He tells the church to love one another, as love is the fulfillment of the law. He tells them to *put aside the deeds of darkness* as the day draws near. And finally, he tells them to clothe themselves with the Lord Jesus Christ: *Rather clothe yourselves with the Lord Jesus Christ and do not think about how to gratify the desires of the sinful nature. (Romans 13:14)*

A s the bride of Christ, the church is reminded that we are preparing ourselves for the return of our groom, Jesus Christ. We must not gratify our sinful nature, but clothe ourselves with the nature and love of Christ. It is natural to want to satisfy our own needs and desires, sometimes at the expense of others, but Jesus is coming for a spotless and holy bride—one who looks like Himself and who is surrendered to His love: *Let us rejoice and be glad and give him glory! For the wedding of the Lamb has come, and his bride has made herself ready. (Revelation 19:7)*

Heavenly Father,
Guide me in my preparation to be Your bride. Clothe me with Your nature and cleanse the attitude of my heart so that I can be Your holy bride, prepared for Your return.
In Jesus' name, Amen

Fear

For God did not give us a spirit of timidity, but a spirit of power, of love and of self-discipline.
II Timothy 1:7

The most important thing to recognize about fear is that it is not of God. Fear is a tactic of the enemy to get us off course, to make us anxious, and to keep us from trusting the Lord. Fear usually begins as an anxious thought. If we allow it to take root in our minds, it becomes embedded in our emotions, where we either feed it or choose to turn it over to God. If we act in fear, we have lost touch with the promises of God, such as, *"(He) will supply all our needs..." (Philippians 4:19), "He will never forsake us" (Deuteronomy 31:6),* and "*He will guard us in all our ways.*" *(Psalm 91:11)* We must be determined to recognize that fear is not of God. We need to rely on the Holy Spirit to keep fear from controlling our thoughts, our emotions, and our actions. Paul writes to Timothy, thanking him for his sincere faith. He reminds Timothy to use his gifts and to remember that God did not give him a spirit of fear but of love and self-discipline. The church was under persecution, and Paul was writing to persevere.

What about you? Has fear taken hold of you? Ask the Holy Spirit to show you what fearful thoughts you have been entertaining and begin to cast them down. In his second letter to the Corinthian church, Paul tells us to take our thoughts captive in obedience to Christ: *We demolish arguments and every pretension that sets up against the knowledge of God, and we take every thought captive to make it obedient to Christ. (2 Corinthians 10:5)* What thoughts have taken you captive? Allow the Lord to fill you with *His* truth. The truth of His Word will drive out all of your fears.

Heavenly Father,
I take captive every fearful thought that I have concerning (fill in the blank). Your Word tells me that You have not given me this spirit of fear, and I claim Your power instead.
In Jesus' name, Amen

June 11

Slaves to Sin

For sin shall not be your master, because you are not under law, but under grace.
Romans 6:14

Why is it easier to live under law and not under grace? It is so difficult to believe that God loved us enough to send His only Son in order for us to live under grace. We are powerless to live a life that is completely free of sin, and the gift of forgiveness through Christ allows us to live in the shadow of His grace. Sure… we don't deserve it. But that is the nature of a gift, isn't it? A gift freely given should be freely received. Grace empowers us to live a godly life. Why, then, do we give in to the temptation of sin when Jesus has given us what we need to defeat sin in our lives? *2 Peter 1:3* puts it this way: *"His divine power has given us everything we need for life and godliness…"* Jesus gave us His Holy Spirit to lead, guide, and direct our paths. His Holy Spirit convicts us of sin and empowers us to turn from the temptation to sin. He did not leave us helpless or alone to fight our sinful nature. Instead, as believers, He gave us a way to obey Him and turn from sin. Why, then, do we fall into sin? Paul makes it clear that we have a choice: to either give ourselves to righteousness or offer ourselves to sin. (*v.13*)

Ask yourself the question, "Does my life reflect a life offered to God, enjoying the freedom from sin that Christ offers, or does it reflect a life that doesn't know this freedom?" When we are able to offer our lives freely back to God, we are able to stand under the shadow of His grace. When we choose to offer ourselves to sin, we stand in the shadow of darkness where confusion reigns and life seems empty. Today, receive the free gift of life knowing that sin no longer needs to be your master because you are no longer under the law of sin, but are under grace.

Heavenly Father,
Thank you for the gift of Your Son, Jesus Christ. He alone has given me the gift of life through forgiveness of sins. Help me to receive this gift of grace and live in the fullness of life in Christ.
In Jesus' name, Amen

Wisdom Through Godly Counsel

May you be blessed for your good judgment and for keeping me from bloodshed this day and from avenging myself with my own hands.
I Samuel 25:33

David sent word to Nabal, who was shearing his sheep, that he would like for Nabal to give his men food and supplies. David's men had at one time guarded Nabal's sheep, and now David sought help from him. However, Nabal told David's servants that he would not give them provisions. Abigail, Nabal's wife, heard from messengers what her husband had done and went to offer David and his men provisions. Abigail's prudent actions and her acknowledgement of David's accession to the throne turned David's heart away from retaliation. Abigail was a wise, godly woman, and David told her, *"Go home in peace. I have heard your words and granted your request." (I Samuel 25:35)*

Courageous leaders are willing to listen and adjust their attitudes and plans accordingly. They have teachable hearts and are willing to listen to the counsel of others. There were other times, however, when David did not listen to the counsel around him. For example, when Abishai told David to kill Saul, David refused to touch God's anointed one. Although courageous leaders are willing to listen to godly counsel, they always seek the Lord's Word as the final authority.

What about you? Do you have godly counselors around you? Consider who in your life offers you godly counsel. Are you willing to listen to their counsel and then take it to the Lord in prayer? If you do not have anyone in your life who seeks to follow God's ways, pray and ask the Lord to send you someone who can fill that role. Pray for an approachable, teachable heart, and always remember to take all counsel to the Lord in prayer.

Heavenly Father,
I desire to be a person who listens to godly counsel. Send people into my life who are seeking You and are willing to guide me on this journey of life. Help me to

always remember to turn to You in prayer, knowing that Your Holy Spirit is my ultimate Counselor and Helper.
In Jesus' name, Amen

The Pride of Moab

He will bring down your high fortified walls and lay them low;
he will bring them down to the ground, to the very dust.
Isaiah 25:12

The self-sufficiency of Babylon, the materialism of Tyre, and the independence of Moab all had pride as the root of their sins. Isaiah describes the people of Moab as *high fortified walls. (Isaiah 25:12)* The pride of these nations caused their destruction. Pride is the insidious enemy within us that tries to destroy humility. Yet God tells us in His Word that He dwells with the humble and contrite of heart *(Isaiah 57:15)* We must also be willing to allow the Lord to bring down the strongholds of pride in our lives so that the humble King of Kings can dwell in us.

Recently, my husband and I were discussing an issue; I thought I was right and he thought he was right. Naturally, I continued to justify and make a point that my way was the right way. I realized that we had locked horns like the buffalo I recently saw on my trip to Montana. Buffalo must be careful when they lock horns because they can die if they are unable to free themselves. I realized that both my husband and I were going to die in the ditch on this issue. Pride was at the root of our disagreement. Both of us wanted to be right.

The Lord desires to find a place in our lives to dwell—a place where He can have room to lead and influence our lives. Wherever pride dwells, we constrict the dwelling place of God in us. Where in your life do you see pride operating? Ask the Lord to remove any stronghold of pride you see operating in your life. You will find freedom and release from the bondage that pride gives.

Heavenly Father,
I pray for a humble and contrite heart—a place for Your Holy Spirit to dwell. Forgive me for my pride, my unwillingness to admit when I am wrong, and my stubbornness when I seek to get my own way.
In Jesus' name, Amen

June 14

Divine Protection

But the Lord is faithful, and he will strengthen and protect you from the evil one.
II Thessalonians 3:3

When the ship that was taking Paul as a prisoner to Rome ran aground off the island of Malta, the soldiers wanted to kill the prisoners before they could swim ashore and escape. But the centurion wanted to spare Paul's life and kept them from carrying out their plans. *(Acts 27:42-43*) Once safely ashore, a deadly viper attached itself onto Paul's hand, but miraculously, he lived. God divinely protected Paul, and He also protects us as He calls us to fulfill His Word and purposes. God told Paul he would reach Rome, and He protected him so that His purposes would not be thwarted.

The enemy seeks to destroy and rob us of the delight of living for God. He seeks to weaken our defenses by causing us to forget that God is faithful and has promised us that He will strengthen us in all things. Paul, a prisoner of Rome, was in a position of weakness, seemingly dependent on the soldiers to protect him. But when his life was threatened, it was *God* who protected him and kept him safe from the schemes of the soldiers. God's purpose to get Paul to Rome could not be thwarted. When we stand in the will of God, seeking to follow Him, He protects us and His plans will be fulfilled through us.

Are you in a place where you sense that the Lord has called you and yet it appears that the enemy has thwarted your plans? Are you only able to see closed doors and feel unprotected from the schemes of the enemy? The servant of Elisha, prophet of Israel, could only see the army of opposition when he looked at the hillside, yet Elisha prayed that he would be able to see the army of God's angels protecting and fighting for them. (*2 Kings 6:15-16*) Ask the Lord to open your spiritual eyes to see the deliverance and protection of the Lord. He will never fail you or leave you unprotected.

Heavenly Father,
Open my eyes like You did for Elisha's servant to see the army of God that fights for me. Help me to believe that although the circumstances appear as though I am defeated, You are with me protecting me from all evil.
In Jesus' name, Amen

Understanding God's Word

. . . all the people assembled as one man in the square before the Water Gate. They told Ezra the scribe to bring out the Book of the Law of Moses, which the LORD had commanded for Israel. So on the first day of the seventh month Ezra the priest brought the Law before the assembly, which was made up of men and women and all who were able to understand. He read it aloud from daybreak till noon as he faced the square before the Water Gate in the presence of the men, women and others who could understand. And all the people listened attentively to the Book of the Law. Ezra the scribe stood on a high wooden platform built for the occasion. Beside him on his right stood Mattithiah, Shema, Anaiah, Uriah, Hilkiah and Maaseiah; and on his left were Pedaiah, Mishael, Malkijah, Hashum, Hashbaddanah, Zechariah and Meshullam. Ezra opened the book. All the people could see him because he was standing above them; and as he opened it, the people all stood up. Ezra praised the LORD, the great God; and all the people lifted their hands and responded, "Amen! Amen!" Then they bowed down and worshiped the LORD with their faces to the ground. The Levites—Jeshua, Bani, Sherebiah, Jamin, Akkub, Shabbethai, Hodiah, Maaseiah, Kelita, Azariah, Jozabad, Hanan and Pelaiah—instructed the people in the Law while the people were standing there. They read from the Book of the Law of God, making it clear and giving the meaning so that the people could understand what was being read.

Nehemiah 8:1-8

The people did not own copies of the Scriptures, so what a thrill it must have been to hear God's Word read aloud! Today most of us have several Bibles on our shelves, and it is hard to imagine the people who did not have access to the Word. Yet throughout the world, many people do not have access to God's Word. Missionaries have risked their lives to take Bibles to countries like China so that people can have the transforming Word of God. Ezra explained what he read to them in a language they could understand. (*v.7-8*) The Levites assisted Ezra in teaching the Law (*v.7*), and together with Ezra helped to bring understanding and application of the Word. I have been told repeatedly by people who long to study and understand God's Word that it is too difficult. I suggest as you study the Bible for the first time, use a modern day paraphrase like *The Message* by Eugene Peterson or the *Life Application Study Bible.* As you become more familiar with the Bible, you will find it helpful to study other translations as well. I am particularly fond of the *Hebrew-Greek Study Bible,* which helps with the translations of the original Hebrew and Greek words. Nehemiah knew it was time for a spiritual revival, and he began by having Ezra open the Word of God to the people. Even as we read God's Word today, we are spiritually revived.

The Word of God is sharper than a two-edged sword. (*Hebrews 4:12*) It separates our soul and spirit and judges the attitudes of our hearts. As you read the Scriptures, ask the Holy Spirit to speak to you; ask the Lord to show you the attitude of your heart and seek to have the Word transform your thoughts and actions.

Heavenly Father,
Speak to me through Your Word. I pray that Your Word will cut through the dark places of my life and bring correction. I pray that Your Word will convict, teach, and bring me closer to You.
In Jesus' name, Amen

Responding to the Invitation

The Lord is not slow in keeping his promise, as some understand slowness. He is patient with you, not wanting anyone to perish, but everyone to come to repentance.
II Peter 3:9

It is the Lord's desire for all people to know Him. He is infinitely more patient than our minds are able to comprehend. He draws people to Himself through cords of love; however, many people choose not to respond to His love. His love is so consuming that He desires no one will perish by not responding to His invitation to know Him. With the Lord, a day is like a thousand years, and a thousand years are like a day. (*v.8*)

The Lord also seeks to deliver us from our sins and those things that keep us in bondage. He continues to reveal to us the things in our lives that hold us captive and keep us from drawing near to Him. I can be so stubborn at times, not able to see the sin in my life. Perhaps I have not forgiven someone or I have allowed a root of bitterness to grow against someone. The Lord continues to pursue me, desiring that I respond to his invitation to turn back to Him.

Why is it so difficult to let go of an unforgiving attitude, pride, or self-centeredness? God is patient with us, and He allows our misery to go unchecked until we recognize how miserable we really are living apart from Him. If you find yourself bogged down in a life, filled with regret, bitterness, or unforgiveness, remember that the Lord is patient. He will tenderly lead you to repentance and restore you. It is His desire that you not perish in your misery, but that you are fulfilled in His love.

Heavenly Father,
Forgive me for not responding to Your invitation to turn back to You. Forgive me for preferring to live a life that is focused on myself. I am grateful for Your patience with me. I am grateful for Your promise of restoration.
In Jesus' name, Amen

June 17

Sin's Consequences

Therefore, since we are surrounded by such a great cloud of witnesses, let us throw off everything that hinders and the sin that so easily entangles, and let us run with perseverance the race marked out for us.
Hebrews 12:1

Sin affects each of us, and it affects the people with whom we are in community. It entangles us and hinders us from running the race that God has set out for each of us. For example, in *Joshua chapter 7*, Achan's greed prompted him to steal a robe and gold from Jericho. The consequences brought about defeat in battle for Israel, and ultimately his sin led to the death of his family and himself. Just as Achan's sin brought about defeat to the Israelites, the same is true of us today. The disobedience of one person can have a profound effect on a whole community. No person is a lone island because whatever we do touches lives, either for good or for evil. Divine justice demands full retribution for the wrong done.

What race has God marked out for you? Is there any sin that is holding you back from God's purposes for your life? Is there any sin that has affected others with whom you are in community? Take gossip for example. It tears down rather than builds up, and God's Word teaches to build one another up: *Therefore encourage one another and build up each other… (I Thessalonians 5:11)* When we gossip, we are not encouraging one another, but instead are tearing each other down. Gossip not only affects you and the person to whom the gossip is directed, but it also affects those who listen or participate. The sin of gossip is like a fire that spreads and affects many people.

What sin has entangled you and perhaps has snared others as well? Ask the Lord to reveal the sin and seek forgiveness. Seek to keep your heart pure, and God's promise is that you will see God: *Blessed are the pure in heart for they will see God. (Matthew 5:8)*

Heavenly Father,
Forgive me for the sin (fill in the blank). Forgive me for the effect this sin has had on others. Untangle me from the power of sin and help me to live with a pure heart so that I am able to see You more clearly.
In Jesus' name, Amen

Laying Down Our Lives

For to me, to live is Christ and to die is gain.
Philippians 1:21

Paul was in prison, in chains, and was ready to die to be with Jesus. He longed to be with the One who had set him free from the chains of his old life and had given him a brand new life. Having offered himself to God as a living sacrifice *(Romans 12:1)*, Paul was willing to lay down his life in any way the Lord chose. Paul grew to find all his life's meaning in Christ and could say with purpose and conviction, "*To live is Christ and to die is gain.*" (*Philippians 1:21)*

As I contemplate what it means to lay my life down for Christ, finding *all* life's meaning in Christ, I realize that I must ask myself the question "Am I willing to lay down my children, my husband, my home, my dreams…?" I can say those words, but what gives them meaning is complete trust in a faithful God. Behind every person or thing that I cling to is a place of lack of trust in my loving Father. So rather than ask yourself if you are willing to lay all down for Christ, a better question is "Do I trust God with all of my relationships, concerns, and all issues of life?"

Paul knew that real life begins and ends with Christ. He had lived life knowing and trusting Jesus Christ, and He had lived a life apart from Christ as a Pharisee. When he penned or spoke these words to a scribe, he was secure that, in life or death and through all things, Christ was his all. He was ready to die and yet willing to live. The physical chains may have kept him bound, but his life was far from bound. He was free in the richest sense—free to live and free to die. He had obtained perfect freedom.

As you reflect on these verses, ask the Lord to show you where you do not trust Him. Deal with issues of trust, and you will be free to lay down all concerns of life.

Heavenly Father,
I am longing to let go of the concerns of this life. I invite the light of Christ to expose any areas where I do not trust You. I pray that You will lay an ax to the

root of my fear, and I release to You and entrust into Your care my very life and the lives of those whom I dearly love.
In Jesus' name, Amen

Willingness to Obey

So if you faithfully obey the commands I am giving you today—to love the LORD your God and to serve him with all your heart and with all your soul—then I will send rain on your land in its season, both autumn and spring rains, so that you may gather in your grain, new wine and oil.
Deuteronomy 11:13-14

God told the Israelites that He had a plan for their lives to be fruitful, but they must first be obedient in order to see the fulfillment of His promises. He told them that they were to love Him with all of their heart, and He would send rain on their land and the land would be fruitful.

Although God knows what is best for us and He is the Promise Keeper, we have a responsibility to obey Him in order to benefit from His provisions. This is where "the rubber meets the road." We can have all the confidence in the world in God's faithfulness and in His knowing what is best for us, but if we do not take this confidence "to the streets," we will never truly know Jehovah Jireh. Abraham had grown to trust Jehovah completely, and now God was going to reveal to him Jehovah Jireh. The condition was that Abraham would have to obey. I don't know about you, but I might have failed the test! Abraham, however, held the Word of God in his heart; he had taken the seeds of faith that God had planted, and he was not willing to let doubt or lack of trust keep him from seeing the promises fulfilled. You see, I think that Abraham's obedience had to be tested in order for the promise to be fulfilled. Are you waiting on a promise to be fulfilled? Your part of obedience is key in seeing that promise fulfilled.

Heavenly Father,
I have been disobedient (fill in the blank). I see barrenness in the places where I desire to see fruitfulness. I chose to serve and love You with my whole heart, soul, strength and mind, and I thank you for Your promise to send rain on the dry places of life.
In Jesus' name, Amen

June 20

The Resurrection and the Life

On his arrival, Jesus found that Lazarus had already been in the tomb for four days. Bethany was less than two miles from Jerusalem, and many Jews had come to Martha and Mary to comfort them in the loss of their brother. When Martha heard that Jesus was coming, she went out to meet him, but Mary stayed at home. "Lord," Martha said to Jesus, "if you had been here, my brother would not have died. But I know that even now God will give you whatever you ask." Jesus said to her, "Your brother will rise again. Martha answered, "I know he will rise again in the resurrection at the last day." Jesus said to her, "I am the resurrection and the life. He who believes in me will live, even though he dies; and whoever lives and believes in me will never die. Do you believe this?" "Yes, Lord," she told him, "I believe that you are the Christ, the Son of God, who was to come into the world."

John 11:17-27

Martha meets Jesus before He enters the village and her words are an affirmation of faith in Jesus' healing ability. Despite what she says, she likely does not expect Jesus to raise Lazarus from death since she objects when Jesus wants to roll back the tomb. Instead, she is expressing faith, not wanting to imply any criticism of Jesus since He was not in Bethany to rescue her brother. Martha's words could be paraphrased, "If you had been here, you COULD have healed Lazarus." Her words were not of reproach but of regret—had Jesus made it in time, her brother would have lived. Nevertheless, she still believed in Him. Similarly, it would be like us saying to the Lord, "Lord, I don't know why You didn't come when I first prayed. I know that with You all things are possible, but I choose to trust in You and know that the outcome is in Your hands and that it will be the best for me." Jesus pushes Martha to a second, deeper level of discussion. *Your brother will rise again.* (*11:23*) Martha understood on one level, based on the Jewish belief in the end time resurrection, that Lazarus would enjoy eternal life. However, Martha misses the more immediate application Jesus has in mind. His correction leads to one of the most famous and significant "I am" sayings in *John's* gospel: "*I AM THE RESURRECTION AND THE LIFE.*" When

Jesus asks her "do you believe this?" He is asking her if her faith can embrace a belief in Jesus—lordship over death itself.

We are often just like Martha. We want to believe that Jesus is all that He says He is, but our minds defy the supernatural love and power of God through Christ. We want to believe that He is the resurrection and the life, but the circumstances of our lives seem to contradict this truth.

Jesus is the same yesterday, today, and tomorrow. (*Hebrews 13:8*) He raised Lazarus from physical death, and He is able to raise us from the shroud of death that defies the life of Christ in us. Where do you need to see the life of Christ in your own life? What has died that you desire to see Him resurrect—a relationship, a promise unfilled? Ask the Lord to bring what seems to be dead back to life. He *is* the resurrection and the life.

Heavenly Father,
I had given up hope in ever seeing (fill in blank) come to life. I look to You as the resurrection and the life and ask You to rekindle life. I give You my hopelessness and ask that You impart new life and hope in me.
In Jesus' name, Amen

June 21

Slaves to Righteousness

You have been set free from sin and have become slaves to righteousness.
Romans 6:18

In our post-modern world today, truth is not absolute; there is no definitive right or wrong. Today's society might view Paul's position—either you are a slave to sin or a slave to righteousness—as narrow-minded. History is proof that societies which have no absolutes, using relativism as their guide, fall into decay, specifically moral decay, and become powerless. God's grace gives us freedom and power to live a life free of sin and dependent on God's truth. Grace is not freedom *from* obedience; it is freedom *for* obedience. Paul exhorts Christians to count themselves dead to sin but alive in Christ. (*v.11*) He continues to address how we do that; it is accomplished by offering our bodies (Greek word indicating all the parts of the body to include body, mind, will, and emotions) to the Lord. In doing so, we become slaves to righteousness. As unbelievers we were slaves to sin, but now, as believers, we are slaves to righteousness, offering ourselves to be servants of the Most High God. One of the names for God in the New Testament is "Adonai," which means master. We are offering ourselves to Adonai as a bondservant, one who *chooses* to be under the Master's authority even if he has already been set free. Experience is often the best teacher, and every time I give in to the temptations of the world, my sinful nature, or the enemy, I lose my peace, joy, and fruitfulness for the Lord.

Paul asks, "Why be enslaved by sin when you can have freedom by living righteously?" Anyone who has given in to sin knows the tyranny of being under the wrong master.

Heavenly Father,
I long to be free from the tyranny of sin. I offer myself to You, Adonai, my Master, choosing to be under Your authority. I pray that You will guide me and direct me in righteousness.
In Jesus' name, Amen

Our Counselor, the Holy Spirit

And I will ask the Father, and he will give you another
Counselor to be with you forever—
John 14:16

Jesus promised His disciples that His Father would send the Counselor, the Holy Spirit, to them when He returned to the Father. The Holy Spirit would lead them into truth and teach them all they needed to know. David was anointed by the Spirit to be king of Israel, but he lived on the other side of the cross, and the Holy Spirit had not yet come to dwell permanently within believers. At Pentecost, the Holy Spirit came upon the believers gathered in Jerusalem and continues to come and to live in believers today.

Jesus told His disciples that apart from Him they could do nothing, but when the Holy Spirit came they had the power to live the Christian life and be witnesses to the world. We all need the power of God to swim upstream against the tide of the world. The world lures us towards material gain and power, but God's power through His Holy Spirit leads us in a life of service and humility. The counsel of the Holy Spirit often runs contrary to the counsel of the world, and it is critical that as believers we willingly yield our lives to Him.

Jesus asked His Father to send the Counselor after He left this earth. He knew that we would need His guidance in order to live a Godly life and impact the world in which we live. Have you asked the Holy Spirit to fill your life with *His power?*

Heavenly Father,
Thank you for the gift of Your Holy Spirit. Fill me with Your power and direct me today as I seek to do Your will.
In Jesus' name, Amen

June 23

Going Down to Egypt

Trust in the LORD with all your heart and lean not on your own understanding.
Proverbs 3:5

Woe to those who go down to Egypt for help, who rely on horses, who trust in the multitude of their chariots and in the great strength of their horseman, but do not look to the Holy One of Israel, or seek help from the Lord. (Isaiah 31:1) These are the words penned by the prophet Isaiah. They describe Israel's reliance on Egypt, who represented wealth, false security, prosperity, and human wisdom. The Israelites had a history of trusting the Lord and then finding their security in other gods. At one time, they found their security in Egypt. After Moses led the Israelites out of Egypt where they had been enslaved, they quickly began to complain and wished they were back in Egypt.

It is so easy to fall into the trap of depending on ourselves or other people for our security. We can depend on our money, our position, or our power which leads us farther and farther away from our dependency on God. All of these things can enslave us. My husband often tells me that we need to be careful that our possessions don't possess us. We also need to be careful to trust in the Lord with all of our heart and to be utterly dependent on Him. The Israelites began to trust in the strength and resources of Egypt, and the Lord warned them that this would lead to bondage.

Do you trust the Lord completely or do you depend on your wisdom, your job, and your abilities to fulfill you? Every time you lean on yourself and away from God, you will find yourself back in Egypt, a place of slavery. Freedom is found in complete dependence and trust in God.

Heavenly Father,
Take me out of my personal "Egypt"—the place where I do not seek You—the place where I trust in myself and my own abilities. Every time I find myself in this place, I only know loneliness and despair. I choose to trust and depend on You.
In Jesus' name, Amen

God With Us

In the beginning was the Word, and the Word was with God, and the Word was God. He was with God in the beginning. Through him all things were made; without him nothing was made that has been made. In him was life, and that life was the light of all people. The light shines in the darkness, and the darkness has not overcome it.
John 1:1-5

In the beginning was the WORD, and the Word was with God; the Word was Jesus. The word means *logos* and is God's utterance on earth. Jesus had a history before He came to earth, and John tells us it was that of the Word. In the book of *Hebrews* we read, "*In many ways God spoke of old to our fathers by the prophets; but in these last days he has spoken to us by His Son. (Hebrews 1:1-2*) Jesus is the eternal Son, the eternal WORD.

God spoke and the world came to life, and He sent His Son to earth to speak and bring life to the desolate, the broken, and the needy. God's Word brought life. The words of Christ brought life, and today His Holy Spirit in us speaks life.

In the beginning was the Word… the Word of life. The author of Hebrews warns us that we must not harden our hearts to God's Word: *Today, if you hear His voice do not harden your hearts as you did in the days of rebellion. (Hebrews 3:15)* This Scripture refers back to the days when the Israelites refused to listen to the voice of God and rebelled in unbelief. They wandered for 40 years in the wilderness, and the entire generation of those who rebelled died before entering the Promised Land.

God is still speaking today, and He is reminding us not to harden our hearts to His Word. He speaks through His Word and His Holy Spirit. When God speaks and you turn away in disobedience, His promise is left unfulfilled. What promises are you waiting for? Ask the Lord if you have been disobedient to His Word and seek to obey.

Heavenly Father,

Forgive me for disobeying Your Word. I turn back to You and ask You to soften my heart so that the next time You speak, I will obey.
In Jesus' name, Amen

Preparing for the Wedding

The kingdom of heaven is like a king who prepared a wedding banquet for his son. He sent His servants to those who had been invited to the banquet to tell them to come but they refused to come.
John 22:2-3

In the passage for today, we read that the king had prepared a wedding banquet for his son. He sent his servants to those who had been invited to the banquet to tell them to come but they refused. He then went to further lengths to insure that they knew he had prepared an elaborate feast and he wanted them to come, but they paid no attention! They even mistreated and killed his servants! The king was enraged and destroyed the murderers. Then he told his servants that those who had been invited did not deserve to come and to go to the street corners and invite anyone they could find to the banquet.

Jesus came first to the Jews, who refused Him, and then He offered the gift of salvation to the Gentiles. The greatest wedding invitation that has ever been issued is the union of Jesus, the groom, to His bride, the body of Christ. Some accept the invitation with joy and others refuse. Jesus sets before us a banquet, a feast fit for a king. We are able to see a vivid picture of a king who offers a banquet in the *Song of Solomon*, *"He has taken me to the banquet hall and the banner over me is love." (Song of Songs 2:4)* Jesus offers us a banquet of His love, and the cost was His very life. He offers us salvation and we can refuse. He further tells us that He has gone ahead and prepared a place for us when we receive Him into our lives: *Do not let your hearts be troubled. Trust in God; trust also in me. In my Father's house there are many rooms; if it were not so, I would have told you. I am going there to prepare a place for you. (John 14:1-2)*

When we prepare to have guests for dinner, we generally take time to plan a menu, shop for the food, and then prepare it. It takes time, but we want to bless our guests. The King in this story was ready for his guests to come. Jesus has gone to great lengths to prepare the way for us to enter His kingdom. He has made a way for us to have eternal life with Him through His death on the cross, and has ascended into heaven to prepare a place for us. Have you entered the banquet hall?

Heavenly Father,
I have refused to accept the invitation to Your wedding feast. Forgive me for turning away and refusing Your invitation. I accept You as my groom and ask You to take me into the banquet hall where the banner over me is love.
In Jesus' name, Amen

Disobedience and Forgiveness

If my people, who are called by my name, will humble themselves and pray and seek my face and turn from their wicked ways, then will I hear from heaven and will forgive their sin and will heal their land.
II Chronicles 7:14

Joshua sent men from Jericho to Ai to spy out the region as they progressed further into the Promised Land. We see no mention that he consulted first with the Lord. The spies' report came back that it was not necessary to send all of the fighting men; the fight could be easily won with a few because there were only a few men in Ai and it could easily be taken. A small army was sent on the advice of the spies, and the men of Ai chased the Israelites from the city, killing thirty-six Israeli men. Joshua, upon hearing the bad news, fell face down before the Lord: *Then Joshua tore his clothes and fell face down to the ground before the ark of the Lord remaining there until evening. The elders of Israel did the same and sprinkled dust on their heads. (Joshua 7:6)* Joshua asked the Lord why He had brought the Israelites across the Jordan only to deliver them into the hands of the enemy. Isn't it like us to blame God for our defeats? God quickly showed Joshua that there had been sin in the camp: *The Lord said to Joshua, "stand up! What are you doing down on your face! Israel has sinned; they have violated my covenant." (v.10)* God reveals to Joshua that defeat was brought on the nation of Israel because someone from the tribe of Judah had disobeyed God and had stolen the riches of Caanan in disobedience to the Lord. Quickly Joshua dealt with the sin in the camp as it had affected them all.

There are times when we experience the effects of sin in our own lives and our sin affects the lives of others as well. The nation of Israel was affected by Achan's sin, and similarly our sin can affect others. God gave instruction in His Word on how to handle sin that has a corporate effect: *If my people, who are called by my name, will humble themselves and pray and seek my face and turn from their wicked ways, then I will hear from heaven and will forgive their sin and will heal their land. (II Chronicles 7:14)*

Is there a sin in your life that is affecting you and others? Are you willing to humble yourself, seek the Lord's forgiveness and ask for pardon? He has promised in His Word that if you are willing to do this, He will heal your land.

Heavenly Father,
I am afraid to let go of my sin. My sin has identified me for so long that I do not know how I could live any other way. But I have seen the destruction that my sin has brought on me and others I love. Forgive me as I turn away from (fill in the blank) and I ask You to bring restoration.
In Jesus' name, Amen

The Banner Before Us

Moses built an altar and called it The LORD is my Banner. He said, "For hands were lifted up to the throne of the LORD. The LORD will be at war against the Amalekites from generation to generation."
Exodus 17:15-16

The whole Israelite community set out from the Desert of Sin, traveling from place to place. When they camped at Rephidim there was no water, so they began to grumble and complain to Moses: *"Why did you bring us out of Egypt to make us and our children and livestock die of thirst?" (Exodus 17:3)* In utter frustration, Moses asks God what he should do as the Israelites were prepared to stone him! God tells Moses to walk on ahead of the people and strike the rock at Mount Horeb and when he did so, the water came forth. After this experience, the Amalekites attacked the Israelites. Moses, Aaron, and Hur went to the top of the hill, and Moses took the staff that God had given him. As long as he held the staff up, there was victory but his hands grew tired. Aaron and Hur held up his hands so that the battle could be brought to final victory. Moses built an altar and called it "The Lord is my Banner" (Jehovah Nissi).

Throughout the Scriptures, we see Jehovah Nissi go before the men and women of God to ensure victory. Sometimes in the battle we need others alongside us to hold up our hands as we tire from the struggles of life. Jehovah Nissi goes before you as you face your trials, and God sends friends to hold you up. We must remember that there is no battle that He hasn't prepared you for, and there are always friends who will help you along the way.

Heavenly Father,
Sometimes I feel so alone in my struggles. Thank you for reminding me that You are always there as Jehovah Nissi, my Banner—the One who goes ahead of me to bring me victory. Thank you for the Christian friends that You send along the way to help me to fight the battle.
In Jesus' name, Amen

June 28

Work of the Holy Spirit

You, however, are controlled not by the sinful nature but by the Spirit, if the Spirit of God lives in you. And if anyone does not have the Spirit of Christ, he does not belong to Christ.
Romans 8:9

Paul identifies three areas where we see the work of the Holy Spirit:

- The higher law of the Spirit superseding the law of sin and death
- The Holy Spirit functioning to transform the life of the believer to be Christ-like
- The Spirit-led Christian living victoriously through the power of the Holy Spirit

The work of the Holy Spirit can be seen in the fruit of the lives of believers. As we yield to His work, we are co-laboring to be more like Christ. The good news is that the law of the Spirit supersedes the law of sin and death, and that is terrific news! Frankly, if this ever made the front page of worldwide newspapers and people believed it, the world would be radically transformed. Humanity goes through the motions of living day in and day out, but imagine humanity transformed by an understanding that Jesus Christ came to set them free from the law of sin and death. Not only that, but He sent His Holy Spirit to enable them to live out their new life in Christ, free from the bondage of sin! This is the good news of Jesus Christ, and this is the message to which Paul dedicated his life.

Do you find yourself in bondage to sin? Perhaps you are thinking of sin in terms of murder, stealing, fraud—but what about greed, anger, lying? All are sins and all make us subject to the law of death! Our lives are filled with areas where we fall short of living in the freedom of obedience to God's Word. Paul writes about the transforming power of God that sets us free from all sin. As Christians he tells us that we are not controlled by the sinful nature, but by the Spirit. Are you willing to surrender to the work of the Spirit in you?

Heavenly Father,
Forgive me for believing that my sins are small and I do not need to worry about them. Forgive me for gossiping, for hurting someone with my words, for being self-centered. As I turn back to You, I pray that Your Holy Spirit will be in control of my life.
In Jesus' name, Amen

June 29

Committed to God

Commit your way to the LORD; trust in him and he will do this: He will make your righteousness shine like the dawn, the justice of your cause like the noonday sun.

Psalm 37:5-6

We live in a world that is stressed by commitment. We are all over-committed, and there is little time left over to commit to the Lord. Today's reading challenges us to commit our ways to God and to trust in Him. This requires our time—time to develop our relationship with God. When trials are upon us we may turn to God, but He desires that we commit to Him daily so that when the trials hit, we will able to trust Him based on our relationship.

If David were to write a purpose statement for his life, it would be to seek his Lord and dwell in His presence forever. He wrote, "*The Lord is my light and my salvation—whom shall I fear? The Lord is the stronghold of my life...*" *(Psalm 27:1)* So great was David's commitment to God, that when his son Absalom rebelled against him and tried to take his throne, he told Zadok, the priest, *"Take the Ark of God back into the city. If I find favor in the Lord's eyes, He will bring me back and let me see it and His dwelling place again. But if He says, 'I am not pleased with you,' then I am ready; let Him do to me whatever seems good to Him." (II Samuel 15:25-26)* His complete trust in the Lord helped him to be wholly committed to Him no matter what happened.

What are the things in your life that keep you from being so committed to God that no matter what is happening in your life, you are still able to trust Him? Commit to spending time daily with Him, and He will bring justice to your cause. (*Psalm 37: 5-6*)

Heavenly Father,
Thank you for Your Word that instructs me to commit my life to You and to trust You. Forgive me that I have neglected my relationship with You and only turn to You in the "storms of life." I thank you that when I spend time with You, my trust will grow and You will bring justice to my cause.
In Jesus' name, Amen

The Gospel Preached to All Nations

And this gospel of the kingdom will be preached in the whole world as a testimony to all nations, and then the end will come.

Matthew 24:14

After Jesus lists a series of events that point to His return, He proclaims that the gospel of the kingdom will be preached in the whole world as a testimony to all nations, and then the end will come. He clearly places that statement between prophecies that seem to predict dire times. Jesus is showing His disciples that a series of events is leading to the most significant event of all the ages: the preaching of the gospel to all nations. He is reminding them that His purpose in all things is to bring the fulfillment of His kingdom to earth, bringing people of all nations into a saving relationship with Jesus Christ. Scripture teaches us that someday every knee will bow and every tongue will confess that Jesus is Lord. *(Philippians 2:10)* Although the events seem frightening, He wanted them (and us today) to know that all things will work together for God's ultimate purpose of redemption and the consummation of the age. Let us remember that God is *patient, not wanting anyone to perish, but for everyone to come to repentance. (II Peter 3:9)* That gives us the reassurance that the Lord always wants to save us. *If God is for us, who can possibly be against us? (Romans 8:31)*

The world today seems upside down. As we read the newspapers and listen to the news, we wonder why the Lord doesn't just return and straighten things out! Jesus Christ came to save the lost, and He still desires that no one perish. He is asking us to continue to share His good news with the people we come in contact with. He is patient, and although the end seems near, according to His Word, He will not return until the gospel is preached to the whole world. We better get busy!

Heavenly Father,

Help me to be a witness of Your love to all I come in contact with. I may not be able to quote Scriptures as I would like or to explain passages of Scripture, but I

am able to share my story of how You have brought me hope. Give me the courage to share my hope with others so that I can be a part of speeding Your return.
In Jesus' name, Amen

God's Rest

Let us, therefore, make every effort to enter that rest, so that no one will perish by following their example of disobedience. For the word of God is alive and active. Sharper than any double-edged sword, it penetrates even to dividing soul and spirit, joints and marrow; it judges the thoughts and attitudes of the heart. Nothing in all creation is hidden from God's sight. Everything is uncovered and laid bare before the eyes of him to whom we must give account.
Hebrews 4:11-13

The author of Hebrews mentions two types of rests that illustrate the spiritual experiences of believers today. The Sabbath rest is a picture of our rest in Christ through salvation. (*Hebrews 4:3, Matt. 11:28*) The Canaan rest is a picture of our rest as we claim our inheritance in Christ. (*Heb. 4:11-13*) We enter the Sabbath rest by turning from our sin and asking Jesus Christ into our lives, but we must also make an effort to enter the rest of Canaan. The Israelites were told by God to enter the land of Cana. The Canaanites were a pagan people, and God told the Israelites that He was giving them the land. The Israelites had to cross the Jordan River and face the battle of Jericho as they entered into the Promised Land. They continued to have to battle the nations that occupied the land. But the victory of battle enabled them to push further and further into the inheritance that God had given them. At each place of victory, they made further inroads into the Promised Land and the victory brought them rest.

Are you at rest as a believer or do you stay very busy, both internally and externally? What does it mean to strive to enter God's rest? God has given you His promises in His Word. You will need to read and meditate on His Word and fight to live in His Word. God will go before you to fight the battle, and as you enter into His promises, you will find the rest that He promises.

Heavenly Father,
You alone offer me rest—the rest of salvation and spending eternity with You, and the rest of Canaan where I enter into the promises in Your Word. Help me to fully enter into this rest. -
In Jesus' name, Amen

July 2

Sacrifice of Worship

But the king replied to Araunah, "No, I insist on paying you for it.
I will not sacrifice to the LORD my God burnt offerings that cost me nothing."
So David bought the threshing floor and the oxen and paid fifty shekels of silver for them.
II Samuel 24:24

The Lord sent a plague on Israel when David sinned by taking a census of his army. His sin was motivated by self-interest and pride. Through a man named Gad, the Lord commanded that David offer an atoning sacrifice. David offered to buy the threshing floor of Araunah so that he could build an altar to the Lord. Araunah offered to give David the land and the animals to be sacrificed, but David refused his offer, insisting that he purchase the land to be used for the sacrifice. He refused to offer a sacrifice that cost him nothing.
How true that is for us today! Worshipping the Lord requires much from us: our time, our commitment, and our very lives! Paul writes, *Therefore, I urge you, brothers, in view of God's mercy, to offer your bodies as living sacrifices, holy and pleasing to God—this is your spiritual act of worship. (Romans 12:1)* What does it mean to offer God our very lives as a living sacrifice? It means that we must be willing to spend time with the Lord in His Word, in prayer, and in worship. The cost is our time. The benefits are eternal.

Heavenly Father,
Help me to give my life over to worshipping You. So much of my time is invested in other things and I find myself empty and searching. I offer myself to You in worship and I'm willing to pay the cost.
In Jesus' name, Amen

Gathering the Troops

Now the city was large and spacious, but there were few people in it, and the houses had not yet been rebuilt.
Nehemiah 7:4

Nehemiah knew the importance of "gathering the troops"—of assembling the people of Judah to begin building their homes. What good would a wall be if there were no people? What good would people be if they didn't begin to gather and build their physical and spiritual homes together? So he found the genealogical record and conducted a census of those who had returned from captivity in Babylon. *Nehemiah 7:1-73* describes the people of the province and the significance of gathering the broken, disgraced, and shamed people of Judah to begin the process of revival.

God the Redeemer repairs the broken places of our lives and revives us so that, as His Redeemed people, we can in turn reach out to a broken world, offering the hope of Jesus Christ. Nehemiah gathered the people who had come out from Babylon and brought them hope once again. God is gathering His troops today, assembling people to begin to build their homes for Christ. He is looking for Christians who are willing to allow the Holy Spirit to repair the damage to their own homes first, and then to send them out to help others. He is gathering an army that may look weary, broken, and destitute, but He is bringing hope and redeeming the lost.

As the Lord works in your life transforming the broken places and strengthening you, He is gathering you to Himself and then joining you to other people whom He has brought hope. Together we are a kingdom united, not divided—united in His love and one in His Spirit.

Heavenly Father,
Thank you for restoring and building me into a "house" to be used for Your glory. Help me to build a house for You to dwell in and to strengthen others as we build one another up with the hope that You bring.
In Jesus' name, Amen

July 4

Removed Hindrances

Therefore, since we are surrounded by such a great cloud of witnesses, let us throw off everything that hinders and the sin that so easily entangles, and let us run with perseverance the race marked out for us. Let us fix our eyes on Jesus, the author and perfecter of our faith, who for the joy set before him endured the cross, scorning its shame, and sat down at the right hand of the throne of God.
Hebrews 12:1-2

In chapter eleven of *Hebrews,* we find a list of men and women of faith. They were able to overcome obstacles because they trusted God. They were willing to press through obstacles to their faith and believe God for the impossible. Obstacles of unbelief hold us back from walking in God's confidence. God's Word promises us that He will remove obstacles from our lives as we seek Him. *Hebrews 12: 1-2* reminds us that we are surrounded by men and women of faith who are an example to us of pressing on in our faith. When we open our hearts to the Lord, He reveals hindrances that stand in the way of our spiritual growth. Paul was able to preach boldly, without hindrance, the Word of God. *(Acts 28:31*) God will remove the obstacles in our lives as we come to Him in prayer so that we will not be hindered in the work He has called us to do.

I was at a retreat and had the privilege of watching young Christian leaders pray that the Lord would remove any hindrances in their lives. At the end of the weekend, I could see that they were free to move forward and boldly teach others about Jesus. I am so thankful that the Lord continues to work in us so that we can become free to be all that He calls us to be.

Heavenly Father,
When I read about the men and women of faith, I am inspired to be like them. Remove the obstacles in my life that keep me from walking in faith.
In Jesus' name, Amen

The Glory of God Most High

The heavens declare the glory of God;
the skies proclaim the work of his hands.
Psalm 19:1

Psalm 19 declares the glory of God, describing God as God Most High. He is above all creation: *In the heavens he has pitched a tent for the sun which is like a bridegroom coming from his pavilion. (v.4)* David describes the skies as proclaiming the work of God's hands. As Elohim God, He is the Creator. As El Elyon, He is God Most High.

El Elyon reveals His power throughout the Old Testament. We see the Red Sea part as the Israelites leave Egypt, their place of bondage. We see the Jordan River part as the people of God cross into the Promised Land. We see El Elyon in the fire with Shadrach, Meshach, and Abednego. We see El Elyon in the New Testament in the person of Jesus Christ, whose power has set us free from the curse of sin and death.

The heavens make a declaration glorifying God, and He is resident on earth through His Holy Spirit in the lives of believers. His desire is to be glorified as El Elyon in your life. When God's power is seen in the life of a believer, evidence of God Most High is seen.

Why is it that we do not always exercise the authority and power we have in Christ? The enemy has contended for our spiritual lives with his lies. One of the places he is at work is in causing God's children to feel powerless against the tide of this present evil age. But the Word of God has given us instructions on how to move in authority and power; we must agree with the Word of God planted in us: *Therefore get rid of all moral filth and the evil that is so prevalent and humbly accept the word planted in you which can save you. (James 1:21)* As believers, the Living Word is planted in us—He is El Elyon, God Most High, and as He lives in us, the glory of God will be seen.

Heavenly Father,
Draw me near to You. Open my eyes that I might see the power of God at work in me. Forgive me when I deny the life of El Elyon at work in and through me, and help me to declare the glory of God so that others might draw near to You.
In Jesus' name, Amen

July 6

Rebuilding Ancient Ruins

Your people will rebuild the ancient ruins and will raise up the age-old foundations; you will be called Repairer of Broken Walls, Restorer of Streets with Dwellings.
Isaiah 58:12

The Lord promised in *Isaiah 58* to satisfy His people in a sun-scorched land and to restore Jerusalem, His holy city. He is the Repairer of Broken Walls and Restorer of Streets with Dwellings. God promised to *loose the chains of injustice and set the oppressed free. (Isaiah 58:6)* When the Lord loosens our chains of oppression, He begins a work of rebuilding "our temple" into a dwelling place for Him. God came to redeem us from our sins and to restore the broken down places in our lives, revealing to us that He is both Savior and Redeemer.

Often we see the Lord as Savior alone, but He is also the Redeemer: *He has sent me to bind up the broken hearted; to proclaim freedom for the captives and release from darkness for the prisoners. (Isaiah 61)* Jesus declared that this passage described His mission on earth. (*Luke 4:15-21*) Jesus came not only to save but to redeem us from our places of darkness and oppression. Redeem means to "deem back"—to give back to us the places that the enemy has stolen. Children are most vulnerable, and at a young age the enemy tries to sew his seeds of destruction, seeking to block the development of our lives in Christ. He may sew seeds of jealousy, envy, unworthiness, and the like. Jesus Christ came to set us free from the seeds of destruction that the enemy has sewn. He saves us from our sin and delivers us from the lies.

God was known as the Repairer of Broken Walls, and through His Son Jesus Christ, He seeks to repair and restore our lives. Are you willing to allow Him to do some repair work? He stands waiting to begin.

Heavenly Father,

I am in need of repair. I can see the seeds of destruction in my life, and I desire for You to restore and rebuild those areas of my life. Thank you that You came to save me, deliver me, and make me whole.
In Jesus' name, Amen

July 7

First Assault: Weak Resources

The LORD turned to him and said, "Go in the strength you have and save Israel out of Midian's hand. Am I not sending you?"
Judges 6:14

The power of the Midianites was so oppressive that the Israelites hid in caves and shelters. The Midianites camped on their land, destroyed their crops, and killed their livestock. An angel then appeared to Gideon and told him to save Israel, calling Gideon a mighty warrior. Gideon, in total disbelief, told the angel, in essence, "Are you out of your mind? I am from the weakest clan and I am the least in my family." The Lord replied by telling him to go in the strength that he has, because He will be with him. God promised to be with him and to use him to defeat the Midianites. The enemy causes us to believe that we are weak. The Lord tells us that with Him we are mighty warriors.

King Sennacherib of Assyria also attempted to cause fear in the Israelites: "*On what are you basing this confidence of yours?*" he asks. *(Isaiah 36:4)* This is the question posed to us today as believers as well, and it would be wise for us to evaluate exactly in what or in whom we place our confidence. The field commander serving as spokesperson for King Sennacherib pointed out that they were depending on Egypt, a splintered reed. *(Isaiah 36:6)* Egypt was known for her resources, particularly her massive army and chariots of horses. If the people of Jerusalem had put their confidence in Egypt, they would have failed. But through the strong, godly leadership of their king, Hezekiah, they chose to believe that God would deliver them. It is an easy trap for us to fall into when we look at the meager or seemingly weak resources we have to defend ourselves against the assaults of the enemy; but we must remember, like Hezekiah and like Gideon, He will surely come and save us!

Where are you experiencing lack? Are you struggling financially or in your job? Or perhaps, like Gideon, God is asking you to do something that requires your complete dependency on Him.

Remember God's words to Gideon, *Go in the strength you have… am I not sending you? (Judges 6:14)*

Heavenly Father,
I confess that I have looked at what appears to be lack of resources when You have asked me to serve You: my fears, my lack of finances, my inadequacies. Today, I choose to believe Your Word that in You I am a mighty warrior, that You will strengthen me and provide what I need to accomplish what You have called me to do.
In Jesus' name, Amen

July 8

Understanding the Times

The Pharisees and Sadducees came to Jesus and tested him by asking him to show them a sign from heaven. He replied, "When evening comes, you say, 'It will be fair weather, for the sky is red,' and in the morning, 'Today it will be stormy, for the sky is red and overcast.' You know how to interpret the appearance of the sky, but you cannot interpret the signs of the times. A wicked and adulterous generation looks for a miraculous sign, but none will be given it except the sign of Jonah." Jesus then left them and went away.
Matthew 16:1-4

The Pharisees and Sadducees came to Jesus and demanded a sign from heaven. *(Matthew 16:1)* They were looking for more compelling proof of Jesus' divine authority. Jesus did not give them a sign and called them a *wicked and adulterous generation* who were looking for miraculous signs while not yet understanding how to interpret the signs of the kingdom of God that were at hand. Kingdom people have a revelation of the times, a revelation that comes from the Holy Spirit, who reveals truth. As kingdom people walking in an understanding of the times, we are able to offer hope and light to those who have not had Jesus and His truth revealed to them. Kingdom people understand the "spiritual climate" of the times and are able to walk in the assurance that God is always with them. The Pharisees demanded a sign. Kingdom people do not need a sign. God has poured out His love into kingdom hearts by the Holy Spirit *(Romans 5:5)* and as seasons of their lives and events in the world come and go, their hearts are able to continue trusting God.

Are you like the Pharisees demanding that God give you a sign? Have you been praying and hoping for something and your prayers have turned from trust to demanding a sign from God? After the resurrection, Jesus appeared to Thomas who had questioned his resurrection and told the Apostles that he would only believe it when he actually saw the nails in Jesus' hands: *Because you have seen me, you have believed; blessed are those who have not seen and yet have believed. (John 20:29)* So often we are like Thomas, demanding a sign, and yet

Heavenly Father,
Open up my eyes to see You at work. Enable me to believe before I see and to walk in the assurance that You are always at work.
In Jesus' name, Amen

July 9

Restoration of Israel

This is what the LORD says "In the time of my favor I will answer you, and in the day of salvation I will help you; I will keep you and will make you to be a covenant for the people, to restore the land and to reassign its desolate inheritances."
Isaiah 49:8

The Lord promises in this passage that He will restore the land of Israel and *reassign its desolate inheritances.* He promises to release the captives, those in darkness, and lead them beside springs of water. Throughout the book of *Isaiah,* we see God as the Sovereign Lord who loves His people, leading through judgment and the consequence of sin, into a place of restoration. What are the "desolate inheritances" in your life—the promises of God that seem empty or desolate in your life? Have you said, like Israel, ...*My way is hidden from the Lord; my cause is disregarded by my God? (Isaiah 40:27) Isaiah* gives us assurance that the Lord never grows tired and that He is always at work in our lives, saying *"The Lord is the everlasting God, the Creator of the ends of the earth. He will not grow tired or weary and His understanding no one can fathom."* *(Isaiah 40: 28)* Throughout *Isaiah*, we see God's faithfulness and restoration to His people. He will indeed restore the "desolate places" of our lives as well.

What in your life appears desolate, barren, or empty? Remember, the Lord promises that He has not disregarded you. He is keenly aware of your needs, and He is at work in restoring your land.

Heavenly Father,
Restore my confidence and trust that You have a great plan for my life. Where I see desolation and barrenness, where I have become disappointed in my plans that have failed, restore my hope in You.
In Jesus' name, Amen

Redirecting Our Faith

Yet the LORD longs to be gracious to you; he rises to show you compassion. For the LORD is a God of justice. Blessed are all who wait for him!
Isaiah 30:18

The Lord longs to be gracious and is full of compassion when He hears our cry for help. *(Isaiah 30:18)* I often find myself straying from the ways of the Lord. It gives me great comfort to know that He longs for me to cry out to Him so He can redirect my path. *Isaiah 28 and 29* describes the six "woes" that we all fall into that take us off course. The first "woe" is written to Ephraim, the northern kingdom of Israel. History tells us that the people of Samaria, the capital city, were given over to the love of fleshly pleasures. With each of the warnings, Isaiah shows a way of escape. The other "woes" were meaningless, empty, religious rituals, hidden evil deeds, rebellion, arrogance, and misplaced confidence. When we fall into any of these traps, *Isaiah* gives us comfort us by saying, *Whether you turn to the right or to the left, your ears will hear a voice behind you saying this is the way; walk in it. (Isaiah 30:21)*

Do you need direction in your life? Check out the six "woes" listed in *Isaiah 28* and *29*. Are you pursuing God or are you pursuing the world? Do you find yourself engaged in empty religious ritual, or are you growing more and more in love and in a relationship with Christ? The Lord longs to be gracious to you, and He is a just God. He seeks to direct your path. When you find yourself in need of direction, ask Him where you have gotten off track and He will show you the way.

Heavenly Father,
I have been struggling to find my way. I am in need of direction in my life. I invite the light of Christ to show me where I am off course and to give me the confidence that You are here.
In Jesus' name, Amen

July 11

Purpose of the Law

Therefore no one will be declared righteous in his sight by observing the law; rather, through the law we become conscious of sin.
Romans 3:20

The Jews thought if they observed the law, they would be righteous (made right by God). Paul explicitly tells them that righteousness *apart from the law* has been made known and that the Law and the Prophets had all testified about this. This righteousness from God comes through faith in Jesus Christ. He explains the purpose of the law is to point to sin, enabling people to see and deal with the sin in their lives. The law was never intended to make them righteous; the law was intended to point them *to* the Righteous One, Jesus Christ, who was the fulfillment of the law. (*Matthew 5:17*) He ends his discussion by reminding them that faith in Jesus Christ does not nullify the law; they are still called to uphold the law, understanding that the purpose of the law is only to point to their sin and to lead them into a living relationship with Jesus Christ.

As Christians, it is hard to understand the meaning of the word "law" as used in the first century church. The word "law" as Paul primarily used it is "nomos," which refers to Mosaic Law or more precisely, the Torah (the law given to Moses on Mount Sinai). Most often, Paul uses the word "law" in this sense, although on occasion he uses the word in a more general sense (the Pentateuch or the Old Testament as a whole). We use the word "law" in a variety of ways, ranging from governmental rule to the natural law of physics. To better understand Paul's argument concerning the law as written to first century Christians, we must be aware of the differences. In life application, as believers, we can find ourselves more interested in following the law than entering into a relationship with Jesus. Jesus put it this way in the gospel of John: *You diligently study the Scriptures because you think that by them you possess eternal life. These testify about me, yet you refuse to come to me to have life. (John 5:39-40)*

Heavenly Father,

Help me to remember that You desire to be in relationship with me. Forgive me where I have been more concerned with studying Your Word than with living Your Word. Forgive me where I have spent time searching for You rather than spending time with You.
In Jesus' name, Amen

July 12

Persistence

May they be brought to complete unity to let the world know that you sent me and have loved them even as you have loved me.
John 17:23

Jesus came to bring us eternal life and to make God known. His prayer was that His disciples would be unified in the same way that He and the Father were unified. He prayed that the same love that the father had for the son would also be in them. In the Old Testament, the prophets wanted to know God. In the New Testament, Jesus tells Phillip that the way to know God is to know Him. (*John 14:9*) In *Exodus 33:13-20*, Moses asked God to teach him His ways that he might know Him. He understood that when we observe someone's ways, we learn a lot about them. Think about your parents. As children we watch our parents and we learn to model their ways. I remember as a child, my parents modeled for me the value of persistence. My father's favorite quote by Calvin Coolidge is, "Nothing in the world can take the place of persistence; talent will not. Nothing is more common than unsuccessful people with talent…" As I observed my parents, they taught me the value of persistence by the way they lived their lives.

What about you? Do you want to know God? If so, observe His Son Jesus Christ. He has made His Father known to us by His actions on earth. He has sent His Holy Spirit to live in us to make Him known. Take the time today to seek to know Him and persist in being one with Jesus, as He and the Father are one.

Heavenly Father,
Give me persistence not to give up in my pursuit of Christ. Teach me His ways so that I might know Him. Enable me to not only observe His ways, but also empower me to live as Christ.
In Jesus' name, Amen

Warning Against Unbelief

So, as the Holy Spirit says: "Today, if you hear his voice, do not harden your hearts as you did in the rebellion, during the time of testing in the desert, where your fathers tested and tried me and for forty years saw what I did. That is why I was angry with that generation, and I said, 'Their hearts are always going astray, and they have not known my ways.' So I declared on oath in my anger, 'They shall never enter my rest.' " See to it, brothers, that none of you has a sinful, unbelieving heart that turns away from the living God. But encourage one another daily, as long as it is called today, so that none of you may be hardened by sin's deceitfulness. We have come to share in Christ if we hold firmly till the end the confidence we had at first. As has just been said: "Today, if you hear his voice, do not harden your hearts as you did in the rebellion." Who were they who heard and rebelled? Were they not all those Moses led out of Egypt? And with whom was he angry for forty years? Was it not with those who sinned, whose bodies fell in the desert? And to whom did God swear that they would never enter his rest if not to those who disobeyed? So we see that they were not able to enter, because of their unbelief.

Hebrews 3:7-5:19

God requires His people to exercise persistent faith, relying on His power to change them and keep them. In *Hebrews 3,* the author describes the disobedience of the Israelites in the wilderness who forgot God's promises and hardened their hearts. The faith of the Israelites was tested in the desert and they failed the test. They grumbled and complained that God had led them into the wilderness. They looked back to Egypt, longing to return. God had told them that their inheritance was the Promised Land and that He would take them there, but their unbelief disqualified a whole generation from entering. In this passage in *Hebrews*, the writer warns the Jewish Christians, to whom this epistle is written, not to harden their hearts as their ancestors had.

This message is still relevant for us today. Has unbelief, doubt, and disobedience hardened your heart? As you wait on God to fulfill your dreams and to fulfill His promises to you, be sure to have a spiritual heart check-up to see if the promise is left unfilled because of your unbelief. The Israelites complained even though God had promised to bring them into the Promised Land. Are you complaining as you wait? Ask the Lord to reveal to you the source of your impatience and seek to trust His Word.

Heavenly Father,
Forgive my unbelief. I have been waiting so long for a promise to be fulfilled. I have begun to complain and lose hope in my dream being fulfilled. Grow patience and trust in me and lead and strengthen me as I place my hope in You.
In Jesus' name, Amen

God Chooses His Leaders

Invite Jesse to the sacrifice, and I will show you what to do.
You are to anoint for me the one I indicate.
I Samuel 16:2-3

The Lord told Samuel the prophet that He would show him who He had called to be the next king of Israel. We see that God calls and anoints individuals for leadership. The Lord told Samuel that He had rejected Saul as the king over Israel. *(I Samuel 16:1)* He then told Samuel to fill his horn with oil and to go to Jesse of Bethlehem because He had chosen one of Jesse's sons to be king. Samuel asked the Lord how he would know which son the Lord had chosen. The Lord said, "*Take a heifer with you and say, 'I have come to sacrifice to the Lord.' Invite Jesse to the sacrifice, and I will show you what to do. You are to anoint for Me the one I indicate." (I Samuel 16:3)*

Has the Lord ever told you to do something without giving you all of the details? Has he told you to "go," maybe even told you where to go, but other than that you have no idea? I don't know about you, but I would prefer instructions, a road map, and all details pertaining to my assignment! But the Lord was giving Samuel the opportunity to exercise his faith and trust in his sovereign God. So it is with us when the Lord calls us and tells us to trust Him. God calls leaders who are men and women after His own heart, and who are willing to go wherever He sends them and trust Him with the details.

Heavenly Father,
Grant me the courage to follow You and trust that where You send me, You will equip me. Anoint me with Your Holy Spirit to do what You have called me to do.
In Jesus' name, Amen

July 15

Purposeful Witnesses

And I will ask the Father, and he will give you another
Counselor to be with you forever – the Spirit of truth.
John 14:16-17

Webster's dictionary defines "purpose" as intention or determination. To be purposeful is to be intentional or deliberate in accomplishing something. Over the past few years, much has been written on being purposeful. All of the writings have had one thing in common: to accomplish something, you have to give it thought, set a goal, and then purpose to do it. It doesn't do any good to have a plan if you aren't intentional about carrying it out. So it is with being a witness for Christ. The Holy Spirit will guide us in what to say, whom to say it to, and how to say it, but we must take the initiative and be obedient.

As citizens of the kingdom of God, we are called to be witnesses of the love of Christ. We must be determined to trust the Holy Spirit to direct us to persons who need Him and be purposeful to share the good news. We do not want to look back on our lives and realize that although the Lord's blessings were bountiful to us, we can hardly remember leading anyone to Christ. I try to remember at the beginning of each day to pray for divine appointments—to pray for God to send people into my life who need to know Christ. It is amazing the opportunities He brings! Being intentional allows us to open our eyes and hearts to see God at work and to participate with His plan.

Jesus promised to send His Holy Spirit to lead us, and when we call on Him, He will direct our path.

Heavenly Father,
Help me to be an intentional witness for You. Lead and empower me by Your Holy Spirit to be deliberate in following You.
In Jesus' name, Amen

Restoring Worship

Now King David was told, "The LORD has blessed the household of Obed-Edom and everything he has, because of the ark of God." So David went down and brought up the ark of God from the house of Obed-Edom to the City of David with rejoicing.
II Samuel 6:12

The Ark of the Lord's covenant, which symbolized the Presence of God, was captured by the Philistines. *(I Samuel 4)* The Philistines carried the Ark into Dagon's temple and set it down. Dagon was the principle god of the Philistines and was worshipped throughout the ancient world. The next day, Dagon was found facedown on the ground, head and hands broken off. The Philistines decided they had angered the God of Israel by bringing the Ark into Dagon's temple. They moved the Ark from place to place, yet the disasters continued. Then the Philistines returned the Ark to Abinadab's house. It remained there until David brought it to Jerusalem. King David knew that the Presence of the Lord embodied by the Ark needed to be with the Israelites. He knew it was time to restore worship in God's people. David's plan to restore worship was to build a temple to house the Ark. However, God had told him that he would not be the one to build this temple. David's son Solomon would build it. David did, however, begin the plans for building the temple by securing the funds and the materials to start the work.

We must also continuously restore worship in our lives. It is easy to get caught up with worshipping other things: family, friends, our homes, or our jobs. Throughout the Scriptures, the Lord has reminded His people to return to Him in worship when they stray. Are you willing to do that?

Heavenly Father,
Restore worship in my life so that I can know Your Presence again. I have been so caught up in doing things for You that I have forgotten to worship You. I feel empty and dry and know that only in You will I find refreshment for my thirsty soul.
In Jesus' name, Amen

July 17

Bold Prayer

For the eyes of the Lord are on the righteous and his ears are attentive to their prayer, but the face of the Lord is against those who do evil.
I Peter 3:12

One of my favorite Scriptures is *Matthew 11:12*: *...the kingdom of heaven has been forcefully advancing, and forceful men lay hold of it.* One aspect of advancing the kingdom of God is by boldly laying hold of the promises of God through prayer. As believers we are called to be bold in prayer, to use prayer as one of the keys of the kingdom, and to believe that the gates of hell cannot prevail against it. *(Matthew 16:17-19)* I used to think of prayer only as something that I was supposed to do to communicate with God, but throughout the years I have learned that prayer is working alongside the Lord to bring *His kingdom* and *His will* to earth! What an awesome responsibility we have to advance His kingdom here on earth through prayer. When we pray the Lord's Prayer, we often do it by rote, but when we really ponder the words that we are saying, they are powerful indeed. *Thy Kingdom come, thy will be done, on earth as it is in heaven.* We must be bold and diligent to go before the Lord in prayer and work towards the advancement of His kingdom here on earth! When we pray for God's will to be done, we are asking for heaven to invade earth; we are asking for God to send the resources of heaven into our families, our workplace, our relationships.

The eyes of God are on the righteous and He hears our prayers. As we grow in our relationship with Christ, we begin to realize that although He already knows what is in our hearts, prayer is the tool that draws us into a closer relationship with Him. Although He knows what we desire in prayer, He longs to communicate with us. Prayer, like communication, is a two-way conversation. The next time you pray, wait and listen to the Lord. He longs to communicate with you, too.

Heavenly Father,

Thank you for the gift of communication through prayer. Thank you for the gift of Your Son, Jesus Christ, who has made a way for me to approach Your throne room. Help me to remember to listen as You communicate Your heart to me.
In Jesus' name, Amen

July 18

Seated in Heavenly Places

In the past God spoke to our ancestors through the prophets at many times and in various ways, but in these last days he has spoken to us by his Son, whom he appointed heir of all things, and through whom also he made the universe. The Son is the radiance of God's glory and the exact representation of his being, sustaining all things by his powerful word. After he had provided purification for sins, he sat down at the right hand of the Majesty in heaven.
Hebrews 1:1-3

Jesus was appointed heir of all things and is now seated at the right hand of God. Paul writes in *Ephesians*, "*I pray that the eyes of your heart may be enlightened in order that you may know the hope to which he has called you, the riches of his glorious inheritance in the saints and His incomparably great power for us who believe. That power is like the working of His mighty strength which he exerted in Christ when he raised him from the dead and seated him at his right hand…" (Ephesians 1:18-20)* Jesus is seated at the right hand of God, and God has raised us up with Christ and seated us with Him in the heavenly realms. (*Ephesians 2:6*) The implications of being seated with Christ are too wonderful to comprehend! In Christ, we are positioned in heavenly places and we live our lives from that position. Think about that for a moment. You are here on earth, but spiritually speaking, in Christ, you have access to heavenly resources! Our lives should be radically influenced by the knowledge that we are positioned to have influence for Christ in everything we do.

When you struggle in your job, when you deal with your difficult teenager, in whatever you face, you face it from a heavenly position with Christ! He is interceding for you, and He is reminding you that in Him you have position of influence. Why do we struggle with circumstances of life and find ourselves without hope? Because we have forgotten that in Christ, we have access to the very throne room of God! Jesus sits at the right hand of the Father and He sees our struggles; He endures our struggles and He delivers us from our troubles! The next time you feel hopeless and powerless over circumstances in life, look up and remember that you are seated with the King of Kings!

Heavenly Father,
Help me to remember that I am seated with Christ in the heavenly realms. Help me not to live under my circumstances, but overcome my circumstances as I live in the place to which You have called me.
In Jesus' name, Amen

July 19

God Works for Good

And we know that in all things God works for the good of those who love him, who have been called according to his purpose.
Romans 8:28

I believe there is no passage of Scripture that has been more comforting for believers during trials than *Romans 8:28*. The verdict is out. We live in a world of tension between good and evil, suffering, and God's glory yet to be revealed. Paul reassures Christians that God is in control, that He will work all things out for good for those who have been called according to His purpose.
Believers have a purpose to love the Lord with all our hearts, souls, minds, and strength, and to love our neighbor as ourselves. Loving the Lord completely does not mean we will not experience trouble, but it does mean that the Lord will take those things in our lives, those "sandpaper" experiences, and turn them into smooth places. He will use those experiences to make us more like Him and to comfort others with the comfort that we have received. (*II Corinthians 7:5-7*) Christians throughout the centuries have been comforted, not only by receiving comfort from God during difficult times, but also by having the privilege of comforting others when they need it, just as they, themselves, were comforted. God does not will all things, but He is at work in all things. I know if I keep my eyes on the One who loves me, I will be strengthened, not just to "endure," but to live victoriously.

Heavenly Father,
Thank you that I have been called for a purpose and that my momentary affliction will be used for good. Help me to keep my eyes on You and remember that Your purpose will prevail.
In Jesus' name, Amen

A Call to Persevere

Therefore, brothers, since we have confidence to enter the Most Holy Place by the blood of Jesus, by a new and living way opened for us through the curtain, that is, his body, and since we have a great priest over the house of God, let us draw near to God with a sincere heart in full assurance of faith, having our hearts sprinkled to cleanse us from a guilty conscience and having our bodies washed with pure water. Let us hold unswervingly to the hope we profess, for he who promised is faithful. And let us consider how we may spur one another on toward love and good deeds.
Hebrews 10:19-24

The word "therefore" in *Hebrews 10:19* refers to the sacrifice Jesus made for our sins once and for all. We should, therefore, have confidence to enter the Most Holy Place. The tabernacle, and later the temple, had three parts: the outer court, the Holy Place, and the Most Holy Place. The Gentiles were allowed in the outer court, the priests (Levites) served in the Holy Place, and only the High Priest was allowed to enter the Most Holy Place. When Jesus died, the veil that separated the Holy Place from the Most Holy Place was torn in two, representing the access we now have into the very Presence of God. The writer of *Hebrews* tells us that now we can draw near because Jesus' blood has cleansed us from sin. As we hold onto this hope, we know that He is faithful, and, out of grateful hearts, we will be able to encourage our brothers and sisters in Christ.

Are you discouraged? Do you know someone who is discouraged? Remember that our High Priest, Jesus Christ, has given us access to His loving Father. Draw near to Him with confidence and He will restore your hope.

Heavenly Father,
As I draw near to You, I am grateful that I need never be alone; I need never fear. Thank you for opening the way so that can be near You.
In Jesus' name, Amen

July 21

Pulling Down Strongholds

Now when Joshua was near Jericho, he looked up and saw a man standing in front of him with a drawn sword in his hand. Joshua went up to him and asked, "Are you for us or for our enemies?" "Neither," he replied, "but as commander of the army of the LORD I have now come." Then Joshua fell facedown to the ground in reverence, and asked him, "What message does my Lord have for his servant?"

Joshua 5:13-14

Joshua was near Jericho, perhaps contemplating a strategy to take down the stronghold. According to Scripture, he saw a man with his sword drawn. Once the man identified himself, Joshua fell facedown on the ground. At the point when Joshua recognized the *Commander of the army of the Lord*, he relinquished his "good ideas" and strategies to take Jericho and submitted to God's. (*v.14*)

Although Joshua may have thought God's plan was a foolish way to conquer Jericho, he followed the Lord's instruction to march around the city for six days with all the armed men. On the seventh day, he was told to march around the city seven times. Then, when the priests blew the trumpets, the people were told to shout and the walls of the city would fall. God's plans may seem foolish or impossible according to our human reasoning, but His plans always work.

What about you? Are you facing strongholds—fortified places in your life where the enemy has held you captive? Are you like Joshua, contemplating a strategy to take down the stronghold? The Lord is standing by with His sword drawn and *His* plan to deliver you. Seek *His* plan and you will have success. It may seem like an impossible task, but He is the Deliverer and He came to set the captives free.

Heavenly Father,
I have been in bondage to (name the stronghold) for years. I have tried over and over again set myself free, and I realize that this is a God-sized task. I surrender to Your plans and trust You to give me Your plan of deliverance.
In Jesus' name, Amen

Taking Our Thoughts Captive

For though we live in the world, we do not wage war as the world does. The weapons we fight with are not the weapons of this world. On the contrary, they have divine power to demolish strongholds. We demolish arguments and every pretension that sets itself up against the knowledge of God, and we take captive every thought to make it obedient to Christ.
2 Corinthians 10:3-5

Strongholds begin in our thoughts. Rather than agreeing with the truth of God's Word, we believe lies and the enemy prowls around seeking to use those lies against us. He distorts the truth and plants seeds of destruction in our thoughts, and eventually a stronghold develops in our mind. Paul addresses the battlefield of our minds and tells us to take our thoughts captive, making them obedient to Christ. The enemy doesn't play fair. He knows if he can get us to agree with his lies, then we are on our way to deception and he can get us to act on our deceived thoughts. Though we live in the world, we do not wage war as the world does. Our weapons are prayer, the Word of God, and the power of His Holy Spirit. These spiritual weapons have the power to demolish strongholds. What must be demolished is any argument, any pretension in our lives that has set itself up against God.

What arguments have you entertained that have persuaded you to turn from God? What pretensions have drawn you from a relationship with Him? God's Word tells us to check out our "thought life" and seek to have the mind of Christ. Be willing to allow the Holy Spirit to examine your thoughts and line them up with God's Word.

Heavenly Father,
My mind has been filled with things that have drawn me away from You. I take my thoughts captive and ask that You give me the mind of Christ. Pull down the strongholds in my mind, so that I might walk in Your will.
In Jesus' name, Amen

July 23

God's Grace Gifts

We have different gifts, according to the grace given us. If a man's gift is prophesying, let him use it in proportion to his faith. If it is serving, let him serve; it if is teaching, let him teach; if it is encouraging, let him encourage; if it is contributing to the needs of others, let him give generously; if it is leadership, let him govern diligently; if it is showing mercy, let him do it cheerfully.

Romans 12:6-8

Paul tells the Christian community that by God's grace we have each been given spiritual gifts to use, serving each other for the glory of God. He describes our mutual dependence on one another and the importance of exercising these gifts with a spirit of humility. Unity in diversity is the theme that runs throughout this passage. As the body of Christ, each part functions differently, supplying the body with what the other parts lack and promoting the common good. When we, as the body of Christ, effectively and with humility operate in our God given gifts, we become a kingdom united, not divided. Jesus tells us that *a kingdom divided cannot stand.* (*Mark 3:24*) No wonder the enemy tries to get a foothold in churches, seeking to divide the body through pride, through competition, and any other means he can use to keep the body from functioning as God intended—in unity and in power. We would be wise to pray for one another, encouraging one another in the gifts that God has given us to be used for His glory!

What gifts has the Lord given you to use to build up the body of Christ? If you are unsure of your gifts, consider the things that you like to do—the things that you are good at and the things at which others say you are good. Pray for opportunities to use your gifts and encourage others in their gifts. Paul tells the Corinthian church to eagerly desire spiritual gifts—that we are one body with different parts. (*I Corinthians 12*) Each part of the body has a function, and without it, the whole body would suffer. As members of Christ's body, let us freely offer our gifts back to the Lord!

Heavenly Father,
I have neglected the gifts You have given me. I offer myself to You as a living sacrifice, using the gifts You have given me for Your glory.
In Jesus' name, Amen

July 24

His Presence Goes Before Us

And the Lord said, I will cause all my goodness to pass in front of you, and I will proclaim my name, the Lord in your presence. I will have mercy on whom I will have mercy, and I will have compassion on whom I will have compassion.
Exodus 33:19

Moses asked the Lord whom he was sending with him to lead the Israelites out of Egypt. He also asked the Lord to teach him His ways so that he would know Him and find favor with Him. The Lord replied that His Presence would go with Moses. I always chuckle when I read the next line in the Scriptures where Moses seemingly didn't hear God say He was going with him or was so busy worrying about who would go with him that he didn't get it: *Then Moses said to him: If Your Presence does not go with us, do not send us from here. (v.15)* We are like that, aren't we? God speaks to us and we are either not listening or are so busy thinking about the next thing we will say that we don't hear His comforting words. God was saying to Moses "listen up, I am going with you—don't worry." Moses just rambles on, asking God "how will your people know that You are pleased with me unless You go with us?" For goodness sake, Moses! God *already* said He was going with you. Moses was anxious to have God with him when he attempted to follow God's call, and he was right to ask God to be with him. But he didn't hear God's response. The Lord, infinitely patient, said to Moses: *I will do the very thing you have asked because I am pleased with you and I know you by name. (v.17)*

Do you believe that God knows you by name? Do you believe that He hears your prayers and desires to answer them? He is delighted with our prayers as we commune with Him, and He responds to us because He knows us by name. He is so patient, even as we refuse to listen to Him answering our prayers; He is watching, listening to our rambling on and on, knowing that if we will settle down and just *listen,* His Presence will go with us. The next time you pray, take time to listen to God. He is waiting for us to listen, and His Presence will go with us.

Heavenly Father,

Thank you that You are always here—waiting, listening and responding to my prayers. Thank you that Your Presence goes before me as I seek to follow Your call.
In Jesus' name, Amen

July 25

Temporary, False Peace

You will keep in perfect peace him whose mind is steadfast, because he trusts in you.Isaiah 26:3

Any peace that we have apart from God's peace is temporary and fleeting. God's peace is dependent on our trusting in Him alone: *You will keep in perfect peace him whose mind is steadfast, because he trusts in you. (Isaiah 26:3)* If our mind is fixed steadfastly on God, then peace will follow. Trusting God helps to keep our minds steadfast and our hearts at peace.

The commander of the Assyrian army told the people of Jerusalem not to listen to their king, Hezekiah, who told them to place their trust in the Lord. *Do not listen to Hezekiah. This is what the king of Assyria says: Make peace with me and come out to me. Then every one of you will eat from his own vine and fig tree (symbols of security and prosperity) and drink water from his own cistern. (Isaiah 36:16)* The Assyrian commander was offering the people a false sense of peace and security by painting a picture for them of prosperity if they would make peace with him. He was their avowed enemy. The enemy tries to lure us into a false sense of peace and security by having us compromise what we believe in and turn from trusting in God. When we feel threatened by an assault, it is easy to seek a solution apart from God. King Hezekiah sent word to Isaiah to pray for the remnant that still survived. We too must remember to turn to the Lord and cry out to Him to save us in the midst of assaults.

Do you find security from trusting in God alone, or are you under assault to trust in something or someone else? Are you tempted to trust in your own resources, friends, anything or anyone other than God? Take a moment to meditate on where you find security and turn to God, seeking to trust Him. He will keep you in perfect peace as you find your security in Him.

Heavenly Father,
You alone are my source of peace and security. Help me to trust You in all things and to turn from any place of false security.
In Jesus' name, Amen

Our Burning Bush

Now Moses was tending the flock of Jethro his father-in-law, the priest of Midian, and he led the flock to the far side of the desert and came to Horeb, the mountain of God. There the angel of the Lord appeared to him in flames of fire from within a bush. Moses saw that though the bush was on fire it did not burn up. So Moses thought, "I will go over and see this strange sight—why the bush does not burn up.
Exodus 3:1-3

Moses was in the middle of doing what he always did—tending the sheep. An ordinary, everyday task was suddenly interrupted by the extraordinary! He sees that the bush was on fire, but it was not burning up. When he went over to the bush to see what it was, the Lord called out to him. God told Moses not to get too close. Was He concerned that Moses might be burned? No, He told Moses that this was a holy place, holy ground, and that he must remove his sandals. I have often wondered what the sandals represent. Perhaps the sandals represent all the places where our feet have tread—all the places where our shoes have gotten dirty and the filth of the world has soiled our lives. In order to stand in front of a holy God, they have to be removed. Or perhaps the sandals represent our humanity—our sin that cannot stand before a holy God. We do not know for certain, but we do know that Moses obeyed and hid his face because He knew that this was a sacred place. Moses was then commissioned by God to lead the Israelites out of Egypt and He promised that he would go with him.

What burning bush experiences have you had? Times when you knew that you were facing a holy God and you trembled in fear? God's Presence is not to be taken lightly; He is a holy God who is seeking to make us holy. What are the sandals in your life that God is asking you to remove that keep you from holiness? What is the burning bush that you face knowing that God is summoning you to follow His call? Just as He told Moses, God promises to go with you: *And God said, "I will be with you." (v.12)* Are you willing to take off your sandals and follow?

Heavenly Father,
I have seen You in the burning bush experiences of my life but have been too afraid to respond and unwilling to count the cost, unwilling to remove my sandals. Forgive me, Lord, for desiring to hold on to the things that keep me from responding to Your call. I choose today to respond to Your call.
In Jesus' name, Amen

Driving Out the Nations

When the Lord your God brings you into the land you are entering to possess and drives out before you many nations—the Hittites, Girgashites, Amorites, Canaanites, Perizzites, Hiites and Jebusites, seven nations larger and stronger than you—and when the Lord your God has delivered them over to you and you have defeated them, then you must destroy them totally. Make no treaty with them and show them no mercy.
Deuteronomy 7:1-2

God promised the Israelites that He would drive out seven nations larger than them so that they could possess the Promised Land. He told them that they must destroy the nations completely—no compromises. The "ite" nations listed in the passage above would bring destruction on the nation of Israel if they were to mingle with them. These were pagan nations and God was warning His people not to have mercy on them but to obliterate them. That sounds harsh, but God knew that if they did not obey, the idolatry of the nations they defeated would creep into their lives.

God has delivered us from those things in us which are opposed to Him. Through His Son, Jesus Christ, He has delivered us from sin and brought us into the Promised Land of eternal life. He has told us to rid ourselves of every evil thing: *Put to death therefore, whatever belongs to your earthly nature; sexual immorality, impurity, lust, evil desires and greed, which is idolatry. (Colossians 3:5)* God is calling us to rid ourselves of the "ites" in our life—no compromises. He desires that we destroy them and have no mercy on the things in our life that separate us from Him.

What "ites" have you made treaty with? God says that we are to show them no mercy. God has given you the land to possess, but you must dispossess those things in the land that will cause you to compromise. He told the Israelites: *Break down their altars, smash their sacred stones, cut down their Asherah poles and burn their idols in the fire. For you are a people holy to the Lord your God. (v.5)* This passage sounds radical! But He desires that nothing stand in the way of our relationship with Him.

Heavenly Father,
As I enter the Promised Land, help me to destroy those things in my life that I still cling to. Forgive me where I have compromised wanting some of You in my life and other things as well. I commit this day to rid myself of anything that stands in the way of my life in You.
In Jesus' name, Amen

Looking Back

Look to the LORD and his strength; seek his face always. Remember the wonders he has done, his miracles, and the judgments he pronounced. I Chronicles 16:11-12

In this passage in *I Chronicles*, we are admonished to look to the Lord and His strength and to remember all that He has done. As we remember the faithfulness of God, we are strengthened in our faith. Healing takes place when we look back and see the faithfulness of God. God encourages people to look back at the rock from which they were hewn. *(Isaiah 51:1-2)* Israel was told to look back to Abraham and examine his faith. They could see that the Lord was true to His promises to bring forth the nation of Israel from Abraham's seed. When we read the story of Abraham and God's faithfulness to him our own faith increases: *By faith, Abraham, even though he was past age and Sarah herself was barren was enabled to become a father because he considered him faithful who had made the promise. (Hebrews 11:11)* Abraham was fully persuaded that God would fulfill His promise to him to have children that would one day become the nation of Israel. As we remember the wonders of the faithfulness of God, our faith grows.

Paul reminded the Corinthian church that they were once adulterers, idolaters, and thieves, but now they were washed, sanctified, and justified as believers in Jesus Christ. *(I Corinthians 6:9-11)* When you are discouraged, look back at all the wonders God has worked in your life and those around you. You may not be where you want to be, but when you look back at where you were in your early walk with the Lord and see how He has changed you, hope increases. Look to the Lord and His strength and remember what He has done. (*I Chronicles 16:11-12*)

Heavenly Father,
Help me to recall all that You have done for me. Let me be ever mindful of Your faithfulness, and when I am discouraged, help me to draw from the past where You have been my rock and have been so faithful.
In Jesus' name, Amen

July 29

Our Inheritance

LORD, you have assigned me my portion and my cup;
you have made my lot secure. The boundary lines have fallen
for me in pleasant places; surely I have a delightful inheritance.
Psalm 16:5-6

In Scripture, we often see actual events, both natural and historical, that point to spiritual truths. In the Old Testament, we see God fulfilling His promise to Abraham to form the nation of Israel. He guided them to the Promised Land which was their inheritance. As a part of the inheritance which God promised Abraham, a new society was established that contrasted greatly with the existing Canaanite society. New boundaries were established as the land was parceled out to the tribes. The tribes had the responsibility to share the land for the benefit of all of the people.

In our spiritual lives, the Lord is our inheritance. The Lord continues to draw us to Himself with *cords of love.* The Holy Spirit is establishing in us the Lord's boundaries in our spiritual land. He is always increasing our spiritual borders so that we can experience more of Him.

Have your boundary lines fallen in pleasant places? Are you increasingly aware of the Lord's Presence in your life? He desires to give you a spiritual inheritance that is the gift of salvation. As He has His way in your life, His boundaries extend to take in more and more of it. Surrendering to Him enables this expansion.

Heavenly Father,
I surrender to You today. Expand my borders to include more of You and less of me. You must increase and I must decrease.
In Jesus' name, Amen

Unbelief

See to it, brothers, that none of you has a sinful, unbelieving heart that turns away from the living God. But encourage one another daily, as long as it is called today, so that none of you may be hardened by sin's deceitfulness. We have come to share in Christ if we hold firmly till the end the confidence we had at first. As has just been said: "Today, if you hear his voice, do not harden your hearts as you did in the rebellion." Who were they who heard and rebelled? Were they not all those Moses led out of Egypt? And with whom was he angry for forty years? Was it not with those who sinned, whose bodies fell in the desert? And to whom did God swear that they would never enter his rest if not to those who disobeyed? So we see that they were not able to enter, because of their unbelief.
Hebrews 3:12-19

In *Hebrews 3:12-13*, the writer warns believers in Christ not to have an unbelieving heart that turns away from the living God. He advises them to *encourage one another daily…so that none of you may be hardened by sin's deceitfulness.(v.13)* This Scripture makes us aware of the importance of Christian fellowship when we are tempted not to believe God's promises or when we are tempted to sin. The writer then recounts the story of the Israelites who were led out of captivity from Egypt and who wandered in the wilderness for 40 years due to their unbelief. Because of their unbelief, they were unable to enter the Promised Land! We too can have hearts hardened by unbelief. Although it may be subtle, we may have bought into a secular worldview without being aware of it. When our hearts are hardened, it prevents us from fully entering into the promises of God. Peter exhorted his readers: *Clothe yourselves with humility toward one another...humble yourselves, therefore, under God's mighty hand, that He may lift you up in due time*". *(I Peter 5:5-6)* If we are willing to follow God's Word, He will keep us from hardening our hearts and from falling into unbelief.

Christian fellowship encourages us in our faith. When we share the stories of God's intervention in our lives with one another, this encourages and builds up our faith as a body. Perhaps if the Israelites had spent their time in community with one another, sharing stories about how God had faithfully led them out of Egypt, parted the Red Sea, and provided them with food and drink, they might not have fallen into unbelief. Instead, they grumbled and complained, forgetting what God had done for them and falling into unbelief.

Do you have Christian friends who encourage you daily in your walk with Christ? If you don't, ask the Lord to connect you with people who will build up your faith, reminding you of the goodness and faithfulness of the Lord.

Heavenly Father,
Forgive me for my unbelief. The voices of the world have been drowning out Your voice—the voice of truth. I pray that You will send me fellow travelers on this journey with You to encourage and build my faith.
In Jesus' name, Amen

The Dawning Light

The Lord is my light and my salvation – whom shall I fear?
The Lord is the stronghold of my life – of whom shall I be afraid?
Psalm 27:1

The people of Isaiah's time walked in darkness, just as many people today walk in darkness. Jesus Christ, the Messiah, came as prophesied in *Isaiah* bringing a "great light" into the world: *The people walking in darkness have seen a great light, on those living in the land of the shadow of death a light has dawned. (Isaiah 9:2)* This great light provides a hope for all mankind. The prophecies in *Isaiah* describe and point to the light of hope for all those in darkness. *Psalm 27,* written by King David, describes the Lord as light and salvation and the stronghold of his life. His light breaks through the darkness and overtakes his fear. This psalm is a confident prayer to God to deliver him from his enemies, saying, *Though an army besiege, me my heart will not fear. (Psalm 27:3)* David knew that the one place where he would be safe was in the light of God—a place where his enemies had to flee. He knew that God would keep him in a safe dwelling place, hiding him in the shelter of his tabernacle. He ends the Psalm with a great statement of confidence that he is certain that he will see the goodness of God in the land of the living. He must wait for the Lord and be strong. (*vv.13-14*)

God is at work in us as we go about our daily routine of life. He is our light and our salvation which enables us to not have fear. God is with us as we seek His help in times of struggle; God is with us as we seek His direction. Immanuel, "God with us," lights our path when the road seems dark.

What are you facing today that makes you fearful? Remember that when your enemies besiege you, God will make them stumble and fall in the darkness. God will light up your path and you will find your way.

Heavenly Father,

You are my light and my salvation; whom shall I fear? You are the stronghold of my life, of whom shall I be afraid? You light my path when I fall into darkness. Blessed be the name of the Lord!
In Jesus' name, Amen

Redirecting Our Faith

The righteous cry out, and the Lord hears them; he delivers them from all their troubles. The Lord is close to the brokenhearted and saves those who are crushed in spirit.
Psalm 34:17-18

The Lord hears the prayers of the righteous, those who are in relationship with Jesus Christ and cry out for help. He is close to the brokenhearted and saves those who are crushed in spirit. Jesus Christ came to save the lost, to set the captives free, and to bind up the broken hearted: *He has sent me to bind up the brokenhearted; to proclaim freedom for the captives and release from darkness for the prisoners. (Isaiah 60:1)* This was and is the mission statement of Jesus. He came to set us free from sin and to mend our broken hearts. The world, the enemy, and sometimes we, ourselves, wreak havoc on our hearts. We protect our hearts from hurt and endlessly build fortresses of protection to ensure that our hearts will be safe. Our hearts are the seat of our emotions, the wellspring of life in us that is vulnerable to heartbreak. King David, pursued by Saul and by his enemies, understood his need for God to save those who are crushed in spirit. He spent years on the run and suffered at the hand of those who were jealous and determined to break him. Yet the Lord delivered him from his enemies and mended his broken heart. He knew heartbreak firsthand when his own son, Absolom, led a rebellion against him.

Are you crushed in spirit? Is your heart suffering from heartache? David remembered that when the righteous cry out, the Lord hears them. He knew this firsthand because it was God who heard his cries and mended his broken heart. The Lord is waiting for you to cry out to Him. His promise is as true today as it was in David's time. He will protect, renew, and restore your life and you will be like King David and proclaim: *My tongue will speak of your righteousness and of your praises all day long. (v.28)*

Heavenly Father,

My heart is broken and my spirit crushed. I am heavy with the weight of disappointment and I cry out to You. You have promised that You are near to the brokenhearted. Draw near to me, Lord, in my time of pain.
In Jesus' name, Amen

Compelled by the Spirit

And now, compelled by the Spirit, I am going to Jerusalem, not knowing what will happen to me there. I only know that in every city the Holy Spirit warns me that prison and hardships are facing me. However, I consider my life worth nothing to me, if only I may finish the race and complete the task the Lord Jesus has given me—the task of testifying to the gospel of God's grace.
Acts 20:22-24

The word compelled means "constrained as through a channel." As we study God's Word and experience God's love, we grow in our desire to serve Him. Little by little, as we are transformed into His image, we increasingly desire to follow Christ wherever He takes us. I remember when the Lord began to stir in my heart to start the ministry of *Drawing Near to God*, I was fearful to step out in faith, but my love for Christ and desire to be obedient compelled me to follow His leading. Often God leads us to do things where we are stretched because then HIS power can be demonstrated through us. It is the sense of the "compelling" of the Spirit that drives us to move forward. In *Acts 20:22-24,* Paul was compelled by the Spirit to go to Jerusalem not knowing what he would face. Paul's life was so completely surrendered to God's will that his only goal was to complete the task the Lord gave him.

Have you ever been compelled by the Spirit to follow wherever God leads? Disobedience was not an option because you were constrained to follow. There have been times in my life when my friends did not understand my call to follow Christ, times when I have been misunderstood, and times when I have had to give up things that I liked to do in order to follow Christ. Paul considered his life nothing if only he could finish the task that the Lord had given him to complete.

Like Paul, when we are compelled by the Spirit to do something, we need to obey whatever it is that God is calling us to do. His grace is sufficient to lead and direct us as we follow the call. Fear may try and disrupt God's plans, but the compelling leadership of the Holy Spirit will continue to keep you in His constraining love and power as you seek to obey. What is God calling you to do today? Are you willing to obey?

Heavenly Father,
For some time now I have been sensing that You have been calling me to do something (fill in the blank). I have been disobedient, and yet Your Holy Spirit continues to draw me into obedience. Today I choose to follow, and, like Paul, I pray for Your grace to accomplish Your will.
In Jesus' name, Amen

Defeat Turned Into Victory

For all have sinned and fall short of the glory of God, and are justified freely by his grace through the redemption that came by Christ Jesus.

Romans 3:23-24

We have all sinned. Our fallen nature causes us to continue to sin, and, like Paul, we are frustrated by doing what we don't want to do. *I do not understand what I do. For what I want to do I do not do, but what I hate I do. (Romans 7:15)* Paul recognized that there was a battle going on in his life between what he knew was right and what was wrong—a battle between his sinful nature and the nature of Christ at work in Him. He recognized that he was powerless to live a blameless life and that only Jesus Christ could save him. *What a wretched man I am! Who will rescue me from this body of death? Thanks be to God—through Jesus Christ our Lord! (Romans 7:24)*

Do you ever feel as though you do things that you don't want to do? Paul's struggle is our struggle as our flesh nature contends with the Holy Spirit in us. Paul's hope is our hope—that Jesus Christ has saved us from this battle and has offered us grace to contend for God's will in our life. As you consider the areas of struggle in your life, think about what might be the root of those struggles. James puts is this way, *What causes fights and quarrels among you? Don't they come from your desires that battle within you? You want something but don't get it. You kill and covet, but you cannot have what you want. (James 4:1-2)* Could it be that the root of our struggles is the sin of pride and not getting our own way? Paul points us to the way out—thanks be to God that we are justified by grace, for we have all sinned.

Heavenly Father,
Thank you for Your Son, Jesus Christ, who turns my defeat into victory. Grant me courage to honestly face the desires that battle within me and to say, like Paul, "thanks be to God through Jesus Christ our Lord!"
In Jesus' name, Amen

August 4

The Benefits of Sonship

Now if we are children, then we are heirs—heirs of God and co-heirs with Christ, if indeed we share in his sufferings in order that we may also share in his glory.
Romans 8:17

As children of God, we are co-heirs with Christ. We have received His Holy Spirit and we must be willing to be led by the Spirit. In doing so, we put the misdeeds of the flesh to death. We have a responsibility, according to Paul, to live by the Spirit. This is a sobering thought! We must co-labor with the Holy Spirit at work in us to be transformed more into the likeness of Christ. The more willing we are to be Spirit-led, the greater our transformation and the freer we become. The kingdom of God is righteousness, joy, and peace, and when Jesus came to earth, He announced His kingdom was near. (*Matthew 4:17*) His kingdom is one of righteousness that produces the fruit of the spirit: love, joy, peace, goodness, and self-control. (*Galatians 5*)

As co-heirs with Christ, we have this fruit as our inheritance. Think about all the misery in the world: frustration, anger, hurt, pain… Christ never promised our lives would be easy. In fact He said, *In this world you will have trouble. But take heart! I have overcome the world.* (*John 16:33*) Jesus did promise in His Word that although we would have trials, He would be with us in the midst of the trials and would help us to overcome our trials. He also taught that the benefits of *His kingdom* would be righteousness, joy, and peace. Another benefit of being a "kingdom people" is the truth that receiving His spirit does not make us slaves to fear; we receive the Spirit of Sonship. As co-heirs with Christ, have you received these benefits—the fruit of righteousness, joy, and peace and the assurance that fear has no place in the life of a believer? If trials have overtaken you and fear has a hold on you, remind yourself that as a child of the King, your inheritance is His peace, joy, and righteousness. If you have agreed with the enemy that you are not entitled to these things, break your agreement and come into agreement with God's Word. Your inheritance is waiting.

Heavenly Father,
I have lived as a pauper—not willing to believe or receive my inheritance as a child of the King. I come into agreement with Your Word that I am a co-heir with Christ, sharing not only in His sufferings, but sharing in His glorious inheritance of peace, joy, and righteousness.
In Jesus' name, Amen

August 5

Committed to His Friend

Greater love has no one than this, that he lay down his life for his friends.
John 15:13

Jesus took his disciples to a vineyard to teach them a spiritual truth. He often used things in the natural to convey a spiritual truth. He looked at the vines and branches in the vineyard and compared His relationship to the disciples to a branch and a vine, saying *I am the vine, you are the branches. If a man remains in me and I in him, he will bear much fruit; apart from me you can do nothing. (John 15:5)* Jesus then described His relationship to His Father and how it related to them: *As the Father has loved me, so I have loved you. (v.9)* Jesus knew that the love He had for his disciples and the world would send Him to the cross; it was His love for them that enabled Him to obey His father and lay His life down for them. He tells His disciples that there is no love greater than laying one's life down for his friends.

Friendships are important. Everyone needs a friend, and everyone needs to be a friend. A true friend will love unconditionally, and a true friend will be willing to set aside his own needs to serve the needs of another. I remember an occasion when some friends at school hurt my feelings. My mother told me that I should feel blessed if, in a lifetime, I had five true friends. Her words have returned to me many times as I have gone through life.

The story of David, who eventually became king of Israel, illustrates a God-ordained friendship in which Jonathan, King Saul's son, willingly lays his life down for David. Jonathan could have been jealous of David, thinking that he should rightfully follow his father as King of Israel. But Jonathan was more concerned with God's will than his own ambition or desires, and he knew that David had been anointed to be the next king. He protected David from Saul, and he did all that he could do to ensure that David would fulfill the call of God: *And Jonathan made a covenant with David because he loved him as himself. (I Samuel 18:3)*

Jesus talked about friendships. He even said that it was His desire that we each are His friend. Friendship with Christ is the most important friendship we have on this earth, and out of our relationship with Him, we will be able to be a true friend to others.

Heavenly Father,
Help me to be a genuine friend, willing to look to serve a friend and consider that friend's interests above my own. Help me to build godly relationships based on my friendship with You.
In Jesus' name, Amen

August 6

Aligning with God

. . .he restores my soul; He guides me in paths of righteousness for his name's sake.
Psalm 23:3

After the Lord shows us that we are on the wrong path, it is our responsibility to accept His plan and follow His way. If we are obstinate and follow our own way, we will be miserable. Isaiah warned the people that they were obstinate because they carried out their own plans rather than the plans of the Lord, forming an alliance, but not by His Spirit. *(Isaiah 30:1)* They consulted with the Pharaoh of Egypt, aligning themselves with ungodly advice (human wisdom and reasoning) and sought protection from the Pharaoh. Their sin, according to Isaiah, was like a *high wall, cracked and bulging, collapsing suddenly. (Isaiah 30:13)* We also have our "high walls" built on human reasoning and unholy alliances. The Lord is calling us to depend on Him, to trust Him, and to come into agreement with His Word laid forth in the Scriptures. The rebellious people in Isaiah's day told the prophets to tell them only pleasant things and to stop confronting them with the Holy One of Israel. *(Isaiah 30:10)* In our nation today and in our personal lives, we can hear the cry of many saying, "Don't tell me any more bad news about God's judgment; don't confront me with the truth of Scripture."

Paul writes to the church in Corinth to beware of leaning on human wisdom or reasoning, saying, *Has not God made foolish the wisdom of the world? (I Corinthians 1:20)* Paul recognized that when we are not in alignment with God's Word and are, instead, dependent on our human wisdom, we are led astray. Seeking God's wisdom enables us to follow His way and His path for us. Recently, I was confronted with a choice. I made a hasty decision and suffered the consequences. The Lord spoke to me in my time with Him one morning, showing me what had happened. I had not consulted with the Lord, and the path that I took was the wrong one.

Joshua fell into the same problem. He did not consult God when the Gibeonites came to seek an alliance with Israel. They deceived him, saying that they were from far away. Joshua did not consult with God, but relied on logic and human reasoning. He soon discovered that he had entered into an alliance with a people not ordained by God. (*Joshua 9*) Remember the next time you need direction to call on the Lord and wait on His leading.

Heavenly Father,
I have been like the Israelites and consulted with many people concerning a decision I have to make. Forgive me for not seeking You first, for relying on human wisdom and not relying on You. I know that You do speak through people, but I have depended solely on them and not committed myself to pray. Today I seek Your wisdom to lead and direct me.
In Jesus' name, Amen

August 7

Trials and Temptations

Consider it pure joy my brothers whenever you face trials of many kinds, because the testing of your faith develops perseverance. Perseverance must finish its work so that you may be mature and complete, not lacking anything.
James 1:2-4

James wrote to the early church which had been dispersed and was facing difficulties. He encouraged them to see their trials as a means for God to develop perseverance and maturity in them. He recognized that God was using their trials to strengthen them so that they would be complete and not lacking.

Trials can either make you bitter or make you better. My mother-in-law told me this after her second adult daughter died. She told me that we have the choice to allow God to use it for our good, or to allow the enemy to use it to destroy us. I will never forget her holding up her arm and telling me that losing her children was like losing an arm; it would never grow back, but the other arm would grow stronger.

Peter, writing to the persecuted church, describes what God has available to us as we face our trials, saying *His divine power has given us everything we need for life and godliness through our knowledge of him who called us by his own glory and goodness. (2 Peter 1:3)* Through the trials that we endure, God gives us His power, but this power is available to us only through our intimate connection with Jesus Christ. He is the vine and we are the branches—a connection that enables us to receive His nourishment and power. Apart from Him we are powerless. I have a cordless vacuum, and if I do not charge it, it is powerless and useless to me. We live charged with God's power when we stay connected to Him.

Are you going through trials? Remember that this is an opportunity for God to make you better, not bitter. It is an opportunity for Him to give you His power not only to endure, but to change and be more like Him. I do not look forward to the rough times in life, but I always know that God is at work in the midst of them.

Heavenly Father,
Help me to use this trial for Your glory. I ask You to give me perseverance so that I will grow to be more like You. Help me to draw from Your power as I stay connected to You.
In Jesus' name, Amen

August 8

Satan, the Father of Lies

And no wonder, for Satan himself masquerades as an angel of light. II Corinthians 11:14

Satan is the enemy of God's people. He is the father of lies: *You belong to your father, the devil, and you want to carry out your father's desire. He was a murderer from the beginning, not holding to the truth, for there is no truth in him. (John 8:44)* Jesus pointed out that the enemy's native language is lies and the Jews were deceived.

The enemy still speaks in his native language today, whispering lies in our ears. His lies bring confusion and disrupt our ability to hear the voice of God. As we recognize and refuse his lies, our spiritual ears are open to hear God's truth. The enemy tempted Jesus and spoke lies to Him in the wilderness, but Jesus combated every lie with God's Word. (*John 4*) We must combat his lies and agree with the truth of God's Word.

Have you believed the lies of the enemy? Are you able to recognize his deception? He prowls around looking to see whom he can devour. (*I Peter 5:8*) He uses his lies to cause you to feel unworthy, rejected, or alone. God's Word builds up; His Word tells us to stand firm and resist the enemy. (*v.9*)

When my daughter went through her rebellious years, the enemy tried to make me believe that I was a terrible parent. I recognized the father of lies trying to cause me to feel defeated, but holding on to God's Word filled me with truth, and the enemy could not get a foothold. There were days when I agreed with the lies, but God in His mercy would remind me of His truth.

The next time you are tempted to agree with the father of lies, remember to hold up God's Word. The enemy will not be able to withstand the truth.

Heavenly Father,
Protect me from believing the lies of the enemy. Help me to stand firm and resist his assaults through the truth of Your Word.
In Jesus' name, Amen

Producing Fruit

Produce fruit in keeping with repentance.

Matthew 3:8

John the Baptist warned the Pharisees to *produce fruit in keeping with repentance. (Matthew 3:8)* He recognized that true repentance would produce good fruit. What is true repentance? It is turning from sin and towards God; it is agreeing with God. Re-pent means we must go back again to "penthouse" thinking—thinking that is higher, like a penthouse, a way of thinking that lines up with God's Word. When we repent, we turn from sin and turn towards God's way of thinking. True repentance will always bear fruit. John the Baptist recognized that the Pharisees were religious on the outside, but their hearts were far from God. He preached repentance to the Jews, declaring that their repentance needed to be genuine and that the evidence would be the fruit seen in their lives. John the Baptist was beheaded because his message was offensive to the king's wife; his strong message offended many.

Jesus entered his ministry on earth with the same message, *Repent for the kingdom of heaven is near. (Matthew 4:17)* Jesus' first message was "repent" so that the people could turn away from those things that blocked a relationship with His Father and turn towards God.

Today, the message of repentance is not always received. People want to feel good, and the message of repentance seems too incriminating. It is easier to preach a message of love than a message of turning from your sins. Most people desire to live a fruitful life in Christ, but we must never forget that the foundation for the fruit is laid by the root. If the root is healthy, then the tree will be healthy and bear fruit. Likewise, if we turn from our sins, the root of our spiritual lives will stay healthy and the fruit of it will follow.

Ask the Holy Spirit to examine your life and reveal to you any attitudes of unforgiveness, bitterness, or anger that are causing you to sin. Seek the Lord in repentance and His forgiveness will make the root healthy; soon you will see the fruit.

Heavenly Father,
Examine my life and see if there is any offensive way in me. (Psalm 139:23-24) I repent for any negative attitudes that I have and turn back to You. I pray that my life will be filled with fruit for Your glory.
In Jesus' name, Amen

Laying Down Idols

Therefore, my dear friends, flee from idolatry.
I Corinthians 10:14

The Old Testament reveals the history of the Israelites when they worshipped Jehovah God and when they fell into worshipping other gods. The Lord sent His prophets time and time again to warn the Israelites to turn from idolatry (worshipping other gods) and turn back to Him. When they were warned, the Israelites suffered the consequences of their idolatry and then turned back to God.

We read in *Acts 19* that many of the people in Ephesus practiced idolatry in the form of sorcery. When a number of these people became believers in Jesus, they burned their magic scrolls, and *the word of the Lord spread widely and grew in power.* (*Acts 19: 20*) The Bible clearly forbids believers to be involved in "occult" practices (*Deuteronomy 18*) because it damages our spiritual lives. We, like the people of Ephesus, must turn from idols and from practices that are contrary to the Word of God so that we will grow in faith and power. Occult practices block our spiritual development because they cause us to depend on false sources of power rather than on God, the true source of power. The reading of horoscopes and tarot cards, going to psychics, fortune-tellers, séances, and using Ouija boards may seem like innocent practices or even games, but they block our spiritual growth. The Word of God teaches that just like the first century church, we must renounce and remove these things from our lives.

If you have sought supernatural power from any other source than the Holy Spirit, renounce those practices, even if they were done in innocence. If you have not engaged in any of those activities, ask the Lord to show you any other areas where you have worshipped anything above Him. It is easy to fall into the idolatry of worshipping money, power, or idolizing people. The Lord is a jealous God; He seeks to have us worship Him alone. *You shall have no other gods before me. (Exodus 20:3)* Take the time today to ensure that you have not put anything above your relationship with the Lord.

Heavenly Father,
Forgive me for worshipping (fill in the blank). I know that my heart has been crowded with other things that have taken Your place. Fill me with Your life-giving Presence as I worship You and You alone.
In Jesus' name, Amen

The Banner Over Us

I am a rose of Sharon, a lily of the valleys. Like a lily among thorns is my darling among the maidens. Like an apple tree among the trees of the forest is my lover among the young men. I delight to sit in his shade and his fruit is sweet to my taste. He has taken me to the banquet hall and his banner over me is love.
Song of Solomon 2:1-4

We see the banner of God being raised in different ways in both the Old and New Testaments. During the battle with the Amalikites, Moses lifted up the rod of God (God's conquering banner): *...tomorrow I will stand on top of the hill with the staff of God in my hands. (Exodus 17:9)* As long as Moses held his arms up, the Israelites prevailed against the Amalekites. The staff of God in Moses' hands was a symbol of the banner of God being raised over the battle. After the battle and the defeat of the enemy, Moses built an altar and called it The Lord is My Banner. (*v.15*)

Another time, the Israelites complained against God *(Numbers 21)* and the Lord sent venomous snakes among them, causing many of them to die. The people recognized that they had sinned against God and asked Moses to pray on their behalf. The Lord told Moses to lift up a bronze snake on a pole so that when the people looked at it, they would live. God raised His banner over the people, and those who obeyed lived.

We read about yet another banner in the *Song of Solomon*—a banner of love. The *Song of Solomon* is about a love relationship between two people pointing to the relationship between Christ and His bride, the church. The writer describes how his loved one is taken to the banquet hall and he places his banner of love over her. (*Song of Solomon 2:4*) God raised His banner of love over us when He sent His Son Jesus Christ to dwell with us. His banner of love was raised in the form of a cross and the death of His Son.

Are you aware that the banner of God is raised over your life? His banner is lifted high over the battles of your life; His banner over you is love.

Heavenly Father,

Thank you that throughout all the struggles of life You are with me, raising Your mighty hand of protection and love.
In Jesus' name, Amen

Do Not Worry

Therefore I tell you, do not worry about your life, what you will eat or drink; or about your body, what you will wear. Is not life more important than food, and the body more important than clothes?
Matthew 6:25

Jesus tells his disciples not to worry about the natural things a person would worry about, like food and clothes. He points out that life is what they should be concerned with, and more specifically, life in Him. He goes on to point out that the birds of the air do not sow or reap or store away in barns, and yet God feeds them. He tells them not to worry, because worrying doesn't add a single hour to life. The reverse of this would be that worry takes away the very life that God intended for us; it steals our joy, our hope, and our zeal for life. Jesus told the disciples to spend their time seeking Him who gives life, and He, in turn, would give them all that they needed.

Jesus told the parable of the sower—how the farmer scattered seeds that fell on the path and the birds ate it up. Some of the seeds fell on rocky places, and without much soil, they withered; others fell among thorns and were choked out. Some seed fell on good soil and produced a bountiful crop. Jesus explained that the one who received the seed (God's Word) that fell among thorns was unfruitful because the worries of this life and the deceitfulness of wealth choked it out. (*Matthew 13*) Worrying will choke out God's Word in our life, and it is His Word that brings us life.

What are you anxious about? Paul tells the Philippians not to be anxious but to rejoice in all things, praying and seeking God, saying, *Rejoice in the Lord always. I will say it again: Rejoice! Let your gentleness be evident to all. The Lord is near. Do not be anxious about anything, but in everything, by prayer and petition, with thanksgiving present your requests to God. And the peace of God, which transcends all understanding, will guard your hearts and minds in Christ Jesus. (Philippians 4:4-7)*

The next time you begin to worry or feel anxious, remember to pray and seek God; rejoice and thank Him. His peace, which is incomprehensible in the midst of anxiety-filled times, will fill your heart.

Heavenly Father,
I pray that You will remove all anxiety from my heart. I lay my burdens down at the foot of the cross and thank you for Your peace.
In Jesus' name, Amen

August 13

Committed to the Call

I am still confident of this; I will see the goodness of the LORD in the land of the living. Wait for the LORD; be strong and take heart and wait for the LORD.
Psalm 27:13-14

David's security in the Lord in the face of his enemies is seen in *Psalm 27*. He is confident that he will see the Lord's faithfulness no matter what happens. He was committed to God and to the call on his life. He knew that he had to wait for the Lord's deliverance when his enemies pursued him, and he knew that he had to be strong and take heart. David had confidence in *God*—not in his own abilities. His confidence was rooted in his understanding that God is good and that His goodness could be seen in the land of the living. I say *could* be seen because it was David's responsibility to see God's goodness; he had a choice to believe God would manifest His goodness towards him, or he could have chosen to believe that God would fail him.

Before David became king of Israel, he was just a shepherd boy, but not an ordinary shepherd boy. What made him extraordinary is that he believed that God was good and that He would deliver the Israelites from the oppression of the Philistine giant. David was an ordinary shepherd boy who believed that he would see the goodness of the Lord deliver the Philistine giant into his hand. *David said to the Philistine, "you come against me with sword and spear and javelin, but I come against you in the name of the Lord almighty, the God of the armies of Israel, whom you have defied. (I Samuel 17:45)* David killed the giant with a sling and a stone because he believed that he would see God in the land of the living. He believed that God would deliver him.

Do you believe that God is active in the world today? Do you have the attitude of David that no matter what you face, God is present and will come to your aid? Sometimes it may seem that God is far away or that He is not aware of your problems. David's words, written so long ago, give us the courage to wait. *Wait for the Lord, be strong and take heart and wait for the Lord. (Psalm 27:14)* He will surely come.

Heavenly Father,
I am weary with defeat. Give me confidence like David to know that You are near. As I wait for You, help me to take heart, knowing that You will come to my rescue.
In Jesus' name, Amen

Dwelling in God's Shelter

He who dwells in the shelter of the Most High will rest in the shadow of the almighty. I will say of the Lord, "He is my fortress, my God in whom I trust."
Psalm 91:1

One of my favorite *Psalms* is *Psalm 91* because it testifies to the security of those who trust God. It may have been written by a priest who wished to assure God's people that if they were willing to trust God and make Him their refuge and dwelling place, no harm would befall them. He recounts that God will save them from the snare of the enemy.

The most common weapon used by the enemy is to ensnare God's people with fear—fear for their health, fear for their children, relationships, job or the future. But God wants His children to dwell in the safety of His shelter; a place of refuge and security. The imagery of God covering them with the feathers of His wings paints a beautiful picture of The Most High God: *Surely he will save you from the fowler's snare and from deadly pestilence. He will cover you with his feathers, and under his wings you will find refuge; his faithfulness will be your shield and rampart. (Psalm 91:3-4)*

God's Word stands true for you today. He covers our fears, our insecurities, and the terror that grips us as we stand under the shadow of His Presence. The key in receiving His protection is that you must *make the Most High your dwelling.* (*v.9*) God is waiting for you to draw near to Him; He is waiting for you to seek Him as your refuge. He has promised that when you do, He will command His angels to guard you in all of your ways. (*v.11*)
Are you overcome with fear today? Stand in the shelter of the Most High and you will find yourself resting in the shadow of His wings.

Heavenly Father,
I am overcome with fear. I choose to make You my dwelling place—to seek You and to draw near to You. Thank you for Your promise that You will protect me and cause me to rest in Your loving arms.
In Jesus' name, Amen

August 15

God's Holy Hill

Lord, who may dwell in your sanctuary? Who may live on your holy hill? He whose walk is blameless and who does what is righteous, who speaks the truth from his heart, and has no slander on his tongue, who does his neighbor no wrong, and casts no slur on his fellow man, who despises a vile man but honors those who fear the Lord…
Psalm 15

The holy hill was the site of Jerusalem's temple. As the people made their way up to the temple, the place where they worshipped God, they were preparing to meet with God. David reflects on who may dwell in God's sanctuary and live in the Presence of God—one whose walk is blameless. As the people ascended the mountain, perhaps it was a time when God was preparing their hearts to be with Him.

God has made a way for Christians to approach Him today through His Son, Jesus Christ. When we invite Him into our lives to dwell in us, He brings His kingdom and begins a process of transformation in us. Our spiritual journey is much like climbing a mountain, as reflected in today's *Psalm.* We accept Christ, and as we climb His mountain of transformation, we become more like Him. There was a high priest in the Old Testament who was the only one who could enter into the Most Holy Place. He did this once a year to offer sacrifices (atonement) for their sins. Jesus is our High Priest who has gone through the heavens to prepare an entrance into God's Presence: *For we do not have a high priest who is unable to sympathize with our weaknesses, but we have one who has been tempted in every way, just as we are—yet was without sin. Let us then approach the throne of grace with confidence, so that we may receive mercy and find grace to help us in our time of need. (Hebrews 4:15-16)*

Jesus, our High Priest, went before us on the holy hill where He died for our sins so that we might be able to approach God. Sinful man could not approach a holy God, and through His atonement on the cross, He made a way for us to approach a holy God. When He was lifted up on the cross at Calvary, He took our sin

with Him and we can now approach the throne of grace with confidence.
The Lord is calling you to the mountain of holiness. His desire is for you to draw near to Him and to be holy as He is holy: *Who may live on your holy hill? He whose walk is blameless and who does what is righteous. (v.1)*

Heavenly Father,
As I climb the mountain of holiness, help me to lead a blameless, righteous life. Keep me from slander and from being deceitful. Convict me of sin so that I might become more like You.
In Jesus' name, Amen

August 16

The Sheep Know His Voice

I tell you the truth, the man who does not enter the sheep pen by the gate, but climbs in by some other way, is a thief and a robber. The man who enters by the gate is the shepherd of his sheep. The watchman opens the gate for him and the sheep listen to His voice. He calls his own sheep by name and leads them out. When he has brought out all of his own, he goes ahead of them, and his sheep follow him because they know his voice.
John 10:1-4

Jesus illustrates the relationship He has with believers by describing sheep and a shepherd, saying, *I am the good shepherd; I know my sheep and my sheep know me—just as the Father knows me and I know the Father. I lay down my life for the sheep." (v.14)* The sheep know the voice of their shepherd and, likewise, believers recognize the voice of Jesus.

There are many voices in the word, voices that lead us astray and voices that discourage, but the voice of God leads us to green pastures and encourages our lives. It is so easy to hear the other voices that clamor for our attention. They become so loud at times, drowning out God's voice. Believers often tell me that they are unable to hear the voice of God, and when I question them, it appears that often they have been listening to so many counterfeit voices that they have not been able to hear the voice of truth. How do we clear out the voices that vie for our attention? We begin by reading and meditating on God's Word. I most often hear the Lord speak to me through Scripture—when I need to make a decision, when I am confused, when I am discouraged, God's Word speaks truth to me. God also speaks to me through people, circumstances, and a variety of other ways, but what I hear will never contradict His Word.

Do you know the Shepherd's voice? Ask the Holy Spirit to search out the conflicting voices that crowd out His voice. His voice will never bring confusion and will always bring His peace.

Heavenly Father,

There are so many voices in my head—the voice of expectation, the voice of shame, guilt, and unworthiness. I pray that You will clear out all the counterfeit voices with Your healing power and enable me to hear Your voice alone.
In Jesus' name, Amen

August 17

Protecting the Wall

Therefore I stationed some of the people behind the lowest points of the wall at the exposed places, posting them by families, with their swords, spears and bows. After I looked things over, I stood up and said to the nobles, the officials and the rest of the people, "Don't be afraid of them. Remember the Lord who is great and awesome and fight for your brothers, your sons and your daughters, your wives and your homes.
Nehemiah 4:13-14

Nehemiah was sent to Jerusalem by God to build a wall around the city. The Babylonians destroyed the city and the Israelites were held in captivity for 70 years. Over a period of years, the exiles returned to Jerusalem, commissioned by Cyrus, King of Persia. Under the leadership of Zerubbabel, the temple was rebuilt. The next wave of exiles returned to rebuild the walls under the leadership of Nehemiah. There was great opposition to the building of the walls, and Nehemiah responded with a strategy. He told the people to continue to work on the wall with spears and bows. They held the spear in one hand and worked with the other hand.

The Holy Spirit desires to rebuild the broken places of our lives—the broken down walls where the enemy has had access to us. The enemy does not want us to walk in freedom, so we must be willing to fight as we work with God to set ourselves free. His Holy Spirit is the "wall examiner," and like David, we must also be willing to allow Him to inspect our broken walls: *Search me, O God, and know my heart; test me and know my anxious thoughts. See if there is any offensive way in me and lead me in the way everlasting. (Psalm 139:23-24)*

Are you willing to allow the Holy Spirit to inspect the hurt, wounded, and broken places of your life? As long as there are wounds, the enemy has access into your life. The Lord is the Healer, and He desires to heal and deliver you from all afflictions. He has promised to be with you throughout the process of setting you free.

Heavenly Father,

I am afraid to open old wounds. It may be easier to ignore the hurt, the rejection, and the fear. Grant me the courage to allow Your light to invade the places of darkness in my life and help me to be set free.
In Jesus' name, Amen

August 18

Present Suffering and Future Glory

I consider that our present sufferings are not worth comparing with the glory that will be revealed in us.
Romans 8:18

We are part of an ongoing story—the story of all times, the story of God's creation of the world, humanity, and the personal ongoing relationship He has with His people. From *Genesis* to *Revelation*, the story consists of one theme: LOVE. God created humanity for fellowship; man was disobedient and fell, and God not only repaired the damage done by sending His Son, He made things even better. Through His Son's death and resurrection, the Holy Spirit was left as a "guarantee," a "first fruits" of the future to come.

The Holy Spirit leads, guides, convicts, and empowers us to live a life of hope as we await Jesus' return and the consummation of His eternal kingdom. Paul describes creation, humanity, and the Holy Spirit groaning as they wait for this future hope. We yearn for something better, and we play a huge role in the unfolding of the story through our prayers of intercession. The groaning that Paul describes is intercession, and often we do not even know how to intercede. The Holy Spirit, Our Helper, prays through us, asking for the will of the Father. That is how we enter into the ongoing story of God's plan, His purpose in salvation as we wait for Jesus' return and the glory that will be revealed. When I consider that I am part of God's plan, I am motivated to pray and to live my life in such a way that I participate with God. When I do not remember there is a higher plan, the trials of life can be overwhelming. This is the hope that Paul shares with the early Christians as they face the trials of life; this is the hope that we share with the saints who went before us.

How about you? Do you recognize that you are part of the ongoing story of God's plan? Do you participate through prayer in laboring for God's glory to be revealed? If you are suffering, remember that God's purpose in allowing the suffering is so that His glory will be revealed through your life.

Heavenly Father,

It gives me hope to know that I am part of an ongoing story—part of a higher purpose that You have for this earth. Help me to remember as I struggle in life that the future with You holds a glory yet to be revealed.
In Jesus' name, Amen

August 19

God's Vision Brings Order

Where there is no revelation, the people cast off restraint;
but blessed is he who keeps the law.
Proverbs 29:18

Proverbs 29:18 indicates that without revelation, God's people cast off restraint. *The Message* puts it this way: *If people can't see what God is doing, they stumble all over themselves; but when they attend to what He reveals, they are most blessed.* God's people need vision and a revelation of God in order to find God's purposes. God's purposes bring order to His people. As believers, we must seek the Lord to find His purposes. *(Jeremiah 29:13)* His Word teaches us that in order to have vision, we must first seek the Lord, not the vision. In seeking the Lord, He will reveal His plan for our lives. So often we get it backwards. We want answers from God and seek those answers. Instead, He tells us to seek Him first and all these things will be given, saying, *But seek first his kingdom and his righteousness and all these things will be given to you. (Matthew 6:33)* Throughout David's life, we see his determination to seek the Lord as he made decisions. We may have many good plans, even godly plans, but it is *God's* plans that will have eternal value: *Many are the plans in a man's heart, but it is the Lord's purpose that prevails. (Proverbs 19:21)*

Recently, I found my life in disorder. I recognized that I had lost the vision that the Lord had given me and I needed to go back to Him and seek Him. I needed to spend daily time with Him, not simply seeking vision, but seeking *Him.* Out of the increased time that I spent with Him, the Lord began to reveal His plan to me. Because of my prayer and meditation on His Word, He began to remove the cloud that surrounded my thoughts. It wasn't an overnight revelation, but I began to discern His will. Trusting Him to lead me became key to knowing the way: *Trust in the Lord with all your heart and lean not on your own understanding; in all your ways acknowledge him, and he will make your path straight. (Proverbs 3:5)*

Heavenly Father,

Thank you for restoring my vision as I seek You. Help me to remember that You are the vision for my life, and it is with You alone that I will find my way.
In Jesus' name, Amen

August 20

In Him We Live and Have Our Being

The God who made the world and everything in it is the Lord of heaven and earth and does not live in temples made by hands. And he is not served by human hands, as if he needed anything, because he himself gives all men life and breath and everything else. From one man he made every nation of men that they should inhabit the whole earth; and he determined the times set for them and the exact places where they should live. God did this so that men would seek him and perhaps reach out for him and find him, though he is not far from each one of us. For in him we move and have our being.
Acts 17:24-28

Recently, we bought a new house before selling our old one. It has been several months since we purchased the new house, and my husband and I have been praying and seeking God's will as to what we should do. I shared our struggle with a friend and she gave me this verse to hold on to: *God has determined the times set for them and the exact places where they should live. (v. 26)* We had been considering putting both houses up for sale and trusting the Lord to give us whichever house he wanted for us to live in. This verse reminded me that God has determined the seasons and times of our lives and that he has a plan, even for where we are to live.

Luke writes in the book of *Acts* that God gives us breath *and everything else. (v. 25)* He is concerned with the details of our lives, and it is comforting to know that He has a great plan. Worrying does not add a thing to His plan! One of the most profound verses in the Scripture above is that it is in God that we live, and move, and have our being. (*v.28*) Living in Christ means that all of the concerns of living are under His care.

Is there anything causing you to worry or be anxious? God's Word has the answer; remember, *Cast all your anxiety on him because he cares for you. (I Peter 5:7)* God will take care of them. He cares for your life and desires that you move and live and have your being totally under the care of His loving Lordship.

Heavenly Father,

I have spent so much time worrying about (fill in the blank). I cast this anxiety up top You, knowing that You care for me. Help me to remember that I am in Christ and that You are in me.
In Jesus' name, Amen

August 21

Philosophies on Trial

Where is the wise man? Where is the scholar? Where is the philosopher of this age? Has not God made foolish the wisdom of the world? Or since in the wisdom of God the world through its wisdom did not know him, God was pleased through the foolishness of what was preached to save those who believe.
I Corinthians 1:20-21

Paul found himself disputing the philosophies of his day. In Athens, the Epicureans and the Stoic philosophers disputed with him as he preached the good news of Jesus Christ and the resurrection. (*Acts 17:18*) The Epicureans were materialists and atheists, and their goal in life was pleasure. The Stoics rejected the idolatry of pagan worship and taught that there was one world-god. They were pantheists whose emphasis was on personal discipline. Today, we also face different philosophies in our society, and we, like Paul, must stand firm in our convictions and boldly share our faith. The world still needs the message of the cross and the hope that it brings. There is no other philosophy that brings the hope of eternal life and the hope of living in Christ.

Paul puts the philosophies of the world on trial knowing that they cannot stand up to the Word of God. He contends that the wisdom of the world is foolishness in comparison with the wisdom of God. Proof of this is that the world's wisdom did not reveal God. It is only by God's Holy Spirit that He is revealed.

What false philosophies have you believed? Today, our society is flooded with self-help books, yet Jesus says *I am the vine; you are the branches. If a man remains in me and I in him, he will bear much fruit; apart from me you can do nothing. (John 15:5)* The philosophies of the world fall short of the wisdom of God. Are you held captive by the philosophies of the world?

Heavenly Father,
Help me to remember that the wisdom of this world is foolishness to You. Help me to depend only on You and not to be captivated by the philosophies that this world offers. In Jesus' name, Amen

Compromising God's Purposes

....when the people of Gibeon heard what Joshua had done to Jericho and Ai, they resorted to a ruse. They went as a delegation whose donkeys were loaded with worn out sacks and old wineskins, cracked and mended. The men put worn and patched sandals on their feet and wore old clothes. All of the bread of their food supply was dry and moldy. Then they went to Joshua in the camp of Gilgal and said to him and the men of Israel, "we have come from a distant country; make a treaty with us."
Joshua 9:3-6

God has a plan, and His plan is perfect. His plan for the world and His plan for our lives will be revealed as we seek Him and as we obey Him. It may seem that your life is spinning out of control, but if you trust God, He will make your path straight. (*Proverbs 3:5*) There are so many things in life that make it appear that God has forgotten us: unanswered prayers, family members or friends that die unexpectedly, opportunities lost. But the truth is that God has not forsaken you. He has a plan, and His purposes will prevail: *Many are the plans in a man's heart, but it is the Lord's purpose that prevails. (Proverbs 19:21)* It is very easy to make plans without consulting the Lord, and yet He wants us to follow *His* plan.

There are times when we forget to seek God's counsel. For example, Joshua did not consult God when the Gibeonites came to make a treaty with the Israelites. The people of Gibeon resorted to a ruse when they heard that the Israelites had defeated Jericho. They were afraid that they would endure the same fate, so they sent a delegation loaded with worn out sacks and old wineskins pretending to have come from far away. They were actually located just North of Jerusalem, but they wanted to trick Joshua and the Israelites into believing that they came from a distant land. Joshua did not consult the Lord. *The men of Israel sampled their provisions, but did not inquire of the Lord. Then Joshua made a treaty of peace with them... (Joshua 9:14-15)* Three days after they made the treaty with the Gibeonites, the Israelites heard that they were neighbors living near them. The Israelites were deceived into making a treaty with the Canaanites, disobeying God's command to destroy them.

When we forget to seek the Lord for *His* purposes and plans, we end up compromising and the consequences can be devastating.

Are you suffering from compromising God's purposes for your life by not seeking Him? Do not be deceived by the enemy. His goal is to thwart God's purposes for your life. Turn back to God and seek Him.

Heavenly Father,
Forgive me for not seeking You. I have been deceived and I ask You to redeem my mistake. Help me to remember to seek You daily so that I can walk in Your plan and purpose for my life.
In Jesus' name, Amen

August 23

Turning Back

. . .if my people, who are called by my name, will humble themselves and pray and seek my face and turn from their wicked ways, then will I hear from heaven and will forgive their sin and will heal their land. Now my eyes will be open and my ears attentive to the prayers offered in this place.

II Chronicles 7:14-15

God has given us a way out when we turn away from Him. The Israelites turned from God and He offered them a way back: to humble themselves, pray and seek God. His promise was if they would do so, He would forgive their sin and heal their land. Solomon prayed to God at the dedication of the temple, offering sacrifices and thanksgiving for God's faithfulness in the building of the temple. The Lord appeared to Solomon acknowledging that He had heard his prayer and reminding him that if the Israelites experienced God's hand of judgment due to their sin, He would hear their prayers if they turned back to Him.

God has given us a way to turn back to Him through His Son, Jesus Christ. There is no sin too great, nothing that we have done that He won't forgive if we humbly turn from our wicked ways. He will bring healing and deliverance. The New Testament passage parallels the grace we are able to turn to in repentance and be healed: *If we claim to be without sin, we deceive ourselves and the truth is not in us. If we confess our sins, he is faithful and just to forgive us our sins and purify us from all unrighteousness.* (*I John 1:8-9*)

Have you committed a sin that you have not taken to God in prayer? What is it? If you are willing to turn back to God, He stands ready to heal the devastation, the brokenness, and the places of desolation in your life that the sin has caused. Will you turn to Him today?

Heavenly Father,
You alone have the power to save and to forgive. I turn back to You and ask that You will hear my prayer and heal my "spiritual land."
In Jesus' name, Amen

August 24

Godly Leadership

I put in charge of Jerusalem my brother Hanani, along with Hananiah the commander of the citadel, because he was a man of integrity and feared God more than most men do.
Nehemiah 7:2

Godly leaders lead by example. Nehemiah modeled integrity and fear of the Lord and won the respect of the people. He also knew that more godly leadership was needed to complete the rebuilding of God's city and His people, and he chose Hananiah because he was a man of integrity and feared the Lord. Nehemiah was unselfish and humble, not needing or seeking to be the only leader, but realizing that more leadership was needed. In the following chapter of Nehemiah, he once again seeks out a leader to come alongside him to revive the people spiritually. Godly leaders realize their limitations and seek to work with other leaders to accomplish God's purposes.

The greatest example of leadership is in Jesus Christ, who described leadership as being a servant, saying, *You call me "Teacher" and Lord, and rightly so for that is what I am. Now that I, your Lord and Teacher have washed your feet, you also should wash one another's feet. (John 13:13-14)*

Paul understood our need for one another as we work together to serve and to fulfill God's call on our lives. He encouraged the church to be aware of the different gifts in the body of Christ and to work together using the gifts for the glory of God: *There are different kinds of gifts, but the same Spirit. There are different kinds of service, but the same Lord. There are different kinds of working, but the same God works all of them in all men. (I Corinthians 12:4-6)*

Nehemiah had reached the point in the rebuilding of the wall of Jerusalem where he needed to bring on other leaders to help, and he chose a man with integrity who feared God. As we work together in the body of Christ, we must be mindful that we need each other to accomplish God's work. When we learn to appreciate the spiritual gifts in others and are not envious or competitive, God's kingdom is advanced and His will is done.

Heavenly Father,
Thank you that I am part of the body of Christ. Help me encourage and appreciate the gifts of others and for us together to use our gifts for Your glory.
In Jesus' name, Amen

August 25

Love Never Fails

If I speak in the tongues of men and of angels, but have not love, I am only a resounding gong or a clanging cymbal. If I have the gift of prophecy and can fathom all mysteries and all knowledge, and if I have a faith that can move mountains, but have not love, I am nothing.
I Corinthians 13:1-2

Love never fails. Love is not just a duty; it is a destiny. Love flows from the heart of God, filling our lives and spilling onto others. We are unable to love unconditionally without the love of God flowing through our lives. The Bible, from *Genesis* to *Revelation,* is a love story—a story of God whose sole desire is to be in relationship with us. When Adam and Eve sinned and broke fellowship with God, God prepared His Son to come to us in order to deliver us.

Jesus Christ came to restore our broken relationship with God, and His love, exemplified on the cross, poured over humanity. Love is the most powerful force on earth. It covers a multitude of sins and it carries the burdens of our losses. Love is our destiny. We are designed to love, and when sin disrupts our life, it disrupts the flow of love and we fail. But love never fails.

Three things remain: faith, hope, and love, and the greatest of these is love. (*v.13*) Paul writes in the book to the Romans that nothing can separate us from the love of God, *For I am convinced that neither angels nor demons, neither the present nor the future, nor any powers, neither height nor depth, nor anything else in all creation, will be able to separate us from the love of God that is in Christ Jesus our Lord. (Romans 8:38-39)*

If you feel separated from God's love, remember that God's love is ever present; it never fails.

Heavenly Father,
Soften my hardened heart and heal my wounds so that I can remain in Your love.
In Jesus' name, Amen

August 26

The Power of God

When I came to you, brothers, I did not come with eloquence or superior wisdom as I proclaimed to you the testimony about God. For I resolved to know nothing while I was with you except Jesus Christ and him crucified. I came to you in weakness and fear, and with much trembling. My message and my preaching were not with wise and persuasive words, but with a demonstration of the Spirit's power, so that your faith might not rest on men's wisdom, but on God's power.
I Corinthians 2:1-5

Webster's dictionary defines reason as "a sufficient ground of explanation or logical defense." *Acts 17:2-3* indicates that Paul reasoned from the Scriptures that Jesus was the Christ and had risen from the dead. Paul had been a Pharisee and had studied under a renowned teacher, Gamaliel. He was powerful, polished in speech, and had a presence of influence. Yet he did not rely on any of these things to present the gospel. He knew that the gospel's message was powerful enough. He did not come with eloquence or superior wisdom; his only resolve was to know Christ and to make Him known.

For years, I was fearful that if I could not adequately quote and defend the Scripture, my attempts at sharing the message of Christ would be hopeless. As I observe Paul's strategy of winning people to Christ, I am astounded at how he simply shared the facts and logically explained the gospel. He even said that it was not by his wise or persuasive words that people would accept the gospel. He knew that it was by God's demonstration of power that those to whom he presented the gospel would be convinced. *(I Corinthians 2:1-5)* It has been so freeing for me to realize that I do not have to convince, and in fact, cannot use persuasion or human wisdom to convince people that Jesus is the Messiah. All I have to do is share my story of what Christ has done for me and leave the results to God.

Heavenly Father,
I pray that others will see the power of God in me as I live my life and share my faith. Forgive me where I have depended on my words of wisdom rather than on the demonstration of the Spirit's power.
In Jesus' name, Amen

August 27

Courageous Action

When the Philistines heard that David had been anointed king over Israel, they went up in full force to search for him, but David heard about it and went down to the stronghold. Now the Philistines had come and spread out in the Valley of Rephaim; so David inquired of the LORD, "Shall I go and attack the Philistines? Will you hand them over to me?" The LORD answered him, "Go, for I will surely hand the Philistines over to you." So David went to Baal Perazim, and there he defeated them. He said, "As waters break out, the LORD has broken out against my enemies before me." So that place was called Baal Perazim. The Philistines abandoned their idols there, and David and his men carried them off. Once more the Philistines came up and spread out in the Valley of Rephaim; so David inquired of the LORD, and he answered, "Do not go straight up, but circle around behind them and attack them in front of the balsam trees. As soon as you hear the sound of marching in the tops of the balsam trees, move quickly, because that will mean the LORD has gone out in front of you to strike the Philistine army." So David did as the LORD commanded him, and he struck down the Philistines all the way from Gibeon to Gezer.
II Samuel 5:17-25

David inquired of the Lord, and he was successful in all that he did. When the Philistine army searched for him, he asked the Lord what to do. God told him to attack and that he would defeat the Philistines. Again the Philistines approached David and his men, and again David inquired of the Lord. This time, the Lord gave him specific instructions for attack, and once again David was successful.

It takes courage to step out in obedience to God, but it takes more than courage. It takes knowing that God has called you to do something. Like David, we must seek the Lord daily as we endeavor to follow Him. The problem is that we are not always sure that the Lord is calling us to action. We may fear that we didn't hear Him correctly, or that it was just our own good idea. I do several things as I seek to know God's will: I pray and fast, check to see if it lines up with Scripture, seek godly counsel, and look to see if circumstances line up. Finally, I check to see if I have peace about my decision. If I sense a green light after going through these steps, then I take action. We often want the Lord to write the steps out in bold letters!

However, as courageous leaders, we must walk by faith and not by sight.

Joshua was told by God to follow the Ark into the Jordan. Then the waters parted. If the Israelites had not put their feet in the water, they would still be beside the riverbank. We need to make the verse in *Proverbs* our motto, *Trust in the Lord with all your heart and lean not on your own understanding; in all your ways acknowledge Him, and He will make your paths straight. (Proverbs 3:5)*

Do you face a decision today? Like David, inquire of the Lord and He will direct your path.

Heavenly Father,
Help me to know Your will today. Lead me in my decision making and help me to obey.
In Jesus' name, Amen

August 28

Third Assault: Misleading Circumstances

He said: "Listen, King Jehoshaphat and all who live in Judah and Jerusalem! This is what the LORD says to you: 'Do not be afraid or discouraged because of this vast army. For the battle is not yours, but God's."
II Chronicles 20:15

The third assault against the people of Jerusalem was to get them to look at the circumstances—the way things appeared. The Assyrian commander threatened the people, *Do not let Hezekiah mislead you when he says, 'The Lord will deliver us.' Has the god of any nation ever delivered his land from the hand of the king of Assyria? (Isaiah 36:18)* The people were reminded that the Assyrians had already defeated and taken most of the cities in Judah. It certainly appeared that the Assyrians had the upper hand and that Jerusalem was a "sitting duck" waiting to be captured! Yet Hezekiah was faithful, and the people were silent in the face of the accusations.

Things are not always as they appear. The enemy distorts our perception of things so that we will feel defeated. The Assyrians used fear to intimidate the Israelites, pointing out their past successes in defeating other nations. The enemy uses the same tactics today. He uses intimidation and fear to discourage the people of God. King Jehoshaphat kept His eyes on God and not on the enemy, reminding the people that the battle belonged to the Lord.

What about you? What battles are you facing? Has the enemy discouraged you by the way things appear? Remember that God is fighting the battle, and though it may look like defeat, God will prevail.

Heavenly Father,
When I look at my circumstances I feel defeated. Help me to get my eyes on You so that I can see that the battle is not mine but Yours.
In Jesus' name, Amen

Surrounded by Witnesses

Therefore, since we are surrounded by such a great cloud of witnesses, let us throw off everything that hinders and the sin that so easily entangles, and let us run with perseverance the race marked out for us. Let us fix our eyes on Jesus, the author and perfecter of our faith, who for the joy set before him endured the cross, scorning its shame, and sat down at the right hand of the throne of God. Consider him who endured such opposition from sinful men, so that you will not grow weary and lose heart.
Hebrews 12:1-3

The eleventh chapter of *Hebrews* is the hall of fame of the Bible. Men and women of faith are commended for walking by faith and not by sight: *All of these people were still living by faith when they died. They did not receive the things promised; they only saw them and welcomed then from a distance. (v.13)* Faith is being sure of what we hope for and certain of what we do not see. (*v.1*) We are surrounded by all the men and women of faith that went before us, and this gives us motivation and hope to keep the faith. The writer of *Hebrews* understands that we must remove anything that hinders us if we are to run the race as the men and women of faith did: *Let us throw off everything that hinders and the sin that so easily entangles... (v.1)*

What keeps you from running the race with perseverance? If there are sins, hurts, resentments, lost hope, or anything at all, your race will slow down. If you are to fix your eyes on Jesus (*v.2*), the hindrances and blocks must be removed. The Christian life is pictured as a long-distance race rather than a sprint, and in order to get to the finish line, those obstacles must be removed. Are you carrying the burden of unforgiveness or the bitterness of a broken relationship?

Fix your eyes on Jesus who perfects your faith and who realized the joy of the cross in the power that it had to break the chains of sin and heal the wounds of life. Consider that He endured opposition from sinful men so that you will not grow weary or lose heart.

Heavenly Father,

I pray that You will remove the chains that have hindered me in the race You have marked out for me. Help me to run the race with endurance and not grow weary or lose heart.
In Jesus' name, Amen

Ongoing Warfare

For our struggle is not against flesh and blood, but against the rulers, against the authorities, against the powers of this dark world and against the spiritual forces of evil in the heavenly realms.
Ephesians 6:12

The struggles that we face on earth are not struggles against people, but against the powers of the dark world. The real enemy is the unseen spiritual force that seeks to rob, steal, and destroy our witness for Christ. Paul describes our struggle in terms of the battle that takes place in the heavenly realms. He writes to the church in Ephesus to be strong in the Lord and to put on God's armor.

David, a shepherd boy, fought the Philistine giant. King Saul offered him his armor to wear, but David refused because he said it was cumbersome. It did not fit him and he wasn't used to wearing armor. Paul tells us that there is armor that we as Christians must all wear. God has ensured that it is a perfect fit to stand against the devil's schemes: *Stand firm then with the belt of truth buckled around your waist, with the breastplate of righteousness in place, and with the feet fitted with the readiness that comes from the gospel of peace. (Ephesians 6:14-15)*

Jesus recognized that Satan was behind Peter's rebuke when he told Jesus that he must not go to the cross. (*Matthew 16:23*) Jesus knew that the internal battle that Peter was facing at the loss of Jesus was driven by Satan. He knew that the battle would continue and culminate in Peter's denial of Jesus. (*Matthew 26:75*)

The battles that we face within ourselves and with others are often spiritual battles driven by forces of evil. We must use the weapons of God to fight these battles, which include the armor of God, the shield of faith, prayer, and the Word of God. Ready yourself with the armor of God. It is impenetrable from the schemes of the enemy.

Heavenly Father,

I arm myself with the full armor of God, standing firm with the belt of truth, the breastplate of righteousness, the Word of God, and the shield of faith. Help me to always be alert, to pray and to be prepared for battle.
In Jesus' name, Amen

Cleansing the Temple

Jesus entered the temple area and drove out all who were buying and selling there. He overturned the tables of the money changers and the benches of those selling doves.
Matthew 21:12

Jesus entered the temple and was angered that His Father's house was being made into a "den of robbers." Jesus was angry when He saw that the temple in Jerusalem was being used for monetary gain instead of being a house of prayer. He overturned the tables and drove out the money changers. He declared that His Father's house would be a house of prayer.

As we prepare to receive the King of Kings, Jesus Christ, we must be willing to drive out or let go of those things (sins) that separate us from Him. He offers us forgiveness for our sins, and when we receive Him, we receive a new, cleansed life. Daily, we must remember to drive out those things that cause us to stumble, those sins that ensnare us. As believers we are the temple of the Holy Spirit (*I Corinthians 6:9*), and our spiritual temple needs to be kept clean. Sometimes our spiritual house gets filled up with the clutter of sin. Things like lying, gossip, love of money, or anger can all clutter our temple. Jesus was angry that God's house, intended to be used for worship, was being used for selfish gain.

God is calling believers to do a house inspection. He desires that our lives be centered on worshipping Him. Anything that blocks our worship must be removed. Invite the Holy Spirit to examine your heart, confess sin, and make room for the King of Kings: *God is light; in him there is no darkness at all. If we claim to have fellowship with him yet walk in the darkness, we lie and do not live by the truth. But if we walk in the light, we have fellowship with one another, and the blood of Jesus his Son, purifies us from all sin. (I John 1:5-7)*

Heavenly Father,
Forgive me for allowing so many things to crowd You out. Remove the clutter of my life that has kept me from worshipping You alone.
In Jesus' name, Amen

September 1

God's Word

Your word is a lamp to my feet and a light for my path.
Psalm 119:105

Faith comes from hearing the message, and the message is heard through the word of Christ. (Romans 10:17) Consequently, the more we meditate on God's Word, the more our faith will increase. *Psalm 119:11* says, *I have hidden your word in my heart that I might not sin against you.* As we meditate on God's Word, it is hidden deep within us, and when we need it and call it forth, we are able to stand in faith. How do we "call forth His Word?" Jesus modeled that for us in *Matthew 4* when He was tempted by the devil. For every temptation that the devil threw at Him, He rebutted it with the Scriptures! As we grow in our knowledge of Scripture, we grow in our authority to stand against the enemy. *Hebrews 4:12* says, *The Word of God is living and active and sharper than any double-edged sword.* If we want to increase our faith, we must meditate on God's Word and remember that it is living and active in our lives.

Where do you have need for God's Word to be a light to your path? Have you come to a crossroad and need to have direction? I remember a time when I was praying for direction. As I prayed, the Lord led me to this Scripture in Isaiah: *I am the Lord your God who teaches you what is best for you, who directs you in the way you should go. If only you had paid attention to my commands your peace would have been like a river. (Isaiah 48:17-18)* I realized at that moment that the Lord would direct me in the way I should go. My part was to be obedient, and the peace followed. God's Word is a lamp to our feet and a light for our path.

Heavenly Father,
Teach me Your Word so that I might not sin against You. Light up my path with Your Word and lead me in the way I should go.
In Jesus' name, Amen

Intimidation

But I said, "Should a man like me run away? Or should one like me go into the temple to save his life? I will not go!" I realized that God had not sent him, but that he had prophesied against me because Tobiah and Sanballat had hired him. He had been hired to intimidate me so that I would commit a sin by doing this, and then they would give me a bad name to discredit me.
Nehemiah 6:11-13

Shemaiah tries to coerce Nehemiah into fleeing to the temple to preserve his life, but Nehemiah discerns the tactic of intimidation being used against him: *I realized that God had not sent him. (v.12)* He refuses to run away in fear for his life and prays that God will vindicate him from those who were trying to intimidate him. (*v.14*) The dictionary defines intimidation "to compel or deter by a threat." From the time when Nehemiah steps out in faith to complete the task that God calls him to do, the enemy uses tactics of ridicule, fear, fatigue, and discouragement. Now he uses deception, false rumors, and intimidation. Every time an attack comes, Nehemiah turns to God in prayer and asks Him to strengthen him. Jesus told us that we would have trials in life, but He gives us hope that He has overcome the world. Nehemiah's relationship with God was strong, and his trust in God helped him to persevere. As we strengthen our relationship with the Lord, we will begin to trust Him more and more and will not lean on our own understanding, but will instead depend on Him to make our paths straight. (*Proverbs 3:5)*

Are you under attack by criticism, intimidation, or false rumors? We all face these things from time to time, but, like Nehemiah, we must face them with God's help. Nehemiah did not run away in fear but stood His ground by seeking God. Jesus Christ was scorned, mocked and beaten; He was nailed to the cross, and yet He endured all of this so that He could carry the sins of the world. He carried *intimidation* on the cross. He carried *scorn* on the cross, and He forgave those who nailed Him to the cross. If you are going through a time of stress, perhaps with false rumors being directed against you like they were against Nehemiah, remember that Jesus Christ carried your burden to the cross. Forgive those who assault you and lovingly confront them with God's help.

Heavenly Father,
My first reaction when I am insulted or intimidated is to flee or fight. Help me instead to stand in prayer and to seek Your help and guidance in dealing with the problem. Thank you that You endured the cross so that I might live in freedom. In Jesus' name, Amen

Discouragement

And he said, "I have been very zealous for the Lord God of hosts; because the children of Israel have forsaken Your covenant, torn down Your altars, and killed Your prophets with the sword. I alone am left; and they seek to take my life.
I Kings 19:14

Elijah, the prophet of God, was exhausted. God used him in a miraculous way to call down fire from heaven, and now he found himself fleeing for his life. He was afraid, alone, and ended up in a cave. The Lord appeared to him to ask what he was doing in the cave, and Elijah replied that after all of his zeal, after all of his hard work, the prophets of God had been killed and the Israelites had forsaken God. He had decided that his hard work in demonstrating God's power was wasted. He was the only one left. God told Elijah to go out on the mountain because He was going to pass by. God was not in the earthquake, fire, or wind. He came with a gentle whisper and spoke to Elijah. God told Elijah that he was mistaken; there were 7,000 in Israel who had not bowed down to Baal—who served God and were standing with him.

Sometimes we find ourselves in a cave like Elijah. We have been zealous for the Lord working hard to serve Him, but discouragement finds a place when we take our eyes off of God. Our perspective can be off and we may fall into believing a lie like Elijah. Suddenly we think we are all alone and we find ourselves in a cave. God comes and reminds us in the whisper of our lives that He is there and that there are other people who stand with us.

Have you found yourself in a cave, burned out and alone? Look up and wait for the Lord to come; He will not be in the earthquakes of life, or the fire; He comes quietly to comfort and point you back home.

Heavenly Father,
I am burned out. I realize that I have lost my perspective and that I have been so busy doing things for You that I have forgotten to spend time with You. Help me

get out of my cave and look up; help me see that there are others who love and serve You and are willing to come alongside me in this journey.
In Jesus' name, Amen

Courageous Follow Through

Not that I have already obtained all this, or have already been made perfect, but I press on to take hold of that for which Christ Jesus took hold of me. Brothers, I do not consider myself yet to have taken hold of it. But one thing I do: Forgetting what is behind and straining toward what is ahead, I press on toward the goal to win the prize for which God has called me heavenward in Christ Jesus.
Philippians 3:12-14

It takes willingness to pursue the Lord and His vision, courage to take action, and perseverance to follow through. Jesus sent His Holy Spirit to lead us into truth and to empower us to advance His kingdom. We have a responsibility as leaders to allow the Holy Spirit to fulfill His plan in us. Paul writes in his letter to the Philippians that he must "strain toward what is ahead." Sometimes we are so burdened with past failures that we are unable to pursue God's plan for our lives. As believers, the foremost plan for us is to witness to the world the saving love and grace of Jesus Christ. We do this differently according to the gifts He has given us and the call on our lives. But in all that we do, the ultimate goal should be to bring others to Christ and to glorify God.

David pursued God's enemies because he knew that God had called him to help preserve a nation for God's purposes. He did not know that the Messiah would come out of this nation to bring salvation to the world. Not only would He come out of this nation, He would come out of David's royal lineage! We may not see the whole picture, but the Lord is sovereign and He fulfills His purposes through us. *(Romans 8:28)* Like David, we must be willing to follow God's call to us and be willing to press on, all the while walking by faith. *(II Corinthians 5:7)*

What has God asked you to do? Are you so burdened with past failures and feelings of unworthiness that you are unable to follow God's call? Paul spoke to the church in Philippi and throughout the ages: *Forgetting what is behind and straining toward what is ahead, I press on toward the goal to win the prize for which God has called me heavenward in Christ Jesus. (Philippians 3:13)*

Heavenly Father,
Help me forget my past failures and to strain forward to accomplish the goal You have called me to. I press on to know You; I press on to follow You. I know that with You I will win the prize.
In Jesus' name, Amen

His Peace

So then, dear friends, since you are looking forward to this, make every effort to be found spotless, blameless and at peace with him.
II Peter 3:14

Believing in Christ gives us peace with God because the righteous blood of Jesus Christ covers our sins and reconciles us to God the Father. By experience we know that we do not always feel peace with God. When we face difficult times we may wonder where God is and if He cares. Peter offers us a clue to the disruption of our peace in terms of our relationship with the Lord. He exhorts the readers in *II Peter 3:14* to *make every effort to be found spotless and blameless and at peace with Him* as they await the return of Jesus Christ. Peace is found *as* we live holy and godly lives. Throughout his letters, Paul tells early Christians that the secret to being at peace with God is to grow to be more like Christ *daily*. Jesus told His disciples in *John 14:27* that He was leaving them with a different kind of peace: *Peace I leave with you; my peace I give you. I do not give to you as the world gives. Do not let your hearts be troubled and do not be afraid.* The world offers us a fleeting peace based on circumstances, success, and material possessions. We are offered a different kind of peace based on the knowledge and grace of Jesus Christ. Peter ends this letter as he began with warnings to the suffering church. They were not to listen to false teachers, but to put their hope in Christ who would be with them always.

Have you lost your peace? Check out any areas of your life where you may need to be reconciled to God: places of disobedience, offenses against others, or anything that blocks holiness. If you are looking for the world to give you peace, remember that God's peace is different. His peace is available when we follow Him: *If only you had paid attention to my commands, your peace would have been like a river, your righteousness like waves of the sea. (Isaiah 48:18)*

Heavenly Father,

Help me in my journey with You to make every effort to be found blameless before You. Restore my peace where I have disobeyed You and help me to remember that Your peace depends on my relationship with You.
In Jesus' name, Amen

September 6

Dominion of Man

God blessed them and said to them, "Be fruitful and increase in number; fill the earth and subdue it. Rule over the fish of the sea and the birds of the air and over every living creature that moves on the ground."
Genesis 1:28

God entrusted the earth to the care of mankind. Earth is the divinely appointed place for mankind where man lives under God's rule and care and enjoys God's abundant blessings. God told man and woman to rule over the earth and subdue it. (*Genesis 1:28*) As God's servants, we are called to share in His kingly rule as stewards of His creation. God's confidence in us, His beloved creation, inspires me to seek God's wisdom, power, and courage to step up to my responsibility to care for the earth and its creatures.

God has entrusted us with the message of the kingdom to be spoken and demonstrated on the earth in our places of work, in our families, our schools. He gave us dominion over the earth and gave us everything we need to do it. But it is our responsibility to carry His message of salvation to a lost world. Salvation is the message of "shalom": wholeness, wellbeing, and peace. He has asked us to rule over the earth and subdue it. All of us have a sphere of influence—a place that God has planted us to insure His kingdom will expand and take root.

Adam and Eve were given authority to rule on earth because they were made in God's image. As God's representatives on earth, they were called to be stewards of God's creation. We are also called to preserve the earth, not to exploit, waste, or destroy the resources of the earth. It is time we remember it is our responsibility to seek ways to care for the earth and the creatures of the earth. Consider what you can do to care for the earth; consider how you can extend the message of "shalom" on earth by words and deeds. God is calling us to remember that in the beginning He created the earth and it was good. (Genesis 1)

Heavenly Father,

Forgive me for not heeding Your Word and accepting responsibility for the welfare of the earth and the creatures of the earth. Help me to remember that You have entrusted me with the message of the kingdom to be spoken and demonstrated on the earth.
In Jesus' name, Amen

The Enemy Destroyed

When they had brought these kings to Joshua, he summoned all the men of Israel and said to the army commanders who had come with him, "Come here and put your feet on the necks of these kings." So they came forward and placed their feet on their necks.
Joshua 10:24

Ancient kings often placed their feet on their enemies as a symbol of their strength and conquering power over them. Joshua told the commanders of the Israelite army to put their feet on the necks of the enemy kings who were captured. Jesus disarmed the power and authority of the evil one when He died on the cross. He put the enemy under His feet signifying His conquering power over Satan, death, and sin. Although the ultimate defeat of the enemy has been accomplished, until the day when Christ returns, the enemy still prowls, trying to disrupt our lives: *Be self-controlled and alert. Your enemy the devil prowls around like a roaring lion looking for someone to devour. Resist, standing firm in the faith. (I Peter 4:8-9)*

Joshua symbolically had the Israelite commanders put their feet on the neck of the defeated kings. Jesus put the enemy under His feet when He disarmed powers and authorities and made them a public spectacle on the cross. (Colossians 2:15) It seemed as though Jesus was defeated on the cross, but on the third day He rose from the grave, and in essence, that day His triumph placed His feet on the neck of Satan.

Life throws a lot of curve balls. Some of those are caused by the poor decisions we make; others are thrown by people who are in opposition to us. But there are times when the enemy seeks to disrupt our lives with his lies and the confusion that his lies bring. His strategy is to have us agree with his lies, and when in agreement, he gains a foothold in our lives. In essence, he places his foot on the neck of our lives: *Do not let the sun go down while you are still angry and do not give the devil a foothold. He who has been stealing must steal no longer. (Ephesians 4:27)* Anger is a key way the enemy gains a foothold in our lives. Anger left unchecked gives the enemy a place in our lives. As we recognize his tactics, we must remember that He who lives in us

(Christ Jesus) is stronger than he who lives in the world (the devil). Thanks be to God that Christ has defeated the enemy on the cross and has placed His feet on the neck of all of his strategies.
Do you need to be rescued from the pit? Call upon the Lord, praise His name, forget not His benefits and remember that He will redeem your life from the pit and will crown you with love and compassion.

Heavenly Father,
I cry out to You for mercy. I am crushed in spirit and need Your healing and deliverance. I cling to Your Word that when I cry out, You will rescue me.
In Jesus' name, Amen

False Rumors

It is reported among the nations—and Geshem says it is true—that you and the Jews are plotting to revolt, and therefore you are building the wall. Moreover, according to these reports you are about to become their king and have even appointed prophets to make this proclamation about you in Jerusalem: 'There is a king in Judah!' Now this report will get back to the king; so come, let us confer together.
Nehemiah 6:6-7

False rumors can be one of the most destructive tools in the arsenal of the enemy. They sometimes begin with a half-truth or a twisting of the truth, but just as often they are not based on truth at all. Rumors often have no validity but are taken as fact. The "rumor mill" can only take root if there is a conduit for the rumor to be spread. It is our responsibility as Christians to stop the gossip. Nehemiah again models godly leadership as he confronts the rumor that his enemies are spreading about Nehemiah himself and the Jewish people. He does not seek to justify his actions by telling them that the project is legitimate because the king gave him authority and supplies to do the work. He does not run to his friends and tell them what terrible things his enemies are saying about him. He goes directly to the source and refutes the lie. The enemy is empowered in darkness; he creeps around in the dark seeking whom he may devour. (*I Peter 5:8*) Scripture tells us to bring all things into the light. That is how we must combat the enemy. Nehemiah brings the truth into the light and then prays that the Lord will strengthen his hands.

Perhaps you have been the victim of vicious rumors, or perhaps you have been a part of spreading false rumors. Ask the Holy Spirit to forgive your participation in spreading rumors through gossip and seek to forgive those who have spread rumors against you.

Heavenly Father,
Forgive me for spreading rumors or for gossiping. I forgive those who have spread false rumors about me. Let me be a godly leader like Nehemiah who chose to live above reproach in all that he did.
In Jesus' name, Amen

September 10

God's Perfect Plan

Not only that, but Rebekah's children had one and the same father, our father Isaac. Yet, before the twins were born or had done anything good or bad—in order that God's purpose in election might stand.
Romans 9:10-11

As Paul struggles with the issue of his fellow Jews' rejection of the Messiah, he describes the favored position the Israelites held, receiving the covenants, the law, temple worship, and the promises of God. The Jews believed that only the children of Abraham could attain salvation. Paul, however, separates believing Israel from unbelieving Israel and begins to build his case that although not biologically descended from Abraham, believing Gentiles are regarded as children of the promise. God's perfect plan is seen throughout the history of Israel, and Paul systematically shows how God's election of Abraham, Isaac, and Jacob fit His plan. Just as Israel was chosen to be a nation separated for God, Abraham, Isaac and Jacob were men elected to fulfill God's plan and purposes. Paul, a Jew, was distressed that those who had been the recipients of God's promises had failed to inherit them. The question then remains: What will happen to God's chosen people? If Israel rejected God's Messiah, would God reject Israel? Does Israel's rejection of the Messiah change the status of "election" for the nation of Israel? It is easy to see Paul's struggle with these questions as he works his way through *Romans 9-11*, but one theme resounds clearly: God's plan is perfect and His promises stand. He used rebellious Israel throughout the Old Testament to keep His plan moving forward, and He will work things out for the ultimate good of the people He created and loves. What hope that should give us, that although the circumstances of our lives seem as though we have been rejected by God, His love is unfailing and His promises to us will always be fulfilled.

What promises have you been waiting on that are yet unfulfilled? Trust in the Lord and remember that He has a plan and that His purposes and plans will stand the test of time.

Heavenly Father,
Thank you that Your plan keeps moving forward and that You will work all things out for my good. Thank you that You used the Israelites, even in their rebellion, to work out Your purposes. My hope is in You and Your unfailing goodness.
In Jesus' name, Amen

September 11

Love Covers Sin

The LORD is slow to anger, abounding in love and forgiving sin and rebellion. Yet he does not leave the guilty unpunished; he punishes the children for the sin of the fathers to the third and fourth generation.
Numbers 14:18

Absalom fled David's kingdom after he killed his brother Amnon for disgracing his sister. *(II Samuel 13)* King David eventually brought Absalom back. Absalom then began a conspiracy to take over the kingdom. He set himself up as judge over the people, sitting by the city gates and dispensing justice. After four years, he led a rebellion against his father. David fled from Jerusalem. In spite of all this, David told his soldiers, *"Be gentle with the young man Absalom for my sake." (II Samuel 18:5)* When Absalom was killed in battle, David mourned, saying, *"O my son Absalom! My son, my son Absalom! If only I had died instead of you." (II Samuel 18:33)* David's love for his son Absalom was extraordinary. It is a love that is not self-seeking, proud, or envious, keeping no record of wrongs. Indeed, we need the power of the Holy Spirit to love others in this way! David had every reason to turn his back on his rebellious son who sought to take his throne from him, but the character of God consumed his life, and, like God, he was slow to anger, abounding in love, and forgiving.

It is easy to love those who are lovable and kind to you, but the true test of the character of Christ in you is to love your enemies: *But I tell you: Love your enemies and pray for those who persecute you that you may be sons of your Father in heaven…If you love those who love you what reward will you get? (Matthew 5:44-46)*

Who is God calling you to love today? Is it someone who has hurt you, someone who has been like Absalom to David and conspired behind your back to harm you? Trust the Lord and seek His love. He is calling you to love your enemies and to do good to all who hate you. (Luke 6:27)

Heavenly Father,

This is a difficult Word. I have been wronged, and yet You are calling me to love my enemy. Pour Your love in me so that I can love those who have hurt me. Apart from You it is impossible to love in this way.
In Jesus' name, Amen

September 12

The Power and Prestige Trap

Everything they do is done for men to see: They make their phylacteries wide and the tassels on their garments long; they love the place of honor at banquets and the most important seats in the synagogues.
Matthew 23:5-6

In *Matthew* 20, the mother of James and John requested that Jesus allow her sons to sit on each side of Jesus in His kingdom. At first glance, we hear a mother's request that spans the ages. A mother today could easily desire for her sons to have a special place of authority. As parents, we wish the highest and best for our children. Parents today naturally seek to advance their children to their highest potential. In my opinion, there is nothing wrong with that; however, when the motive is to have power or prestige, or even authority that God has not ordained, we can fall into a trap of self-promotion, or in this case of promoting our children apart from the will of God. In the same story in *Mark*, the mother is never mentioned. Instead, the sons ask for this special position of favor. Regardless of who made the request to Jesus, the deeper truth here is that we are to humbly serve the Lord and others, seek Him and His will in all things, and trust *Him* to place us in positions where *He* has called us.

Jesus tells the crowds and His disciples that the Pharisees did everything for men to see. Their religious activities were a sham because they did not practice what they preached. *(Matthew 23:5-6)* The Pharisees were more concerned with their power and position than they were with their relationship with God.

In the case of the promotion of James and John and the hypocrisy of the Pharisees, we see a common problem. The concern was for themselves, not for others. Their desire was to self-promote—to have the position of honor, and in the case of the Pharisees, the coveted title of Rabbi. The Lord came as a humble servant, and He modeled a servant's heart throughout His ministry on earth. As He went to the cross, He did not consider equality with God as something He needed to attain; after all, He *was* God. He could have told His Father, I would like plan "B" please—not the cross. He could have reminded His Father that He was the

King's Son. No, He chose to become a servant, to die as a criminal taking the lowest position of all. He has paid for our freedom so that we will never need prestige or power; we only need Him.

Heavenly Father,

Forgive me for desiring prestige and power. Sometimes I get so caught up in the world, thinking that the world will offer me something that I don't have. Forgive my discontentment and enable me to have a servant's heart.

In Jesus' name, Amen

September 13

Believing Prayer

And without faith it is impossible to please God, because anyone who comes to him must believe that he exists and that he rewards those who earnestly seek him.
Hebrews 11:6

The godly men and women of the Old Testament prayed with great devotion to God, believing that He would hear their cry. Daniel, for example, prayed three times a day to God and believed that God would save him even when thrown in the lions' den and in the fiery pit. The psalmist knew that God would answer his prayers: *I waited patiently for the Lord; He turned to me and heard my cry. (Psalm 40)* Hezekiah turned to prayer when faced with the armed Assyrians and all seemed hopeless, and God heard his cry and saved him and the people of Jerusalem. *(Isaiah 37:21-35)*

Jesus, God with flesh, came to earth and commended those with faith, those who would believe that through prayer that all things are possible with God. God not only hears our prayers, He also answers them. It may not be in the way we expect, but He will indeed answer!

Have you been praying for God to answer a prayer for some time now? As you pray, do you really believe that He hears your prayers? Do you believe that He desires to answer your prayers? The key is this: He wants you to delight in Him so that He can give you the desires of your heart. (Psalm 37:4) He wants you to be so close to Him that you will know His will and pray for His will to come and His kingdom to be released in your circumstances. He wants you to be so connected to His heart that your prayers become His prayers and His prayers become your prayers. That is the prayer of the faithful; that is the prayer that moves heaven to invade earth.

Heavenly Father,
My prayers have been filled with selfish requests. I have not sought You as much as I sought for You to answer my prayers. I am turning back to You to love You, to know You, and to delight in You, and I know that You will take care of all my needs.
In Jesus' name, Amen

Taking the Land Back for God

Now then, you and all these people, get ready to cross the
Jordan River into the land I am about to give them—to the Israelites.
I will give you every place where you set your foot.
Joshua 1:2-3

Moses, the leader of Israel, died and the baton was passed to Joshua. God instructed Joshua to get ready to cross into the Promised Land—the place of their inheritance—the place they had been traveling to for so many years. Now the time had come to finally see the fulfillment of the long awaited promise, and Joshua was probably afraid. Did he have what it took to lead these people? Was he a strong leader like Moses, or would he crack under the pressure? Would others compare him to Moses, or worse still, would *he* compare himself to Moses? God must have heard his thoughts because he spoke to Joshua words that have been quoted throughout the ages—*I will give you every place where you set your foot*—and then words that drove his fears away: *Be strong and courageous. Do not be terrified; do not be discouraged, for the Lord your God will be with you wherever you go. (v.9)*

Have you ever had to follow another leader wondering if you could ever fill their shoes? Have you ever wondered why God would ask you to do something that you did not feel qualified to do? God is not looking for qualified people to answer His call. He is looking to qualify those who look to Him to answer the call. Joshua had been with Moses and had observed and participated in leadership. In many ways, he was equipped to do the job, but God knew that Joshua needed words of encouragement because Joshua was dependent on God. Joshua had spent many hours outside of the tent of meeting when Moses met with God and knew that He needed God to go wherever he went.

Has God called you to do the impossible? Have you told Him that you are under qualified for the job? Remember that He gives grace to the humble and strengthens the weak.

Heavenly Father,

I confess that I am afraid to step out in faith and do what You have called me to do. Give me the courage to trust You and know that You will be with me wherever I go.
In Jesus' name, Amen

Abundant Peace

The fruit of righteousness will be peace; the effect of righteousness will be quietness and confidence forever.
Isaiah 32:17

Jehovah Shalom promises that our peace will be like a river. *(Isaiah 66:12)* When we accept Jesus as our Savior, He comes into us in the form of His Holy Spirit and becomes our "living water" and our peace. Jesus Christ told the Samaritan woman at the well, *If you knew the gift of God and who it is that asks you for a drink, you would have asked Him and He would have given you living water. (John 4:10)* As we then continue to drink of the well of living water through His Holy Spirit, we are filled with supernatural peace. Jehovah Shalom longs to give us abundant peace if we are willing to drink from the river of life.

Shalom means peace, well-being, and wholeness. Jesus offers us eternal life when we turn from our sins and turn to Him. Salvation is at work from the moment we receive Him into our lives. From that moment, the Prince of Peace resides in us to work His salvation into us—His shalom, peace, well-being, and wholeness. Our anxiety is replaced with His peace. Our fears are replaced with His peace. Our anger, our disappointments are all replaced with "shalom." Quiet confidence replaces self-confidence.

Years ago I met a young woman who exuded this peace. It was her peace that led me to desire more and more of Jesus. I wanted what she had. Does your life reflect the fruit of righteousness which is peace and the effect of righteousness which is quietness and confidence? If not, ask the Holy Spirit to bring His healing and deliverance into any part of your life where you are experiencing anxiety or loss of peace.

Heavenly Father,
Help me to trust You to let go of the things that I worry about. I desire for Your peace to be like a river in my life, flowing to all of the people around me.
In Jesus' name, Amen

September 16

Deception

When word came to Sanballat, Tobiah, Geshem the Arab and the rest of our enemies that I had rebuilt the wall and not a gap was left in it—though up to that time I had not set the doors in the gates—Sanballat and Geshem sent me this message: "Come, let us meet together in one of the villages on the plain of Ono." But they were scheming to harm me.
Nehemiah 6:1-2

When the enemies heard that the wall had been rebuilt and there were no gaps left, they stepped up their tactics of intimidation. They sent word to Nehemiah to leave his work and meet them. The enemy begins to notice when the Lord "closes the gaps" in our broken walls as well. Where he once had access to our thought life, our emotions, and the ability to affect our actions, he now is being closed out. The Holy Spirit is always at work when we surrender to Him and bring our lives in closer union with Christ. The enemy seeks to interfere with this process of spiritual transformation. Sanballat, Tobiah, Geshem, and the rest of the enemies became fearful that the position of the Jews would be strengthened and this would undermine the authority and power that they now held in that region.

The enemy thrives on having power and authority, but he can only have that kind of influence in the places where we are weakened. A significant way the enemy finds access is through deception. He may even use partial truths to throw us off course and have us believe a lie. Scripture tells us we must be alert to the schemes of the evil one. Believers throughout the ages have sought God for discernment: *I am your servant; give me discernment that I may understand your statutes. (Psalm 119:125)* Deception began in the Garden of Eden when the serpent deceived Eve into eating the apple. Jesus warned us of "deceivers" who would come. (*Luke 21:8*) Deception has been a tool in the enemy's arsenal throughout the ages; however, the Lord has given us the Counselor, His Holy Spirit, to discern deception and to know the truth. (*John 16:12-13*)

Heavenly Father,

Close the gaps of my life where the enemy has access; the broken-down places; the places of unbelief and lack of trust. Protect me from the deception of the enemy, and lead me in the truth of Your Word.
In Jesus' name, Amen

September 17

God's Unfailing Mercy

It does not, therefore, depend on man's desire or effort, but on God's mercy.
Romans 9:16

Paul makes a radical statement in *Romans 9:15*: *What then shall we say? Is God unjust? Not at all! For He says to Moses: I will have mercy on whom I have mercy, and I will have compassion on whom I have compassion.* After writing that, God chose Jacob over Esau in order that His purpose in election might stand. Paul tells Christians that God is sovereign, and He can show mercy and have compassion on whomever He wishes. Paul is underscoring that God's mercy is not as we imagine it or as we hope it will be. His mercy is much greater than we can comprehend. The Lord has the "bigger picture" in mind, and His highest form of mercy is seen in His fulfilling His plan and purpose. We cannot always see where God is going, but we can learn to trust His character.

Moses discovered God's character when he asked God to send His glory to help him to lead the Israelites out of Egypt. God described His glory to Moses as His goodness in the following passage of Scripture in *Exodus 33: I will cause my goodness to pass in front of you, and I will proclaim my name, the Lord in your presence. I will have mercy on whom I will have mercy, and I will have compassion on whom I will have compassion.* Paul emphasizes God's mercy to those who are destined for destruction as He patiently waits for their repentance. He points to His highest purpose of mercy leaving a remnant to carry out His purposes. *(vv.28-29)*

I have a gift of mercy. In God's hands it is a beautiful thing, but in the hands of the enemy it becomes people-pleasing. God's mercy is strong, truthful, and full of God's highest purposes. Mercy manipulated by the evil one is masked in seeking approval, which is self-centered rather than God- centered. God's mercy may be seen in the form of tough love. Man's mercy may be seen in indulgence.

Heavenly Father,
I desire to have Your mercy, motivated by love and truth. Lead me, Holy Spirit, to be merciful God's way. - In Jesus' name, Amen

Name Above all Names

My prayer is not that you take them out of the world, but that you protect them from the evil one.
John 17:15

Jesus prayed to His Father and asked Him to protect His disciples. He did not pray that they be taken out of the world, but that they would be protected while in the world. The world is where His disciples would do their work of advancing the kingdom. He knew that the enemy would seek to keep them from doing the Father's will. Jesus prayed to the Father that they would be protected by the power of His name: *Holy Father, protect them by the power of your name—the name you gave me—so that they may be one as we are one. (v.11)* There is power in the name of Jesus Christ.

In the Old Testament, the men and women of God came to know and understand the character of God through His name. Every time they experienced a side of God, they discovered another facet of His nature that was given a name. For example, God called Abraham to sacrifice his son Isaac on the altar. God had promised Abraham that from his seed would come many nations, and Isaac was the first installment on His promise. Now God asks him to sacrifice the only possibility for fulfillment of this promise. Abraham obeyed and prepared to sacrifice his son, but God intervened and provided another sacrifice. That day Abraham came face to face with God the Provider, Jehovah Jireh. Throughout the Old Testament, we meet Jehovah Rohi (our Shepherd), Elohim (our Creator), and Jehovah Raphe (our Healer).

The name of God is powerful, and through His Son Jesus Christ we are faced with the name above all names: *Therefore God exalted him to the highest place and gave him the name above every name, that at the name of Jesus every knee should bow in heaven and on earth and under the earth, and every tongue confess that Jesus Christ is Lord to the glory of God the Father. (Philippians 2:9-11)*

Heavenly Father,
Protect me and my family by the power of Your name. I exalt You to the highest place as Messiah, King of Kings and Lord of Lords.
In Jesus' name, Amen

Answered Prayer

. . .he was chosen by lot, according to the custom of the priesthood, to go into the temple of the Lord and burn incense. And when the time for the burning of incense came, all the assembled worshipers were praying outside.
Luke 1:9-10

The angel of the Lord appeared to Zechariah when he was in the temple of the Lord praying that his wife would bear a son named John. His son John, later to be known as John the Baptist, prepared the way for the coming Messiah. Zechariah did not believe God, so God made him silent until the baby was born. What catches my attention in this story is that Zechariah had been praying when God appeared and spoke. Zechariah was in the Presence of God, praying to God, and yet he did not believe God.

Sometimes we pray, and when God answers our prayers we do not recognize His answer, or we choose not to believe this is His answer. Scriptures tell us that God is attentive to our prayers, and when we pray in faith, we must believe that He answers. The problem is that we don't believe. Perhaps the answer to our prayer is different than we expect, or perhaps our prayers do not line up with the will of God. Nevertheless, when we pray, we are called to believe and expect that God will answer.

Prayer is communicating with God, seeking His will, and sharing our heart. Luke tells us in the gospel of Luke that we must ask, seek, and knock with bold prayers, expecting God to answer: *So I say to you: Ask and it will be given to you; seek and you will find; knock and the door will be opened to you. For everyone who asks receives; he who seeks finds; and to him who knocks the door will be opened. (Luke 11:9-10)*

James explains that we do not get answers to our prayers because we ask with the wrong motives: *When you ask you do not receive, because you ask with wrong motives, that you may spend on your own pleasures. (James 4:3)* Prayer is not intended to procure what we want for ourselves; prayer is our communication with God, connecting with Him to understand what is on His heart. Naturally we pray for things on our hearts, our concerns and needs, but the distinguishing factor is our motive.

Jesus said the prayer that touches the heart of God begins with *your kingdom come, your will be done on earth as it is in heaven. (Matthew 6:9)* When we seek God in prayer, our ultimate goal is for God's will to be done.

Heavenly Father,
Forgive me for my selfish prayers. Thank you for reminding me that prayer is communicating with You and sharing my heart. My desire is that You will share Your heart with me.
In Jesus' name, Amen

Accomplishing God's Purpose through His Strength

Now then, just as the LORD promised, he has kept me alive for forty-five years since the time he said this to Moses, while Israel moved about in the desert. So here I am today, eighty-five years old!
Joshua 14:10

When we depend on God, He gives us strength for each season of our lives. He is not concerned with how old we are in numeric terms. He is concerned with how mature we are in Him. Throughout our lives, the Lord calls us to serve Him as part of His army of soldiers. We never retire from God's army. Joshua was over 85 years old when the Lord spoke to him in *Joshua 13:1*. There was a lot of work yet to be accomplished for the Lord. Large areas of land still needed to be taken, and these lands needed to be divided up among the tribes.

Joshua and the apostle Paul both knew that their years were numbered, yet a vast amount of work remained to be accomplished to fulfill God's purposes. Throughout their lives, both continued to fight the battles that were before them. Joshua continued to work into his old age to fulfill what God had called him to do. I imagine there were times when both men were tired or discouraged or felt like giving up before their tasks were completed. Yet God gave them the strength to persevere. The Lord has numbered our days and has given us all a purpose to glorify Him on this earth and to spread His Word. As I write this devotional, I feel as though there are not enough hours in the day. Yet, the Lord reassures me that *I can seek Him and His strength, that I can do all things in Christ who strengthens me*, and that *He will renew my strength each day. (Philippians 4:13)* As I depend on Him, I will be able to accomplish all of the things He would have me do. It is the same for you. Remember, retirement is not an option for a child of the King!

Heavenly Father,

Strengthen me to do the things You have called me to do. Help me to remember that I can do all things through You.
In Jesus' name, Amen

Boomerang Judgment

Do not judge or you too will be judged. For in the same way you judge others, you will be judged, and with the measure you use, it will be measured to you.
Matthew 7:1-2

Judging others has a boomerang effect on our lives. When we judge others, the judgment comes back on us. With the same measure we judge, it will be measured back to us. For example, you may decide never to be like one of your parents, and yet you find that you are doing the same things they did. The judgments that you made against them found a way back to you! Although we are called to judge between good and evil, we are not to judge a person; only God knows what is in their heart. Sometimes it is easy to be the judge and jury, but only God is the righteous judge. Jesus warned us not to judge because He knew that this is an area of great temptation for all of us. We judge because we see a speck in someone's eye and Jesus tells us: *Why do you look at the speck of sawdust in your brother's eye and pay no attention to the plank in your own eye? (v.3)* What we see in other people and judge, God locates in us. We find it easy to judge because we are familiar with the very action that we are judging.

God's Word tells us that mercy triumphs over judgment. *(James 2:13)* Grace sees the sin in someone, mercy sees the misery, and judgment sees neither. Think of someone you have judged. Ask the Lord to give you "kingdom lenses" to see this person as He sees them. Chances are the person you are judging has issues that run deeper than you are able to see. Man sees the outward appearances; God sees the heart. *(I Samuel 16:7)* Make a commitment today to leave judgment to God.

Heavenly Father,
Help me to see others as You see them. Forgive me where I have judged others harshly. Forgive me where I have judged myself harshly, and lead me in Your mercy.
In Jesus' name, Amen

September 22

Setting a Godly Example

But the earlier governors—those preceding me—placed a heavy burden on the people and took forty shekels of silver from them in addition to food and wine. Their assistants also lorded it over the people. But out of reverence for God, I did not act like that. Instead, I devoted myself to the work on this wall. All my men were assembled there for the work; we did not acquire any land.
Nehemiah 5:15-16

Nehemiah rebuked the nobles for exacting usury from their Jewish brothers, and he implemented a plan of correction. He then told the nobles how he had set an example for them of how to treat their Jewish brothers fairly. He told them that it was out of reverence for God that he did not take advantage of his Jewish brethren as they had done. Once again, Nehemiah displays godly leadership as he devotes himself to the work alongside the Jews and contributes to the welfare of the people monetarily. As Christian leaders, God calls us to set an example in thought, word, and deed as we do His work. Nehemiah worked on the wall and he supplied food for the officials and the Jews: *I never demanded the food allotted to the governor, because the demands were heavy on these people. (5:18b)* The governors before Nehemiah had placed a heavy burden on the people and took forty shekels of silver from them in addition to food and wine. Nehemiah's success in motivating the people was due to his humility and concern for the people. Christian leaders have a responsibility to lead by example. Leadership is defined as "influence."

Recently a young woman approached me and shared with me that her mother had rejected her and that she had not seen her in years. She subsequently has had a problem with women in authority. One day she saw me talking in the church with some other women and decided that I was just like other women in authority who would reject her. She had come to the class that I teach and was looking for her group. I left the room and the Lord nudged me to turn back and ask her if she needed any help in finding her group. The young woman told me later that in that moment she realized someone cared. I learned something important—we never know who is watching us. I had no idea that young woman had pressing needs and that a simple kind gesture from me would have such an impact on her. Consider your sphere of influence and the affect you have on others. Ask the Lord to help you be like Nehemiah who led by example and did not consider his leadership position to be a place of honor, but a place of service.

Heavenly Father,
Help me to be a godly leader who serves rather than expects to be served, who looks out for the needs of others rather than seeking to have my own needs met.
In Jesus' name, Amen

September 23

Life Worthy of the Calling

As a prisoner of the Lord, then I urge you to live a life worthy of the calling you have received. Be completely humble and gentle; be patient, bearing with one another in love. Make every effort to keep the unity of the Spirit through the bond of peace.

Ephesians 4:1-3

It is believed that Paul penned these words while he was a prisoner in Rome. He was writing to the church in Ephesus, and this was probably a circular letter intended for other churches as well. Perhaps Paul was reflecting on his own life. Had he led a life worthy of the calling? He knew that the life of the church was dependent on believers fulfilling their calling with humility and love towards one another. He knew that it would take effort to keep the unity of the Spirit through the bond of peace. Christians needed to bear with one another, exhibiting patience and humility. Why was this so important to Paul? As a missionary he had worked with believers. He had seen the intensity, pressure and opposition against those who sought to spread the gospel. He knew first hand the abuse suffered on account of his sharing the gospel in hostile places. But he also had seen the church united, the church fighting for God's kingdom to come and for His will to be done. He knew that a church united would stand and a church divided would fall. It is interesting to note that Paul follows up in this same passage in Ephesians with a description of individuals using their gifts for God in order to prepare God's people for works of service: *It was he who gave some to be apostles, some to be prophets, some to be evangelists, and some to be pastors and teachers, to prepare God's people for works of service, so that the body of Christ may be built up...(Ephesians 4:11-12)*

God is still calling us to make every effort to keep the unity of the Spirit. He is calling us to be patient and humble and to use the gifts He has apportioned to us to build up the body of believers in preparation for service.

Are you living a life worthy of the calling you have received? Seek to be patient and gentle, making every effort to keep the unity of the Spirit. God will meet you daily as you join with others as one body seeking to grow His kingdom.

Heavenly Father,
I recognize that I have made very little effort to be patient and work with others to keep the unity of the Spirit. Help me to bear with one another and to be willing to exercise my gifts in order to build up the body of Christ.
In Jesus' name, Amen

September 24

Love Keeps No Record of Wrongs

Make sure that nobody pays back wrong for wrong, but always try to be kind to each other and to everyone else.
I Thessalonians 5:15

One of Paul's descriptions of love is not keeping a record of wrongs. *(I Corinthians 13:6)* I would need a volume of books to record all the times I have kept a record of those I felt had wronged me! Fortunately, the Lord in His mercy and love has shown me a better way. He has helped me burn the records and replace them with His love. Love covers a multitude of sins, including my record keeping! The Lord wants us to be record keepers of love. We need the power of the Holy Spirit to live a life of love. Paul knew that the key to growing spiritually was to leave the past behind and strain to what is ahead. *(Philippians 3:12-14)*

David was wronged in many ways by Saul, by Absalom, and by those who did not remain loyal to him. He "pressed on," however, knowing that he was a man of vision on a mission. We also must respond to God's vision and mission. We must press on in love so that the enemy cannot gain a foothold in our lives. David could have ended his mission at any time if he had focused on the wrongs committed against him, but he made a choice to love.

What does it mean to love with Christ's love? Christ's love is unconditional, expecting nothing in return; Christ's love sees the best in us; Christ's love sees our hurts, our desires, and our needs. Think about someone in your life who is difficult to love. Ask the Lord to help you to overlook the wrongs they have done and to see them through God's eyes. Many years ago I did just that. There was someone in my life who was very difficult. I prayed unceasingly that the Lord would give me love for him and that I would be able to see him through God's eyes. The Lord began to reveal to me *His* heart for this person, and compassion, understanding and love began to grow in me. I learned in this season of growth that I did not have to overlook the wrong done to me, but I also did not have to keep a record of the wrong. Keeping a record of the wrong was like keeping a score card, and the negative points kept adding up. It left no room in my heart to see through "kingdom eyes."

Heavenly Father,
Help me to throw away my score card when someone has hurt me. Forgive me where I have at times enjoyed keeping score. Help me to see people through Your eyes of love.
In Jesus' name, Amen

September 25

The Son of Man Returns

At that time the sign of the Son of Man will appear in the sky,
and all the nations of the earth will mourn. They will see the Son of Man
coming on the clouds of the sky, with power and great glory.
Matthew 24:30

Jesus ends the Olivet Discourse with the disciples proclaiming that *the Son of Man will appear in the sky, and the nations of the earth will mourn. (Matthew 24:30)* They will see the Son of Man coming on the clouds of the sky with power and great glory. He reminds them that heaven and earth will pass away, but that His words will remain forever. *(Matthew 24:35)* In a world constantly changing, it is reassuring to know that God's words are true. Although we live in an isolated segment of time, what is happening in the affairs of men and the events of our day are fulfilling what our Lord said would occur.

Jesus asks this question: *when the Son of Man comes, will he find faith on the earth? (Luke 18:8)* This question follows the parable of the persistent widow who kept going to the judge pleading for justice against her adversary. For some time he refused, but finally because of her persistence, he made sure that she received justice. Jesus commends those who cry out for justice in a demonstration of their faith in God. The Son of Man will be returning, and in the meantime He has told us to keep the faith, to be persistent in prayer, and to seek justice through His mercy. It is easy to continue in our lives disregarding the fact that Jesus will one day return. He is preparing His bride, the church, for His return, and He is looking for faith on the earth upon His return.

As you look to the return of Jesus Christ, are you endeavoring to fulfill your part in bringing God's kingdom to earth? Are there areas of your life where you have not been persistent in prayer? Is your faith a demonstration of your trust that God is in control? There will come a time, according to God' Word, where persecution will increase; a time of spiritual decline and a time where the Christian message is considered obsolete. I believe that time is drawing near. Jesus is warning us to stand firm and persevere just as the widow did in the parable: *When the Son of Man comes, will he find faith on the earth? (Luke 18:8)*

Heavenly Father,
Increase my faith that I may persevere in my faith. Help me to overcome my complacency and give me renewed passion for Your Word. Heaven and earth will someday pass away, but Your Word will remain forever.
In Jesus' name, Amen

September 26

Preparing the Way

A voice of one calling: "In the desert prepare the way for the LORD; make straight in the wilderness a highway for our God. Every valley shall be raised up, every mountain and hill made low; the rough ground shall become level, the rugged places a plain. And the glory of the LORD will be revealed, and all mankind together will see it. For the mouth of the LORD has spoken."
Isaiah 40:3-5

The picture we have in *Isaiah 40:3-5* is that of repairing roads, removing obstacles, and preparing the way for the coming of a king. The image of a highway is frequently used in Isaiah's prophecy. Isaiah prophesied against the Assyrian threat to Jerusalem, and now He points to the fulfillment of God's comfort for the captives in Babylon. He describes God's deliverance of the captive Israelites in the midst of the wilderness describing a highway fit for a king.

This Word is fulfilled in the ministry of John the Baptist who came to prepare the way for the ministry of Jesus Christ. Just like the days when the roads were prepared for a king's arrival, John the Baptist prepared the way for Christ to come. He removed the obstacles from the roads of life by preaching repentance. When John the Baptist began his ministry of preparation, the gospel of Mark points to the fulfillment of Isaiah's prophecy: *It is written in Isaiah the prophet: I will send a messenger ahead of you, who will prepare the way—a voice of one calling in the desert, prepare the way for the Lord, make straight paths for him. (Mark 1:1-3)*

We can take comfort that God goes before us even in the most difficult of times, preparing the roads in our lives by removing the obstacles so that we can draw near to Him. What obstacles do you have that need to be removed to make way for King Jesus? Seek the Lord and trust Him with the roadblocks of your life. He is calling to you in the desert places of life; He is seeking to come into the places of your life where rubble and obstacles have stood in the way. He is calling to you to prepare the way—a voice crying out in the wilderness.

Heavenly Father,
I can hear You calling as a voice in the wilderness of my life. I desire for You to remove anything that separates me from Your love and cry out to You to make the rough parts of my life level.
In Jesus' name, Amen

September 27

His Promised Return

But the day of the Lord will come like a thief. The heavens will disappear with a roar; the elements will be destroyed by fire, and the earth and everything in it will be laid bare.
II Peter 3:10

The disciples asked Jesus to describe the sign of His coming again. In the gospel of *Matthew,* Jesus described the signs that would precede His coming. However, He also told them that they would not know the time of His return. Peter stresses in his letter that believers are not to be swayed by false teachers or scoffers, those who say Jesus will not return, or those who claim to know the specific date of His return. It is important that we wait patiently, always being prepared for His return. Peter tells us that the Lord is infinitely patient. He desires that no one perish but that everyone is given the opportunity to repent and come to salvation before He returns. For some, the wait for Christ's return has caused laziness and lack of commitment to a holy life. The materialism of the world has captured hearts, and little concern is given to the return of the Messiah. In fact, the thought of His return is disconcerting because enjoying of the pleasures of this earth is paramount. Some tend to ignore things like environmental concerns and social issues, believing that when Christ returns, He will transform the earth.

Peter tells us, however, that the day of the Lord's return will come like a thief in the night. In the meantime, we must take seriously Peter's admonition to live holy and godly lives as we look forward to the day of Christ's return. *(II Peter 3:12)*

Holiness means "being set apart" for God. In what ways do you need to be set apart from the world? Do you spend endless hours watching TV programs that do not edify God? Do you spend time on the phone gossiping or judging others? Ask the Holy Spirit to do a heart exam and be open to the possibility that He is calling you to make some changes. Without holiness, no one will see the Lord. *(Hebrews 12:14)* He is calling us to holiness so that we will be able to behold Him

Heavenly Father,
Prepare me for Your return. Keep me from the things of the world that separate me from You. Give me a pure heart so that I might see You.
In Jesus' name, Amen

September 28

The Envy Trap

But if you harbor bitter envy and selfish ambition in your hearts, do not boast about it or deny the truth. Such "wisdom" does not come down from heaven but is earthly, unspiritual, of the devil. For where you have envy and selfish ambition, there you find disorder and every evil practice. But the wisdom that comes from heaven is first of all pure; then peace-loving, considerate, submissive, full of mercy and good fruit, impartial and sincere. Peacemakers who sow in peace raise a harvest of righteousness.
James 3:14-18

As I read through the parable of the workers in the vineyard *(Matthew 20),* I am struck by how human nature is the same throughout history. Jesus tells the story about men working in the vineyard, and although some of the workers came in later to work, all of the workers were paid the same wage. I don't know about you, but I would have been just like the men who grumbled that it wasn't fair to pay everyone the same wages because some had worked longer hours and should be compensated for more work. Jesus' response to their grumbling has caused me to search for the point that He was trying to make. Jesus was demonstrating grace—getting what you do not deserve. Grace simply does not come naturally to most of us. It is far easier to demand fairness than to administer God's grace. Are you struggling with the unfairness of life, trying to equalize it? Life does not always seem to be fair; however, a life of undeserved grace eliminates our need for fairness and causes us to live above the place of mediocrity into a place of unmerited favor—a place of incomparable peace and joy.

When you expect everything to always be fair, this sets you up for the "envy trap," such as desiring something that someone else has or pursuing a goal only to have someone else achieve it. James warned us that selfish ambition and envy are traps where disorder reigns. *(James 3:16)* Ask the Lord to search your heart and show you if there is any envy or selfish ambition. Choose to trust the Lord to give you what you need, and do not envy what others have. It is liberating to know that God has a plan for those who love Him. We need not envy the plans He has for others; we need only to trust Him with His plan for us.

Heavenly Father,
Help me not to be envious of what others have or what others have accomplished. Help me to remember that You have a plan and purpose for all of Your children and that I will not be left out of Your plan.
In Jesus' name, Amen

September 29

Jesus Reinstates Us

When they had finished eating, Jesus said to Simon Peter, "Simon son of John, do you truly love me more than these? "Yes Lord, he said, "you know that I love you." Jesus said, "Feed my lambs." Again Jesus said, Simon son of John, do you truly love me?" He answered, "Yes Lord, you know that I love you." Jesus said, "Take care of my sheep." The third time he said to him," Simon son of John, do you love me?" Peter was hurt because Jesus had asked him the third time, "Do you love me?" He said, "Lord you know all things; you know that I love you." Jesus said, "Feed my sheep."
John 21:15-17

Jesus warned Peter that after He died Peter would deny Him. That seemed preposterous to Peter at the time, but when the rooster began to crow, Peter knew that what Jesus had told him now had come true: *Will you really lay down your life for me? I tell you the truth, before the rooster crows, you will disown me three times. (John 13:38)* And Peter did. After Jesus was arrested, Peter denied Him three times when questioned whether or not he had been with Jesus. I cannot imagine how Peter must have felt when the rooster began to crow and Jesus' words came back to haunt him. I suspect that in that moment his heart broke knowing that he had denied Christ, his Savior…his friend. If the story had ended here, it would have been tragic—the story of a broken man named Peter who lived the rest of his life in shame and guilt. No, the story had an ending of redemption and grace. After the resurrection, Jesus appears to Peter and reinstates him. He commissions Peter to feed His sheep, meaning the people who were broken and needy—people just like Peter. You see, Peter needed to experience the pain of separation from God, the conviction of needing God, and the pain of deserting God so that he could in turn help others. Jesus began by asking Peter if he loved Him using the Greek word "agape." Each time Jesus asked if Peter loved him, He commissioned him to feed and care for His sheep. It may not have any true significance, but it is interesting to note that the first time Jesus asked Peter if he loved Him, He used the word "agape," which means "to love with the same love that God loves us." The third time He uses the word for love "filios," which means "to love with a brotherly love." Perhaps Jesus recognized that Peter was not able to love Him with agape love, so He met Peter where his heart was. As we follow Peter in his walk with Christ throughout the New Testament, we see a man who grows more and more in love with Christ. It is evident from his willingness to lay down his life for His Lord that over the course of his life he grew to love Christ with agape love.

Have you ever denied Christ? You may say, "Of course not!" But when you refuse to tell others about Him because of fear of rejection, you deny Him. Like Peter, Jesus is telling you to feed and care for His sheep. Are you willing?

Heavenly Father,
Forgive me for denying You with my words and actions. Grow the love of Christ deeply in my heart so that I can tenderly care for Your sheep.
In Jesus' name, Amen

September 30

God's Strength Brings Peace

I can do everything through him who gives me strength.
Philippians 4:13

Jehovah Shalom tells Gideon through the visitation of an angel that Gideon is a mighty warrior. Gideon is stunned and explains to the angel that his clan is the weakest in Manasseh and that he is the least in his family. The angel of the Lord reveals the key to the peace God gives us when we are faced with difficult circumstances: he tells Gideon to go in the strength that he has because *God is with him.* Gideon made all sorts of excuses when the angel told him that God wanted him to deliver the Israelites out of the hands of the Midianites: *But Lord, Gideon asked, how can I save Israel? My clan is the weakest in Manasseh, and I am the least in my family. (Judges 6:15)*

Moses was also full of excuses when God called him to lead the Israelites out of Egypt. He asked God who would go with him; he told God that he wasn't an eloquent speaker and that he couldn't talk to Pharaoh; he told the Lord that he didn't even know God's name! Moses was a basket case!

How like Moses and Gideon we are! God calls us to do something and we are full of excuses! It's not that we don't want to obey, but we simply fear our inadequacy to do it. Paul understood the problem. He had been a powerful man—a Pharisee—respected by Israelites until he met Jesus on the road to Damascus. He was ruined forever. Jesus blinded his eyes and Paul groped his way back home. I imagine losing your eyesight gives one a vastly different perspective on life. He was on top of the world one moment and at the bottom of the cave the next...in darkness. I imagine that during that time before Jesus sent Ananias to open his eyes, Paul had time to think about this man Jesus, the one he had been persecuting.

Sometimes it takes "cave" times to recognize our weaknesses and utter dependency on God. We can be so self secure and independent that we do not see the need for God. Maybe we keep God at a distance so that when we do need Him we can call on Him, but most days we are fine without Him. It often takes a crisis for us to recognize our need. Paul figured it out. We know that he recognized his need for God when he wrote to the Philippians and said that he could do everything only through God's strength. What a long way he had come from the self-sufficient days on the road to Damascus!

Do you recognize daily your need for God, or does it take a crisis for you to turn to Him? He is calling you today to depend on Him daily and acknowledge that apart from Him you can do nothing. When we acknowledge our weaknesses, He makes us strong. *(II Corinthians 12:9)*

Heavenly Father,
Forgive me for turning to You only in times of distress. Help me to recognize that I can do all things only in Your strength.
In Jesus' name, Amen

October 1

Fully Persuaded

Against all hope, Abraham in hope believed and so became the Father of many nations, just as it had been said to him, "So shall your offspring be." Without weakening in his faith, he faced the fact that his body was as good as dead—since he was about a hundred years old—and that Sarah's womb was also dead. Yet he did not waver through unbelief regarding the promise of God but was strengthened in his faith and gave glory to God, being fully persuaded that God had the power to do what he had promised.
Romans 4:18-20

Abraham was fully persuaded—period. There was no question at all that he believed God when the odds seemed impossible. God told him that he would be the father of many nations. But Sarah's womb had been closed for years, and Abraham was old enough to be a grandfather or even a great grandfather! But God spoke and Abraham believed. Sarah, on the other hand, laughed when she heard about it. Sarah even tried to make it happen in someone else's womb by giving her handmaiden to Abraham. But God promised, and He never breaks His promises. Paul writes in the book of Romans that Abraham was fully persuaded and did not waver in unbelief regarding God's promise. Then why did he listen to Sarah and agree to try to fulfill the promise another way? Still God saw his heart. Abraham did give in to Sarah and had Ishmael who was not the promised child from Sarah's womb. But God saw that Abraham still believed.

We all have moments when we doubt what God has told us. We may try to take the matter into our own hands to make the promise happen ourselves and make a mess of things, but God does not give up on us. He wants us to be like Abraham who had some anxious moments, but he was still persuaded. Persuaded for what? Persuaded that *he* could not make it happen himself, but that God had the power to do what He promised.

What promises have you been waiting on for God to fulfill? Are you fully persuaded that God has the power to do it? You may think it depends on you, but God is able and does not want us to waver in unbelief. James writes that we must not be like a wave of the sea, blown and tossed by the wind, but when we ask, we must believe and not doubt. *(James 1:6)* Are you being blown by the wind, double-minded and unbelieving? God is looking for people who are fully persuaded that He has the power to do all things.

Are you willing to trust Him?

Heavenly Father,
Forgive me for my unbelief. Help me to be fully persuaded that You have the power to do what You have promised. Give me the courage to let go and wait patiently on You.
In Jesus' name, Amen

October 2

Christ the Stumbling Stone

As it is written: "See, I lay in Zion a stone that causes men to stumble and a rock that makes them fall, and the one who trusts in him will never be put to shame."
Romans 9:33

In this passage in *Romans 9,* starting with *verse 30,* Paul concludes the chapter with a comparison of believing Gentiles and unbelieving Jews. The Gentiles obtained righteousness because they trusted in the Messiah; the Jews stumbled over the Messiah and were rejected by God. Israel stumbled because they refused to recognize the fulfillment of the law in Jesus Christ. In both the New and Old Testament, we find many references to a "stone." The stone references in the Old Testament point to the Christ of the New Testament. The Jews were looking for a triumphant king to come as the Messiah, so the most significant place of their stumbling was the cross. They were looking for a king to set them free from Roman domination, not a man who called Himself "king of the Jews" and yet died on a cross.

Today we can still fall prey to stumbling over Christ. In examining *Romans 10:2,* we read that the Jews had a zeal not based on knowledge. We can have misdirected zeal that is not based on the knowledge of God's Word or His saving grace. As believers, we can stumble by trying to please God through works. Unbelievers stumble because their knowledge of the work of the cross is incomplete. The Jews, not knowing the righteousness that comes from God, sought to establish their own righteousness based on the law.

Are there "laws" you have imposed on yourself that keep you from *accepting* Christ as your Savior? Are there "laws" you have imposed on yourself that keep you from *surrendering* to Christ as "Lord"?

Heavenly Father,
I sometimes have self-imposed laws that have caused me to stumble. I have set expectations for myself that You never placed on me, and it has led me to believe that

I must be in control of my life. Forgive me for stumbling over Your grace. Help me to surrender my will.
In Jesus' name, Amen

October 3

Sin

I have hidden your word in my heart that I might not sin against you.
Psalm 119:11

The Greek translation for sin is *amartia.* It means "missing the mark." Sin begins with temptation. It doesn't become sin until you give in to the temptation. As courageous leaders, we must resist temptation by having the Word of God in our hearts. David missed the mark when he disobeyed God's Word: *"You shall not commit adultery." (Exodus 20:14)* Another time, the Lord was angered by David's actions when he took a military census to see how many fighting men there were. *(II Samuel 24)* Although Joab questioned David's actions, David overruled him and the census was taken. It is assumed that David's action was motivated by pride in the size of his military and in his own power rather than recognizing the gifts of the Lord. David became "conscience stricken," *(v.10)* confessed to the Lord that he had sinned, and asked for forgiveness. In both David's sin with Bathsheba and his sin of taking the census, there were consequences for David and for his kingdom.

Psalm 119 points to God's Word as the assurance against sin: *How can a man keep his way pure? By living according to your word, I seek you with all my heart; do not let me stray from your commands. I have hidden your word in my heart that I might not sin against you. (vv.9-11)* God's Word leads us in paths of righteousness and keeps us from temptation. Temptation is not sin. Sin is giving in to temptation. The Lord's Prayer seeks protection from the temptation to sin: *...and lead us not into temptation, but deliver us from the evil one. (Matthew 6:13)*

Have you hidden God's Word in your heart? Reading and meditating on God's Word provides the means for us to keep our hearts right before God. His Word brings us instruction and helps us to know God's will. David missed the mark some of the time, but he always knew that he could turn back to God.

Jesus is the Living Word, and when He was with His disciples, He told them that they were already clean because of the words He had spoken to them. *(John 15:3)* He is calling you to hide His words in your heart so that you will not be tempted to sin.

Heavenly Father,
Create a clean heart in me and renew a right spirit within. (Psalm 51:10) Help me hide Your Word in my heart so that sin will not find a place in me.
In Jesus' name, Amen

October 4

Turning Darkness into Light

The people living in darkness have seen a great light; on those living in the land of the shadow of death a light has dawned."
Matthew 4:16

After Jesus was led into the desert and was tempted by Satan, He began to preach to the people. He came preaching with power and was filled with the Spirit, fulfilling the prophecy in *Isaiah 9:2*: *The people walking in darkness have seen a great light; on those living in the land of the shadow of death, a light has dawned.* From that point on Jesus began to preach that the kingdom of God was near. Today's Scripture reading in *Matthew* points to Jesus as the great light who had come to those living in the shadow of death. Reminiscent of the *23rd Psalm*, Jesus came as our Shepherd, the One who leads us out of the shadow of death and into the light: *The Lord is my Shepherd; I shall not be in want... Even though I walk through the valley of the shadow of death, I will fear no evil...* Jesus came to lead us out of darkness into light—out of the shadow of death and into the light of eternity.

God tells the people through Isaiah: *I will lead the blind by ways they have not known, along unfamiliar paths I will guide them; I will turn the darkness into light before them and make rough places smooth. (Isaiah 42:16)* God was bringing comfort to His people as He lead them out of captivity, guiding them each step of the way.

Jesus Christ came to be a light to the Gentiles, to those who did not know Him, to a people living in darkness. He brought salvation and eternal life to those who believed. Peter describes believers as chosen people, a royal priesthood who were called out of darkness into Christ's wonderful light.

Sometimes we forget that we no longer live in the shadow of death, that we have been called out of darkness into light. We forget and our lives are darkened by struggles, perhaps life-threatening issues, disappointments, or depression. Darkness tries to lure us into standing under the shadow of death, but as believers we are called to the light; we are called to life and not death. We must agree with the life of Christ in us that cries out for the light.

Heavenly Father,
I have at times forgotten that I am a child of Christ called out of darkness into the light. Help me to live in agreement with the life of Christ in me and no longer stand under the shadow of death.
In Jesus' name, Amen

October 5

Turning Complaints into Constructive Action

Miriam and Aaron began to talk against Moses because of his Cushite wife, for he had married a Cushite. "Has the Lord spoken only through Moses?" they asked. "Hasn't he also spoken through us?"
Numbers 12:1-2

Miriam and Aaron complained about Moses' wife being a Cushite. Their complaining turned into judgment of Moses and his ability to lead. Many times as they traveled through the desert, the children of Israel complained against Moses and Aaron. The Israelites told them that they wished they had died at the hands of the Egyptians. Now they were in the desert and were going to starve to death! The Lord rained down bread from heaven and Moses said to them: *You are not grumbling against us, but against the Lord. (Exodus 16:8)* Even after they were in the Promised Land, the tribe of Joseph complained because they wanted more land. They feared they didn't have enough land for the numbers in their tribe, and they feared the Canaanites who had chariots and power.

Too often, we, like the Israelites of old, are guilty of complaining about our leaders, what we have to do, what we don't have—the list goes on and on. Sometimes it is easier to complain than to turn to God. Paul reminds the people of Philippi to remember that they need to shine like stars as they represent the gospel: *Do everything without complaining or arguing, so that you may become blameless and pure, children of God without fault in a crooked and depraved generation, in which you should shine like stars in the universe as you hold out the word of life. (Philippians 2:14-16)* Paul encourages Christians, then and now, to be light in a dark and unbelieving world. When we complain, we agree with the darkness and do not reflect Christ's light. We have a choice to complain or to be thankful. Thankfulness is the anecdote to discontentment, and it is discontentment that causes us to complain.

What circumstances are you in that have caused you to complain? Start thanking the Lord in *all* things and your light will shine, drawing others to Christ. Today a friend told me that she was choosing to hang out with positive people. I would like to be the kind of person that she enjoys being with—one who is content, who doesn't complain, and has a grateful heart. You can choose today to be that kind of person, too.

Heavenly Father,
I often choose to complain because for the moment it makes me feel better. I think that if I have my pity party when I am discontent, it will help me get through the day. The truth is I feel worse. Forgive my complaining today, Lord. Thank you for the many blessings of this life. Help me to always have a grateful heart and be someone who others enjoy.
In Jesus' name, Amen

October 6

Standing Strong against Opposition

Moses answered the people, "Do not be afraid. Stand firm and you will see the deliverance the LORD will bring you today. The Egyptians you see today you will never see again.
Exodus 14:13

Although Pharaoh released the Israelites to leave Egypt, he later changed his mind. So he took 600 of his best chariots and fighting men and took off after the Israelites. The Egyptians pursued the Israelites and overtook them as they camped by the sea near Pi Hahiroth. As Pharaoh approached, the Israelites were terrified and cried out to Moses: *Was it because there were no graves in Egypt that you brought us to the desert to die? (v.11)* If I were Moses I would have been terrified also. Not only did he have the Egyptians breathing down his neck, he had the whole nation of Israel terrified and now furious with him for leading them out! Talk about being caught between a rock and a hard place! But Moses, a man of God, knew that God would deliver them because he trusted his God. He told the people to stand firm, not to fear; they would see the deliverance of the Lord. At this point, God told Moses to raise his staff, and all night the Lord drove the sea back and turned it into dry land. All of the Israelites passed through the Red Sea. When the Egyptians pursued them, the Lord made the waters flow back, and Pharaoh and his army were killed.

God reminded Moses that he had His staff of authority in his hand. It was God who had given him the staff to use as a symbol of God's mighty power because He knew that Moses would face opposition. Later on we see Moses raise his staff when Israel fought the Amalekites. When he raised his arms, the enemy was defeated.

The Lord has placed the authority of Christ in us. When Jesus Christ was nailed to the cross, He took with Him our sin, our sickness, our sorrow, and our struggles. As believers, He gives us His authority through His Holy Spirit to stand against all those things that oppose us. Christians face difficult circumstances just like unbelievers do, but there is a difference—we are more than conquerors because of the shed blood of Christ: *And we know that in all things God works for the good for those who love him who have been called according to his purpose. (Romans 8:28)* God stands in opposition to everything in our lives that opposes His purposes. Stand firm today and see the deliverance of the Lord. Take up your staff and remember that God fights for you.

Heavenly Father,
Thank you, Lord, for reminding me that I am more than a conqueror because of what You did for me on the cross. Victory in times of struggle is mine when I have the faith to stand and wait for Your deliverance.
In Jesus' name, Amen

October 7

No Power Apart From God

This is what the Lord says to you: Do not be afraid or discouraged because of this vast army. For the battle is not yours but God's.
2 Chronicles 20:15

The Moabites and the Amnonites came to wage war against King Jehoshaphat of Judah. Some men came and told the king that a vast army was coming against them, and the king's first response was to inquire of the Lord. He proclaimed a fast for all of Judah, and the people came together to seek the Lord. The king prayed in front of the people and declared the faithfulness of God, knowing that God would hear his cry and save them. (v.9) Jehoshaphat tells God that he knows they have no power to face this vast opposing army, but they would keep their eyes on God. What a statement of faith! The godly King Jehoshaphat knew that there is no power apart from God. The prophet then told all of the people not to fear or be discouraged: the battle belonged to God. As the people of God began to praise the Lord, God set up ambushes for their enemy and defeat of the enemy followed.

The Lord knows the struggles you face—the opposition of the enemy who seeks to destroy you. His Word today is a reminder that no matter what you face, when you seek the Lord, when you pray and fast, He will defeat your enemies. God is looking for people of faith who will trust His faithfulness—people who will not fall into the trap of the enemy but will look to God.

Do you face an impossible circumstance with impossible odds? Does life seem overwhelming and you are faced with a vast army of opposition? Seek the Lord; pray and fast; believe that the battle is the Lord's. When the people of Judah were at the end of their rope, they tossed out their hands to the Lord and He grabbed it to save them. Let go of the rope and reach up to God. He will fight the battle.

Heavenly Father,
I feel like I am in a war zone. I look to You and Your power to fight this battle. I have no place to turn save to You, for You alone are able to bring victory.
In Jesus' name, Amen

The Secret of Oil

At that time the kingdom of heaven will be like ten virgins who took their lamps and went out to meet the bridegroom. Five of them were foolish and five were wise. The foolish ones took their lamps but did not take any oil with them. The wise, however, took oil in jars along with their lamps.
Matthew 25:4

In the Scriptures, oil is used to anoint individuals for God's service. In the Old Testament, Aaron and his sons are anointed as priests with oil *(Exodus 29)* and David is anointed by Samuel to be the King of Israel. *(I Samuel 16:13)* In the New Testament, believers are filled with the Holy Spirit to be empowered for God's service and to spread the gospel. As believers, God anoints us and sets His seal of ownership upon us, putting His Holy Spirit in our hearts as a deposit, guaranteeing what is to come. (2 Corinthians 1:22)

The parable in *Matthew 25* tells of the ten virgins who took their lamps to meet the bridegroom. Five of them were foolish because they took their lamps but did not take any oil with them. The other five took their filled lamps along with extra jars of oil. When the bridegroom was late in coming, the oil began to run low and the five who had not taken an extra supply were left behind when they went to buy more oil. As the bride of Christ, we must remember to keep our lamps filled with the oil of His Holy Spirit so that we will be prepared for His return. We need to be filled with His Spirit to accomplish His will on earth. As we believe in Christ and invite Him into our hearts, God anoints and seals us with the oil of His Spirit. He wants to release His Holy Spirit in our hearts so that we can live powerful lives for Him. The foolish virgins were not prepared for the bridegroom. When he arrived they did not have enough oil in their lamps. Let us be like the wise virgins who were prepared for His coming by keeping their lamps filled.

Have you asked the Lord to fill you with His Spirit? He wants to anoint and empower you daily to live as a powerful witness to the gospel. Daily seek His filling and you will never run short of His supply of oil.

Heavenly Father,
Fill me with Your Holy Spirit. Release the life of Christ in me as I surrender to Your will. Empower me to be a witness for Christ.
In Jesus' name, Amen

Outcry for Justice

Now the men and their wives raised a great outcry against their Jewish brothers. Some were saying, "We and our sons and daughters are numerous; in order for us to eat and stay alive we must get grain. Others were saying, "We are mortgaging our fields, our vineyards and our homes to get grain during the famine." Still others were saying, "We have had to borrow money to pay the king's tax on our fields and vineyards. Although we are of the same flesh and blood of our countrymen and though our sons and daughters are as good as theirs, yet we have to subject our sons and daughters to slavery. Some of our daughters have already been enslaved, but we are powerless, because our fields and our vineyards belong to others." When I heard their outcry and these charges, I was very angry.
Nehemiah 5:6

Nehemiah heard the outcry of the people who were oppressed; their children were being sold into slavery and their land was being taken from them in order to pay their debts. Nehemiah was outraged. He accused the nobles and officials of exacting usury from their own countrymen. He told them that what they were doing was not right and took action to rectify the social injustice.

When you hear the outcry of social injustice today, do you respond as Nehemiah did? Christ's compassion for the poor, the needy, the hurt, and the broken is evident throughout Scripture: *The Spirit of the Lord is on me, because He has anointed me to preach good news to the poor. He has sent me to proclaim freedom for the prisoners and recovery of sight for the blind, to release the oppressed. (Luke 4:18)* As ambassadors for Christ, we are also called to have compassion on the needy, the oppressed, and the down-trodden. We should be outraged when we see the condition of those in need and see others taking advantage of the poor.

As I read about the complaints of the Jews in Nehemiah's day, I am convicted that there are people in my community, state, and country crying out for help. In truth, I spend most of my time with people like myself who have plenty of food, clothes, and so much more than just the necessities of life. I hear the outcry for justice, the outcry for help, and I am overwhelmed with the needs. If each one of us does one thing a day to help relieve the needs of others, we *will* make a difference. Sometimes it seems as though what we do is only a ripple in a sea of need, but if each one of us throws a pebble in the water, we will make a tidal wave of assistance to those crying out for help.

Heavenly Father,
I take my one pebble and cast it into the lake of need. Give me eyes to see the broken, the needy, the poor, and the outcast. Help me to be like Nehemiah and not turn my back on those in need but be outraged enough to take action.
In Jesus' name, Amen

Praising the Lord

Praise the Lord, O my soul; all my inmost being, praise his holy name. Praise the Lord, O my soul and forget not all his benefits—who forgives all your sins and heals all your diseases, who redeems your life from the pit and crowns you with love and compassion, who satisfies your desires with good things so that your youth is renewed like the eagle's.
Psalm 103:1-5

David knew the benefits of the Lord. He had been anointed to be king of Israel and from that time on, he had been pursued by his enemies. He had experienced the forgiveness of God when he sinned; he had been healed from his broken heart when he experienced the consequences of his sin with Bathsheba. He had been redeemed from the pit and had experienced the compassion and love of God through it all. "O my soul" is a conventional Hebrew way of addressing oneself. David looked into his soul and saw the love of God that had been poured in; he looked into the pit and saw that he was no longer there. He looked up and saw the hand of God who had been gracious and compassionate towards him.

Like David, we must praise the Lord for His benefits as He lifts us from the pits of life that we sometimes fall into. He heals, redeems, and satisfies our desires with good things. I wonder how many of us really believe this. Do we know God as the Redeemer who is compassionate and gracious, slow to anger and abounding in love? *(v.8)*

He satisfies our desires with good things. *(v. 5)* This one verse alone is worth meditating on every day. God wants to give us the desires of our hearts! One of my favorite scriptures that reinforces this is *Psalm 37: Trust in the Lord and do good; dwell in the land and enjoy safe pasture. Delight yourself in the Lord and he will give you the desires of your heart.* The key to the benefits of God is trust; the key to achieving the desires of our heart is trust.

David trusted the Lord with all of his heart. When he killed the Philistine giant with a few pebbles and a sling, he knew that His God would prevail. As he recalled how God had been present in his life over the years he could say with assurance: *Praise the Lord, O my soul; all my inmost being, praise his holy name.*

Heavenly Father,
Praise the Lord, O my soul! You are my Redeemer and my Healer, and You satisfy my desires with good things. Help me to remember Your benefits and to always have a grateful heart.
In Jesus' name, Amen

Concealing Sins

So do not be afraid of them. There is nothing concealed that will not be disclosed, or hidden that will not be made known.
Matthew 10:26

Jesus Christ told His disciples that all hidden things will be revealed. David walked with God and writes: *Search me, O God, and know my heart; test me and know my anxious thoughts. See if there is any offensive way in me, and lead me in the way everlasting. (Psalm 139:22-23)* One day David fell. When he saw something he wanted, he took it. Then he tried to conceal it with another sin. Yet he was the one who prayed for God to expose his dark and offensive ways.

Paul also understood the trap of temptation and writes: *For I have the desire to do what is good, but I cannot carry it out. For what I do is not the good I want to do; no the evil I do not want to do—this I keep on doing. (Romans 7:18)* He struggled with doing those things he did not want to do and recognized the futility of his struggle with sin apart from Christ. He knew that only God, through Jesus Christ, could offer him hope. *(Romans 7:25)*

As believers, we have been called to walk in the light of Christ and to have a willingness to allow the Holy Spirit to bring truth and correction into the dark places of our lives. When we find ourselves in sin, we must be willing to expose the sin to the light of Christ, seek forgiveness, and turn back to Him. Today's Scripture reading in *Matthew* reminds us that all hidden things will be made known, and it is best to ask the Holy Spirit to reveal those things so that we can deal with them.

What secrets does the Lord wish to come into the light? Do you need to ask someone to forgive you because you have held onto a grudge or perhaps have not dealt with them fairly? Have you been dishonest in any way assuming no one would find out? Have you lied about something? Ask the Lord to reveal what is in your heart and bring all things into the light. You will find freedom when He brings you out of the darkness into the light.

Heavenly Father,

I have held onto (fill in the blank) for so long. I know that it has been a place of darkness in my life and I desire to bring it into Your light. Search my heart for all offensive ways and lead me back to You.
In Jesus' name, Amen

Bringing His Comforting Presence

Shout for joy, O heavens; rejoice, O earth; burst into song, O mountains! For the LORD comforts his people and will have compassion on his afflicted ones.
Isaiah 49:13

Isaiah told the people that God would bring strength to the weary, increase the power of the weak, and bring streams in the desert. Although the people returning from captivity were weary and discouraged, He promised them that He would give them strength to rebuild their land from a desert into fertile ground again.

The Jewish rabbis refer to *Isaiah 40-66* as the "Book of Consolation." Isaiah sought to comfort the Jewish remnant in Babylon after their years of captivity and assure them that God was with them and would take them safely home. The Israelites were in captivity in Babylon for 70 years before they returned to Jerusalem. These were desert times where they were in an unfamiliar land filled with false gods. Their world was turned upside down as they sought to make a life for themselves in a foreign place. But God in His mercy enabled them to grow as a nation, and eventually He brought them out of captivity. They found that even in captivity, their God promised them streams in the desert: *I will make rivers flow on barren heights, and springs within the valleys. I will turn the desert into pools of water, and the parched ground into springs. (Isaiah 41:18)*

We often find ourselves in seasons of our lives where we are physically or spiritually dry, feeling as though we are in a desert, discouraged and weary. Today, we can be comforted during our hard times by knowing that God's presence brings us strength and power.

Are you weary or discouraged? God may not remove you from the desert when you wish, but He will surely bring you streams of water in the desert. Jesus told the woman at the well that if she was spiritually thirsty, she needed only to drink from *the* living water. Jesus Christ is the only well that never runs dry; He is living water for our times in the desert.

Heavenly Father,
I pray for Your Presence in the dry and thirsty places of my life. Comfort me with Your Word and bring me safely out of captivity and into newness of life in You.
In Jesus' name, Amen

October 13

Timetable

But do not forget this one thing, dear friends: With the Lord a day is like a thousand years, and a thousand years are like a day. The Lord is not slow in keeping his promise, as some understand slowness. He is patient with you, not wanting anyone to perish, but everyone to come to repentance.
II Peter 3:8-9

Peter, writing to the persecuted church, reminds them that time is not the same to God as it is to man. Believers were waiting for the promises of God to be fulfilled as they endured the persecution. They were waiting for His return when Jesus would right every wrong and turn their sorrow into joy, when He would come and every knee would bow to His Lordship. Peter describes the character of God as patient, not wanting anyone to perish. God was giving people time to come to know Him because of His infinite love for people.

This fundamental truth brings understanding to us today as we await His promised return. Peter makes two points to strengthen the believers' position of trust as they await the second coming of Christ. These are the relativity of time and the loving forbearance of God. What man regards as a long time is like a mere day to God because He operates from an eternal perspective. We see time in terms of minutes, hours, days, months, and years. However, God's view of time is not the same as ours, and He is sovereign over time. This is exceedingly helpful as we grow in knowledge and grace.

We all wait for something, such as a wayward child to come home, a job opportunity to come through, or a financial breakthrough. As we pray, seek, and wait on the Lord, God is working His character in us. He is able to answer our prayers in an instant, but He desires that we draw near to Him and become more like Him. In the process of waiting, we are transformed as we turn to God. The Lord is infinitely patient with us and desires that we know Him; that is His ultimate goal.

The Lord waits patiently for unbelievers to know Him. It may seem to us that He is slow in coming, but His timing is eternal and His desire is for all to know Him.

Heavenly Father,
Help me to trust You with the timing of things in my life. Forgive my impatience as I wait on You to respond to my prayers. Thank you that Your concern is not just for my good but for my best.
In Jesus' name, Amen

The Money Trap

For the love of money is a root of all kinds of evil. Some people, eager for money, have wandered from the faith and pierced themselves with many griefs.
I Timothy 6:10

A man came up to Jesus and asked him how he could receive eternal life. Jesus replied that he must keep the commandments and quoted several, omitting the commandment *thou shalt not covet.* Quickly the man responded that he had kept all the commandments and asked Jesus if there was any other area where he still fell short. Jesus told him, *Go, sell your possessions and give to the poor.* The young man *went away sad because he had great wealth. (Matthew 19:16-22)* Jesus had purposefully left out the commandment, "Do not covet," because He knew that wealth was a stumbling block for this man. Jesus never says that wealth or having possessions is a bad thing; He simply points out that the love of things over the love of Christ is a stumbling block in our relationship with Him. I imagine that the man went away burdened with the love for his things and yet he missed the one thing that could bring him all that he ever needed—Jesus Christ.

Peter recognized that Jesus and His message were stumbling blocks for some people: *Now to you who believe, this stone is precious. But to those who do not believe, "The stone the builders rejected has become the cornerstone, and a stone that causes men to stumble and a rock that makes them fall." They stumble because they disobey the message—which is also what they were destined for. (I Peter 2:7-8)* Christ, the Cornerstone, was rejected by some, becoming a stumbling block; but for believers, He was and still is precious. The man who came to Jesus desiring eternal life found Christ's message to be a stumbling block. We don't know for certain, but it appears that he was unwilling to surrender his whole heart to Christ; material possessions had left no room for Jesus, the Cornerstone.

How do you view your money and possessions? Do they interfere with your relationship with Christ? I have found that possessions can easily slip into center stage in my life. Possessions can vie for the chief place in my heart where Jesus longs to be. I must always check myself and ask if anything that I own, anything that I have achieved, has slipped into the place where Christ desires to be. Let us keep checking our hearts so that the things of this world will not take the place of God or interfere with our relationship with God. Money in and of itself is not evil; it is the *love* of money that causes us to stumble.

Heavenly Father,
Forgive me where the things of this world crowd You out. Help me to surrender daily all that You have given me back to You. Help me to remember that all that I have is a gift from You to be used for Your glory.
In Jesus' name, Amen

October 15

Faith and Deeds

What good is it, my brothers, if a man claims to have faith but has no deeds? Can such faith save him? Suppose a brother or sister is without clothes and daily food. If one of you says to him, "Go, I wish you well; keep warm and fed," but does nothing about his physical needs, what good is it? In the same way, faith by itself, if it is not accompanied by action is dead.
James 2:14-17

Faith, according to Scripture, is being sure of what you hope for and certain of what you do not see. *(Hebrews 11:1)* Faith is the certainty of God at work even though we don't physically see Him. If we open our spiritual eyes and ears, however, we will see God at work in amazing ways in our daily lives. Faith, however, is not activated until we take action, applying what we hope for and what we are certain of through our actions. We can pray for days or weeks for something and never participate with God to bring results. I remember counseling a young woman who said her family was in financial stress. Her husband told her that she did not have enough faith that God would provide, but he refused to go to work! That is not faith. Faith prays and seeks God to lead and direct and is demonstrated through action. True faith is exhibited when we step out to do something that we believe God is calling us to do after seeking Him through prayer.

Joshua and the Israelites had to step out in faith to cross the Jordan River into the Promised Land. They had to believe that God was with them and they had to be certain of what they did not see. What they saw with their natural eyes was a swollen river that was impassable. But God promised them that He would take them into the Promised Land, and in order to do that they had to cross the river. God told Joshua to be strong and courageous and to keep the faith. And God sent His Presence in the form of the ark ahead of them and the Jordan parted. But, and this is a big "but," the Israelites had to cross over; they had to believe that God would part the waters and they had to believe that when they got into the middle of the river, the waters would stay parted.

In our Scripture reading for today, James reminds us that our faith is not sincere if it is not accompanied by actions. When we see someone in need, we must help in any way that we are able. Ask the Lord to increase your faith in the unseen and your willingness to take action.

Heavenly Father,
Forgive me when I have passed up opportunities to put my faith to action. Give me eyes to see those around me who need my help. Increase my faith to walk in the places where You have called me, knowing that You go before me and prepare the way.
In Jesus' name, Amen

Worship Opens the Prison Doors

About midnight, Paul and Silas were praying and singing hymns to God and the other prisoners were listening to them. Suddenly, there was such a violent earthquake that the foundations of the prison door were shaken. At once all the prison doors flew open, and everybody's chains came loose.
Acts 16:25-26

Paul and Silas were accused of advocating customs that were unlawful for the Romans to practice. They were beaten and thrown into prison and the jailer was commanded to guard them carefully. The jailer put them in the inner cell and fastened their feet in the stocks. Around midnight, Paul and Silas were praying and singing hymns to God and suddenly the prison doors flew open. When the jailer woke up, he saw that the doors were open and the chains were loosed. He assumed that the prisoners had escaped, but Paul and Silas remained in the prison. The trembling jailer came to them and asked how he could be saved. He knew that he stood in the presence of holy men. Paul and Silas shared the message of Christ, and that night the jailer and his whole household accepted Christ!

There are several amazing things about this story recounted in Scripture. The Lord intervened to free Paul and Silas from the prison when they prayed and worshipped Him. The prison doors were opened and their chains loosed, but Paul and Silas remained there, knowing they had a mission to accomplish for God.

As believers, we know from Scripture that the Lord inhabits our praises. When we praise Him, He draws near and His Presence sets the captive free. *Psalm 100* describes entering the courts of God through the doors of praise and thanksgiving: *Worship the Lord with gladness; come before him with songs. Know that the Lord is God. It is he who made us, and we are his; we are his people, the sheep of his pasture. Enter his gates with thanksgiving and his courts with praise. (Psalm 100:1-4)*

The author of *Hebrews* tells us to offer a sacrifice of praise to God through Jesus. Sometimes praising and worshipping God can be a sacrifice. We may not feel like it because our lives have been shipwrecked, or we may not wish to sacrifice the time worshipping

God. But the sacrifice of praise—the fruit of our lips—is precious to Him. *(Hebrews 13:15)*
Practice praising and thanking God daily. Even when you find yourself in the dark times of life, praise Him like Paul and Silas. Your praise will open the prison doors and set you free.

Heavenly Father,
In my darkest hour I will praise You; in the places of freedom and in the places of captivity I will praise You. For You alone are worthy of praise and You alone set my soul free.
In Jesus' name, Amen

God Fights our Battles

After I looked things over, I stood up and said to the nobles, the officials and the rest of the people, "Don't be afraid of them. Remember the Lord, who is great and awesome, and fight for your brothers, your sons and your daughters, your wives and your homes."
Nehemiah 4:14b

The people were becoming discouraged when they saw the huge pile of rubble that needed to be built up into a wall. Already feeling beaten down, they were easy targets for the enemy. Their enemies moved in for the kill, telling the people of Judah that they were going to kill them and put an end to their work. (*4:10*)

The enemy uses our times of discouragement and our weakened states to send his destructive attacks. Like Nehemiah, we must remember that the Lord will fight for us. In fact, Paul writes in his letter to the Corinthians that God is the strongest in us when we are in a weakened state! *(II Corinthians 12:10*) Nehemiah tells the people not to be afraid and reminds them that the battle belongs to the Lord. Throughout the Scriptures, when people are given assignments by the Lord, it is interesting to note that the Lord sends an angel to tell them not to be afraid.

The Lord has given us His Word, His Holy Spirit, and the assembly of saints to empower us with courage and strength when we face the challenges of life as we seek to accomplish what God has called us to do. Nehemiah's trust in God is contagious and motivating to the people. He tells them to strap their swords to their side and get to work, for the Lord will fight for them. What an encouraging word this is for us today as we face life's challenges!

Heavenly Father,
I am discouraged and overwhelmed trying to accomplish the tasks before me. Help me to remember that You are with me; help me to recognize the source of my fear and turn to You as the source of my courage, remembering that I can do all things through Christ who strengthens me.
In Jesus' name, Amen

October 18

The Secret of Using Talents

Again, it will be like a man going on a journey, who called his servants and entrusted his property to them. To one he gave five talents of money, to another two talents, and to another one talent, each according to his ability. Then he went on his journey. The man who had received the five talents went at once and put his money to work and gained five more.
Matthew 25:14-16

In the parable of the talents in *Matthew 25*, two of the servants doubled their talents (coins) that were given to them by their master. The other servant who was given one talent buried it for fear that he would lose it. He played it safe whereas the other servants worked to produce more. The master told the two servants who doubled their money that because they were faithful in a little thing, he would entrust them with more. I suppose that the man who hid his one talent did so because he was fearful of losing it or squandering it. He thought that his master would be pleased that he did not take a risk with the money he was given. Using this analogy in terms of the talents, or gifts, that God has given each of us, we too easily bury our gifts because it may seem too risky to use them. It may even be that we do not recognize our gifts or are unwilling to open them. Whatever the reason, many of the gifts that God has given us remain unused.

Think about some of the men and women of the Bible: Abraham, David, Rebecca, Paul, and Peter. Each of them was obedient and each had to use the resources, gifts, and talents that the Lord had given them to follow the call. Abraham had the gift of faith. David had a heart of worship. Rebecca was strong, resilient and faithful. Paul was brilliant, and Peter was impetuous. Yes, God could even use impetuous Peter because Peter was willing not to bury his talents but to use all that he had for the glory of God.

God has entrusted us with many talents or gifts that He expects us to use to advance His kingdom. He does not want us to bury our talents but to use them for His glory. What gifts has God given you that you have buried? If you are uncertain of your gift, ask a trusted friend and seek the Lord for ways that you can use your God-given gifts. Do you have the ability to sing, to paint, to organize, to teach? There are many ways that you can serve the Lord. If He has given you a gift, He is waiting for you to use it for His glory!

Heavenly Father,
I am unable to see how You have gifted me. Perhaps I have been looking for a big sensational gift and have not noticed some of the quiet ways that You use me. Open my eyes to see the gift; open my heart to receive the gift; open my arms to extend the gift to others so that I bring honor and glory to Your name.
In Jesus' name, Amen

October 19

Faithful Response

Remember me for this, O my God, and do not blot out what I have so faithfully done for the house of my God and its services.
Nehemiah 13:14

When Nehemiah heard about the broken promises of the people, he immediately initiated reforms. His faithful response as the leader of the people was to set things in order. He began by throwing Tobiah's household goods out of the rooms, purifying the rooms and restoring the equipment of the house of God. *(13:8-9)* He restored the tithes and appointed Shelemiah, the priest, and Zadok, the scribe, to be in charge of the storerooms. He closed the doors to Jerusalem so that no "loads" (labor) could be brought in on the Sabbath day. Lastly, he rebuked those who disobeyed the Lord by intermarrying. He purified the priests and Levites of everything foreign. *(v.30)* As faithful followers of Jesus Christ, we are called to be obedient to God's commands.

As believers, we *are* the temple of the Holy Spirit (*I Corinthians 6:19*) called to be pure and holy. The Lord calls His people to a higher standard than that of the world. We have His Word to guide us, convict us of sin, and lead us into truth. The church today in many ways is beginning to resemble the world. As believers, are you willing to raise the standard by following God's Word? When you fail, are you willing to faithfully respond by repenting and turning back to the Lord? The Lord is looking for a remnant who will faithfully seek to follow His ways.

What ways need to be "reformed" in your life? God is calling you to a higher standard and seeks to have your whole heart. He stands ready to clean out *His* temple where He resides in you; He seeks to purify and to restore His dwelling place. Today, as you surrender to His will, He will remove the rubble and make way for His Presence.

Heavenly Father,

I surrender my heart, my mind and my will to You. I pray that You will cleanse the thoughts of my heart and remove all the debris in the way that separates my life from You.
In Jesus' name, Amen

October 20

Strategies for Evangelizing

Be wise in the way you act toward outsiders; make the most of every opportunity. Let your conversation be always full of grace, seasoned with salt, so that you may know how to answer everyone.
Colossians 4:5-6

Although Paul realized that circumcision was not necessary for salvation, he knew that in order for Timothy to be effective as a missionary spreading the word of Jesus Christ, he would need to be circumcised. The Jews were more apt to hear his message if he were circumcised. It is often prudent to be sensitive to the ways of the people we are trying to bring to the Lord. We should also be strategic or mindful of the best places, time, and recipients of the message we bring. For example, the apostles chose to teach about Jesus in the synagogues where the people were more likely to listen to what they had to say. Paul was also sensitive in considering the best strategy for evangelism when he was in Philippi. He was wise to go to the river, the place of prayer, to share about Jesus. The place of prayer by the river was likely to be filled with people ready to hear the Word of God. We, too, must carefully consider the most effective place and the most effective way to share our faith.

Consider whom the Lord has placed in your life: people in the workplace, in your home, and your friends. As you build relationships and sensitivity to the people He places around you, your effectiveness in living the gospel before them will increase. God is not looking for "super saints" to spread His message of salvation. He is looking for ordinary people living among ordinary people who are willing to share an *extra*ordinary faith. We earn the right to be heard when we care for the people around us. Often it is more effective to preach the gospel with actions, not with words. Sometimes what we do speaks louder than what we say.

Paul, in his letter to the Colossians, reminded them to be wise in the way they acted towards outsiders, filling their conversations with grace. He recognized that the world of unbelievers is watching us. They want to believe in a God who cares, but they first want to see if *you* care.

Heavenly Father,
Use me for Your glory in my home and in my relationships, and especially allow outsiders to see my love for You through how I care for them. I want to draw people into Your kingdom with love.
In Jesus' name, Amen

October 21

Pondering God's Word

So they hurried off and found Mary and Joseph, and the baby who was lying in the manger. When they had seen him, they spread the word concerning what had been told them about the child, and all who heard it were amazed at what the shepherds said to them. But Mary treasured up all these things and pondered them in her heart.
Luke 2:16-19

The shepherds were keeping watch over their flocks one night, and an angel of the Lord appeared to them. The angel told them not to be afraid; a baby had been born in Jerusalem and He was the Christ, the Son of God. They decided to go and see the baby, and they found Jesus lying in a manger. Afterward, they spread the word about Jesus and everyone was amazed. The Scriptures do not say that Mary was amazed, but instead state that she pondered all of this in her heart.

Have you ever sensed God speaking to you and you did not even want to share it with anyone else? His words were too precious, too personal, too close to home. Do you ever read a Scripture and the words leap off the pages into your heart and you know God is speaking? Or perhaps a friend tells you something and you know that God is speaking to you through that friend? Sometimes a circumstance in your life points to the voice or thumbprint of God. And yet all you can do is treasure His Word in your heart, pondering what it means and weighing it carefully.

Years ago I read a passage in Isaiah and I knew that God was speaking to me. I sensed that He was giving me direction for the future, but it did not make sense at the time. I did not share it with anyone because it made no sense to me and I was not able to even articulate what I thought it might be saying. As the years passed, that same verse would come back to me. On several occasions, friends would share this verse with me and say that they thought it was for me. All the while, I meditated on it, pondered and treasured it in my heart. A few years ago, the verse began to unfold, and the years of treasuring it in my heart began to find wings.

Mary knew that what the angel had told her had come true. Now she listened as others recognized her son as the Messiah. She held onto the words of the angel; she held on to the words of people, pondering them in her heart. She did not rush out to make it happen. She just waited. And God fulfilled all of His Word that He had spoken to her heart.

Heavenly Father,
I am clinging to Your Word. I will treasure Your Word in my heart and trust You to fulfill Your promises.
In Jesus' name, Amen

October 22

Consequences and Restoration

And the God of all grace, who called you to his eternal glory in Christ, after you have suffered a little while, will himself restore you and make you strong, firm and steadfast.
I Peter 5:10

Sin causes us to suffer. You may be in denial that you are suffering because of a sin in your life, but eventually and undoubtedly sin causes pain and suffering. Peter reminds us that there is a devil who prowls around seeking those whom he can devour. He uses our sin to make us stumble and suffer. The good news is that the Lord will restore us and enable us to stand firm and steadfast. Paul questions, "*What shall we say, then? Shall we go on sinning so that grace may increase? By no means! We died to sin; how can we live in it any longer?*" *(Romans 6:1)* It is tempting to think that if we intentionally commit sin, we can draw on God's grace after the fact. This is faulty thinking. First, there are consequences for sin, and secondly, we are to consider ourselves dead to sin. David suffered the consequences each time he sinned. When he sinned with Bathsheba, the Lord allowed their first son to die. When he sinned by taking the census, David had to choose which consequences he and Israel would suffer. It is inevitable that we all will suffer consequences when we sin. The good news is that the Lord offers us His forgiveness, and His mercy triumphs over His judgment. *(James 2:13)*

Are you suffering because of sin? Is there an area of your life where the Lord desires to bring you restoration? As you seek to align your heart with God's heart, He will show you where you have fallen. The enemy is subtle and sometimes we do not know when we have fallen into one of his land mines until our foot is blown off. We are unable to walk without pain, but the Lord seeks to restore us.

Joseph sinned when he bragged about his dream to his brothers. The spirit of jealousy went after him through his brothers and he was thrown into a pit. From the moment he landed in the pit of death, God sought to restore him. He was retrieved by a caravan of Egyptians, sold into slavery, and spent time in prison. Eventually he was restored to be the right-hand-man to Pharaoh. His position afforded him the ability to bring restoration to his whole family. God will always restore us, even from the deepest pit!

Heavenly Father,
I waited patiently for the Lord; He turned to me and heard my cry. He lifted me out of the slimy pit, out of the mud and mire; He set my feet on a rock and gave me a firm place to stand. (Psalm 40:1-2)
In Jesus' name, Amen

October 23

Ministers of Reconciliation

All this is from God who reconciled us to himself through Christ and gave us the ministry of reconciliation; that God was reconciling the world to himself in Christ, not counting men's sins against them. And he has committed to us the message of reconciliation.
2 Corinthians 5:18-19

In Paul's letter to the Corinthians, he describes the ministry of reconciliation to which believers are called. He writes that God reconciled us to Himself through Christ, and now we are called to reconcile the world to Christ. He calls us Christ's ambassadors, representing Christ and sharing His good news to a broken world. I marvel that we are called to carry the most incredible message of all time to the world! I wonder how many of us take this seriously—this business of being an ambassador. I imagine that the ambassadors all over the world take their job seriously, but do we?

What does it require of us to take the message of the gospel out to others? There is a cost involved—a willingness to be bold and to share what Christ has done for us. Paul writes in *II Corinthians, Chapter 4* that God has made His light shine in our hearts so that we now have the light of the knowledge of the glory of God in the face of Christ. The light God shines in us reflects *His* face in His Son's face. As we carry the message of Christ to others, they will see the face of God in us! Paul drives his message home by telling us that we are jars of clay that carry this treasure of Christ: Christ broken in us as seen in our lives that are pressed in by despair, persecution, and the struggles of life. *(II Corinthians 4:7)* The fact that we carry the sufferings of Christ and do not despair gives our life power to be witnesses for Christ, sharing His message of reconciliation: *...pressed on every side but not crushed, perplexed, but not in despair, persecuted, but not abandoned; struck down, but not destroyed. We always carry around in our body the death of Jesus, so that the life of Jesus may also be revealed. (v.7-10)*

Let us be a people willing to be broken, willing to carry the message of Christ out to a broken world to bring hope and reconciliation.

Heavenly Father,
Help me to remember that I carry this treasure (Christ) in a jar of clay (my body) to show that all power within me comes from You. I call on Your power within me to share the message of Christ and His gift of reconciliation and hope.
In Jesus' name, Amen

October 24

Transformation Through Worship

Come, let us bow down in worship, let us kneel before the LORD our Maker.
Psalm 95:6

The people of Israel turned from their Creator, choosing to worship other gods. *Isaiah 44* describes the idols that the people made: *They know nothing, they understand nothing; their eyes are plastered over so they cannot see, and their minds closed so they cannot understand. (Isaiah 44:18)* It is interesting to note that although this is a description of the wooden idols, it also describes the people to whom Isaiah was sent to prophesy. God told Isaiah, "*Go and tell this people: 'Be ever hearing, but never understanding; be ever seeing but never perceiving. Make the heart of this people callused; make their ears dull, close their eyes.*" *(Isaiah 6:9)* The Israelites worshipped wooden false gods, and they as a people took on the same characteristics as the gods they worshipped.

I once heard that we become like whomever or whatever we choose to worship. The Psalmist exhorts us to bow down in worship, kneeling before the Lord, our Maker. (*Psalm 95*) There are so many things that we bow down to—the gods of money, power, reputation. But God wants us to bow down to Him alone. The Israelites became like the idols they worshipped with eyes closed and ears too dull to hear. When they worshipped God, their spiritual eyes and ears were opened.

Worship transforms us. If we worship God, we will be like God. If we worship other things, we will become absorbed in those things. American Idol has become one of the most popular shows on TV. I love to watch the young talented (and not so talented) people as they pursue their dream to become a famous star. I believe the show has become successful because it is thrilling to see an unknown person become famous overnight. What strikes me the most is America's obsession with stardom. Magazines about the rich and famous fill our stores, and even national news focuses on the lives of stars. In many ways we idolize them and long to live the life of the rich and famous. The problem is we fall prey to the desire to emulate them.

God is calling us to be like Him—to be transformed through worshipping God into His image. We will become like Him when we worship Him alone.

Heavenly Father,
You alone are worthy of all of my worship. Transform me into Your likeness that I might reflect Your glory and draw others to You.
In Jesus' name, Amen

October 25

Count It All Joy

Consider it pure joy, my brothers, whenever you face trials of many kinds, because you know that the testing of your faith develops perseverance. Perseverance must finish its work so that you may be mature and complete, not lacking anything.
James 1:2

James writes to the twelve scattered tribes who were being persecuted for their faith. He tells them that they should count it joy when they face trials. Now I don't know about you, but I might not have been willing to stay to hear the rest of his message! Who in their right mind counts trials as joy? But reading on we see that our trials bring us joy because ultimately our trials will bring us to a place where we will be lacking nothing—a place of true freedom. Perseverance is a quality that is developed under trial. We do not grow perseverance unless we have to persevere. Once we have persevered and pressed through our difficulties, we become mature, attaining the character of Christ.

My Dad always taught me to persevere. He valued persistence and modeled an attitude of never giving up. He taught me that a person of perseverance must finish his work in order to go on to the next level of achievement.

My sister-in-law was bedridden until she went to be with Jesus. She was 40 years old when she died, and she persevered under each trial that she faced in terms of her health. Her attitude was always the same: God will never give you more than you can handle. She knew that God was faithful and trustworthy and that with Him she could handle anything.

James knew that if God's people were to press on to the higher goal, they would have to be willing to undergo trials and difficulties and never give up. Are you facing trials that cause you to want to give up? Today's Scripture reading points you to the end result of the trial—the maturation of your faith. Ask the Lord to help you see the finish line so that you can run the race with perseverance, knowing that the end is worth the suffering.

Heavenly Father,
Help me to see the finish line of this trial, knowing that I will become more like You as I persevere to the end. Give me the courage to press on and a willing heart to believe.
In Jesus' name, Amen

October 26

Commander in Chief of Our Lives

David said to the Philistine, "You come against me with sword and spear and javelin, but I come against you in the name of the LORD Almighty, the God of the armies of Israel, whom you have defied.
I Samuel 17:45

One of my favorite stories in the Bible is the one where David, a shepherd boy, defeats the Philistine giant. As a child, I remember thinking how courageous young David was. Now I realize that David's courage came from his trust in Jehovah Tsebaoth, the One who enabled David to defeat the giant.

Jehovah Tsebaoth came to earth in the person of Jesus Christ and defeated Satan, the giant of all times. The enemy is looking for a foothold in our lives. He is like the Philistine giant who mocks and torments us, causing us to feel defeated. He may cause us to *feel* defeated, but we are not defeated…we have victory through Christ. All the enemy can do is lure us into agreement with his lies so that we can *feel* defeated. When we agree with him, we lose perspective and forget the truth—that Christ came and defeated Satan on the cross. The enemy cannot cause defeat; he can only make you think that you are defeated.

David picked up his five stones and took off the armor of King Saul. It was nice of the king to offer David his armor; the problem is that it did not fit David. David knew that the only armor that fit was God's armor, the truth of His Word and the truth of God's character. He was Jehovah Tsebaoth, captain of all the hosts of armies. David only needed His captain to fight for him! And with just a few pebbles in his hand, the Lord directed his aim at the giant and the giant came down.

What giants do you face? What armor are you wearing that does not fit, that is cumbersome and preventing you from victory? Is it the armor of seeming defeat? Is it the armor of feeling overwhelmed by your enemy? Is it the armor of lies? Jesus came to earth and conquered death, offering us eternal life. He came to earth to conquer the giants we face in our everyday lives. The enemy is a defeated foe. One small stone in the form of agreeing with God's Word will send him fleeing!

Heavenly Father,
I have believed a lie. I have been discouraged and have felt defeated. I come into agreement with Your Word and break all agreements I have made with the father of lies. All victory is Yours!
In Jesus' name, Amen

October 27

Stationed at the Lowest Point

Therefore I stationed some of the people behind the lowest points of the wall at the exposed places, posting them by families, with their swords, spears and bows.
Nehemiah 4:13

As the enemy spread unsettling rumors, I imagine that Nehemiah consulted with the Lord many times. He did not allow fear or the concern of the people to deflect his God-given task of rebuilding the wall. He immediately stationed guards on the most vulnerable places of the wall with spears, swords, and bows. He knew that he must rebuild and strengthen every section of the wall that enabled the enemy to have access.

As believers, it is tempting to allow the enemy to instill fear in us, but God has promised us that He has not given us a spirit of fear but of power along with a sound mind. (*II Timothy 1:7*) When attacks come, we must seek the Lord for wisdom and discernment about what to do and ask Him to show us where our vulnerable places are, the places where the enemy has easy access. The Lord is faithful and will reveal our areas of weakness, both through His Word and through our faithful Christian friends and intercessors. The way to close the gap in our places of vulnerability is to "post guards" at those places.

It is interesting to note that the enemy spread rumors about Nehemiah and the Israelites in order to prevent the rebuilding of the wall. The enemy seeks to do the same to us. He distracts us with all sorts of things to take our attention away from allowing the Lord to repair the broken down places of our lives that give the enemy places to slip in. When we are distracted by his tactics, he comes into our places of vulnerability.

Where do you see the enemy at work in your life? Do you have any places in your life that are vulnerable to his attacks—unforgiveness, bitterness, anger? Are there things that the Lord has asked you to do but you have rebelled and refused? Seek the Lord today for the places of vulnerability in the walls of your spiritual life and ask Him to restore and rebuild them so that only the Lord can have access into your life.

Heavenly Father,
Close the gaps in my life that allowed the enemy access. Strengthen and post Your guards in the places where I have been most vulnerable.
In Jesus' name, Amen

October 28

Intimacy with Christ

If you have any encouragement from being united with Christ, if any comfort from his love, if any fellowship with the Spirit, if any tenderness and compassion, then make my joy complete by being like-minded, having the same love, being one in spirit and purpose.
Philippians 2:1-2

Jesus gives the disciples a very poignant description of the relationship they are invited to have with Him. He describes in *John 15:1-13* what this relationship should look like and compares His relationship with them to a vine and its branches. He is the Vine and believers are the branches. The vine gives strength and nourishment to the branches and cannot exist apart from the vine. So it is with us as we walk with Christ. We are to be so closely connected with Him that *apart from Him, we can do nothing.* I remember as a young Christian observing a couple who obviously were connected to Jesus in a way that I did not think was possible. When I asked them what their secret was, they said it was spending time "abiding" in Christ. Just as the union of the vine and the branch is vital, so is our time spent connecting with Christ, receiving our nourishment and very existence from Him. So it was with Paul that his life was so connected with Jesus that he lived only to know Him and to make Him known. He knew that his encouragement came from his union with Christ, and that union allowed him unity in spirit with others.

Intimacy with Christ fills us with agape love. There are several kinds of love: *filos*, brotherly love; *eros*, sexual love; and *agape,* a love that emanates from the Father's heart. Jesus described the love that he had for His Father in their intimate relationship: *Father, just as you are in me and I am in you, may they also be in us so that the world may believe that you have sent me. (John 17:21)* Jesus wanted us to be united to Him as He and the Father were united. In turn He desired that believers would be united in His love. *(v.23)* The unity of the body of Christ will demonstrate the love of Christ.

You may not have experienced a close relationship with your father on earth, but God the Father seeks to draw you near to Him. He sacrificed His only Son so that you could be in a close relationship with Him—so close that you can hear His heartbeat! His heart beats for you. He is tender and full of compassion, and His loving eyes are on you. Are you willing to open your heart?

Heavenly Father,
Help me to receive Your unconditional love. So many conditions for love have been put on my life that it is difficult to receive Your love. I open my heart to receive from You; I open my arms to embrace You; I open my eyes to see You.
In Jesus' name, Amen

October 29

Spiritual Act of Worship

Therefore, I urge you, brothers, in view of God's mercy, to offer your bodies as living sacrifices, holy and pleasing to God—this is your spiritual act of worship.
Romans 12:1

God's mercy, having redeemed us from the world, now demands a response—a response of nothing less than the offering of ourselves entirely to the Lord. We are only able to do this by surrendering ourselves through the power of the Holy Spirit at work in us; He transforms our minds, wills, and bodies from conforming to the world to conforming to the image of Christ. Paul describes this process of transformation as our "spiritual act of worship," beginning with the renewal of our mind: *Do not be conformed to the pattern of this world but be transformed by the renewing of your mind. Then you will be able to test and approve what God's will is—his good, pleasing, and perfect will. (Romans 12:2)*

When our minds are washed and renewed by the Word and cleansed of the effects of world thinking, we will then be able to live according to God's will. As Christians we pray: *thy will by done, thy kingdom come.* We seek to know and to obey God's will, but the world view has confused our thinking and ability to test and approve what God's will is. God, who created our mind for His use, desires that we have the mind of Christ because what we think is reflected in our actions. Another translation of spiritual act of worship is "reasonable service," which implies that it is reasonable for us to expect to respond to God's mercy by offering our lives back to Him in gratitude.

Every morning and every evening the Israelites offered sacrifices as an act of worship to the Lord. I try to remember to consciously offer myself as a sacrifice to the Lord when I first awaken and just before I go to bed at night. It is my way of remembering God's mercy and love and responding by giving Him back the very life He has given to me.

Heavenly Father,
I present myself to You as a living sacrifice to worship You. I surrender to Your Holy Spirit at work in me and pray that my mind will be renewed and that I will know Your perfect will.
In Jesus' name, Amen

October 30

God's Promises

Praise be to the LORD, who has given rest to his people Israel just as he promised. Not one word has failed of all the good promises he gave through his servant Moses.
I Kings 8:56

After the Lord delivered David from his enemies, he sang praises to the Lord, *As for God, his way is perfect; the word of the Lord is flawless. (II Samuel 22:31)* David knew God's Word to be flawless and His ways to be perfect. The last words of testimony that David gave indicate his absolute trust that the Lord would fulfill every promise that He made to him: *Is not my house right with God? Has He not made with me an everlasting covenant, arranged and secured in every part? Will He not bring to fruition my salvation and grant me my every desire? (II Samuel 23:5)*

God is The Promise Keeper; He keeps His Word and His Word never fails! Life causes us to doubt and lose trust in promises given and promises received. Everywhere we turn we see broken promises: marriages that break up, parents that are inconsistent with their promises, books that promise us security, and health that fails us. We put our hope in promises, and when they are unfulfilled, disillusionment crouches at the door of our hearts. God promised Moses that He would take the Israelites into the Promised Land. Although the people grumbled, doubted God's Word, and failed to live up to their promise to worship God alone, God took them into His Promised Land. There was one problem, however. The generation of Israelites that disobeyed and did not trust the Lord were not welcomed into God's Promised Land.

Like the Israelites, we fall into doubting God's promises to us in His Word. We lean on our own understanding and past experiences where we have been let down by a word of promise and trust has been eroded. Proverbs addresses this problem: *Trust in the Lord with all of your heart and lean not on your own understanding; in all your ways acknowledge him and he will make your paths straight. (Proverbs 3:5)* The key to entering into the promises of God is trusting *Him*—not leaning on your own understanding or experiences, but looking to

God to make your path straight. Be secure in the knowledge that the Lord will fulfill every promise to us because His Word is trustworthy.

What about you? Have you doubted that the Lord will fulfill His promises to you? Look up rather than down at the circumstances that cause you to doubt. His promises never fail.

Heavenly Father,
I choose to trust You today in all things. I have doubted that You would ever answer my prayers or fulfill my dreams. I have believed that You planted the seeds of promise in my heart, but I have refused to water them by trusting You. Forgive me for leaning on my past experiences and for doubting Your Word.
In Jesus' name, Amen

October 31

The Furnace of Affliction

See, I have refined you, though not as silver;
I have tested you in the furnace of affliction.
Isaiah 48:10

According to the words of Isaiah, God would have given the Israelites peace and protection if only they had obeyed God: *I am the Lord your God who teaches you what is best for you, who directs you in the way you should go. If only you had paid attention to my commands, your peace would have been like a river. (Isaiah 48:17-18)* God's chosen people turned from the Lord, and in His love and mercy for them, He allowed them to suffer the consequences. Yet God proclaims through Isaiah that He will carry them, sustain them, and ultimately rescue them. *(Isaiah 46:4)*

Obedience is the key to peace and prosperity. The Israelites continued to disobey God and turn to other gods, and the Lord allowed His testing in the furnace of affliction to draw them back. They ended up in captivity for 70 years suffering the consequences of their disobedience. But God, the Redeemer and the Restorer, directed them back so that their peace would be restored and the river of God's love could be restored. God never stopped loving them; He withdrew His hand of protection to allow consequences because He loved them. He led them back as a shepherd gently leads his sheep.

God allows us to be tested in the furnace of affliction as well. Again, because of His deep love and care for us He uses our trials and difficulties of life to draw us back. It is our disobedience that leaves us as prey for the enemy to sneak in. Think about Eve in the Garden of Eden. She had the perfect life—a loving husband and a God who walked with her, protected her, and talked with her. Yet when Satan tempted her with his lie, she sinned by disobeying God. The flow of God's peace ended as she and her husband were cast out of the garden. Yet God had already planned a way to bring them back—to restore their peace and communion with Him through His Son, Jesus Christ.

The Lord will never forsake us even though we often forsake Him. As we walk through the furnace of affliction, whether caused by our disobedience to Him or simply trials of life, He will draw us to Himself. He promises to pour out water on our thirsty land because we belong to Him. *(Isaiah 44:3-4)*

Heavenly Father,
"Where can I go to flee from Your Presence? If I go to the heavens, You are there; if I make my bed in the depths, You are there. If I rise up on the wings of dawn, if I settle on the far side of the sea, even there Your hand will guide me." (Psalm 139:8-9) Thank you, Lord, that You are always there by my side.
In Jesus' name, Amen

November 1

Finding Refuge in Jesus

Come to me, all you who are weary and burdened, and I will give you rest. Take my yoke upon you and learn from me, for I am gentle and humble in heart, and you will find rest for your souls. For my yoke is easy and my burden is light.
Matthew 11:28-31

Jesus carries our burdens. He tells us in *Matthew* that His yoke is easy and His burden is light. A yoke is a wooden harness that fits over the shoulders of a pair of oxen. Jesus wants us to be yoked with Him. Recently I was carrying some heavy burdens. This passage reminded me that Jesus is willing to carry my burdens, but it is up to me to let go and allow Him to carry them. Jesus is a willing partner and waits on us to come to Him.

Jesus had just praised His father because He had hidden things from the wise and revealed them to children. What had He hidden? Why did He hide things from the wise and reveal them to children? Following His prayer, He relates that the Son is only known to those whom God reveals Him. Jesus turns to encourage all who are weary to come to Him. Leading up to our Scripture reading for today, Jesus seems to be saying that a childlike faith is what it takes to know God, the Son. Think about children for a moment. They are dependent on their parents or those in authority to lead them. They learn from them and life is revealed to them through household and parental guidance. If children are in a secure home, they have no concern about having their needs met. They relax in a safe environment, resting in the security of trust. Jesus suggests that if we are weary and need rest, then we need to give our burdens to Him. Just as a child trusts his parents, we must lay our burdens on Him. We learn from Him and He reveals Himself to us. As the revelation of Jesus awakens our hearts, we will find rest for our weary souls. Our souls are never at rest apart from knowing God.

We are sometimes like fugitives running from our own fears, lack of trust, or other obstacles in our lives. Just as the roads were marked and in good repair to the cities of refuge in the Old Testament, so the Lord has made a way for us that is free and clear. He longs for us to run to Him. The roads clearly mark the way: *Come to me all you who are weary and burdened…* Come with a childlike faith and an expectation that you will find rest.

Heavenly Father,
I have been carrying heavy burdens. I release them to You and I take Your yoke upon me that is easy and light. Where I have not trusted You, forgive me; where I have doubted You, bring truth; where I have lost my way, I come.
In Jesus' name, Amen

November 2

God's Judgment

Do not show partiality in judging; hear both small and great alike.
Do not be afraid of any man, for judgment belongs to God.
Bring me any case too hard for you, and I will hear it.
Deuteronomy 1:17

Deuteronomy 1:17 points out that God is the ultimate Judge. His name Jehovah means Righteous Judge, and we are called to entrust all judgment to Him.

Peter tells us that judgment must first begin with the household of God. *(I Peter 4:14-18)* We must be willing to have the Holy Spirit examine *our* lives, bring conviction, and, most importantly, bring us to repentance. David was quick to ask God to search his heart to see if there was any offense in him. *(Psalm 139)* It is sometimes easier not to have God examine our hearts because we may not want to see what is there; perhaps we know what is there and do not wish to deal with it. Often when we judge others harshly, it is because we have not allowed God to judge us in the same area. Isn't it interesting that what we criticize in others is often found in ourselves? Jesus warned us to be sure to check out our sins before we pass judgment on another person: *Why do you look at the speck of sawdust in your brother's eye and pay not attention to the plank in your own eye? (Matthew 7:3)*

It is also interesting to note in the passage from *Matthew* that we will be judged by the same measure that we judge others. *(v.1)* Have you ever noticed that the judgments you have made seem to come back to you? For example, you may have judged one of your parents and determined never to be like them. Years later you find yourself doing the same things that you vowed you would never do. Judgment apart from God causes us to bring judgment on ourselves. Our Scripture reading today in *Deuteronomy* reminds us that judgment belongs to God. Although we are called to be discerning and to judge good from evil in others, the Lord ultimately is the One who makes the final judgment. We are called to speak the truth in love, stand on our convictions, and gently lead others to Christ. We must always remember that we will all stand before God and give an account for how we handled His truth. *(Romans 14:10)*

Did we judge others or did we bring them to the Righteous Judge? Did we criticize others or did we pray for them? Did we see a speck in our brother's eye and refuse to take the plank out of our own eye? Ask the Lord to help you today to discern good from evil, to examine your own heart, and leave the judging to Him. He is indeed a Righteous Judge!

Heavenly Father,
I am so quick to judge. Forgive me. Help me to turn to You in prayer and not in judgment of others. Help me to speak the truth in love without judgment to others and to always be willing to allow You to examine the motives of my heart.
In Jesus' name, Amen

November 3

The Secret of Helping Others in Need

The King will reply, "I tell you the truth, whatever you did for one of the least of these brothers of mine, you did for me."
Matthew 25:40

When the Son of Man comes, all nations will be gathered before Him and He will separate the "sheep" from the "goats." The sheep will be blessed by the Father and will receive the inheritance of the kingdom. The goats will be cursed and thrown into the eternal fire prepared for the devil. Jesus further describes that the sheep, His own, will be the ones who took care of the sick, clothed the poor, and fed the hungry. Our actions truly reveal whether or not we are Christ's own—the sheep of His pasture that hear and obey His voice. (*John 10*) Jesus taught the principles of "kingdom living" to His disciples, to those who had faith in Him. His words remind us today of the principles of kingdom living and the importance of our being obedient to them.

Kingdom living means we live for God and others and not for ourselves. It means that we are not self-motivated but God-motivated so that others can see Christ through us. I grieve to think of the people the Lord has called me to reach out to but I did not respond because my eyes were on self. Our world is increasingly self-centered. As globalization spreads, the world that we live in shrinks. We are becoming more dependent worldwide on one another. Jesus came over 2,000 years ago with His message that the kingdom is near. He taught principles for kingdom living that highlighted His desire for us to care for the poor, the needy, and the destitute. He made it clear when we care for one another in need—the sick, the impoverished—we are serving our Lord.

Where has God called you to serve? Ministry means serving, and kingdom ministry means serving the "least of these." Ask the Holy Spirit to lead you as you seek to serve others. As you serve Christ's brothers you will be serving Him: *I tell you the truth, whatever you did for the least of these brothers of mine, you did for me.*

Heavenly Father,
Open my eyes to the needs around me. Where I have been blinded to the plight of the poor and needy, forgive me. Open my heart to serve, and help me to remember that as I look into their eyes, I will see You.
In Jesus' name, Amen

November 4

Jehovah Rohi Cares for Us

The Lord is my shepherd, I shall not be in want. He makes me lie down in green pastures, he leads me beside quiet waters, he restores my soul.
Psalm 23

David grew up as a shepherd who understood the significant role the shepherd has in the lives of his sheep. He knew that he must care for them and keep constant watch over them. The sheep could wander away and get lost; a predator could kill the sheep; the sheep needed food and fresh water. It was a full time job caring for sheep! But God knew that David needed to understand the role of a shepherd because He had chosen David to be King of Israel someday; He needed to train him to lead gently but aggressively, teaching the sheep to follow the master.

Jehovah Rohi, our Shepherd, searches for His lost sheep, those who don't know Him. He binds up the wounded. The prophet Isaiah prophesied that the Messiah would come to "bind up the brokenhearted, to proclaim freedom for the captives." *(Isaiah 61:1-2)* Jesus Christ came as the fulfillment of that prophecy. He was the One who was sent to care for us as our Great Shepherd. *(Luke 4:18)* He was the promised Shepherd who would lead His sheep to safety, restore souls, and take them to safe pasture.

We are like sheep needing a shepherd to guide us to green pastures, protect us, and save us from predators. Peter writes that we are to cast all of our anxieties on Him because He cares for us. *(I Peter 5:7)* As we begin to know and trust the Lord to care for us, our lives will be filled with peace and confidence because Our Shepherd cares deeply for us.

Has the Lord been trying to lead you to green pastures, but you refuse to go? Has He tried to restore your broken soul, but you are afraid to let Him visit there? If you find yourself in turbulent waters, seek the Good Shepherd and ask Him to lead you beside quiet waters.

Heavenly Father,
I have been afraid to let You lead me into the unknown. It has been easier to stay in turbulent waters that are familiar than to allow You to lead me out. Your Word promises me that You will be with me, and goodness and love will follow me wherever I go if I am willing to let go. Help me to believe; help me to surrender.
In Jesus' name, Amen

November 5

Sword, Plough, Trumpet

From that day on, half of my men did the work, while the other half were equipped with spears, shields, bows and armor. The officers posted themselves behind all the people of Judah who were building the wall. Those who carried materials did their work with one hand and held a weapon in the other, and each of the builders wore his sword at his side as he worked. But the man who sounded the trumpet stayed with me.
Nehemiah 4:16-18

Nehemiah's plan of counterattack is described: *From that day on half of my men did the work while the other half were equipped with spears, shields, bows and armor. (v.4:16)* Even the builders wore a sword at their side. In addition to that, Nehemiah was aware of the wide separation between the people doing the work, so he set up a warning system to warn the people of impending danger. He told them to gather together when the trumpet sounded so that their God could fight for them. Watchmen were normally posted on the walls of a city to warn the people of danger, but watchmen were also needed in the rebuilding of the walls.

We need a "watchman" posted on the walls of our life. The Lord has given us His Holy Spirit to do that work. The Holy Spirit warns us of danger and empowers us to stand up to the distractions and attacks that keep us from the work that God calls us to do. The Scriptures tell us that we are the temple of God's Holy Spirit and that we are being built into spiritual houses. (*I Corinthians 3:16* and *I Peter 2:5*) The enemy will seek to stop the building up of our spiritual lives, but we have a model found in Nehemiah's strategy to combat these attacks. We must put on the armor of God (our sword and bow) and pick up our plough (the work to be done); only then will we be able to stand up to the challenges that face us.

Where do you feel challenged in your walk with Christ? Is He asking you to step out in faith against the scheme of the enemy? Ask the Holy Spirit to post a watchman on your spiritual walls and forge ahead into whatever He is calling you to do. With the armor of God secure and the watchman ready to sound the trumpet for danger, you can trust that the Lord will fight for you. Anything that God calls you to do, He will equip and empower you to do. Never allow fear of attack to stop you from the things of God. Silence the voice of the enemy by strapping on God's Word and start building!

Heavenly Father,
Fill me with Your Holy Spirit to begin the work to which You have called me, and post guards over my life. Thank you for the knowledge that where You send me, You have already gone to prepare the way.
In Jesus' name, Amen

November 6

Neglecting Salvation

We must pay more careful attention, therefore, to what we have heard, so that we do not drift away. For if the message spoken by angels was binding, and every violation and disobedience received its just punishment, how shall we escape if we ignore such a great salvation? This salvation, which was first announced by the Lord, was confirmed to us by those who heard him. God also testified to it by signs, wonders and various miracles, and gifts of the Holy Spirit distributed according to his will
Hebrews 2:-4

The first of five admonitions in *Hebrews* is found in *Chapter 2, Verses 1-4*. The warnings become stronger as we progress through the book from drifting from God's Word to defying God's Word. *(Hebrews 12:14-29)* The danger noted here is that of neglecting salvation, not rejecting it. How are we neglectful as Christians? The translation here says that the danger is in ignorance. The word *salvation* means to save, wholeness, and well-being. We must not be ignorant of the full meaning of salvation. When we receive Christ into our lives, we are saved from our sin, but this is just the beginning of living in Christ. He came to set us free from sin, bind up the broken-hearted and set the captive free. Although in Christ we are new creations, we bow down to the old creation, the one that is in chains, the one that believes the lies of the enemy. Jesus continues His work on earth through His Holy Spirit, and the process of sanctification—becoming holy and set apart for Christ to live His life through us—begins. It is a journey of surrender, a journey of willingness to allow the Lord to bring healing into our lives.

The writer of *Hebrews* knew that careful attention needed to be paid to the gift of salvation that we are given. It must not be neglected or ignored. The gift of salvation was confirmed by God with signs and wonders and gifts of the Holy Spirit. *(Hebrews 2:4)* As we journey with Christ, He calls us to live as children of the light. Too often we continue to live in darkness. Our chains are broken and our freedom is won through the blood of Christ, but yet we live as if we are still in prison! As children of light, Paul writes that we must no longer live in the futility of our old thinking: *So I tell you this, and insist on it in the Lord, that you must no longer live as the Gentiles do, in the futility of thinking. They are darkened in their understanding and separated from the life of God because of the ignorance that is in them due to the hardening of their hearts. (Ephesians 4:17-18)*

Have you hardened your heart in terms of allowing God to bring His light and healing presence into the dark corners of your life? Embrace the fullness of salvation and recognize that your chains are removed. If your heart is hardened by disappointments, remember Jesus died not only to take you to heaven one day, but for you to experience His freedom through salvation on this side of heaven.

Heavenly Father,
Forgive my hardened heart. Soften my heart to know and love You and to receive Your love and freedom through Christ.
In Jesus' name, Amen

November 7

Removing the Scales

Your word is a lamp to my feet and a light for my path.
Psalm 119:105

In *Acts 8*, Saul set out to destroy the Christians. He was highly educated, came from a prominent family, and described himself as "a Hebrew of Hebrews." One day, God's plan for his life intersected his self-prescribed plans. He met the very One whom he had been persecuting, the Lord Jesus Himself. I cannot imagine how he must have felt when he heard the Lord say to him on the road to Damascus, *Saul, Saul, why do you persecute Me?* (*Acts 9:4*) Saul was blinded for three days until God sent a disciple named Ananias to place his hands on Saul and pray that he be filled with the Holy Spirit. Immediately, the scales fell from his eyes and he could see again. Have you ever wondered what Saul (later known as Paul) thought about those three days? He had been on a mission to persecute and kill Christians, and now his whole life was turned upside down. He was a scholar, and now he could not see to read. He was a man of prestige and influence, and now others would have to lead him everywhere he went. I imagine during those lonely three days, Saul did some soul searching, and by the time that Ananias knocked on his door, he was a broken man. The Scriptures tell us that after spending several days with the disciples, he went out at once to preach in the synagogue that Jesus is the Son of God. *(Acts 9:19-20)*

The story of Saul is our story. We were once blind to God, and Jesus spoke to our hearts to turn us to Him. He removed the scales from our eyes and set us free to serve Him. Yet there are times in our walk with Christ that we resist His Word that would set us free, times where we would rather not have the scales removed so we can do our own thing. On occasion, I have heard the Lord saying to me: "Why are you resisting me? Why do you continue to struggle with where I am leading you?" Those times, like Saul, I find myself in the darkness of my own prison, captured by my self-absorbed thoughts or my unwillingness to hear His voice and obey.

Do you have scales over your eyes? Do you struggle with wanting to know God's will but feel blinded by doubt and unbelief that He will lead you? Ask the Holy Spirit to remove the scales, whatever might be blinding you from the truth. Then, like Saul, "at once" begin to preach the good news.

Heavenly Father,
Illuminate my path with Your Word which lights my path and removes the scales from my eyes. Give me fresh, clear vision to go out and be a witness for You.
In Jesus' name, Amen

November 8

Ordinary Men

When they saw the courage of Peter and John and realized that they were unschooled, ordinary men, they were astonished and they took note that these men had been with Jesus.
Acts 4:13

After Jesus had died and resurrected, Peter and John were questioned by the rulers, elders, and teachers of the day in Jerusalem about the healing of a cripple: *By what power or what name did you do this? (Acts 4:7)* Peter, filled with the Holy Spirit, boldly declared that it was by the name of Jesus Christ that the man had been healed. Peter could have made his point and stopped there. He would have been faithful to God and proved that he was courageous. But Peter decided to go one step further and declare that it was by the name of Jesus the man was healed and that it was this same Jesus whom they had crucified! Talk about courage. He simply added fuel to the fire of their rage. Just hearing the name of Jesus sent them into orbit, but to be blamed for His death must have been over the top for them. When they saw the courage of Peter and John and realized that they were unschooled ordinary men, they were astonished! The next statement of Scripture could easily go unnoticed but it is one of the most profound statements in the Holy Scriptures. The chief priests and Sadducees took note that Peter and John had been with Jesus. They knew right then that these unschooled ordinary men were extraordinary, bold and courageous *because* they had been with Jesus.

As ordinary people, we are transformed when we spend time with Jesus. In close relationship with Jesus, we exchange our "ordinariness" with men and women filled with the Holy Spirit, empowered with courage and boldness to live for Christ. Jesus has a plan for your life, and as you live in close relationship with Him, He will empower you to live boldly for Him.

Peter and John were told to no longer preach in the name of Jesus, and they replied: *Judge for yourselves if it is right to obey you rather than God. For we cannot help speaking about what we have seen and heard. (vv.19-20)*

When you start to think that you are just an ordinary person unable to make a difference in this world, remember Peter and John and how time spent with Jesus empowered them to spark a fire for Christ all over the world. When you spend time with Jesus, He will pour His very life into you.

Heavenly Father,
I pray that I will be in union with Christ as the vine is to the branches. May my life be spent in union with You so that I might do extraordinary things in Your name.
In Jesus' name, Amen

November 9

Persecuted for Righteousness Sake

Blessed are those who are persecuted because of righteousness,for theirs is the kingdom of heaven.
Matthew 5:11

Jesus taught in the Beatitudes that you are blessed when persecuted for *His* sake. He goes on to say that you are blessed when people insult you and make evil accusations against you because of your love for Christ. The Greek word for blessed, *mekarios,* means "filled with joy that comes only from a relationship with Christ." It is not dependent on happiness, which depends on circumstances; it comes from deep within as a soul satisfied and content. In the state of blessedness, deep security and love are felt amidst persecution. It does not matter what is said about you, your inner soul rises above the intended arrows.

Stephen, a man full of God's grace and power, did great wonders and miracles among the people. *(Acts 6:8)* Opposition arose among members of the synagogue, and these men began to argue with Stephen. However, they could not stand up against his wisdom or the Spirit by whom he spoke. *(v.10)* So they stirred up the people against him, seized him and brought him before the Sanhedrin. They produced false witnesses against him and charged him with death by stoning. When Stephen listened to their false testimony, his face shone like the face of an angel. *(v.15)*

What catches my attention in the story about Stephen is that his face displayed what was going on inside of his soul. He visually expressed the state of "blessedness" that Jesus describes when persecuted—rising above the circumstances—filled with peace.

You may not recall being persecuted directly for your faith, but what about the time where you mentioned the name of Jesus and people recoiled? Or perhaps the time where you mentioned to someone that you read your Bible and they looked at you like you were an alien. Persecution may seem like a strong word in those cases, but nevertheless, every time you witness for Christ you may face rejection.

Have you been fearful to share your faith in concern for persecution, or more likely rejection? Ask the Lord to fill you with His righteousness, bearing rejection for the sake of entering the kingdom.

Heavenly Father,
I have feared being persecuted for my faith and have been unwilling to share my faith with others. Fill me with Your righteousness so that I will not fear what men can do, but only fear what denying You could mean.
In Jesus' name, Amen

November 10

Priesthood of Believers

As you come to him, the living Stone—rejected by men but chosen by God and precious to him—you also, like living stones, are being built into a spiritual house to be a holy priesthood, offering spiritual sacrifices acceptable to God through Jesus Christ.
I Peter 2:4

You are being built into a spiritual house for God. As a believer, His Holy Spirit dwells in you, and He is building your spiritual house so that His Spirit fills every room in your house. Peter tells believers that the purpose of this house as a holy priesthood is to offer spiritual sacrifices acceptable to God through Christ. What does it mean to be a holy priesthood?

The priests in the Old Testament were in charge of the worship in the temple. They made sure that the Holy Place was kept in order by keeping the lamp stand lit, the 12 loaves of bread on the table, and the holy fires kept blazing. The High Priest was the only one allowed in the Holiest Place to offer sacrifices for the sins of the people. He entered into the Holiest Place once a year, and a rope was tied around him in case the glory of God struck him dead and they needed to pull him out. He was our representative offering our worship and sacrifice before God. Jesus, our High Priest, has made a way for us to approach God's throne. His death on the cross tore the veil that separated the Holy Place from the Holiest Place so that we can enter the tabernacle of worship from the outer courts, through the Holy Place and into the Holiest Place as believers: *When Christ came as high priest of the good things that are already here, he went through the greater and more perfect tabernacle that is not man made, that is to say, not a part of this creation. He did not enter by means of the blood of calves and goats but he entered the Most High Place once and for all by his own blood. (Hebrews 9:11-12)*

Believers are the new priesthood, the place where Christ dwells offering sacrifices of worship to God. We are being built into a spiritual house that expands with His life and is consumed with His love.

Are you willing to surrender your life to God's plans of building you into a spiritual house? Are there any rooms in your house you would rather leave the door closed and not have the Lord clean and renovate for His use? Remember, you are called as a priest to offer sacrifices of praise and worship to God, and He desires you to worship Him with *all* of your heart, soul, strength and mind. Don't withhold any rooms from His Presence. Invite Him in to build a house for His glory.

Heavenly Father,
Build my life into a place where Your Presence dwells. I open the rooms of my heart to You so that my life will be a place of worship.
In Jesus' name, Amen

November 11

The River of Life

The man brought me back to the entrance of the temple, and I saw water coming out from under the threshold of the temple toward the east…
Ezekiel 47:1

Ezekiel the prophet was led by a man of God to the entrance of the temple. Ezekiel was among the Jews exiled to Babylon by Nebuchadnezzar in 597 B.C. He was of a priestly family and served as a priest-prophet in his day. During the first seven years of his ministry, he relayed to his fellow Jews the harsh reality that Jerusalem would fall. After the fall of Jerusalem, he began to deliver the hope of restoration and revival for the future. In one of his visions, the man of God took him to the entrance of the temple to show him the glory that would one day be returned to the temple. Our Scripture reading today speaks of the vision of water—a river flowing under the door of the temple. The man measured the water knee deep, waist deep, and finally too deep to cross. Then he was led to the bank of the river where he saw a number of trees on each side of the river. He was told that the river emptied into the sea where the water becomes fresh and living creatures thrive. Wherever the river flowed, everything would live.

The picture of the restoration of the temple is a picture of our spiritual life—our life in Christ. Jesus tells the woman at the well that He is the living water that she thirsts for: *If you knew the gift of God and who it is that asks you for a drink, you would have asked him and he would have given you living water. (John 4:10)* Jesus, our living water, wants to come into the temple of our lives. Paul describes our lives as homes for His spirit to dwell, and the river of life in Christ longs to fill our temple. For some, it is enough for His river to fill knee deep, and for others, waist deep. But it takes a leap of faith to allow His living water to fill us so that we are unable to touch the bottom of the river bed. We are no longer in control when the river goes beyond waist deep. As long as we are waist deep, we can still go back to shore. When the river goes over our head, we are offering our lives to God completely—no longer in control—willing to surrender to the Master's hand.

Are you willing to surrender completely to the living water of Christ? If you are knee deep, ask Him to take you further (waist deep). If you are waist deep, ask Him to take you over your head. Offer your life in complete surrender, and when you do, you will find that floating in the river of His Presence is complete freedom.

Heavenly Father,
I surrender all control. Send forth Your river of life throughout my temple so that I may be truly set free.
In Jesus' name, Amen

November 12

Fear

There is no fear in love. But perfect love drives out fear, because fear has to do with punishment. The one who fears is not made perfect in love.
I John 4:18

Fear, according to Webster, is a "strong emotion caused by anticipation of danger." Fear produces anxiety and is a tactic the enemy uses to discourage God's people. *Dis*courage means to take away courage, and Nehemiah's enemies knew that if they could make the Jews fearful, their courage to complete the task would be taken away. The enemies said: *Before they know it or see us, we will be right there among them and will kill them and put an end to the work.* (*v.11*) The Jews responded by saying they feared being attacked. Nehemiah did not give in to the fear and quickly responded by posting men with swords, spears, and bows on the lowest point of the wall at the exposed places. He then reminded them that the Lord is great and awesome and that they should go and fight for their homes and family. (*v.14*) Nehemiah did not allow fear to discourage the people, but instead instilled courage in them by encouraging them to have a plan and be prepared to fight.

Fear can be contagious if we are not careful. The enemy tries to take our courage away, but the Lord has a plan to fight for us when we turn to Him in prayer. He will encourage us as we prepare to stand against fear, and He will fight for us. *Isaiah 43: 1-2* reminds us that the Lord is with us during anxious, fear-provoking times: *Fear not, for I have redeemed you; I have summoned you by name, you are mine. When you pass through the waters, I will be with you; and when you pass through the rivers, they will not sweep over you. When you walk through the fire, you will not be burned.*

Heavenly Father,
Fear has come in like a raging storm and continues to try to break me. Encourage me with Your Word and through prayer so that fear can be driven back, sending the storm out to sea.
In Jesus' name, Amen

Recognizing Heresy

Many will follow their shameful ways and will bring the way of truth into disrepute.
II Peter 2:2

The false teachings Peter addresses center on two errors: denial of the return of Christ in judgment *(II Peter 3:3-10)* and moral failure. *(II Peter 2:2,10-22)* Peter claims that their teachings were heretical, refuting the fundamental doctrine of salvation. The word *heresy* originally meant "to choose." Peter alludes that false teachers brought their self-chosen teachings, persuading people to believe things they wished were true rather than the truth that God revealed to them.

False teachings can be subtle and bring destruction to those who have not built a strong foundation on Jesus Christ and His Word. False teachers prey on those who are new converts *(II Peter 2:18),* seeking to uproot the seeds of God's Word that have been planted but have not yet taken root. *Matthew 13* describes how vulnerable new believers can be to false teachings because they do not have God's Word firmly planted in their heart. Jesus describes a new believer as one who receives the message of the kingdom. When the seed, however, falls on rocky soil, it is snatched away because it has no roots. False teachers find easy prey in those who have not had a chance to allow the "root" of the Word to ground them in God's truth.

False teachers often promise freedom by casting off all moral restraints. They teach that the Bible is too narrow, not relevant for today. There is a temptation to revise the more difficult teachings of Holy Scripture to allow freedom from moral restraints.

Peter warned the early church, and likewise the church throughout the ages, to be careful not to bring the way of truth into disrepute. *(II Peter 2:2)* He spoke of the false teachers in severe language, claiming that the blackest darkness is reserved for them: *These men are springs without water and mists driven by storm. Blackest darkness is reserved for them. For they mouth empty, boastful words and by appealing to the lustful desires of sinful human nature, they entice people who are just escaping from those who live in error. (2 Peter 2:17-18)*

We must hide the Word of God in our hearts so that we are able to stand against false teachings. In every generation, there rises up those who refuse to believe God's Word, but we must not allow the way of truth to fall into disrepute.

Heavenly Father,
I pray that the seeds of Your Word will take root in my life. Help me to recognize false teachings and to bring Your truth into the light.
In Jesus' name, Amen

Brotherly Love

Love must be sincere. Hate what is evil; cling to what is good. Be devoted to one another in brotherly love. Honor one another above yourselves.
Romans 12:9-10

Unconditional love, *agape* love, must be the basis for all that we do. Paul exhorts Christians in the 1st century church, and likewise today, to be sincere in love with the motive to build up the body of Christ. Paul suggests that believers must live in harmony with one another, not being filled with pride or conceit. Prior to this, Paul described the different gifts that are evidenced in the body of Christ: encouragement, giving, mercy, and teaching. He says that each member of the body must work together using his gift for the benefit of all. Love is the key to the Christian community, and it is through love that we must exercise our gifts.

There is nothing more powerful than love that is genuine, devotion to one another, and honoring others above ourselves. A community of believers devoted to Christ and to one another could feasibly change the course of the whole world! Paul suggests that the key to living in harmony with one another is humbly living at peace with all persons. Love in action calls us to care for our enemies: *If your enemy is hungry, feed him; if he is thirsty, give him something to drink. (v.20)* We are called to love even those who are unlovable and extend a hand even to our enemies. Only through the power of the Holy Spirit and a surrendered life are we able to love in the way Christ calls us.

When we honor others above ourselves, we crucify the flesh that demands our own way and extend the hand of grace that offers unconditional love. Paul knew that to be an effective community for Christ, using individual gifts for the good of the whole, would require humility and a willingness to serve others.

Where has God called you to serve? Who has He called you to honor above yourself? Paul's words ring true for us today: *Be devoted to one another in brotherly love…*

Heavenly Father,
Why is it so hard to let go of my own needs in order to honor others above myself? Why do I cling to my own desires and resist the call to love? Help me to be devoted to others, serving them with Your love which is sincere and selfless.
In Jesus' name, Amen

Our Faithful Promises

For this reason Christ is the mediator of a new covenant, that those who are called may receive the promised eternal inheritance—now that he has died as a ransom to set them free from the sins committed under the first covenant.
Hebrews 9:15

Believers are in covenant with God. When we receive Jesus Christ as our Lord and Savior, we come into a covenant with God and must be committed to respond in love and obedience to Him. We fulfill our commitment to love and serve God to the best of our ability. The world is watching to see if our walk and our talk line up in our commitment to love and serve God. In a world with a lost sense of commitment, we must take our covenant with God seriously. The writer of *Hebrews* challenges the church to persevere in attaining the promises that our commitment to Christ brings.

As faithful followers of Christ, we have a responsibility to show integrity in our relationships with other people. One way we do this is by being faithful to our commitments, or in a sense, covenants we make with them. If we tell someone we are going to do something, we must follow through.

Jesus Christ was the ultimate example of following through on His commitment to the Father to die on the cross for the sins of the world. At any moment He could have said, "I have changed my mind; this is too difficult." But He loved His Father, He loved humanity, and He obeyed.

David set an example as leader of Israel by being faithful to his word. We need to follow the example of these great men. Pay attention to your words and to the commitments you have made to people. Determine to be committed to persevere. Remember, the world is watching to see if there are men and women who are trustworthy. Many will let them down. Work diligently not to be one of them.

Heavenly Father,
Help me to only commit to those things which I am able and willing to follow through. Keep ever before me the standard of the covenant relationship and

commitment I have with You and help me to bring this standard into my every day commitments.
In Jesus' name, Amen

Receiving Divine Direction

At Caesarea there was a man named Cornelius, a centurion in what was known as the Italian Regiment. He and all his family were devout and God fearing; he gave generously to those in need and prayed to God regularly. One day at about three in the afternoon, he had a vision…
Acts 10:1-3

Cornelius heard from God because he was a man of prayer. He sought God in his day-to-day life and God spoke back through a vision. He told Cornelius to go to Joppa bring back a man named Simon who is called Peter. In the meantime, God directed Peter through a dream. Peter saw heaven open up and a large sheet descend to earth. It contained all kinds of animals, reptiles, and birds. God spoke to Peter telling him to get up and eat and not to call anything impure that God has made clean. *(v.15)* I can only imagine how puzzled Peter must have been as he pondered the meaning of his dream. Meanwhile, the men sent by Cornelius arrived at Peter's door, and the Holy Spirit told Peter to open the door and go with these men whom God had sent.

It amazes me how tuned in to God's voice both Cornelius and Peter were! Both men of God stepped out in faith to trust God's divine direction. God called Peter to go into the house of a Gentile (Cornelius) to tell them about Jesus. When Peter stepped out in obedience, he began to understand the dream that God had given him. The dream had deeper significance than declaring food clean or unclean. He saw that salvation was not intended for the Jews only; it was intended for Gentiles as well. The barrier had been lifted between Jew and Gentile. God orchestrated their coming together to fulfill His eternal purpose of bringing the Gentiles into the Kingdom of God. God knew He could trust Cornelius and Peter because they spent time with Him in prayer and they had learned to both hear and to obey His voice.

God still speaks today: *He is the same yesterday, today, and tomorrow.* (Hebrews 13:8) As we commit our lives to Him, He speaks and gives divine direction through His Word, through visions, and through dreams. He has not stopped speaking. We have stopped listening.

Heavenly Father,
Open my ears so that I can be attentive to Your voice. Open my eyes so that I can see You more clearly. Open my heart so that I can respond in obedience to Your direction.
In Jesus' name, Amen

God's Word Is Fulfilled

...so is my word that goes out from my mouth; it will not return empty, but will accomplish what I desire and achieve the purpose for which I sent it.
Isaiah 55:11

Isaiah reminds us that God's Word will never return empty—it will always accomplish its purpose in fulfillment. God promised the Israelites that one day they would return from captivity and back to their homeland, and He fulfilled His promise. Isaiah writes that God's ways and thoughts are not like our ways and thoughts—His ways and thoughts are higher. When God's Word goes forth, it reflects His ways and thoughts.

Our words are often spoken in haste, sometimes untrue, and often unfulfilled. We speak what is in our hearts, and often our hearts are filled with impurities. James wonders how we speak words of blessing and words that are destructive from the same mouth: *Out of the same mouth comes praise and cursing. (James 3:10)* Scripture tells us that we will be held accountable for every careless word that we speak.

Jesus told His disciples that His words would never pass away: *Heaven and earth will pass away, but my words will never pass away. (Matthew 24:35)* The word of God will never pass away; it will accomplish the purpose for which it was sent.

Perhaps God has spoken a word to you and you have been waiting for the fulfillment. I remember when my daughter was eight years old and I sensed the Lord speaking to me. He told me that she was going to be a powerful woman for God. The years that followed were stormy, and it looked as though His Word would not be fulfilled. Finally, I began to see her life turn towards Christ. She began to develop into the most amazing young woman! As I waited on His Word to be fulfilled, I doubted I had heard it. I wondered if He had changed His mind, but I kept going back to the time when I heard Him speak. He had confirmed it in His Word, and I clung to the hope in Isaiah's word that *God's Word never fails, never returns empty, and always accomplishes what it has purposed. (v. 11)*

What promise are you waiting for God to fulfill? Trust His Word. It never fails. Sometimes the waiting *is* the fulfillment of His Word, but we don't even see it.

Heavenly Father,
I cling to your promise that Your Word will never return empty. Grant me patience and trust as I wait on Your promise to be fulfilled.
In Jesus' name, Amen

Intimate Worship

Six days before the Passover, Jesus arrived at Bethany, where Lazarus lived whom Jesus had raised from the dead. Here a dinner was given in Jesus' honor. Martha served while Lazarus was among those reclining at the table with him. Then Mary took about a pint of pure nard, an expensive perfume; she poured it on Jesus' feet and wiped his feet with her hair.
John 12:1-3

Mary knew how to worship Jesus with all of her heart, soul, strength and mind. She offered Him everything that she had in complete surrender. The expensive perfume may have been her dowry, the only thing that she had of value. It represented the one thing that she had to offer if she hoped to marry. She unbound her hair, which respectable women of that day did not do, because she was not concerned with what people thought. She took her hair and wiped His feet with the perfume. I can only imagine the scene... everyone was prepared to eat, perhaps the room was filled with laughter and talking, and then a loud sound… a broken bottle and a fragrance filled the room. The people were silenced; the stares were threatening. But Mary only had eyes for Jesus. She came to worship, and worship she would do. Her reputation did not concern her; she was caught up in worship. One of the disciples, Judas, scolded her for wasting such a costly gift. In pretense of being pious, he suggested that she could have sold it for the poor, but Mary did not flinch. She had eyes only for her Lord. Jesus knew that His day of betrayal was near and that Mary's act of worship had a deeper significance; it was the preparation for His burial.

As you read through the story of Mary in today's Scripture reading, could you put yourself in Mary's place? Could you relate to her act of worship and her determination to keep her eyes on Christ alone?

Jesus is calling us to Himself. He desires intimacy with His bride, the church. He is calling to you today to sit at His feet and worship—leaving the crowds, laying aside the busyness of the day or the concern over what others will think. He is calling you to sit at His feet. It is the sweet fragrance of worship that will fill the room.

Heavenly Father,
I praise and worship You, closing out the world and the things that cry out for attention. I sit at Your feet and break open the jar of my life, offering You the fragrance that comes from brokenness as I worship You.
In Jesus' name, Amen

November 19

Believing is Seeing

Then Jesus told him, "because you have seen me, you have believed; blessed are those who have not seen and yet have believed."
John 20:29

Thomas was not with the other disciples when Jesus appeared after His resurrection. After hearing that Jesus had appeared, Thomas told the others that unless he saw the nail marks in the hands of Jesus and put his hand into His side, he would not believe. Thomas needed to see evidence that Jesus had risen from the dead. A week later, the disciples were in the house again, and this time Thomas was with them. Though the doors were locked, Jesus entered the room and looked at Thomas: *Put your finger here; see my hands. Reach out your hand and put it into my side. Stop doubting and believe. (v.27)* Thomas responded in utter belief! Jesus told them He recognized that Thomas needed to see to believe, but the ones who would be truly blessed were those who have not seen, yet believe.

What are you having trouble believing? Jesus may be asking you to exercise faith in order to see. *Faith is being sure of what we hope for and certain of what we do not see. (Hebrews 11:1)* It is stepping out to believe God even though there is no concrete evidence. It is having the certainty that God is able to do what He promised. It is the assurance that your faith will allow you to see. God may be calling you to a higher level of faith. It may appear that He has forgotten or abandoned you, but He has promised to never leave and never fail you. Wait on His Word; step out in faith trusting His Word, and He will bring His promise to pass.

Heavenly Father,
I can relate to Thomas. I need to see things to believe, and I desire to be a person of faith that is certain of the things that I don't see—assured of Your promises and trusting of Your Word. Help me to grow in faith and to be blessed as You promised through not seeing but believing.
In Jesus' name, Amen

November 20

Lukewarm Faith

These are the faithful words of the Amen, the faithful and true witness, the ruler of God's creation. I know your deeds, that you are neither cold nor hot. I wish you were either one or the other! So because you are lukewarm—neither hot nor cold—I am about to spit you out of my mouth.
Revelation 3:14-16

The church in Laodicea was the wealthiest city in Phrygia during Roman times. It was known for its banking, textile industry, and medical school. Its major weakness was lack of water supply. God speaks through the writer, John, to describe the community at Laodicea as rich and in need of nothing. Yet God sees their cold and empty hearts—their need is great, they just don't see it. They are lukewarm in their commitment to God, and He will not tolerate it.

God is judging our churches today; in those that are lukewarm, He is removing His Presence. Those who are on fire for Him are growing, and the Holy Spirit is moving in amazing ways. The church today has become infiltrated by the world and the pressure to conform to its ways. God is looking for the passion for Christ to be restored—for the zeal of His church to return with the message of salvation.

I have a friend who is a missionary to Third World countries, and each time she returns from the mission field, she recounts stories about the Lord being present in her work. She has witnessed God working in miraculous ways, setting the captives free and delivering the people through spiritual, emotional and physical healings. The people are desperate for a Savior, and their faith is simple; they choose to believe. They have nowhere to look but up. The Western world has less need for Christ: materialism, intellectualism, power and prestige—the gods of this age—have eroded our faith. We run after so many things and have so many resources available to us that the need for Christ drowns in the deluge of plenty.

Before Jesus left this earth, He asked the question: *When I return will I find faith on this earth? (Luke 18:8)* He is not looking for a lukewarm church; He is looking for a church that is totally committed, charged with faith, and trusting Him in all things. It would do us all good to check the temperature of our faith and see if we are totally relying on God or if we are simply lukewarm Christians, forgetting our need for Him.

Heavenly Father,
When I honestly evaluate my Christian walk, I am able to see that I am often a lukewarm Christian. Forgive me for allowing the world to fill my life rather than seeking You alone. Give me a passion to believe, a heart on fire, and a willingness to put You first in all things.
In Jesus' name, Amen

November 21

Jehovah Rohi Leads Us

They will neither hunger nor thirst, nor will the desert heat or the sun beat upon them. He who has compassion on them will guide them and lead them beside springs of water.
Isaiah 49:10

The Lord is our Shepherd. We shall not want. He leads us beside quiet waters. (Psalm 23) I love to go the mountains and sit beside a mountain stream. The quiet ripple of the water is soothing and the beauty of the water fills my soul. God has promised us that He will provide a spring of water to those in the desert.

We all have "desert times"—times where our lives seem dry, flat, and without purpose. During those times, the Lord seeks to send our roots down deep in Him as we search for His spring within us. Jesus told the woman at the well that He was the spring of Living Water—that the water He offered would cause her to never thirst again. *(John 4)* The times when we are spiritually thirsty and dry are the times when the Lord has us search for Him; these are the times when our spiritually dry land searches for the streams of His Presence.

The Israelites were the chosen people of God, yet they were a fickle people. They would turn from God, and then they would find themselves in the desert wondering why God had abandoned them. How like the Israelites we are! We suddenly find ourselves away from the mountain streams, away from the place of life in Christ, and we end up in the desert. When Israel was in exile God spoke to them: *The poor and needy search for water; but there is none; their tongues are parched with thirst. But I the Lord will answer them. I will make rivers flow on barren heights, and springs within the valleys. I will turn the desert into pools of water and the parched ground into springs. (Isaiah 41:17-18)* God saw their thirst and parched souls in the desert of exile, and He promised them streams in the desert.

God, through His Son Jesus Christ, has provided Living Water to our thirsty souls. When it seems as though the wellspring of life has gone dry, He leads us besides the still waters and refreshes us; He may not lead us out of the desert, but He will surely provide water in the desert.

Are you thirsty and dry? *Come all you who are thirsty, come to the waters…(Isaiah 55:1)*

Heavenly Father,
As a deer pants for streams of water, so my soul pants for You, O God. My soul thirsts for God, the living God. (Psalm 42:1) Fill me today with Your Living Presence.
In Jesus' name, Amen

November 22

Perseverance with Determination

Not that I have already obtained all this, or have already been made perfect, but I press on to take hold of that for which Christ Jesus took hold of me. Brothers, I do not consider myself yet to have taken hold of it. But one thing I do: Forgetting what is behind and straining toward what is ahead, I press on toward the goal to win the prize for which God has called me heavenward in Christ Jesus.
Philippians 3:12-14

Paul was determined to know Christ and the power of His resurrection. *(Philippians 3:10)* In order to know Christ in that way, he knew he would have to forget the past and look ahead. He knew that in order to press on toward the goal of knowing Christ, he could not be burdened with his past sins, his failures, or the poor decisions he had made. Paul had been a Pharisee, and his goal at one time had been to annihilate Christians. After his conversion on the road to Damascus, he was forgiven and it was time to move on into the purpose to which God had called him.

In order for us to fulfill the call that the Lord has on our lives, we must be willing to accept the forgiveness that Christ offers us when we turn to Him. You may think that God will never use you because of your past. Shame or a feeling of unworthiness may be holding you back. But Jesus is calling you to forget the past through His gift of forgiveness, and it is His desire for you to look to what lies ahead. The past may be haunting you and the future may frighten you, but the Lord is inviting you to follow Him. He has a plan and a purpose for your life: *"I know the plans I have for you," declares the Lord, "plans to prosper you and not to harm you, plans to give you hope and a future." (Jeremiah 29:11)*

Have you put plans on hold because your past is holding you back? What lies have you believed that make you unable to press on towards the goal and purpose that God has for your life?

The Israelites were reminded that dwelling on the past prevented them from seeing hope for the future: *Forget the former things; do not dwell on the past. See I am doing a new thing! Now it springs up; do you not perceive it? (Isaiah 43:18-19)* Are you willing to forget the past? The moment you turned to Jesus and asked Him to forgive you, He forgave and removed your sin forever. Forget the former things and look and respond to His calling for you.

Heavenly Father,
Help me to put the past behind, to believe that You have forgiven me, and to forgive myself. Help me to see the new thing that lies ahead and to press on towards the purposes to which You have called me.
In Jesus' name, Amen

November 23

Prayer, Praise, and Thanksgiving

Rejoice in the Lord always. I will say it again: Rejoice! Let your gentleness be evident to all. The Lord is near. Do not be anxious about anything, but in everything, by prayer and petition, with thanksgiving, present your requests to God. And the peace of God, which transcends all understanding, will guard your hearts and your minds in Christ Jesus. Finally, brothers, whatever is true, whatever is noble, whatever is right, whatever is pure, whatever is lovely, whatever is admirable—if anything is excellent or praiseworthy—think about such things. Whatever you have learned or received or heard from me, or seen in me—put it into practice. And the God of peace will be with you.
Philippians 4:4-9

In *Philippians 4:4-9,* Paul underscores the importance of fighting the schemes of the enemy through prayer, praise, and thanksgiving. He also reminds us to *rejoice in the Lord always. (v. 4)* Every time I read this verse, I underscore the word *always.* It doesn't say "sometimes" or "when I feel like it." I am supposed to praise God no matter what battles I face, no matter how discouraged I am, or even if my world seems to be falling apart. Paul was able to do it, but that was *Paul*, the saint of saints! Surely, I am not supposed to rejoice in *all* things. The truth is, when I do, things change. Perhaps the circumstance doesn't change; it may even get worse. Something changes, however, inside me when I am faithful to praise the Lord, rejoicing in *all* things! I become less self-centered and more God-centered.

Paul tells us not to be anxious, but always present our prayer requests to the Lord *with thanksgiving.* The remedy for taking our eyes off our problems is to remember God's faithfulness and to be thankful. Again in his letter to the Thessalonians, Paul says: *Be joyful always; pray continually; give thanks in all circumstances for this is God's will for you in Christ Jesus. (I Thessalonians 5:16-17)* Be joyful in all things for this is the will of Christ. We rejoice because Christ has set us free from sin and death; He is setting us free from the things that oppress us—from our hurts, our past, our places of defeat. We have so much to be thankful for, and we have so much joy to share with people who do not have this hope. What differentiates believers from the rest of the world is the hope we have in Christ. Jesus never promised us that our lives would be easy; in fact, He says we *will* have trials and troubles. But He did promise us that in the midst of our trials, He will be there.

Are you overwhelmed with trials, sorrow, and circumstances of life? Rejoice in the Lord because He is near and He will see you through.

Heavenly Father,
I turn to You in praise and thanksgiving for Your faithfulness. Instead of being anxious, I present my requests to You knowing that You will hear my prayer and care for my needs.
In Jesus' name, Amen

November 24

Setting the Captives Free

The Spirit of the Sovereign LORD is on me, because the LORD has anointed me to preach good news to the poor. He has sent me to bind up the brokenhearted, to proclaim freedom for the captives and release from darkness for the prisoners, to proclaim the year of the Lord's favor and the day of vengeance of our God, to comfort all who mourn.
Isaiah 61:1-2

The Lord is near to the brokenhearted and saves those who are crushed in spirit. *(Psalm 34:18)* At times we all experience a broken heart. Illness, death of loved ones, loss, and broken relationships all contribute to broken hearts. But God has promised that He is near us when our spirits are crushed.

I always wanted to protect my children from having their hearts broken. Children can be so cruel, and it was so hard when my children were the recipients of harsh words or rejection from friends. We all have been there at some time. We all have experienced the heartache when a friend lets us down or an opportunity we had been hoping for passes us by. *Psalm 34* reminds us that when the righteous cry out, the Lord delivers us from our troubles. What a comfort it is to know that God stands by on the playground of life with our children, in our homes, and in the workplace ready to comfort us when the arrows come our way.

God speaks to Israel in her time of need: *Fear not, for I have redeemed you, I have summoned you by name; you are mine. When you pass through the waters, I will be with you; and when you pass through the rivers, they will not sweep over you. When you walk through the fire, you will not be burned. (Isaiah 43:1-2)*

Oh, beloved child of God, He will never forsake you in your hour of need. He sees your hurts and disappointments—the rivers that threaten to overtake you and the fires that threaten to burn you. He sees your heartaches for your loved ones; He knows them by name. He has engraved you on the palms of His hands and never forgets you. *(Isaiah 49:16)*

When you go through times where the enemy throws arrows in your heart, remember to put up your shield of faith: *...take up the shield of faith with which you can extinguish the flaming arrows of the evil one. (Ephesians 6:16)* God will not only carry you through the heartache, He will tenderly remove every arrow of hurt and replace it with His love.

Heavenly Father,
My heart is filled with arrows of hurt. I look to You as my source of healing and comfort. Thank you that You hear my cry and carry my sorrow.
In Jesus' name, Amen

November 25

Spiritual Rest

He who dwells in the shelter of the Most High will rest in the shadow of the Almighty. I will say of the LORD, "He is my refuge and my fortress, my God, in whom I trust."
Psalm 91:1-2

There are two kingdoms at war—the kingdom of God and the kingdom of darkness. The kingdom of God is righteousness, joy and peace; the kingdom of darkness brings destruction and robs us of peace and joy. There are likewise two strongholds—the stronghold of God and the counterfeit stronghold of the prince of this world.

Just before Jesus went to the cross, He said that the time for judgment had come and the prince of the world (Satan) would be driven out. *(John 12:31)* Satan's mission is to rob, steal and destroy, setting up strongholds or counterfeit fortresses in our minds, our wills and in our lives. His strongholds begin in our thought life with his lies and accusations. When we agree with his lies, he gets a foothold or access into our lives. When we refuse the lie and agree with God's Word, we find ourselves in the fortress or stronghold of God's protection.

God's kingdom is at work in setting the captives free *(Isaiah 61)* and the enemy is at work capturing our thoughts with lies and setting up a place where he can have further dominion. *Psalm 91* describes the stronghold of God, the place of refuge, the place of rest for us: *He who dwells in the shelter of the Most High will rest in the shadow of the Almighty. I will say of the Lord, "He is my refuge and my fortress, my God in whom I trust. Surely he will save you from the fowler's snare and from deadly pestilence. He will cover you with his feathers and under his wings you will find refuge."*

The place of rest from the accusations of the enemy is in the arms of God; His Word is our fortress and His Presence overshadows the snare of the enemy. Our place of immunity from the schemes of the enemy is under the shadow of His wings.

Are you being attacked by the evil one? He is the father of lies. *(John 8:44)* He doesn't play fair as he preys on our insecurities, our wounds—the places in our lives that need to be healed and delivered through Christ. In order to stand against his accusations, allow Jesus to heal and deliver you from sin in areas you need healing. God gives grace to the humble and those who turn to Him in faith. He waits for you now to rest in His shadow—in the place of refuge. His faithfulness will be your shield. *(v.4)*

Heavenly Father,
Your Word says that if I make You my place of refuge, no harm will befall me. (Psalm 91:9) I run to You for shelter from the arrows of the enemy, asking You to help me agree with Your word and close the door to any accusations and lies that the enemy feeds on. You have promised to save me and to hide me within the shelter of Your wings.
In Jesus' name, Amen

November 26

The Lord's Requirements

He has showed you, O man, what is good. And what does the Lord require of you? To act justly, and to love mercy and to walk humbly with your God.
Micah 6:8

Micah the prophet states his case against the people of God. God brought them out of slavery in Egypt and had been faithful to them. Israel is speaking and wondering what sacrifices would be acceptable to God: *With what shall I come before the Lord and bow down before the exalted God? (v.6)* Israel begins to suggest sacrifices and offerings that may please the Lord, and Micah responds: *He has showed you, O man, what is good. And what does the Lord require of you? To act justly, and to love mercy, and to walk humbly with your God. (v.8)* Micah is not denying that sacrifices are good and desirable; he simply wants the nation of Israel to recognize that sacrifices do not take the place of love, mercy and humility towards their God and others.

We often think that we must "do" things for God. We place expectations on ourselves that God never intended for us. We find ourselves burnt out and wondering if God has deserted us amidst all of the wonderful sacrifices that we have made for Him. Yet God has not called us to sacrifice; He has called us to be merciful. He has not called us to do things *for* Him; He has called us to love Him. He has not called us to take pride in the things that we do. He has called us to walk humbly with Him.

The nation of Israel had gotten off track. The ritual of sacrifice had replaced their heart for God. Their hearts had grown cold doing things *for* God because they were no longer walking *with* God. Has your heart grown cold towards God? Are you burnt out with the burden of serving Him, but feel distant from Him? Remember... the highest calling is to love God and to walk in mercy and humility. Examine your heart's attitude. Are you growing closer to the Lord, or are you growing distant? Surrender the things that you are doing *for* Him, and seek to be *with* Him.

Heavenly Father,
I have been burdened by the busyness of serving and doing rather than spending time with You. I lay down the expectations I have placed on myself and draw near to You.
In Jesus' name, Amen

November 27

Transitions

Now that the LORD your God has given your brothers rest as he promised, return to your homes in the land that Moses the servant of the LORD gave you on the other side of the Jordan.
Joshua 22:4

The tribes of Reuben, Gad, and the half-tribe of Manasseh returned to the eastern side of the Jordan. They had fulfilled their promise to Moses and Joshua by joining the fight to assure the other tribes had a secure foothold in the land west of the Jordan. Therefore, the time had come for them to leave the other nine and one-half tribes and go back to their families. The common task of securing the land had kept all of the tribes unified.

The relationships that the tribes of Israel experienced would never again be the same. Change can be bittersweet, evoking both happy and sad emotions. Death, illness, divorce, and job changes produce many different emotions. The Lord directs us in His Word in ways to remain stable as we go through these changes, looking to Him for stability. God never changes, and when our lives feel like shifting sand, He is always our sure foundation. James writes that God does not change like shifting shadows. *(James 1:17)*

Most people do not like change. It is easier to live with the familiar than to experience change, but the Lord calls us to be willing to change as He directs. God called Abraham to leave the familiar—his country, his home, his friends—and go to a distant land: *The Lord had said to Abram, "leave your country, your people and your father's household and go to the land I will show you." (Genesis 12:1)* He was called out of the familiar into a place that God would show him! It must have been hard enough to leave, but to leave and not know where you were going had to be difficult. But Abraham was able to endure the change with all of its uncertainty because he trusted God.

Change produces anxiety because we like the familiar, but change that the Lord brings produces peace and joy as we step into the place to which we are called. Has the Lord called you to a season of change? The only way you can enter fully into the new season is to let go of the old. God will bless you as he did Abraham when you step out and trust him.

Heavenly Father,
Change produces fear and anxiety in me. I am comfortable with my life, but I recognize that You are taking me to a new place. I release the familiar to You and embrace this season of change.
In Jesus' name, Amen

November 28

The Glory of God Most High

The king of Sodom said to Abram, "Give me the people and keep the goods for yourself." But Abram said to the king of Sodom, "I have raised my hand to the Lord, God Most High, Creator of heaven and earth, and have taken an oath that I will accept nothing belonging to you, not even a thread or the thong or sandal, so that you will never be able to say I made Abram rich."
Genesis 14:22-23

When Abram tells the king of Sodom, *"I have raised my hand to the LORD, God Most High, Creator of heaven and earth,"* he is telling him that God is his leader and he is God's servant. He makes a declaration that he will not be obligated to anyone but the Lord. Raising one's hand in ancient times was a standard oath taking practice. Abram would only take an oath with His God. Had Abram taken the goods that the king of Sodom offered him, this Canaanite king might later have claimed the right of kingship over Abram. Abraham knew all that he had came from God and that all of his successes were because of God's faithfulness. He did not wish to take any rewards but only to honor His God. The king of Sodom was a Canaanite king who might have been seeking a way to have Abram's allegiance.

We must declare that all we have and all we are comes from our God Most High and be willing to submit to His authority alone. Our allegiance to God is constantly being challenged by the pull of the world. Prestige, power, and influence all strain our dependency on God. James writes: *Every good and perfect gift is from above, coming down from the Father of the heavenly light... (James 1:17)* James tells the Jewish Christians that they must not be deceived into thinking that the gifts that we have and the successes we have come from our own hand. Abram understood this and refused to accept anything from the Canaanite king.

Satan sought to have Jesus bow down to him and tempted Him in the wilderness with power: *Again the devil took him to a very high mountain and showed him all the kingdoms of this world and their splendor. "All this I will give you," he said, "if you will bow down and worship me." Jesus said to him, "Away from me, Satan! For it is written: Worship the Lord your God, and serve him only." (Matthew 4:8-10)*

Satan still works to get believers to worship anything but Jesus. He lures us with money, with self-interest, preying on our weaknesses and tempting us with worldly things. But like Abram, we must say "no thank you" to the goods he promises. If we fall into his trap, our allegiance to God Most High is compromised.

Heavenly Father,
Every good gift is from You. Thank you for all that You have given me. Protect me from the evil one who tempts me with the things of this world. Help me to be like Abram and raise my hand to God alone.
In Jesus' name, Amen

November 29

Strengthening the Weak

The word of the Lord came to me: "Son of man, prophesy against the shepherds of Israel; prophesy and say to them: 'This is what the Sovereign Lord says: Woe to the shepherds of Israel who only take care of themselves! Should not shepherds take care of their flock?'"
Ezekiel 34:1-2

God spoke to Ezekiel about the state of the shepherds in Israel—those who were in authority over the people of Israel. They were taking care of themselves and neglecting the people. They were not strengthening the weak, healing the sick, or binding up the injured. They did not look out for those who had strayed or were lost and without hope. *(v.4)* They ruled the people harshly and brutally so the people were scattered without a shepherd.

Jesus called Himself the Great Shepherd. He stands in sharp contrast to the shepherds of Israel. He looked at the crowd with compassion: *Jesus went through all the towns and villages, teaching in their synagogues, preaching the good news of the kingdom and healing every disease and sickness. When he saw the crowds, he had compassion on them, because they were harassed and helpless, like sheep without a shepherd. (Matthew 9:35-36)* Jesus told the parable of the lost sheep and how a shepherd who has 100 sheep will leave the 99 in order to go and look for the one lost sheep. Jesus explains that His Father in heaven will do the same; He is not willing to lose any of His sheep. How comforting to know that as the sheep of God's pasture, He will come and get us if we lose our way.

Jesus, the Good Shepherd, laid His life down for His own sheep. *(John 10:14)* He made Himself nothing, humbled Himself, and became obedient to death. *(Philippians 2)* He searches for the lost, binds up the broken-hearted, and strengthens the weak. Unlike the shepherds in Israel, Jesus cares deeply for His sheep, even to the point of laying down His own life.

Are you in need of comfort? Turn to Jesus. He waits with open arms.

Heavenly Father,
I have felt so alone, harassed and in need of comfort. I turn to you as my Shepherd, knowing that Your care will bring me back to a safe place in You.
In Jesus' name, Amen

November 30

Lack of Trust

Trust in the LORD with all your heart and lean not on your own understanding;
Proverbs 3:5

Sometimes it is the way we perceive a situation that causes us to be anxious. We try to determine with our own understanding what is going on. It is just human nature that our perspective is filtered by our past experiences, both good and bad. Paul was clear in his letter to the Corinthians that the wisdom of the world is foolishness to God. *(I Corinthians 1:20)* We must not lean on our own understanding, but instead, we must trust in God to reveal truth, to dispel lies, and to lead us on a straight path. Sometimes trust has been eroded by past disappointments, like when we have chosen to trust someone, only to have that person let us down. We erroneously equate our experiences with people with the truth of God's Word.

Are you willing to come out from under the law, recognize God's truths, and trust Him to care for you? Peter knew as he wrote his letter to the scattered exiles that they needed to trust the Lord completely if they were to sustain the difficult times ahead and be a light to a broken world. The enemy will use our false perceptions to disrupt relationships and cause division. Recently, I filtered something my daughter said to me and decided that I was a terrible mother. When I spoke to the Lord about it and committed it to prayer, I recognized that I had believed a lie based on my false interpretation and perception of what she had said. The Lord showed me an area of weakness in me that desired to be the perfect mother, and I used that filter to misinterpret what my daughter had said. When we lean on our own understanding, we can be fooled because our understanding is sometimes askew. But when we turn to the Lord for truth and wisdom, He brings us clarity and understanding. He is in the business of building up, and the enemy is in the business of tearing down.

Heavenly Father,
Give me wisdom and direction today and keep me from my faulty reasoning and understanding. Where I have faulty perceptions, bring me Your truth.
In Jesus' name, Amen

December 1

Rumors

When they came to Geliloth near the Jordan in the land of Canaan, the Reubenites, the Gadites and the half-tribe of Manasseh built an imposing altar there by the Jordan. And when the Israelites heard that they had built the altar on the border of Canaan at Geliloth near the Jordan on the Israelite side, the whole assembly of Israel gathered at Shiloh to go to war against them. So the Israelites sent Phinehas son of Eleazar, the priest, to the land of Gilead—to Reuben, Gad and the half-tribe of Manasseh.
Joshua 22:10-13

A true accounting of events helps clarify a situation, but a false accounting can turn into a rumor and create a volatile situation. The tribes that crossed back to the east side of the Jordan built an altar as a memorial, or "witness," to remind future generations that they worshipped the one true God. They feared the possible apostasy of future generations who might forget the commandments of the Lord. The other Israelite tribes, however, thought they were setting up a separate altar which had been forbidden.
Phinehas and a representative from each of the tribes went to find out if the other tribes were "breaking faith." The representatives told the tribes their concerns and listened and accepted their reply. Phinehas was able to discern the truth—the tribes east of the Jordan were not worshipping false Gods—and his report stopped the false rumors. Had the nine tribes not sent Phinehas and representatives to bring the truth into the light, the tribes may have gone to war.

Bringing controversies into the light weakens the position of the enemy, not allowing him to gain a foothold into the situation. If you hear a rumor about someone or something and are involved in the situation, always go to the source to seek the truth. If you are not part of the problem, or part of the solution, it is wise not to get involved. James writes that the tongue is a fire that sets a forest on fire with just a spark. (*James 2:6*) That is how rumors begin—with one false word—and spread like wildfire.

Have you ever been a part of a rumor that caused someone great hurt or harm? Have you ever been on the receiving side of a false rumor? You know the destruction that is sown and the effects that are lasting. If you have been involved either way, ask the Lord to forgive you. Forgive those who have spread false rumors against you, and the Lord will free you from resentment.

Heavenly Father,
Forgive me where I have gossiped or been part of false rumors. Help me remember that one spark can cause a fire that has hurtful effects. I forgive those who have spread false rumors against me. Give me courage to seek the truth when false rumors are spoken and to keep silent when temptation to spread gossip presents itself.
In Jesus' name, Amen

December 2

The Authority of God Most High

Then Jesus came to them and said, "All authority in heaven and on earth has been given to me. Therefore go and make disciples of all nations baptizing them in the name of the Father and of the Son and of the Holy Spirit and teaching them to obey everything I have commanded you."
Matthew 28:18-29

Jesus commissioned His disciples to go and make disciples of all nations. A disciple is one who learns from a teacher. Jesus taught His disciples by modeling servant leadership. For three years the disciples watched Jesus before He sent them out to do greater works than He did: *I tell you the truth, anyone who has faith in me will do what I have been doing. He will do even greater things than these because I am going to the Father. (John 14:12)* The disciples watched Jesus, they asked Him questions, and they modeled what He did. And now as disciples of Christ, He calls us to do even greater things!

Jesus told His disciples there were two things required of them: that they bear fruit in His name and that they love others as He had loved them.*(John 15:8 and 13:35)* Paul describes the fruit of a disciple as Christlikeness: *joy, peace, patience, kindness, goodness, gentleness and self-control. (Galatians 5:22)*

Jesus describes the love of a disciple as the love He had displayed to them: *A new command I give you: Love one another. As I have loved you, so you must love one another. By this all men will know that you are my disciples, if you love one another. (John 13:34-35)* The character of Christ and the love of Christ are reflected in the lives of disciples.

For us to be a disciple of Christ, we must learn from Jesus, our Teacher, obeying His commands to love and bear fruit in His name. As we love one another and display the fruit of the Spirit, we will draw others to Christ and fulfill the Great Commandment. The world is literally dying to see Christ in action through our love and through our actions. We are called to *be* disciples and to *make* disciples. As we model Christ in all that we do, we successfully nurture others to the ways of Christ.

Is God calling you to love someone and reflect the character of Christ? God leads us to reach out to certain people. Seek His will and look for them. As you obey and reach out with Christ's love, you will be amazed at the response.

Heavenly Father,
Direct me to those who You are calling me to reach out to. Give me eyes to see them as You see them and a heart to love them with Your agape love, that they may know You.
In Jesus' name, Amen

December 3

Working Out Your Salvation

Therefore, my dear friends, as you have always obeyed—not only in my presence, but now much more in my absence—continue to work out your salvation with fear and trembling.
Philippians 2:12

As we grow in Christ-like character, we are called to progress in holiness and godliness. Paul tells the people of Philippi that when he is gone, they must continually seek to grow in Christ and work out their salvation. Salvation begins with our acceptance of Jesus Christ as our Lord and Savior, and it continues as we allow the Lord to work in us to become more like Christ. The process of working out salvation is called sanctification; it is the process of growing more holy as we draw near to God.

Peter describes the process of sanctification as participating in the divine nature of Christ: *His divine power has given us everything we need for life and godliness through our knowledge of him who called us by his own glory and goodness. (2 Peter 1:3)* He does not say that we *have* a divine nature, but that we *participate* in HIS divine nature. Here, Peter is talking about growth in holiness. In addition, he says that believers are called to separate themselves from the corruption of the world. *(II Peter 1:4b)* When we receive Jesus Christ into our lives, we become a new creation. We are then called to grow in Christ's character and to daily work out our salvation by allowing God to work in and through us. *(Philippians 2:12-13)*

The evidence of growing in holiness can be seen in our lifestyle changes—by the books we read, the movies we attend, the people we spend time with. The Lord calls us daily to grow in holiness, separated from the world but still a part of the world. We must never have the attitude that if we are holy we must separate from the world. The world is our mission field! Jesus was clear that we are called to holiness *in order to* influence the world.

Jesus said that as believers we are lights on a hill; the salt of the earth. *(Matthew 5:13-14)* As we allow our light to shine before men, they will see our good deeds and praise our Father in heaven. Holiness is not a call to superiority; it is a call to humility.

Are you growing in holiness? Are you able to see that your lifestyle has changed since you came to know Christ? He is calling you to be set apart for His glory so that others can see His light shine through you.

Heavenly Father,
Help me to display Your light to others. I pray that I will grow in holiness and that You will draw me away from those things that are displeasing to You. Give me a willing heart to respond to Your love by yielding to the process of growing to be more like You.
In Jesus' name, Amen

December 4

The Spirit of the Pharisee

Woe to you teachers of the law and Pharisees, you hypocrites! You clean the outside of the cup and dish, but inside they are full of greed and self-indulgence. Blind Pharisee! First clean the inside of the cup and dish, and then the outside will be clean.
Matthew 23:25-26

Jesus confronted the Pharisees on numerous occasions. The Pharisees were the teachers of the Law of Moses. They adhered to the law but missed the intent of the law. The laws became burdensome dealing with the external life of the people, but they did not deal with the internal or heart of the people. Jesus knew that the intent of the law was to bring structure and stability to God's people and to point them to God, not from God. They began to exalt the law above a relationship with God.

Jesus came confronting the religious people of His time—the Pharisees and the Sadducees. He boldly spoke about the hypocrisy of the Pharisees: *In the same way on the outside you appear righteous but on the inside you are full of hypocrisy and wickedness. (v.28)* Jesus was not speaking against observing the requirements of the law, but rather against Pharisaical legalism. Such legalism was keeping the letter of the law to gain merit with God but ignoring the spirit of the law. He aptly describes how they did this in contrasting the external interpretation of the rabbinic tradition of the law with Jesus' correct interpretation of the law: *You have heard that it was said to the people long ago, Do not murder and anyone who murders will be subject to judgment. But I tell you that anyone who is angry with his brother will be subject to judgment. (Matthew 5:21-22)*

Jesus came not to abolish the law but to fulfill it. *(Matthew 5:17)* He fulfilled the law in the sense that He gave it its full meaning. He emphasized the underlying principles rather than merely external obedience.

Applying this to our lives, we are called to be filled with the Holy Spirit who will guide and lead us into truth. *(John 16:12)* As you yield to the Holy Spirit, He will lead you into freedom to follow Christ in obedience, not by a set of rules, but by a loving relationship. As you surrender to His love and receive His grace, your life will reflect a life of freedom in following God's commands. Unlike legalism and the life of the Pharisees, love, not rules, will dictate your living.

Sometimes in our walk with Christ we are faced with people who are not living for Christ. Some are even opposed to Christ. It is not the rules of the Christian faith—it is not even the doctrine of the Christian faith—that will draw them. It is the love of Christ that will impact them to make a decision for Christ. Good doctrine is important. Obedience to God's commands is central to our growing in holiness, but if people are not drawn by God's love and filled with His love, their faith will be externally driven by works and not by grace.

Does your life in Christ reflect a life of grace? Are you still striving to be justified by works and not by faith? Ask the Holy Spirit to show you where you are under the law, and draw near to His love and place of freedom.

Heavenly Father,
I recognize that in some ways I have the spirit of a Pharisee. I am striving to do things for You; I am seeking to follow Your commands by the letter of the law rather than through a transformed heart. Your Word tells me to seek You first, to draw near to You and from the outflow of this relationship will flow a heart to serve.
In Jesus' name, Amen

December 5

Worshipping and Fasting

While they were worshipping the Lord and fasting, the Holy Spirit said, "Set apart for me Barnabas and Saul for the work to which I have called them." So after they had fasted and prayed, they placed their hands on them and sent them off.
Acts 13:2-3

Paul's first missionary journey was birthed by the Holy Spirit when believers in Antioch were fasting and praying. As we fast and pray, the Holy Spirit will guide us as He did the early church. As we practice the spiritual disciplines of prayer, fasting, and worship, our lives increasingly will reflect the presence of the Holy Spirit and lead us into God's will.

Some people asked Jesus why His disciples were not fasting like the Pharisees and the disciples of John. He replied: *How can the guests of the bridegroom fast while he is with them*? (Matthew 9:14-15) Jesus told them that the time would come when He, the bridegroom, would be taken away, and on that day they would fast. After He was taken from them, fasting became a part of the spiritual discipline of His disciples.

After Jesus' death and resurrection, the disciples fasted as they sought direction from the Lord: *Paul and Barnabas appointed elders for them in each church and with prayer and fasting, committed them to the Lord, in whom they had put their trust. (Acts 14:23)* The early church knew that the spiritual disciplines of worship, prayer, and fasting were needed to draw them near to their Lord. Fasting is a tool that helped them focus on Him rather than on satisfying their flesh. As they drew near to Him, He drew near to them and they received direction from God.

In the place of intimacy when we worship, pray, and fast, the sheep hear the voice of the Shepherd. *(John 10)* As we are intentional to draw near to the Lord, He leads, guides, and directs our path.

Recently I was praying about a decision facing me. I sought the Lord's will and made a decision. When things did not seem to line up in my timing, I began to second guess that my decision was in line with God's will. But when I remembered that I had sought the Lord through prayer and fasting, I gained confidence that He was directing my path. The issue for me was trust. Was I going to lean on my own understanding of how things appeared, or was I going to trust His Word that when I seek Him I will find Him? *(Jeremiah 29)* Holding fast to His Word in all things has made my path straight.

Have you set aside time recently to fast and pray? The Lord will meet you in the time that you set aside to seek Him. He inhabits the praises of His people and He gives grace to the humble—those who seek Him wholeheartedly.

Heavenly Father,
Help me set aside time to fast, pray and seek Your will in my life. Where I am weak, make me strong; where I am too busy, forgive me; where I am in unbelief that You will meet me as I seek You, show me the truth.
In Jesus' name, Amen

December 6

The Spirit of Elijah

At the time of the sacrifice, the prophet Elijah stepped forward and prayed: "O Lord, God of Abraham, Isaac, and Israel, let it be known today that you are God in Israel and that I am your servant and have done all these things at your command."
I Kings 18:36

Elijah was the prophet of Israel. A prophet spoke the word of the Lord to God's people to bring truth and conviction and turn them back to God. King Ahab was king of Israel, and his queen Jezebel worshipped the pagan god Baal. King Ahab allowed the worship of Baal: *Ahab also made an Asherah pole and did more to provoke the Lord, the God of Israel, to anger him than did all of the kings of Israel before him. (I Kings 16:33)* Ahab elevated the worship of Baal to an official status in the northern kingdom at the beginning of his reign. God sent His judgment on Israel by causing a draught for three years. Then he called Elijah the prophet to present himself to Ahab to tell him that the source of the drought was the breach of covenant with the one true God. Elijah went to Ahab and told him that because he and his people had abandoned all of God's commands, it was time to see the display of God's power. Elijah told Ahab to summon all Israel and the 400 prophets of Baal. He instructed the prophets of Baal to prepare a sacrifice with a bull offering and put it on wood but to not light fire under it. The god who answered by fire would be the true God. From morning until noon, the prophets of Baal cried out to their god but he did not show up with fire. Elijah called on Jehovah God, and after pouring water on his altar of sacrifice three times, he prayed: *O Lord, God of Abraham, Isaac, and Israel, let it be known today that you are God in Israel and that I am your servant. (v.36)* God sent fire and the sacrifice was consumed. Elijah had the false prophets of Baal killed, and Jezebel threatened to have Elijah killed. He ran away, ending up in a cave of despair when God showed up and spoke to him. Elijah represents the people of God who share His Word, His truth. He saw God move in a miraculous way and then he fled in fear.

The spirit of Jezebel causes fear and seeks to destroy the prophets of God. Are you walking in the spirit of Elijah, proclaiming God's Word, or has the spirit of Jezebel caused you to be fearful, placing you in the cave of despair? When God spoke to Elijah on the mountain, he was strengthened in his call and able to obey God's next command. If you are discouraged by your influence in a world that does not care to hear about God, be careful not to fall into the trap of fear, but stand on the truth of God's Word. He will deliver you as you stand on His Word.

Heavenly Father,
I have tried to live Your Word and to speak Your Word, but I have been rejected and am hiding in the cave of disappointment and discouragement. Like Elijah, I have believed a lie that I am the only one who seeks Your truth. Forgive my agreement with that lie and show me, as You did Elijah, my fellow Christians who stand beside me in the fight.
In Jesus' name, Amen

December 7

Wounded for Us

We all, like sheep, have gone astray, each of us has turned to his own way; and the LORD has laid on him the iniquity of us all.
Isaiah 53:6

Isaiah 53 describes Jesus growing up as a tender shoot, marred beyond recognition as He went to the cross, a man of sorrow familiar with suffering. It is a sobering thought to think about the sufferings of Christ. The death that He suffered was what we deserved, yet our sins were laid on Him even though He was sinless. Man was created in God's image but allowed sin to infiltrate his life. We were separated from God by the sin in our human hearts: *We all, like sheep, have gone astray. (Isaiah 53:6) But He was pierced for our transgressions, He was crushed for our iniquities; the punishment that brought us peace was upon Him, and by His wounds we are healed. (Isaiah 53:5)* Sin, our rebellion against God, mortally wounded humanity, bringing about physical and spiritual sickness and death.

Jesus knew that His time had come to judge the prince of the world (Satan), and He willingly went to the cross: *The reason my Father loves me is that I lay down my life—only to take it up again. No one takes it from me, but I lay it down of my own accord. (John 10:17-18)* Jesus willingly laid His life down so that our sins would be forgiven and we could be reconciled to God. He had the authority to lay it down and the authority to take it up again. *(v.18)*

We are like sheep, gone astray, turning to our own way. The picture of the shepherd who cares for his sheep is the picture of Jesus as He leads His sheep out of harms way: *I tell you the truth, I am the gate for the sheep. All who ever came before me were thieves and robbers, but the sheep did not listen to them. I am the gate; whoever enters through me will be saved. (v.7-8)* Jesus is the gateway to forgiveness, and when He hung on the cross as our sins were heavy upon His soul, He cried out to His Father. He had not been separated from His Father, but as He carried our sins to the cross, the separation was unbearable: *He took up our infirmities and carried our sorrows…*

We *are* forgiven and healed by the completed work on the cross. Jesus Christ bore our sins, healed our wounds, and set us free!

Heavenly Father,
I have taken for granted what You did for me on the cross. I have looked the other way, not wanting to picture Your agony and suffering—only receiving the benefits of Your grace and salvation. My heart grieves that I have been so blind. Help me remember the great cost You paid for a debt that You didn't even owe.
In Jesus' name, Amen

December 8

Life in Relationship

You diligently study the Scripture because you think that by them you possess eternal life. These are the Scriptures that testify about me, yet you refuse to come to me to have life.
John 5:39-40

The Pharisees were the educated men of their time. They knew the Scriptures and were the experts on application of Scripture, but they missed the Messiah when He came. The Scriptures pointed to Christ through prophecy, but they refused to believe. Have you ever wondered why they refused to believe? I have. I wonder if they were so caught up in their study of the Word that they missed *The Word.* Jesus said that He had come to the lost sheep of Israel; they were lost, but they didn't know it. The Scripture reading today says that they studied the Scripture to find eternal life. Jesus said that the Scriptures only testify *about* Him; they do not give eternal life. Only a relationship with Christ offers the gift of salvation. Jesus recognized that if they did not believe Moses and the prophets who wrote about Him, they would not recognize what He was telling them as the truth. *(John 5:46)*

It is possible to study the Scriptures and never receive Christ into your life. There are religion professors who study God's Word and English teachers who study the Word as literature who will never come to know The Living Word, Jesus Christ. Jesus tells the unbelieving Jews that John the Baptist gave testimony to Christ, yet they did not believe.

What can we do to draw others to Christ? We know that it is His power that draws them and it is His Word that brings the truth. But it is the testimony of our lives that will make a difference for Christ; it is the world that sees the light of Christ in us that will respond in faith. The only Bible that some people may read is you. There is no substitute for studying the Word, but to lead people to Christ, we must live the Word. Are others able to see the reflection of your relationship with Christ by your actions?

Heavenly Father,
Forgive me where I have diligently studied Your Word but have not sought You, the Living Word. Sometimes in my desire to understand Your Word, I have overlooked my relationship with You. Help me to draw near to You.
In Jesus' name, Amen

December 9

God's Covenant of Faithfulness

As for me, this is my covenant with you: You will be the father of many nations. No longer will you be called Abram; your name will be Abraham, for I have made you a father of many nations. I will make you very fruitful; I will make nations of you, and kings will come from you. I will establish my covenant as an everlasting covenant between me and you and your descendants after you for the generations to come, to be your God and the God of your descendants after you.
Genesis 17:4-7

The Lord promised Abraham in *Genesis 17* that he would be the father of many nations. We see the fulfillment of that promise beginning in *Genesis 21* with the birth of Isaac. It required faith on the part of Abraham and Sarah to believe that the Lord would fulfill His promise to them. In fact, Abraham and Sarah initially laughed when they heard that two people their age would have a child. Sarah even tried to fulfill the promise herself by giving her servant Hagar to Abraham to produce the promised child.

Followers of Christ enter into a covenant with God to obey His Word and to enter into His promises. Often we struggle believing these promises. We try to control situations rather than choosing to trust the Lord and allow Him to fulfill His promises. Joseph learned in a dream that He would be a man of influence and that even his brothers would one day bow down to him. God had promised him that his life would be one of influence and power. But he ended up in prison. I imagine he wondered if God's promise was really true or if it was just his active imagination.

Has God spoken a promise to you and now you wonder if it was just your wishful thinking? He has promised that He is faithful to His Word and that His purposes will stand the test of time. God's timing is often not our timing and His ways are not our ways, which causes us trouble as we wait on His promises to be fulfilled.

Peter writes that God has given us everything that we need through our knowledge of Him. *(2 Peter 1:3)* As we grow in our understanding of the character of God, we will be better equipped to hold onto His promises. As we learn that He is faithful, consistent, full of compassion, and understanding, we will be able to trust Him.

He wants what is best for us, and all of His promises are for our good.

Are you discouraged as you wait on the fulfillment of His promise? Seek to know God, and He will disclose His Word to you. Wait on His promises. He never fails.

Heavenly Father,
Lord, I knock and keep on asking for doors to open in my life. Forgive me where I have spent more time seeking those things than searching for You. Help me trust You and know that Your timing is perfect.
In Jesus' name, Amen

December 10

Drawing Us Back

For a brief moment I abandoned you, but with deep compassion I will bring you back.
Isaiah 54:7

The Lord speaks to the people of Israel: though they were abandoned for a brief moment, with deep compassion He will bring them back. *(Isaiah 54:7)* God judges us and allows us to feel the consequences of our turning away from Him. The people of Israel, God's covenant people, had turned to other gods and had rejected the God of Abraham, Isaac, and Jacob. Throughout the book of Isaiah, we see God's compassion as He reaches down to call His people back to Him. The prophet Isaiah describes how God's brief abandonment of His people felt to them: *as if you were a wife deserted and distressed in spirit. . . (Isaiah 54:6)* Sometimes, we feel as though God has abandoned us, but He draws us back with *cords of love,* drawing those who are weary and thirsty back into His life-giving presence.

Surely Peter felt abandoned when Jesus died. We know from his actions that he denied Christ out of fear, and he must have wondered why things turned out this way. But when he heard that the tomb was empty, he ran as fast as he could to check it out and spread the word that the Messiah, His trusted friend, was alive. Peter had known abandonment, and he had, in turn, abandoned Christ when he denied Him. When Jesus appeared to Him, I suspect that Peter was ashamed. He recalled that Jesus had told him that he would deny the Lord, but Peter refused to listen. *(John 13:38)* When Jesus spoke to Peter after the resurrection, He commissioned Peter to feed and care for His sheep. He didn't condemn Peter for denying Him. Filled with compassion, He drew Peter back.

That is what our Scripture reading for today conveys: God may seem to abandon us for a brief moment, but with deep compassion, He brings us back.

Are you in a season of feeling abandoned by God? Does He seem distant and now you are distancing yourself from Him? Though your emotions tell you to run away, draw near to Him because He is waiting to bring you back.

Heavenly Father,
Things have not been going the way that I had hoped. I am disappointed with life and have denied that You care about me. Forgive me for abandoning my relationship with You, as I have been drowning in self pity. Draw me back. I need You.
In Jesus' name, Amen

December 11

Philip and the Ethiopian

Now an angel of the Lord said to Philip, "Go south to the road—the desert road—that goes down from Jerusalem to Gaza." So he started out, and on his way he met an Ethiopian eunuch, an important official in charge of al the treasury of Candace, the queen of the Ethiopians.
Acts 8:26-27

God had a special assignment for Philip. He sent an angel to direct him to an influential Ethiopian man to share the gospel. The Ethiopian had gone to Jerusalem to worship and on his way home was sitting in his chariot reading the book of Isaiah. The Holy Spirit told Philip to go to his chariot and listen. Philip heard the man reading Isaiah, the prophet, and asked him if he understood what he was reading. The Ethiopian immediately responded that he could not know if someone did not explain it to him.

The Holy Spirit directs us to people who need to know Jesus Christ—who need to understand His Word and the good news of salvation. He directs us to people who may have never read God's Word and to people who may be trying to read the Word but do not understand it. We may sense God telling us something or leading us to someone, but often it is easy to assume that it is our overly active imagination. It is tempting to persuade ourselves that it isn't God speaking. But God speaks all the time. He is looking for people who are sensitive to His Holy Spirit's leading and who are willing to respond. Fear of rejection can be a huge deterrent in responding, but if we press through our fear, God will be with us as we seek to obey.

I am always grateful for the times when I act on what I think may be God leading me to share my faith or do something that He calls me to do. There have been times when I have stepped out in faith and wondered if it was really God's leading, but I know that it is better to step out in faith than to miss an opportunity to obey God. He has always been faithful when I have sought to obey.

Has the Lord asked you to do something and you have come up with a thousand reasons that it can't be God speaking? If you are asking the Holy Spirit to lead you daily, it is better to assume that

God will lead. Pray for God's timing and His open doors, and trust Him to help you obey.

Heavenly Father,
I have feared rejection when You have called me to step out in faith. Help me to be like Philip who was led by Your Spirit to help the eunuch understand Your Word. Drive far from me all of my excuses that hold me back from obedience.
In Jesus' name, Amen

December 12

Living in the Power of Christ

His divine power has given us everything we need for life and godliness through our knowledge of him who called us by his own glory and goodness. Through these he has given us his very great and precious promises, so that through them you may participate in the divine nature and escape the corruption in the world caused by evil desires.
2 Peter 1:3-4

Peter writes that the power of God has given us all that we need to live a godly life. It is through our knowledge of Christ and His promises that we participate in what God is doing on earth. We actually participate in His divine nature and are protected from world corruption when we walk in the promises of God. The New Age movement which has become popular in the Western world teaches a counterfeit version of our Scripture reading for today. New Age believes that we *are* divine—in a sense, that we are gods. Our Scripture reading for today relates that we *participate* in God's divine nature, a vastly different concept. It is through Christ living in us that the power of God is available to us—the power for us to live godly lives.

The divine nature of Christ runs contrary to the world's standards and views. For example, Jesus tells us to love those who hate us and to bless those who persecute us. That is definitely not the worldview held in society today! Just watch the news to see that the worldview today is to seek revenge. Christ taught us to live another way, one that is only possible with His power, His authority, and His love—all divine qualities that require a supernatural God. It is through the promises of God in His Word that we are able to participate in the divine nature and escape the corruption in the world.

Paul prays for the people of Ephesus to be empowered by God so that they can live a godly life: *I pray that the eyes of your heart may be enlightened in order that you may know the hope to which he has called you, the riches of his glorious inheritance in the saints, and his incomparably great power for us who believe. (Ephesians 1:18-19)* Paul knew that the

Ephesians needed God's power to live the life to which they were called. He described the power available to Christians as the same power exerted when Christ was raised from the dead. *(v.20)* Knowing that this is the power available to us in Christ Jesus gives us hope to live as Christ, not as the world dictates. Are you appropriating His power today?

Heavenly Father,
I pray that You will demonstrate Your power today as I live my life for You. Thank you for allowing me to participate in Your divine nature as I hold on to the promises in Your Word.
In Jesus' name, Amen

December 13

Our Obedience and Faithfulness

Be very strong; be careful to obey all that is written in the Book of the Law of Moses, without turning aside to the right or to the left. Do not associate with these nations that remain among you; do not invoke the names of their gods or swear by them. You must not serve them or bow down to them. But you are to hold fast to the Lord your God as you have until now.
Joshua 23:6

When someone is close to death, we usually give full attention to what he or she says. I remember a few days before my grandfather died, he told me that he thought he was going to die. Of course, I told him that he should not talk that way, but when he repeated it to me, I began to pay attention.

When Joshua knew that he was going to die soon, he gave the Israelites their final instructions and they paid attention. Joshua emphasized that they must refuse to ally themselves with the enemy who remains in the land. He warned them not to associate with the pagan nations or to serve false gods. Joshua knew from their past history, the people of God from time to time had become idolatrous, forgetting their God. Before he died, he warned them not to assimilate into the pagan culture.

Shortly before Jesus died, He prayed to God the Father. *(John 17)* We pay special attention to these words. He prayed and gave instructions to His disciples before He went back to be with the Father.

In the book of *Deuteronomy*, Moses warned the Israelites that when they entered the Promised Land they must be careful to observe His commands: *See, I have taught you decrees and laws as the Lord my God commanded me, so that you may follow them in the land you are entering to take possession of it. (Deuteronomy 4:5)* He reminded them to be careful not to fall into idolatry: *Therefore watch yourselves very carefully, so that you do not become corrupt and make for yourselves an idol, an image of any shape…(v.15-16)* God warned the people through Moses that they were to destroy the enemy in the land lest they be tempted to fall into their pagan ways.

We should take note of Joshua's admonitions. As children of God, we are grafted into the same covenant with Him and therefore have the same call to obedience if we are to receive the privileges and blessings of God. We sometimes find ourselves making peace with our enemies when the Lord wants us to destroy them. Our enemies today are the things that tempt us to turn from God. Idolatry in today's world takes on many forms, such as worshipping money, power, or prestige. Idolatry can be worshipping people rather than God or living a life that is contrary to God's commands. The world today is full of temptations, but we are not to ally ourselves with them.

Heavenly Father,
Forgive me where I have allowed idolatry into my life—where I have entertained the "enemies" of God, the things that draw me away from You. You are calling me to live a life fully devoted to You, and I let go of all the things (fill in the blank) that separate me from You.
In Jesus' name, Amen

December 14

Comforting the Contrite

For this is what the high and lofty One says—he who lives forever, whose name is holy: "I live in a high and holy place, but also with him who is contrite and lowly in spirit, to revive the spirit of the lowly and to revive the heart of the contrite."
Isaiah 57:15

God dwells in a humble heart. He always seeks out the places of humility in which to dwell. When Jesus Christ came to earth, He did not come as the conquering King, but as a lowly servant; He did not choose to be born in a palace fit for kings, but in a stable; He did not dwell while on earth in a palace, but claimed that He had no place to rest His head. When we receive Christ into our lives, He comes to revive the heart of the contrite—the humble in heart. When we turn to Him in repentance seeking to draw near to God, He hears our prayers: *If my people who are called by my name, will humble themselves and pray and seek my face and turn from their wicked ways, then will I hear from heaven and will forgive their sin and will heal their land. (2 Chronicles 7:14)* God sent His Son, Jesus Christ, to dwell in willing humble hearts—hearts seeking God and His ways.

In *Isaiah 59:1-2*, the people are reminded that the arm of the Lord is not too short to save, nor is His ear too dull to hear. It is our sins that have separated us from God. *(Psalm 66:18)* When we turn back to Him in humility and true repentance, the Lord, our Redeemer, listens and comforts us. Our children often do things that displease us, but we are quick to comfort them when they recognize and ask forgiveness for their wrong behavior. God is our loving Father who *revives the spirit of the contrite. (Isaiah 57:15)*

Does your heart need to be revived? Has pride found its way into you and crowded out the Presence of Christ? As you humbly turn to Jesus, He will forgive, heal and comfort you. Humility brings not only the comfort and restoration of God, but it also brings the power and presence of God into your life.

Heavenly Father,
Forgive me for turning away from You. I have been caught in the trap of believing that I can do all things in my own strength. Forgive my arrogance and pride. I acknowledge today that I can do nothing apart from You.
In Jesus' name, Amen

December 15

From Obedience to Love

One of you routs a thousand, because the LORD your God fights for you, just as he promised. So be very careful to love the LORD your God.
Joshua 23:10-11

Christ set us free from the law of sin when He died on the cross. This was and is His greatest gift of love to us. He gave His all for us, so how can we do less than give our all to Him? As we give Him our love, we need to remember that love and obedience go hand in hand. Just as children are more willing to obey when they know that they are loved, we return God's love through obedience.

Jesus commands us to love. It is through our obedience that love reaches fulfillment. The ultimate display of Christ's love was His obedience to die on the cross. He lay His life down for us because of His great love for us: *As the Father has loved me, so have I loved you. Now remain in my love. If you obey my commands, you will remain in my love, just as I have obeyed my Father's commands and remain in his love. (John 15:9-10)* Jesus told his disciples to love one another as He has loved us and to demonstrate love by laying our lives down for others. In the self-centered world in which we live, this is a tall order!

What does it mean to lay our lives down for one another? I believe that when we consider the interests of others above our own interests, we are displaying true love. When our world is no longer "us" centered but "other" centered, the love of Christ flows through us. It is difficult to die to self, and yet Christ tells us that it is through taking up His cross—dying to self—that we are united with Him: *If anyone would come after me, he must deny himself and take up his cross daily and follow me. For whoever wants to save his life will lose it, but whoever loses his life for me will save it. (Luke 9:23-24)* The key to following Christ and becoming Christlike is denying oneself. As we love Christ and take up His cross of self-denial, we will in turn love others selflessly.

Heavenly Father,
I surrender to Your love. Such love is impossible for me to comprehend! Help me to love You with all of my heart, soul, and mind, and to love my neighbor as myself. - In Jesus' name, Amen

December 16

Confined to the Moment

As he was praying, the appearance of his face changed, and his clothes became as bright as a flash of lightening. Two men, Moses and Elijah, appeared in glorious splendor, talking with Jesus. They spoke about his departure, which he was about to bring to fulfillment at Jerusalem
Luke 9:29-31

Jesus took Peter, John, and James with Him up onto a mountain to pray. They were His closest disciples, having formed a bond that enabled Jesus to take them to the intimate place of prayer. Jesus prayed to His Father, and His intimacy with His Father was evident as He prayed: ...*his face changed.* He modeled His intimacy with God the Father, and undoubtedly His disciples learned a valuable lesson in being in the Presence of God. I suspect that their prayer life was transformed on the mountain that day. As Jesus prayed, Moses and Elijah appeared, speaking to Jesus. The presence of Moses and Elijah pointed to the time when Jesus' death and resurrection would fulfill the law and all the prophecies of the Old Testament. Moses represented the Law and Elijah represented the prophets.

Peter and his companions were sleepy, but when they saw the glory of Christ and the two men standing with Him, they became fully awake. *(v.32)* Isn't it interesting that they became sleepy as they prayed with Christ? We see this happening again in the Garden of Gethsemane when Jesus asks them to stay alert in prayer and they fall asleep. Without an awareness of the Presence of God, with only a call to obedience apart from relationship, the disciples found prayer boring—lulling them to sleep. But when God's Presence was revealed through His glory, they awoke and responded.

Our prayer life takes wings when we know we are in the Presence of God. Suddenly, our spirit is awakened to the glory of God, and the intimacy that Jesus had with His father is seen in our relationship with Christ through prayer. The Lord does not want us to pray by rote, but by our relationship and awareness of the Presence of God.

Peter responded as Elijah and Moses were leaving Jesus: *Master it is good for us to be here. Let us put up three shelters—one for you and one for Moses and Elijah. (v.33)* Peter had a new experience on the mountain that day. He saw the intimacy that Jesus had with His Father. He saw the glory of God displayed on the mountain, and then he wished to capture the moment by building structures around his mountain top experience.

We sometimes are tempted to recapture our mountain top experiences—times when we have prayed and known the strong Presence of God. But we are not called to stay on the mountain top. We are called to take the Presence of God into the valley of our lives.

Heavenly Father,
I long for intimacy with Christ as Christ had with His Father. Invigorate my prayers with Your Presence. I seek You, Lord—not an experience, only You. Fill me with the glory of God in my times with You so that I might reflect Your glory in the valley of life.
In Jesus' name, Amen

December 17

Salvation in Jesus

And everyone who calls on the name of the Lord will be saved.
Acts 2:21

As I write this devotion on drawing from the springs of salvation, we are in the season of Advent, anticipating the celebration of Christmas, the birth of Christ. In *Isaiah 7:13*, Isaiah prophesies to King Ahaz: *Hear now, you house of David!... The Lord will give you a sign: The virgin will be with child and will give birth to a son, and will call Him Immanuel.* Seven hundred and fifty years later, God carried out His promise through the birth of His Son, Jesus Christ. Jesus said that He was the fulfillment of the prophecies concerning the Messiah, the One who would ultimately bring freedom to the captives. *(Matthew 4:18-21)* During the Advent season, I am reminded that Jesus came to earth to save us and everyone who calls on His name. The Messiah, Jesus Christ, grew as a shoot from the stump of David *(Isaiah 53)* and His kingdom will have no end: *For unto us a child is born, to us a son is given, and the government will be on his shoulders. And he will be called Wonderful Counselor, Mighty God, Everlasting Father, Prince of Peace. Of the increase of his government and peace there will be no end… (Isaiah 9:6-7)*

Is His kingdom ruling and reigning in your heart? Jesus came to save us from our sins and to give us eternal life. He came to rule in our hearts today as we live our lives for Him. As we surrender to God's kingdom rule, it will affect everything we do. For example, you may no longer desire to go to places that you went before or to be with people who lead you to sin. You may notice that your life changes in ways that you never thought possible.

Jesus came to seek and save the lost, and He came to give the saved an abundant life. After Jesus' resurrection, He sent the promised Holy Spirit to dwell in the hearts of believers. He is our Counselor and brings us peace. As the government of Christ grows in our lives, the increase of His peace and His counsel will grow in us. The key to the kingdom rule of Christ in us is the surrender to His Spirit. The Holy Spirit lives in us but must be released in us. We may choose to ignore Him or release His Presence into every facet of our lives.

Over the years, the Lord has called me to surrender different parts of my life to Him. Sometimes I readily obey Him, and other times I struggle and fight surrendering to Him that which I hold dear. As I release those things, I make room in my heart for more of Christ to dwell. As I let go of those things that I think I must control, His Presence fills the void.

Today, allow His kingdom to come and His will to be done in your life as you surrender the things that have inhibited His Presence.

Heavenly Father,
Release Your Holy Spirit in me. Enable me to surrender all of my life to You so that more of Your Presence will be evident in my life.
In Jesus' name, Amen

December 18

Responding to God's Word

One of them, when he saw he was healed, came back, praising God in a loud voice. He threw himself at Jesus' feet and thanked him—and he was a Samaritan. Jesus asked, "Were not all ten cleansed? Where are the other nine? Was no one found to return and give praise to God except this foreigner?"
Luke 17:15-18

On His way to Jerusalem, Jesus traveled along the border between Samaria and Galilee. Along the road, ten lepers cried out to Him to be healed. Jesus told them to go show themselves to the priest, as this was dictated by the law after a cure. On their way, they were cleansed. One of the lepers who had been healed returned to Jesus, thanking and praising God for his healing. Jesus commended him for his grateful heart and rebuked the nine who did not give thanks.

Several things jump out at me in our Scripture reading for today. First of all, it was the Samaritan who gave thanks to God. Normally Jews did not associate with Samaritans, and the Samaritans were not considered on an equal footing with the Jews, socially or religiously. Yet, the Samaritan gave thanks. It is easy to get caught up with "religion" and not relationship. The Samaritan's heart was touched by Jesus' extended mercy, and he responded with gratitude. As the Lord is faithful to us, it is natural to grow in our relationship with Him and respond with gratitude.

The other thing that catches my attention in the reading is that the lepers were healed "on the way" to presenting themselves to the priest. The lepers were not healed until they responded in faith to the words of Christ. It must have been difficult to leave the leper camp still covered in the effects of leprosy, believing that they were healed. As they went, they were cleansed and their faith grew.

We must respond to God's Word in faith. On our spiritual journey with Christ, we sometimes must believe before we see rather than see before we believe. Faith grows when we choose to believe God's Word.

Are you responding to God's faithfulness in your life with a heart filled with gratitude? Are you responding to God's Word in faith, believing before you see results? Praise God in all things; believe God in all things; trust Him as you walk with Him today.

Heavenly Father,
Thank you for Your faithfulness in my everyday life. Forgive me when I am ungrateful. Help me to respond to Your Word, believing before I am able to see.
In Jesus' name, Amen

December 19

Responding to the Message

He who listens to you listens to me; he who rejects you rejects me;
but he who rejects me rejects him who sent me.
Luke 10:16

Jesus told the disciples that the harvest was plentiful but the workers were few. *(Luke 10:2)* Jesus knew that His disciples would not be received everywhere they went and forewarned them: *When you enter a town and are welcomed, eat what is set before you. Heal the sick who are there and tell them: "The kingdom of God is near you." But when you enter a town and are not welcomed, go into its streets and say: "Even the dust of your town that sticks to our feet we wipe off against you." (vv.8-11)*

Whenever God's Word goes out, the enemy begins to stir up trouble because God's Word in our lives is active and transforming. As we testify to God's faithfulness in our lives, the message is often opposed. Jesus told His disciples to heal the sick to bring evidence that His kingdom was near, but to leave any place that His kingdom was not received. In the gospel of Luke, Jesus tells His disciples that when they are rejected, it is the same as rejecting Him. *(Luke 10:16)*

Throughout the Scriptures, Paul spoke about God's faithfulness. Some people responded positively, but some became jealous and fearful. In the city of Iconium, Paul and Barnabas went as usual into the Jewish synagogue where they would share the message about Christ. They spoke so effectively that a great number of Jews and Gentiles believed. But the Jews who refused to believe stirred up the Gentiles and poisoned their minds against their brothers. *(Acts 14:1-2)* Wherever the gospel is preached, there will be those who respond and those who oppose the message. Paul writes that the message of the cross is foolishness to those who are perishing, but to those who choose to believe, it brings the power of God. *(1 Corinthians 1:18)*

As we share the gospel of Christ, it is easy to despair when people do not respond positively. The truth is that our responsibility is only to share the "good news" of Christ. We cannot control the response of others. Paul recognized that his eloquent speech and persuasive words had no effect on people. He knew that it was the power of God to reach the people. *(1 Corinthians 2:4)*

Remember that it is our responsibility only to share His Word, but it is God's work that brings His Word to fruition. The most powerful message to others is a message without words—it is the power of a transformed life. As people see the change in you as you grow in Christ, it will impact them in ways you never imagined!

Heavenly Father,
Fill me with Your power to spread Your Word. Help me to remember that I am only the messenger and that You will cause the seeds that I plant to grow.
In Jesus' name, Amen

December 20

Choosing Whom We Will Serve

But if serving the LORD seems undesirable to you, then choose for yourselves this day whom you will serve, whether the gods your forefathers served beyond the River, or the gods of the Amorites, in whose land you are living. But as for me and my household, we will serve the LORD.
Joshua 24:15

Joshua testified of the faithfulness of God to the Israelites. He recounted the goodness of the Lord as He faithfully brought them out of Egypt and led them into the Promised Land. God was also faithful to defeat all of their enemies. Joshua had followed the Lord all the days of his life and his testimony was sincere. In other words, his "walk" matched his "talk." He had chosen to faithfully serve God, and as his days were numbered, he reminded the Israelites that they had a choice—to serve God or to serve the gods of the Amorites.

The Christmas season is full of choices. We are reminded that this is the season that we celebrate the birth of Christ, but as you read this, are you filled with the delight of His birth, or are you caught up in the frantic secular activities that have invaded this holy season? I find myself in a war zone during this time of year—the war between following the world's ways and the ways of Christ. I am caught up in the tide that sweeps me out into the sea of spending, of people pleasing, and stress.

The Scripture reading for today reminds us that we have a choice to serve God or the god of Mammon. Jesus has given us this same admonition: *No one can serve two masters. Either he will hate the one and love the other, or he will be devoted to the one and despise the other. You cannot serve both God and money. (Matthew 6:24)* As I write, I am keenly aware of how I easily fall prey into doing things during this time of year that draw me away from Christ rather than toward Him. Reading the word of Joshua, I am reminded that I have a choice to draw near to Christ or to get caught up in the frenzy of the secular idea of Christmas. Will you choose with me to remember the real reason for the season?

Heavenly Father,
Help me to remember the reason for this holy season—the birth of Your Son Jesus Christ. Help me avoid getting caught up in the tide of busyness that threatens to draw me away from God.
In Jesus' name, Amen

December 21

New Resolve

The people of Israel, including the Levites, are to bring their contributions of grain, new wine and oil to the storerooms where the articles for the sanctuary are kept and where the ministering priests, the gatekeepers and the singers stay. We will not neglect the house of our God.
Nehemiah 10:39b

The Israelites confessed their sins and were now determined to start over again, assuming the responsibilities and duties of the people of God. *Nehemiah 10* describes the commitment that the people made before God and the agreement they signed to insure that they fulfilled their commitment. They agreed to keep the Sabbath holy since they had defiled it by conducting business on the Sabbath. They agreed to continue the appointed feasts and to make offerings of tithes. They concluded with a resounding word as one new man: *We will not neglect the house of our God. (v.15b)* The spiritual revival at Water Gate began a time of reflection on God's Word, of confession of sins, of worship, and now a time to take action in obedience by following God's laws.

God's people also need a "spiritual revival." Perhaps we have neglected studying God's Word, neglected to pray, or have not been in fellowship with other believers. It is also possible that we are going through difficult times, and although we are practicing the disciplines of the faith, we are still feeling spiritually dull or dry. During those times, it is good to pray for the Lord to revive you, and often renewal begins with a heart of thanksgiving and a willingness to repent. *James 4:8* reminds us that if we draw near to God, He will draw near to us. Sometimes just having a new resolve isn't enough. We need Christian friends to pray with us or help us to draw near to the Lord. God's Word brought a new resolve to the people to turn back to God and to follow His ways. *Nehemiah 11* describes that after their determination to assume the responsibilities of God's people, the people were able to work together to begin to reestablish the city of Jerusalem. As the body of Christ, we need times of revival to draw us back to the Lord and to cause us to have a new resolve to establish His kingdom here on earth.

How about you? Are you in a spiritually dry place? You may need to have new resolve to seek the Lord and obey His commands, and like the people of Nehemiah's day, proclaim that you will no longer neglect the house of God. Revival means to "bring to life again." As you resolve to turn back to God, He will bring you new life.

Heavenly Father,
I am spiritually dry and in need of revival. I turn back to You with new resolve and commitment to seek You with all of my heart.
In Jesus' name, Amen

December 22

Made for Noble Purposes

In a large house there are many articles not only of gold and silver, but also of wood and clay; some are for noble purposes and some for ignoble.
2 Timothy 2:20

Paul wrote *II Timothy* while imprisoned under Emperor Nero. The church was under persecution, and he was concerned about the welfare of the churches during this time of persecution. In his letter to Timothy, he warns the church to guard itself against foolish controversies. He reminds the church to avoid godless chatter because those who indulge in it will become ungodly. *(v.16)* The early church was being threatened with a form of Gnosticism, and he warned them not to engage in arguments surrounding heresy but to concentrate efforts on correctly handling the word of truth. After describing the heresy, Timothy continues by describing a large house filled with articles made for noble purposes of gold and silver and those made for ignoble purposes. He calls for Christians to be noble and holy, useful for the Master's purposes.

Paul further qualifies holiness and the standard for noble purposes: *And the Lord's servant must not quarrel; instead he must be kind to everyone, able to teach, not resentful. Those who oppose him he must gently instruct. (vv.24-25)*

We are temples of the Holy Spirit and are called to fill our spiritual temples with noble articles of silver and gold, preparing a place fit for King Jesus. As we surrender to His purposes, His Holy Spirit will do house cleaning by removing the articles that are ignoble and filling the house with holiness. Paul writes that we must pursue righteousness, faith, and love and have nothing to do with foolish arguments and quarrels. We are called to be kind to everyone, able to teach, and not be resentful.

You are made for noble purposes. The Lord seeks to fill you with His Holy Spirit. He is seeking a willing heart ready to discard the ungodly attitudes of the heart and pursue righteousness. Are you prepared today to open the doors of the temple of your heart and allow Him to do housecleaning? Are you willing to pursue righteousness, preparing your house for the noble purposes of God?

Heavenly Father,
I surrender to the work of Your Holy Spirit in me. I desire to be filled with the noble purposes of God. Forgive me where I have been a part of godless chatter and cause me to pursue righteousness, peace, and love.
In Jesus' name, Amen

December 23

Brotherly Love

For this very reason, make every effort to add to your faith goodness; and to goodness, knowledge; and to knowledge, self-control; and to self-control, perseverance; and to perseverance, godliness; and to godliness, brotherly kindness; and to brotherly kindness, love. For if you possess these qualities in increasing measure, they will keep you from being ineffective and unproductive in your knowledge of our Lord Jesus Christ.
II Peter 1:5-8

Peter describes the importance of pursuing godly character such as self-control, perseverance, brotherly kindness, and love. He identifies that these qualities in increasing measure will keep us from becoming ineffective and unproductive in our Christian walk. Peter sought to strengthen the persecuted church by issuing a call to Christian growth. He emphasized the need for love and kindness as we deal with people.

Paul describes brotherly love in his letter to the Romans: *Love must be sincere. Hate what is evil; cling to what is good. Be devoted to one another in brotherly love. Honor one another above yourselves. (Romans 12:9-10)* Paul understood the need for Christians to live in harmony with one another. *(v.16)* He speaks to us throughout the ages as we are called to reflect the character of Christ.

Brothers and sisters in Christ are called to deal with conflict differently than the world. In *Matthew 18*, Jesus gives us a model to follow when we confront someone. He tells His disciples to first go to the brother who has sinned and confront him one on one. If he does not listen, go back again with a witness, and then to the church if the issue is not resolved. It takes maturity and spiritual character to lovingly confront someone and discipline to take the steps as described by Jesus to resolve the conflict. It is sometimes easier and certainly quicker to skip the steps and go straight to others to straighten things out. I think that Jesus gave us these steps so that we could grow in His character as we pursue God's way to handle difficult situations.

Are you faced with conflict in a relationship? Remember that the Lord is calling you to grow in brotherly love by practicing self-control and kindness. As you possess these qualities in increasing measure, you will be more effective and productive in your witness to others of the love of Christ. Consider following the steps in Scripture towards reconciliation. As you pursue God's ways, you will reflect Him and others will be drawn to Him as well.

Heavenly Father,
Help me to reflect the character of Christ as I deal with people with whom I am in conflict. I pray that I will possess the qualities of Christ in increasing measure and become an effective witness for Christ.
In Jesus' name, Amen

December 24

Nothing is Impossible with God

The angel answered, "The Holy Spirit will come upon you, and the power of the Most High will overshadow you. So the holy one to be born will be called the Son of God. Even Elizabeth your relative is going to have a child in her old age, and she who was said to be barren is in her sixth month. For nothing is impossible with God." "I am the Lord's servant," Mary answered. "May it be as you have said..."

Luke 1:35-38

God sent the angel Gabriel to Nazareth to a virgin pledged to be married to Joseph. Her name was Mary, and the angel told her the Lord was with her and she was highly favored. The angel's words troubled Mary because she did not understand what he meant. But the angel told her not to be afraid because she had found favor with God; she would give birth to a baby named Jesus. He would be the Son of the Most High and God would give Him the throne of David. Can you imagine what must have gone through Mary's head at that moment? We do know from Scripture that she questioned how this could happen since she was a virgin. The angel explained that the Holy Spirit would come upon her, overshadowing her and she would be with child. The angel said that even her cousin Elizabeth would have a baby in her old age.

All of these things must have seemed impossible to young Mary, but her response reflected her trust in God: *with God all things are possible.* With these things swirling in her head, she could have questioned the angel further; she could have been in disbelief, but instead she chose to believe, knowing that her God could do anything. Not only was she certain that her God was able to do these things, but she did not ask him to reconsider. What would people think? She was a virgin and would disgrace her family because no one would believe her. Would Joseph still marry her? Surely these things troubled her, but she chose to trust: *May it be as you have said.*

On the eve of Christmas, the celebration of the birth of Jesus Christ, consider those things that seem impossible in your life—a broken relationship, a suffering friend, an issue of poor health.

Whatever it may be, nothing is impossible for God. He sent His Son, Jesus Christ, to do the impossible—what we could not do ourselves. He saved us from our sin and suffering, and in the midst of the seemingly impossible, He breaks through as the great Morning Star. His light shines in the darkest places, in the places of uncertainty, and a new day dawns.

Heavenly Father,
I give You all my fears for the New Year—the places of uncertainty, the things that seem impossible. Like Mary, I declare that with You all things are possible as I wait for the dawning of a new day.
In Jesus' name, Amen

December 25

Pondering in Our Hearts

So they hurried off and found Mary and Joseph and the baby who was lying in the manger. When they had seen him, they spread the word concerning what had been told them about this child, and all who heard it were amazed at what the shepherds said to them. But Mary treasured up all these things and pondered them in her heart.
Luke 2:16-19

The shepherds were living out in the fields near where Jesus was born. As they watched over their flocks, an angel appeared and told them to not be afraid. They were terrified! The angel announced the birth of Christ, the Savior. I wonder what went through their minds as the angel spoke and the glory of God shone around them. Perhaps they were in disbelief; perhaps they were so amazed that they could not even comprehend what the angel was saying. As the shepherds were trying to take in all that was going on around them, suddenly a *great company of the heavenly host* appeared with the angel. *(v.13)* At this point, maybe they considered running away; perhaps they fell to the ground. We do know that they responded by saying to one another: *Let's go to Bethlehem and see this thing that has happened which the Lord has told us about. (v.15)*

The shepherds responded by going to see the baby—the Savior. They could have stayed in the fields watching their flocks, but they knew that they must go. The shepherds hurried off and found Mary and Joseph and the baby. They spread the word about what they had seen and all who heard were amazed. But Mary took all of these things and stored them in her heart. While the shepherds ran and told everyone, Mary quietly took it all in. Just as she carried the Son of God in her womb, she now carried the glory of the moment in her heart, treasuring the gift that she had been given.

Sometimes the Lord does something so extraordinary in our lives that we can't help sharing our experience with a multitude of others. Yet there are times when the Lord does something so awesome, so incredible, that all we can do is pray and ponder these things in our heart. The treasure of the experience is beyond words, beyond understanding, and to share it at first would take away the mystery and awe. Sometimes we must process it before we are able to share. Other times we may choose not to share because it is too close to our heart.

Perhaps today the Lord has touched you in a way that is too awesome for words. Like Mary, ponder these things in your heart and give thanks to the Lord.

Heavenly Father,
Today as I celebrate the birth of Your Son, help me to treasure Your coming and place deep in my heart the joy and gratefulness of the miracle of His birth.
In Jesus' name, Amen

December 26

Seated with Christ

And God raised us up with Christ in the heavenly realms in Christ Jesus, in order that in the coming ages he might show the incomparable riches of his grace, expressed in his kindness to us in Christ Jesus. For it is by grace you have been saved, through faith—and this not from yourselves, it is the gift of God—not by works, so that no one can boast.
Ephesians 2:6-9

Paul writes to the Ephesians to help them understand God's eternal purposes and grace. He reminds the Ephesians and believers throughout the ages that we are saved by grace through our faith in Jesus Christ. And now we are seated with Christ in heavenly realms. It is hard to wrap my mind around the fact that those of us who are "in Christ" are seated with Him in heavenly places. The term "heavenly realms" occurs five times in Ephesians, emphasizing our union with Christ, making us beneficiaries of every spiritual blessing from above. Although we are positioned on earth physically, we are spiritually positioned in heaven! If we were to live our lives in the shadow of this truth, I believe we would have victory over many of the issues that plague us. Paul writes: *Praise be to God and Father of our Lord Jesus Christ, who has blessed us in the heavenly realms with every spiritual blessing in Christ. (Ephesians 1:3)*

There were times when Paul yearned to leave this earth and be with Christ. He was persecuted, beaten, misunderstood and broken—yet never destroyed. At times he lived in the shadow of death, but all the while he clung to his position in heaven: *But we have this treasure in jars of clay to show that this all surpassing power is from God and not from us. We are hard pressed on every side, but not crushed; perplexed, but not in despair; persecuted, but not abandoned; struck down, but not destroyed. (2 Corinthians 4:7-9)* Paul's earthly life carried the death of Jesus so that the life of Jesus could be revealed. He knew that though his body and emotions were beaten down, his spirit all the more was alive. He knew that his position on earth was temporal—his true home was in heaven. As he endured his trials, he was strengthened in his position in Christ.

What trials have you endured that have caused you to suffer? Remember that you are seated in heavenly places with Christ Jesus, and from heaven's perspective, you will always be victorious!

Heavenly Father,
Help me remember that I am seated with You in the place of spiritual blessings.
In my times of trial, give me heaven's perspective so that I can stand in victory.
In Jesus' name, Amen

December 27

Dreaming with God

Write down the revelation and make it plain on tablets so that a herald may run with it. For the revelation awaits an appointed time; it speaks of the end and will not prove false. Though it linger wait for it; it will certainly not delay.
Habakkuk 2:2-3

The prophet Habakkuk receives a revelation from God concerning the fall of Babylon, which occurred in 539 BC, about 66 years after Habakkuk's prophecy. The Lord told him to write the revelation down plainly so messengers could deliver the message. The Lord delivered His message through Habakkuk that the fall of Babylon would come only in the time appointed by God. In the meantime, Judah needed to be faithful to God and await His justice to be meted out.

Years ago as I read this Scripture, the Holy Spirit spoke to me concerning a ministry called Drawing Near to God that the Lord was leading me to establish. He told me to write out the vision that He gave me, making it plain so that others could run with the vision. The ministry began as a Bible study and grew into a ministry of prayer, compassionate care, and a Bible program for children. The Lord laid on my heart a course for the ministry. After several years, I became discouraged as I worked toward the fulfillment of this vision. The Lord spoke again as I grew impatient. He reminded me that the revelation or vision awaited an appointed time. God may give us vision and direction, but we have to wait on *His* timing. I remembered the scripture in *Habakkuk* describing Habakkuk's word concerning Babylon: even though the fulfillment of the prophecy may linger, the people were instructed to wait expectantly. *(v.3)*

Proverbs 29:18 tells us that where there is no revelation (vision), people perish or cast off restraints. People need God-ordained vision in order to follow a course and purpose in life. Without vision, we perish because we are created to fulfill God's purposes on earth. Sometimes we become discouraged as we sense that God is calling us to do something, yet doors do not open as we anticipate and things do not work out as we expect. If God has given you the vision, He will fulfill it in *His* time. Remain faithful to the vision and He will bring it to pass.

As you approach the New Year, you may have considered making a New Year's resolution. This year, seek the Lord's heart and ask Him to give you vision and revelation of His call for the New Year. Then faithfully follow His lead and wait on His timing. Though the fulfillment may linger, it will surely come to pass.

Heavenly Father,
As the New Year approaches, give me eyes to see and ears to hear Your vision for my life. Give me a fresh perspective on old visions unfulfilled and an expectant and trusting heart to know that what You ordain, You will fulfill.
In Jesus' name, Amen

December 28

Humility

Young men, in the same way be submissive to those who are older. All of you, clothe yourselves with humility toward one another, because, God opposes the proud but gives grace to the humble. Humble yourselves, therefore, under God's mighty hand, that he may lift you up in due time.
I Peter 5:5-6

Human nature has remained the same throughout the ages. The disciples of Jesus were very much like His disciples today, seeking truth, longing to be like Jesus, yet fighting their sinful, human nature. People in the time of Jesus, like today, wanted to be great; they wanted recognition and an elevated position. The disciples asked Jesus, *Who is the greatest in the kingdom of heaven?* Jesus responded to them in a way that surprised them: *He called a little child and had him stand among them. And he said: "I tell you the truth, unless you change and become like little children, you will never enter the kingdom of heaven. Therefore, whoever humbles himself like this child is the greatest in the kingdom of heaven." (Matthew 18:1-4)* We see from this teaching that humility is valued in the kingdom of God. The world exalts those who have power and prestige, yet God exalts the humble.

Joseph had a dream that his brothers would all bow down to him, and his pride got him into a lot of trouble. His brothers threw him into a pit and he ended up in slavery. A little time in prison humbled Joseph, and by the end of his life he was a man of humility who extended kindness to his brothers. He did not end up embittered over what his brothers had done to him; instead, he allowed the Lord to grow humility and mercy in his heart.

God gives grace to the humble, so where we are willing to be humbled, He will grow His grace in us. Pride can grow like a weed and take over the garden of our spiritual lives if we leave it unattended. Pride subtly makes its way into facets of our lives, seeking to root out humility and cause us to exalt ourselves, thereby bringing destruction. *(Proverbs 16:18)*

God's Word tells us to humble ourselves under God's mighty hand so that He may lift us up. *(I Peter 5:5-6)* Where do you need to humble yourself under His mighty hand? He has promised in due time to lift you up and pour out His grace upon you.

Heavenly Father,
I have been boastful and proud (fill in the blank). I acknowledge that apart from You, I can do nothing. I seek Your forgiveness for my pride. I humble myself under Your mighty hand, knowing that You will restore me.
In Jesus' name, Amen

December 29

God's Faithfulness

They refused to listen and failed to remember the miracles you performed among them. They became stiff-necked and in their rebellion appointed a leader in order to return to their slavery. But you are a forgiving God, gracious and compassionate, slow to anger and abounding in love. Therefore you did not desert them.
Nehemiah 9:17b

After the reading of God's Word and the recounting of all of the promises of God, the people praised the Lord for not abandoning them even though time and time again they had been rebellious. Even when the Israelites worshipped idols, the Lord never deserted them. There were consequences for their disobedience and the Israelites wandered in the desert for 40 years. But all the time in the desert, God instructed them, provided food and water, and gave them clothes that did not wear out. (*9:20-21*) God is faithful to us even when we forsake Him, even when we turn to our "idols" of money, pride, or success. There are consequences for us as well when we turn away from the Lord. Our sins separate us from God and keep us from walking in the fullness of the promises of God. The Lord, however, never forsakes us because of His compassion. (*v.19*) He longs for us to turn back to Him so that we do not have to suffer further consequences.

Nehemiah 9:28 describes what happened to the Israelites when they did evil in God's sight: *Then you abandoned them to the hand of their enemies so that they ruled over them. And when they cried out to you again, you heard from heaven and in your compassion you delivered them time after time.*

Beloved friend, in what circumstances are you being disobedient to the Lord? He longs for you to turn back to Him. He has seen the devastation and turmoil that you are in, and He will be faithful to restore you when you return to Him.

Heavenly Father,
My soul thirsts for You in this dry and weary land. (Psalm 42:2) I have been wandering in the desert, refusing to listen to what You have been telling me. Forgive me, Lord, for my hard heart, and thank you for receiving me back again.

In Jesus' name, Amen

December 30

Plans to Prosper

"I know the plans I have for you," declares the Lord, "plans to prosper you and not to harm you, plans to give you a hope and a future. Then you will call upon me and come and pray to me and I will listen to you. You will seek me and find me when you seek me with all of your heart. I will be found by you," declares the Lord, "and will bring you back from captivity.
Jeremiah 29:11-14

Jeremiah the prophet speaks words of hope to the Israelites in exile. They must have wondered if God had forsaken them as they found themselves in captivity in a foreign country. Jeremiah told them that after 70 years were completed, He would come to them and fulfill His promise to return them to their homeland. We know from history that the Israelites returned to Jerusalem after 70 years, and they rebuilt their temple and restored their city. The Lord reminds His people through Jeremiah that He has a plan and purpose for them—plans that included a hope for the future. He knew that the Israelites would once again call on Him and He would hear their cry and deliver them.

Sometimes we find ourselves in captivity wondering if God has forsaken us. We question if He has a plan for us and wonder if the chains that hold us will ever be broken. God has promised in His Word that it is in the places of bondage—the places where we are held captive—that He hears our cry and gives us hope for the future. Peter found himself in a prison for sharing the good news of Christ. He could have wondered if God had forsaken him, but instead he began to worship and praise the Lord. He *knew* that God had a plan for him, and whether it was in prison or in the free world, God would be exalted. His assurance of his future is indicative of his trust in God. Peter knew that God's plan for him was not to harm him, but to use him to bring others to Christ. His mission was fulfilled even in the prison when the guards accepted Christ, and he continued upon his release to preach and demonstrate the good news.

Do you feel forsaken by God? Are you wondering if He has plans for you that are good? Today's Scripture reading reminds us that when we call out to Him, He will hear. The key is to seek Him wholeheartedly, and when you do, He will bring you back from captivity.

Heavenly Father,
My future is uncertain and I need the hope that You bring. Help me to keep my eyes on You and to trust You with my future.
In Jesus' name, Amen

December 31

Continuing Our Spiritual Journey

Therefore, my dear friends, as you have always obeyed—not only in my presence, but now much more in my absence—continue to work out your salvation with fear and trembling for it is God who works in you to will and to act according to his good purposes.
Philippians 2:12

As you approach the New Year, God is challenging you to continue in your spiritual journey of transformation. The Holy Spirit will continue His work daily in your life, forming the image of Christ in the heart of your life. Paul told his friends in Philippi that they must continue to work out their salvation. He knew how easy it was to become discouraged, give up, or even become lazy in their spiritual growth. Paul reminded them that God was working His purposes in them and that it would require their diligence in obedience to press on in their spiritual journey as they responded to God's grace.

Paul continues to tell the Philippians that they are called to live blamelessly in the midst of a crooked generation, that they are called to shine as they hold out God's Word of truth. And we, too, are called to live blamelessly—to shine as stars in a world that is crooked and depraved. *(Philippians 2:15)* People are looking for hope, for truth, and for light in the darkness, and as believers we hold the light of Christ in our hearts and the truth that will set them free.

Later in his letter to the Philippians, Paul writes that he must forget what lies behind and press on to what lies ahead. *(Philippians 3:12-14)* He recognized that spiritual growth is hindered when we live in the past with our sins, our regrets, and our shame. He knew that in order to go forward, he had to forget what was behind and strain toward what was ahead. He longed to take hold of that which Christ had procured for him.

What is it that keeps you from pressing on in your spiritual journey? What do you need to let go of so that you can grab hold of the promises that God has for you? The goal is spiritual transformation. The Christian life is like a race. Just as the winner of the Greek races received a wreath of leaves, the Christian receives an award of salvation. Paul reminds us in his letter that we run the race to continue to work out this gift of salvation, allowing God to work His purposes into our lives. A whole New Year lies in front of you. Are you ready to press on in the race and claim your reward? Consider how the Lord is calling you to fulfill His purposes.

Heavenly Father,
Help me to let go of the past—those things that haunt me and stunt my spiritual growth. I long to go forward in my journey with You, to lay hold of the promises of God, and to press on into the purposes You have for me.
In Jesus' name, Amen

Made in the USA
Middletown, DE
04 May 2021